Practical help for your church in the Decade of Evangelism

GW01466386

Reaching the Men

Using this Book

This is the fifth in the series of CPAS evangelism resource books. These books are designed to be a practical resource for local churches. Written mainly with Anglican Churches in mind, we hope they will be useful to churches of other denominations too.

This book is intended as a tool for church leaders, evangelism committees and church councils, house groups and other groups concerned to make their church a place where men can easily feel at home. It can be read by interested individuals like any other book, but its main aim is to provide leaders with photocopyable resources to generate discussion and decisions. It attempts to explain why there are more women than men in the church today. The author then goes on to suggest concrete ways in which churches can re-address this balance and make their churches friendly and relevant for men.

What's what?

The resource material falls into five sections, each with some or all of the following:

An *Introduction* page which outlines the contents of the section. It also gives extra group activities and ideas on how to use the materials.

A *Briefing* paper on the subject or evangelistic idea. This is either for a leader's own information or for photocopying and distribution to members of a planning group or church council.

One or more *Discussion* papers for group members. Again, these are designed for photocopying. These discussion papers may not refer directly to the briefing papers and so may be used on their own.

A collection of *Ideas* for further discussion. These provide starting points for discussion and planning.

One or more *Illustrations* for sermons, talks or group work. They may contain cartoons or graphics. These illustrations may be photocopied on to acetate sheets for use with an overhead projector.

Is it a course?

The material has not been set out as a five-part course. However, it is possible for church leaders to form a course by picking various discussion papers from the five chapters. This book is packed tight with good ideas on how to reach men with the gospel. Therefore the key is to do what suits your situation.

Lifeboat Churches: Women & Children First

Contents

A two-page *Briefing* paper giving possible reasons why there are more women than men in the church and ideas on how to reverse this trend.

A *Discussion* paper including several mini Bible studies on Jesus' encounters with men.

A *Discussion* paper on 'What is my church doing to reach men and women?'

Two *Illustrations*, one showing how often women frogmarch their partners unwillingly to a meeting and the other showing the embarrassing lack of men in a congregation.

Extras

What does he see?

Try this bit of market research with non-Christian friends, relatives or work-colleagues.

'John (or Peter, Fred, Brian), we really need your help. We are trying to take a look at our church from the visitor's point of view. Will you come some time at your convenience and look round? Tell us what your first impressions are. Please be honest; it will help us to make visitors more welcome.'

Don't be surprised if the person invited decides that he needs to come along to an actual service to check things out properly. You've given him an excuse for coming. Then do something about at least one of his recommendations. Better still, enlist his help along with his non-Christian friends, to make the changes.

Restoring the vision

It is possible that you have a men's group in your church already, but one which perhaps has lost its vision of reaching out to non-Christian men. Edward de Bono, talking about secular work patterns says, 'Organizational patterns tend to outlive their usefulness and become powerful negative weapons. All organizations seek to maintain their own existence; they finish up existing on sentiment, not on rationality.' If that describes your church situation then take a look at the words of Isaiah: 'Do not dwell on the past. See, I am doing a new thing! Now it springs up' (Isaiah 43:18).

How about praying for one man a month to be added to your church? The key, I'm sure, is to start something new with what we already have and then set a realistic target which will challenge us to grow.

What's missing

Leaders and groups will find the author's book *Men! What's Missing in Today's Church* published by HarperCollins invaluable for further ideas and insights.

Lifeboat Churches: Women & Children First

Men matter in our churches today. But unless we start building bridges that men can cross over in order to enter the kingdom of God, we are not giving them a chance to respond to the power of God demonstrated in the God/man, Jesus.

> 'Tradition is the democracy of the dead.'
>
> **G.K. Chesterton**

> 'Learn to build upon the strengths which you can already see rather than bemoan the weaknesses which the devil keeps reminding you about. We can't do everything but everyone can do something. Look for the obvious 'somethings' rather than trying to be too clever and developing obscure plans which have no realistic hope of success.'
>
> **Derek Cook**

Why the men aren't there

The number of churches where men outnumber women can almost be counted on one hand. Is yours one of them? If not, I hope this book will help your church to discuss the issues and be able to take steps to become more 'man friendly'.

First, let me suggest three basic reasons why we seem to have successfully reached more women and their young children with the Christian message than men.

1 In the 1914-18 war, a whole generation of church-going men were wiped out. Many of those who didn't die physically, died to God. Their war experiences made them lose all belief in a God who is good, and so they turned their backs on both God and the church.

2 For many years ministers of all denominations have been trained by theological colleges to be pastors, teachers and carers. Anyone who didn't fit into that mould was either squeezed into it or rejected as a candidate. Pastors are good at pastoral duties. Teachers are good at teaching believers. Carers respond to situations of need. So churches became internal market-driven groups rather than enterprises concerned with outreach.

Women needed daytime activities locally, and these were provided by the churches. There was a need for support groups, and these became supportive. Most of these activities were geared to meet the needs of women and pre-school children. Almost all were daytime events when these people had time on their hands.

No one gave any strategic thought to the effect that all of this would have upon men, especially the husbands in these families. Subtly, but certainly, many churches have become need-orientated.

3 Because an increasing amount of time was spent in contact with women and children, most ministers learned the language of communication to such groupings. They assumed that the same words would do when they spoke about God to men. 'Loving Jesus with all your heart' makes sense to most women.

Ministers talk a lot about faith. Women can comprehend that. They are aware of exercising faith every day. Tell them the story of Elijah and the widow's handful of flour, and they will all respond with a miracle of their own when 'a little went a long way' (see 1 Kings 17:9-16).

But the man wants to know how it happened. Facts are at the forefront in his mind. When he asks questions he may come across to Christians as aggressive and unbelieving, when in fact he is 'only asking'.

Reversing the trend

The place to start is so obvious that we neglect it. We start with the men that we have in our churches. We start by helping *these men* to get to know one another so that they can strengthen one another.

I have acted as a consultant on evangelism for a number of churches. They often have a predominantly male leadership team. Yet often the

few men that they do have in church are so busy conducting the business of the church that they never have time for the business of extending the kingdom of God.

But here is what has surprised me most of all. Most of these Christian men inside the church didn't even know each other. Their links were only on the surface. Few of them knew how any of the others had come to believe in God. When they did discover the facts, they were immensely encouraged. They knew little about each other's daily work and so could not really pray for one another. They had failed to see themselves as comrades. Fellowship is a lovely female Christian word. The man outside the church is looking for those who will stand with him in the battle of life. When we realize what we are, we can draw others into the kingdom.

Spiritual abuse

So, our starting point as men is to get to know each other. Then, once we have done that we can turn our attention to the next obvious group of men: our present circle of contacts. These will certainly include the neglected group of husbands of Christian wives. These men have been spiritually abused! We have put pressure on their marriages by helping to change the woman that they married into a very different person. Don't blame all the changes in her life upon God. The Holy Spirit is responsible for her new birth and for the emerging fruits of 'love, joy, peace, patience, kindness, goodness, faithfulness, gentleness and self-control' (Galatians 5:22). But it is our particular brand of church culture which has resulted in her being overloaded with meetings to attend or organizations to support and run.

In communicating with the non-Christian husband, we must learn that he will probably not come to God in the same way that his wife did. In a recent survey conducted by Maranatha Ministries, more than 60% of the Christian women who responded said that 'need' or 'crisis' was a major factor in their search for God. If that same 'need' message had been relevant for the man, he would already be converted. We can't keep hammering, 'You need Jesus', 'You need God in your life', 'You need forgiveness'. The self-sufficient man doesn't recognize need at all or, if he does, he cannot admit it, not even to himself.

I hear many preachers talk about how special we are to God's heart. That is a lovely thought which makes immediate sense to the mind of a woman. But it is not a good image for the man. He needs to hear about his significance to God's *plan*. And the church needs to start thinking about how to present the Christian message to a strong person who is an unbeliever. Is there something in it that is worth discovering? How can we present the truth to the man who has everything?

Fair shares for men

In this workbook I will argue for fair shares for the men. I will also ague that in the church today we must all do the hard work involved in learning how to communicate with men so that they can become Christ's men.

> *'We are overlooking the important in favour of the urgent.'*
> **Derek Cook**

> *'In England we rely on a time lag of fifty years between the perception that something ought to be done and a serious attempt to do it.'*
> **H.G. Wells**

Think about it!

Most churches and Christian fellowships have spent the last few years either lurching from one crisis to another or leaping from one special programme of events to the next. I call it 'flavour-of-the-month Christianity'.

Few churches do any strategic medium-term or long-range planning. Most leadership groups haven't the courage to ask the serious question, 'Is what we are doing having any effect?'

5

Lifeboat Churches: Women & Children First

Jesus and men

The purpose of this study is to examine Jesus' approach to men in the Gospels. The incidents are focused on the practical, everyday issues that are equally valid to us today.

Jesus' approach to men was not totally different from the way he dealt with women. But there are certain remarkable common features in these passages from which we may learn a good deal.

Read:–

- Mark 1:14-18 (Simon and Andrew)
- Mark 3:13-15 (The Twelve)
- Mark 8:27-33 (Simon and Peter)
- Mark 10:17-22 (Rich young ruler)
- Luke 19:1-10 (Zacchaeus)
- John 3:1-15 (Nicodemus)
- John 21:15-19 (Simon Peter)

1 What features of Jesus' approach to men do you notice in the text?

2 Do these features apply specially to men, or equally to women?

'If there is time, look also at Luke 10:38-42 and John 4:1-42.'

3 What can we learn from Jesus about the way in which the gospel should be offered to men today?

4 Deborah Tannen, an American Professor of Linguistics, once said:

'Women speak and hear a language of connection and intimacy, while men speak and hear a language of status and independence. Instead of different dialects, it has been said they speak different genderlects.'

In the light of these Bible passages and your own experiences, do you agree with her?

Lifeboat Churches: Women & Children First

What is my church doing to reach men and women?

Think about your church and fill in the list below indicating the men's and women's activities or groups within your church.

For men	If yes, tick here	For women	If yes, tick here
Family Service	☐	Family Service	☐
Men's Breakfast	☐	Babies and Toddlers	☐
Football team	☐	Daytime Bible Studies	☐
Add other outreach activities that you do for men.		Aerobics/Keep Fit	☐
		Mother's Union/ Young Wives Group	☐
....		Others	
....		....	
....		....	
....		....	
....		....	
....		....	
....		....	

1 Looking at your list, is there an imbalance in activities for men and women? If this is the case, why do you think this imbalance exists?

2 The birth rate is 52% male, 48% female. Yet often congregations are 30% or less male, 70% or more female. What is the ratio in your own church e.g. out of fifty people, how many are men and how many are women?

3 How important do you think it is for men to meet in groups? Or do you think it's only necessary for women to do this? Do men meet together in secular groupings?

4 Are there any particular groups for men which are needed in your church? What might be the first steps in setting them up?

Notes

'I knew men would be excited about going to a football ground.'

'...and now to illustrate my sermon, I need one man to come to the front.'

The Male Handicap

Contents

A two-page *Briefing* paper looking at the male make-up and how often it appears harder for a man to believe in Christ than a woman.

A *Discussion* paper on the Godness of Jesus. It may be helpful to gather together half a dozen men to work through this study

A *Discussion* paper on communication and the need to be up to date with current issues and TV programmes.

A *Discussion* paper on developing a strategy to reach men.

An *Illustration* listing some of things that make a man tick.

An *Ideas* list giving some do's and don'ts for reaching men.

Extras

Form a problem-solving group for men.

Topics to look at:

'Getting on Top of Stress'

'Preparation for Fatherhood'

'How to be a Better Father'

'Retirement Planning'

'Controlling Credit Cards'

'Attitudes to Pornography'

'Green Issues'

Agenda for change

Every Christian should know:

1 How to say what they believe about God.

2 How to say why they became a Christian.

3 How to say what is now important to them about being a Christian.

'Always be prepared to give an answer to everyone who asks you to give the reason for the hope that you have' (1 Peter 3:15).

The Male Handicap

There would appear to be a basic gender problem, a male-female difference in attitude and approach to life. Understanding and coming to terms with that difference is the first step to making the Christian faith accessible to men.

How men think

Why is it more difficult for a man to believe than a woman? In debating this issue I have heard Christians suggest that it isn't more difficult, it is just that men have more pride. So I then want to know why a man generally has more pride than a woman. What is it that makes him more intent on getting there by his own efforts? Is this pride a genetic factor in men or is it culturally induced? Can we use it as an *advantage* in presenting our message? Can we talk about being *proud* to be a Christian? Is that the meaning of Paul's words: 'Let him who boasts boast in the Lord' (2 Corinthians 10:17)?

Over the last few years I have been conducting my own research into how men think when it comes to religious issues. To me there do seem to be some differences in the way that a man's mind reacts to religious matters. As a man, I want proof, actual evidence for things. My favourite saying is, 'seeing is believing'. A Christian message is based upon actual events and upon well-attested historical evidence. For the Christian faith, that's fine. But we have got into the habit of failing to quote, or forgetting to quote, all the evidence at our disposal.

Perhaps women do not need quite so much proof before they are ready to take a step of faith. Men are not as good at 'walking on water', and tend to panic much more easily. Women seem to possess more spiritual sensitivity. The man, on the other hand, wants details of how it will all work out. Women seem more prepared to sense the rightness of Christian truth. They trust their instinct and their feelings more. They see reality in faith and value in belonging to the wider Christian family.

These are generalizations, but many appear to fit the stereotype! Certainly most women have to deal with life and death issues at first hand at an earlier stage than most men. Women find in childbirth and in nursing sick children or elderly parents that eternal matters are brought into sharp focus. In the past men have often not come up against the same kind of crucial events until mid-life crisis or the threat of redundancy faces them. Now a growing number of men are present at the birth of their child and this is a moment of profound meeting with eternal reality. At times such as these it is possible to talk with men seriously about creation and creativity.

'I am driving around an estate in Macclesfield with my wife, Lilian. We are looking for a house where we are to have an evening meal. It is about five years since we were there and my memory isn't as good as it was once upon a time.

'Lilian suggests that we should stop and ask someone for directions. I am convinced that I will spot some corner that I recognize in a moment or so. Ten minutes later, Lilian suggests again that we ask the lady walking down the road ahead of us. 'She won't know,' I say, and drive straight past her.

'Five minutes later Lilian points out another couple of pedestrians. 'Oh,' I reply, 'they might give us wrong directions.' Then I produce one of those useless pieces of information which men keep in reserve for such situations. 'Did you know,' I say, 'that in Mexico if you stop someone and ask for directions, they often guess at the directions because it would be impolite not to help you.'

'Lilian makes the point that we are in Macclesfield, not in Mexico!

'The real point is that finding one's own way is an essential part of the independence that I need in order to keep my self-respect. I feel uncomfortable asking for help.

'When I do eventually stop, I send Lilian out to ask for the directions!'

Does it work?

As a man, I want to know how Christianity will work out in real life. Real life often means the workplace. Many men spend more hours involved in work and travelling to work than they do at home. So the man is not generally looking for help within family relationships, and he *is* wondering if Christianity will seriously weaken his bargaining power at work.

In this area most ministers are unable to offer realistic teaching because many of them have not held responsible positions in industry or the commercial world; or at least, not for long periods and not recently.

So churches must release their laymen to teach the reality of working for God in the workplace. One man said to me recently, 'I can't ask the vicar for help over my work problems. He just wouldn't understand.' But that church did have a few men who could understand given the chance. They were tied up with the Church Fabric Committee and so had no time available to provide instruction on how Christianity could work in the workplace. Most men need mentors; let's offer some Christian ones.

Competition

Of course the church should talk to women about the Christian family. But it should also balance it for men by talking about the modern-day Christian army. Men are competitive. I'm not sure whether this is a genetic issue or culturally induced but I observe it everyday in men's work and play.

The competitive edge is there even in men's friendly sports. Then there is the aggression on the motorway. I'm not saying that all women are angels, but at least they're generally on the same side. More women are prepared to enjoy playing the game and who wins is incidental.

Men seem to see life much more as individuals in a hierarchy in which they are either one up on other men or one down. I am either the leader of the pack or the follower. Either I give the orders or I receive the orders. For men, life is a continual contest. It involves a regular struggle to preserve independence and especially to avoid failure.

Fear of failure

Men find it very difficult to come to church services. Much of this is due to the real fear of being embarrassed. Embarrassment comes through not knowing exactly what to do or when to do it. Women can smile and shrug off things that go deep down into a man because he perceives that he has failed.

'You go on your own, darling,' one man said to his wife. 'I might just embarrass you.' It was a rare moment of honesty, but his real reason for absence was to protect himself from failure.

Women see themselves much more within the context of community. They look for a part to play in a network of connections.

One woman who has recently moved to a new area told me sadly that because she is working in the daytime and no longer has tiny children she hasn't been able to get into the circle of mums in her village. She doesn't feel that she has settled into the new area because she hasn't fitted into the network. Her husband is oblivious to her need and finds it difficult to understand her problem.

Men concentrate on avoiding failure; women concentrate on avoiding isolation.

Let's be radical

Release men from routine church committee work to concentrate on helping men who are asking questions about Christianity.

Most men need mentors

The Male Handicap

The GODNESS of Jesus

There is a basic minimum which people need to know in order to be Christians. We cannot agree with those who say it doesn't matter what you believe as long as you are sincere. It does matter; it makes all the difference between heaven and hell, both now on earth, and in the eternal future.

How much does a person need to know? The Christian message centres around Christ. People need to grasp at least a little of the following four concepts: Maybe they need to know all the areas covered in the Gospel of Mark.

Jesus as Saviour

He is the one sent from heaven to earth. He gave his life in our place because of our sin. He purchased our salvation. Our sin is abhorrent to God. There is salvation in no other name. There is no other way back to the Father. Jesus alone and Jesus only.

1 Can you think of any Bible verses to support this?

Jesus as Lord

It was not only the beliefs of the early Christians which turned the world upside down; it was also their lifestyle. Christianity offers a realistic alternative strategy to that pursued by our present Western society. You cannot believe in Jesus and live as you like.

2 Can you think of any Bible verses and present-day examples to support this?

Jesus as Enabler

Jesus' own life was lived in constant touch with the Father (with one exception on the cross!). Communion-contact was possible because his life was filled with the Holy Spirit. That same Holy Spirit now indwells the lives of all those who believe.

3 Can you back this up with Bible verses and illustrations of how the Spirit dwells within?

Jesus as Leader

Jesus does not merely guide the *individual*. He is the leader of the greatest group in all the world – the church. Belonging to him integrates us with all saints of all time. The New Testament is full of 'plural' promises made to the Christian community.

4 Produce Bible verses which show this and try to see why it is important for modern man, a product of the nuclear family, to belong together in a secure group.

5 Let half the group pretend to be non-believers, each choosing an idea of God in which they refuse to believe. In turn, the other half of the group discuss their unbelief with them. The non-believers press their case. Don't be thrown if the Christians lose the argument. Remember, this is only an exercise. Sometimes in real life you will find that the non-believer suddenly does want to know about the real thing. Never be too keen on winning an argument; concentrate on being a witness to the truth. Effective evangelism doesn't depend on our cleverness but on the power of the Holy Spirit working through us.

6 Finish your time together by reading Colossians 1: 15-29 and praying for one another and for any men that you have mentioned in your conversation.

The Male Handicap

- Bosses (CEOs, senior officers) want <u>strategic</u> answers: Why should we be in this market? What's the long-term impact? What trends are we anticipating?

- Peers (vice presidents, department heads) want <u>tactical</u> answers. How much will this cost? How will it make my job easier? How will it improve my bottom line?

- Subordinates (line managers, engineers) want <u>technical</u> details. How does it work? Will it last? Does it fit?

As a general rule, there's no point in talking long-term strategy with technicians, and there's no excuse for boring the CEO with nuts-and-bolts details.

Success Secrets
Mark H. McCormack

? 1 The lesson is to tailor your communication to your target. What lessons can you learn from the above quotation as you plan to reach out in evangelism for men?

We must learn to talk with each other about the problems of the real world. We may disagree on the solutions. We may have different perspectives or different political persuasions. Even if we disagree, we must respect one another and accept that other Christians are looking for the best solutions even when they see things differently from us.

If we cannot debate issues among ourselves we will never be equipped to talk about them with the men outside our church circle. The impression we will give to friends and colleagues is that our beliefs are irrelevant to living in the real world. But by knowing what is going on in the world and what the 'world' is watching on television, listening to on the radio and reading in the media, we will automatically have points of contact to share our faith.

? 2
- Do you agree ?

- How often do you watch documentaries and news programmes on television with your friends and work colleagues, do you feel in touch?

- Which magazines do you buy? Do you have time to read them?

Notes

The Male Handicap

Notes

Peer groups for men

It has often been suggested that in order to combat a culture which is antipathetic to church-going, it is necessary to set up peer groups for men to provide the support they need in order to identify with the Christian faith. In this group they can find friendship and the opportunity to bring into the open the problems they have to grapple with.

In small groups look at the list of points about how a man ticks.

1 Do you agree with them? Are there any other points which are missing?

_____

_____

_____

2 Still bearing in mind the list, consider these questions:

• If you had an opportunity of creating a men's group from scratch, what would it be like?

• Where would it meet?

• How often would it meet?

• What would be the content of the programme?

• Would you target it at any particular group?

3 Now turn these ideas into a strategy.

• What is the aim of this strategy?

• What steps are needed to achieve this aim?

• What happens if one of these steps goes wrong?

• How can you sell this approach to everyone in your church?

What makes a man tick?

Here are some of the things that a man might aim for:

1 Finding a niche for himself in the adult world.

2 Success – at home, at work and in his leisure – and yet he needs to be cared for and wanted.

3 Standards to live by. These are often set by parents and peers and may depend upon cultural upbringing.

4 Fulfilment as a husband, father, colleague, etc. Improvement of self-worth, improvement materially, and sexual fulfilment.

5 Satisfaction – he needs goals to aim at to give a sense of achievement.

2 The Male Handicap

Some do's and don'ts on reaching men

✔ **DO** find out what is already happening in your area.

✗ **DON'T** write off what other people are doing.

✔ **DO** consider doing one or two things well to start with.

✗ **DON'T** do too much too soon or your standards will slip.

✔ **DO** remember that God creates us as individuals with differing characteristics and gifts.

✗ **DON'T** create an unbiblical stereotype of the Christian man, e.g. a saintly Rambo surrounded by a subservient wife and children!

✔ **DO** continue or start encouraging women to share in church leadership. They have a unique contribution.

✗ **DON'T** let ministry to men lead to male domination.

✔ **DO** make sure your criticisms of your church's record of reaching men are targeted at men.

✗ **DON'T** let your criticism result in devaluing or knocking the often saintly lives of women, who have often kept the ship afloat in hard times.

✔ **DO** make sure you are promoting the Christian faith and following Christ.

✗ **DON'T** simply create another male club or clique. The church is not a club.

✔ **DO** remember the needs of all groups of men. In some areas it could be the 'few' who do have jobs, those who are on shift work, men looking after children or visiting them at weekends, men with non-Christian wives.

✗ **DON'T** lose sight of the goal: reaching men, with the truth and strength of the gospel.

Being Man-friendly

Contents

A three-page *Briefing* paper outlining five ways to make your church more man-friendly.

A *Discussion* paper helping us to understand why some men feel at home in a pub, which in turn will help us to know whether they will feel at home in their local church.

A *Discussion* paper helping us to review our friendships with men.

An *Ideas* sheet using a questionnaire to research men's views on religion. This has been widely used in door-to-door calling for the last fifteen years.

An *Illustration* listing five ways to make your church more man-friendly which are mentioned in the briefing sheet.

Extras

Questionnaire

Why not visit an area collecting only men's views? Here's your opening sentence: 'We are researching men's views on religion. It takes only a few minutes, and there are no trick questions. Will you help us please?' After your research why not set up a men's evening in a pub or community hall and address some of their issues? You could re-visit and invite them to your group church.

For extra help with taking a survey look up
pages 28-9 in *Practical Ideas for Evangelism* by John Young, CPAS, or
pages 54-8 in *Evangelism Cookbook* by Derek Cook, Paternoster Press.

Story Time

Every outreach service should include a man or a couple telling 'their story'. It needs real skill to cut it down to 3-5 minutes but it can be done and it will be powerful. The person speaking needs too put himself into the male outsider's skin. He should cut out or explain words that sound like a foreign language. Get rid of all asides and cross-references and in-jokes. Practise saying it out loud. Above all, the person needs to refine it so that the greatness of God shines through.

For those who are shy about standing in front of a congregation, use a short interview style. They can talk just to the presenter who will put them so much at ease that they will forget all about the audience. By the way don't try to cover their whole life story in a five minute interview.

Prayers down your street

You may have used the approach in your neighbourhood of praying for the people in a particular street at a particular Sunday service (see pages 28-9, of *Practical Ideas in Evangelism* by John Young, CPAS).

Why not adapt that idea and request prayers just from the men of the households that you visit? You may get fewer prayer requests, but you will have shown your concern for men. Then, in church, have Christian men leading prayers for the men of your area. It's been known for some non-Christian men to come along just to make sure that their prayer request was included. Ensure some prayers are world-centred rather than self-centred.

Being Man-friendly

What you see beats what you hear every time. Any television producer will tell you that. They go to a lot of trouble to set up a Victorian scene for a television play only to discover that one of the extras was wearing a modern-day wrist watch! It all has to be shot again.

The eye gate is more powerful than the ear gate. That is why the old rule is: 'Never perform with children or animals.' They are sure to do something that steals the show away from you.

What will a man see when he does find his way into a Church?

Church or fortress?

I visit many churches, of all denominations, in the course of my evangelistic work. I have the luxury of seeing these churches as an outsider would see them, from the point of view of someone attending for the first time.

Men do find it difficult to enter a church building. Many buildings are imposing places and it isn't even always obvious which door will be open to let you in. I've walked all round a parish church before now, trying to find the right entrance. Some doors were locked; one just needed a shoulder charge.

Some buildings are surrounded by iron railings that give the impression that we should keep out. Some churches look closed even when they are open. Shouldn't we do something about this? How about a hanging sign — like a pub sign — to replace the noticeboard?

First impressions

What will a man see when he does find his way in? Will all the visual impact confirm his prejudice that church is for women and children? The only decent notices are the ones advertising the young wives' group or the children's outing. There are several of those lovely little posters with pictures of animals or little children. They are very sweet but not very manly.

Why does no one ever throw out the old hymn books? What about that broken bench or chair? Are there no men here to repair them? Try to look at your church through the eyes of a male outsider.

There is another reason why men have problems coming through the doors of our church buildings. For many men, their previous visits have been associated with what in the trade is called 'rites of passage': baptisms, weddings, funerals. At all of these events there are sets of rules. There is a code of practice about where people will sit. Some will be at the front. Some will have certain words to say. There is a pattern of seating, especially at a wedding where you are expected to be on the bride's side or a friend of the bridegroom.

Incidentally, baptisms, weddings and funerals are also times when emotion often surfaces. That in itself is enough to frighten most men off. How does he know that at a normal service there won't be even more sniffing and hankies? We are so used to our services that we don't even realize that for a visiting man they provide a real fear barrier. What does he do when he doesn't know the rules? Remember that he doesn't want to fail.

A man-friendly alternative

Let me propose five ways to make your church more man-friendly.

1 Accept him as he is

Recognize that as a man he will respond differently from a woman. His confrontational questioning is not committed unbelief but genuine searching. It seems like a trial of strength to us, but he is actually looking for reality and checking it out. Let him compare his quality of life to yours.

2 Treat him as a potential leader

There's the old management rule called the Pygmalion Effect: 'Our expectations for others condition our behaviour toward them, which in turn affects how they behave toward us.'

Begin nudging people in the right direction. Treat men as if they *were* what they could be, not what you think they are. Our faith is not a juvenile matter. Give the man asking serious questions a Christian book to read, not just a four-page tract.

John's Gospel may be theologically deep, but it is not the easiest for most men to read, especially men who want to see some action. Mark's Gospel in the Good News translation might be the best approach.

Expect a mature man to make rapid strides after his conversion. Realize that his contacts are new potential members of the kingdom of God. Accept that he will have better insights into how the outsider thinks and feels than you do. Let him advise you about ideas for winning more men.

3 Build him some bridges

Give him the chance to meet people at normal events, e.g. trips out to the theatre, a sporting event, Sunday lunch at church. Help him to save face. Organize some food events.

Then he has the excuse of the meal: 'I'm only going for the food.' *A Just Men* evening gives him another reason: 'It's only for men.'

Let him help in the church in some practical way. Maybe the church window frames need painting or the path levelling. Perhaps he could play double bass in the worship group? Now there is a real dilemma. Would his presence compromise the group or would their reality of faith and worship lead to his conversion?

Can you get rid of those uncomfortable pews? They were built for the men of the 1890s and were only just reasonable then. Nowadays, when everyone is bigger, they fit the women of the 1990s but are agony for most men. That man squirming in the pew is not under the conviction of the Holy Spirit: he is just tremendously uncomfortable on that kind of seat. An ancient Chinese proverb says: 'The mind can only absorb what the bottom can endure.'

4 Help him to overcome the fear barrier

Take note of a man's serious fear of failure.

Take the time to give him an explanation of Christianity if his wife has become a believer. Do it within the first month. Follow up your visit with a telephone call and a letter.

Label the loos. On arrival at church, a man not used to attending is tense. He needs toilet facilities. Where are they? He shouldn't have to ask; it puts him at an immediate disadvantage (Incidentally, does your men's toilet have a mirror? Men have hair to comb as well.)

Announce the page numbers of any service book and don't use abbreviations that only the initiated will understand.

uncomfortable pews?

Being Man-friendly

Women do have a real religious advantage when attending church. They have better peripheral vision! They see things better out of the corner of their eye. There are more receptor cones on the retina giving the woman better edge vision. So she comes along to church and spots things out of the corner of her eye. She notices that everyone is about to sit down, and she sits down with them even when no announcement has been made. The man, from his blinkered viewpoint, finds himself still standing up. That is very embarrassing. It wouldn't be so bad if he were on the back row out of sight, but all the Christians have filled the back rows and he is probably on display near the front.

Explain each stage of the service, in terms that the outsider will understand.

5 Avoid the cringe factor

Dr Peter Cotterell recently wrote:

'There really can be little doubt that the churches' ministers represent a major problem to the churches. Perhaps the TV caricature of the ministry is the best illustration of that fact. They are presented as wet, elderly, absurd, oddly dressed, homosexual, bleating, bumbling, five-miles-an-hour car drivers.

'The New Testament picture of the Christian is the converse of all that. Of course, it can be argued that the caricature is just that — a caricature.

'But there would be no caricature, no exaggeration, unless there is something there to be caricatured, to be exaggerated.'

Put a man's man up front some of the time. I am not making a value judgement here, only a realistic assessment of what is appropriate.

Don't force everyone to take part in the singing and don't ask men to do

the actions. 'Now we will all be Wiggly Worms,' said a Joyce Grenfell-like woman as she encouraged everyone to join in the song for the little children. The visiting father near to me was a Professor of Physics at the local university, and he didn't want to be a wiggly worm that day. You need to be able to say about your Guest Services, 'This is the best programme that is on today.' That will mean rehearsing your material until it is really good, and then making it even better.

Rehearse your material until it is really good

Being Man-friendly

The pub and the church

The purpose of this exercise is to demonstrate the point that a good pub fulfils a number of needs within a man. It is first and foremost a meeting point for men where they feel relaxed and at home.

List below why it is that a man feels at home in a pub. Then, looking at this list, think how you can translate those welcoming features into local church characteristics.

Notes

My local pub is friendly and welcoming because...	My local church could be more friendly and welcoming if...
1 _____	1 _____
2 _____	2 _____
3 _____	3 _____
4 _____	4 _____
5 _____	5 _____
6 _____	6 _____
7 _____	7 _____
8 _____	8 _____
9 _____	9 _____
10 _____	10 _____

Being Man-friendly

A day in the life of ....

For a typical week, list on the chart the places you meet other men: at work, in the pub, in church ...

1? What percentage or proportion are non-Christians?

2? In each context, are there men you know well – men you would call friends? Make a note on the chart of how many?

Place	Christians/non-Christians	Friends

3? Would it be helpful if the balance between Christian and non-Christian contacts was changed? If so, which way, and why?

4? What are the reasons it is difficult to share Christian convictions and experiences with other men? (If in a group, you may wish to consider this individually and then come together to compare notes.)

1. _____

2. _____

3. _____

4. _____

5. _____

Questionnaire

---

1   **Do you believe there is a God?**

☐ YES ☐ NO ☐ NOT SURE

---

2   **What do you think Christianity is all about?**

....

---

3   **Do you attend a church?**

☐ REGULARLY ☐ OCCASIONALLY ☐ RARELY ☐ NEVER

---

4   **What do you believe is the purpose in living?**

....

---

5   **What is your ambition in life?**

....

---

6   **What do you think is the cause of all the unhappiness in the world?**

....

---

7   **Do you think there is any life after death?**

☐ YES ☐ NO ☐ NOT SURE

---

8   **Would you like to know God better than you do?**

☐ YES ☐ NO ☐ NOT SURE

---

9   **Other Comments / Queries**

Five ways to make your church more man-friendly.

- Accept him as he is

- Treat him as a potential leader

- Build him some bridges

- Help him to overcome the fear barrier

- Avoid the cringe factor

Action Outreach

Contents

An *Ideas* sheet listing twenty ideas on how to build contact bridges with men.

A *Discussion* paper on men's ten dreams of fame.

An *Ideas* sheet giving a checklist for organizing men's events.

An *Illustration* using a cartoon on misleading publicity!

An *Illustration* of what not to do at a men's supper. (For ideas on how to run food events for men, see chapter 5, pages 34-36.)

A two-page *Briefing* paper looking at using sports and 'D-I-Y' to reach men.

Extras

Football pursuits

Derek Jefferson an ex-premier league football player and qualified Football Association Coach has set up his own Trust called 'Football Pursuits'. He is mainly concerned with running skill-training sessions for 7-11 year-olds. However, he is available to speak at men's events on his experience as a football player and more importantly on his Christian faith.

To contact him write to: Derek Jefferson, 12 Oldberrow Close, Monkspath, Solihull, West Midlands, B90 4LX. Tel: 021-745 7420

Prayerful focus

If you have a six-month programme of events for men, concentrate your invitation on any one man prayerfully for each event. Go for the obvious. If he is keen on watching sport, choose that style of event for your invitation. If he is a player, go for the participation night. Pray before you invite any man to do anything.

A useful resource

Sport and Recreation, and Evangelism in the Local Church by Leonard Browne, Grove booklet on Evangelism, no. 13, 1991.

Available from:

Grove Books Ltd, St John's College, Chilwell Lane, Bramcote, Nottingham NG9 3DS.

Action Outreach

Find out what a man thinks, and then talk about it. Find out what a man does, then organize it. Find out what a man wants, and make it happen. Use whatever means possible, in any appropriate location, to present the truth about God to men.

Keeping informed

Why does a man sit at breakfast time reading his newspaper? Why doesn't he talk about things to his wife? Have you seen the advert where, in order to get his attention, the young wife pinches her husband's spoonful of cereal?

The reason for the man's newspaper addiction is another of the gender differences. Women collect much of their news by talking together. They exchange news about items and especially about people, and use their network of contacts both locally and further afield to build up their picture of the world. Men, on the other hand, use the news from the paper to give them their way into a conversation with other men.

If they are to be seen as informed and knowledgeable they must keep up on some international news, environmental issues and especially sport.

Sporting interest

I wanted to make a comment to the man in our petrol station, just to be friendly. It was no good talking about people, even though we live in the same village, so we talked about football. Now I don't play that game; I've only ever played the kind where you can pick up the ball and run with it. But I had to know enough to appear informed, and we passed a pleasant few minutes.

The majority of men have some level of interest in matters of sport. As an increasing number of sports people are becoming Christians we obviously have a great opportunity to link sport with Christian commitment. Of course, not all Christian sports

people are saints. I heard one of them utter a couple of swear words during one of his Wimbledon matches. But that surely makes it all the more real.

We can utilize the sports link to present the truth about God. One way is to use the video programmes which a number of companies are producing about sports personalities. While you cannot afford to fly some of these superstars in from the United States, you can get hold of a video interview and use that effectively. You will need to buy or hire the video and watch it yourself beforehand. There is no reason to use all of the video if it is a long one. You can run part of the video, conduct a short interview with a local Christian sportsman and then go back to finish the video. It's worth remembering that videos do have pause buttons.

It may be that one of your local pubs has a projection video. They can fill a whole wall with a programme rather than a small television screen. It's great for impact and the curiosity value factor can attract one or two technically-minded men to the showing.

'But that might mean we have to do the event in the pub.' 'Yes,' I reply. 'But then we'd have to go to them.' 'Yes,' I say. 'But they would be on their home ground and we might be at a definite disadvantage.' 'Yes, of course. That's possible.' 'And there might be more of them than of us.' 'Praise the Lord,' I reply, 'isn't that the whole idea?'

A variation of the video theme is to make your own video featuring two

or three men from your own church or local Christian sportsmen. Ask someone who is really into making videos (perhaps on a semi-professional basis) to help you make the programme. If that man is not yet a committed Christian then this may be the way God will use to draw him in.

The other way to link into men's interest in sport is to run a sports evening. Hire the local badminton court and organize a knock-out competition. Alternatively, you may be able to hire the sports hall at the YMCA or local community school to run a five-a-side competition. You may well have to ask for help from the friends and colleagues who never come to church, either to make up the teams or to provide the competition.

You will find a number of men who would like to have a work-out with the weights. Organize it as a fun night. Show that Christians are not averse to keeping fit physically as well as spiritually, and ask the minister to preach on 1 Corinthians 9:25 the following Sunday.

Do-it-yourself

Some men who are not into the fitness scene are very keen on D-I-Y projects.

One of the ways in which a man is prepared to learn is if you give him the chance to listen to an expert.

Lots of younger men never picked up D-I-Y skills from their fathers. This is partly due to parents and children living at opposite ends of the country and partly due to the fact that the father didn't know how to do it either. In my rural area, the youngsters are still expected to help on the farm alongside Dad. Our industrialised society has destroyed this kind of learning.

There are other areas of education and help which men will be interested in attending. Could we save some money by doing the simple oil change service on the car for ourselves? Have you got an expert who can demonstrate the 'how to' factor? Use whatever experts you do have. Is there a basic building task which can be taught over a couple of evenings? You could tackle 'Brick laying for Beginners with hands on experience', or 'How to lay a garden patio that stays level', and many other such projects.

Then, when it comes to gardening, there is a huge reservoir of eagerness to pick up the tricks of the trade. Men want to do things right; the talk by an expert will attract numbers of 'fringe' men.

Why not have a Saturday when some of the church members' gardens - the really good ones - are open for visitors? A ticket, with the money going to a local charity, gains entrance to all the gardens any time between 2 p.m. and 7 p.m. A map gives their location. Some of them serve teas as well. Church members may be so booked up with church meetings that they haven't had time to develop their gardens. If so, you may need to postpone the 'open gardens day' to the next year and reduce the number of church business meetings in the meantime. Or perhaps you can open the gardens of half a dozen sympathetic non-church attenders.

All these events can simply be contact events: building bridges with activities. Or they can include a specific Christian comment time. Your builder can give an epilogue on 'Building God's Kingdom'. The Christian gardening expert can include a section on 'The Tree of Life'. (Did I hear a groan? Well, come up with something better then!)

'Give the new Christian man the chance to lead you in effective outreach. After all he knows how the uncommitted man is thinking better than you do.'
Derek Cook

Use your experts

Action Outreach

Bridge Builders for Men

1. Give High Profile to the men that you do have already in your church.

2. Place photographs of men in the church entrance which say: 'We are here to help you.'

3. Produce beer mats with gospel messages.

4. Give free lifts home from the local pubs at closing time.

5. Place Christian reading material at the launderette, doctor's, dentist's.

6. Encourage men to share their testimonies in church services.

7. Take over leisure centre or squash courts for the night.

8. Hold a men's night in local restaurant/hotel.

9. Invite a Christian sportsman to give a demonstration of his skills.

10. Organize and run an 'It's a Knockout' Competition.

11. Hire the local cinema and show a film with a Christian meaning which can be discussed later over a pint of beer.

12. Organize a car treasure hunt (many men want to be racing drivers).

13. Hire a premier division football ground for a game.

14. Sponsor a parachute jump for local charity.

15. Run aerobics classes for men over 50!

16. Organize a flight on Concorde, or an airship, or a hot air balloon.

17. Hire a stand at agricultural shows or town carnivals and then use your men to run it.

18. Study Christians through the ages. Then write in your local newspaper about men who have changed society.

19. Appoint a media rep.

20. Go hospital visiting in the men's wards

Notes

Action Outreach

Men's ten dreams of fame

In a survey men were asked:

'What do you really want to achieve in life?'

'How would you like to be remembered?'

'What do you want from life itself?'

In their replies, some of the more common phrases were:

I want to...

- *make a difference.*
- *have an impact.*
- *make a contribution.*
- *do something important with my life.*
- *prove myself.*
- *be somebody.*
- *achieve something worthwhile.*

I want my life to...

- *be significant.*
- *count.*
- *have meaning.*

?
1 Do these phrases ring true?

?
2 Are there other points you would have expected to see?

?
3 Is the 'want' driven by a need for recognition *now* or a desire to be remembered long after we've died—a form of immortality?

?
4 For Christians, is 'success' a good, bad or neutral thing?

?
5 What difference might Christianity make to a person's 'dreams of fame'? And would the difference be 'exciting and challenging' or 'irrelevant and off-putting' to someone without Christian faith?

Action Outreach

Action checklist

Here's an action checklist to use when planning an event to which men who seldom come to church are invited.

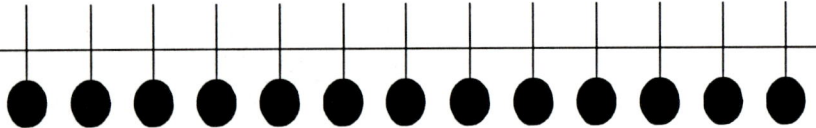

Tick when completed

The idea _____

- [ ] Date _____   - [ ] Venue? _____

Speaker? _____

- [ ] Invited   - [ ] Accepted
- [ ] Who is looking after the speaker? _____

Follow up. What is it? _____

- [ ] Planned
- [ ] Who is responsible? _____

Publicity. Who is responsible? _____

- [ ] Publicity ordered
- [ ] Invites given out personally at church

Prayer. Who is responsible? _____

- [ ] Organized
- [ ] Will there be a special time of prayer? If so,
- [ ] Where? _____   - [ ] When? _____

- [ ] Event evaluated. By whom? _____

- [ ] Publicity planned for next event

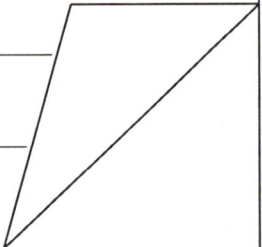

TONIGHT 'CHRISTINA REVEALS ALL'

MEN ONLY

'Oh, no! They've got the 'n' and the 'a' the wrong way round.'

'But, look at the crowds!'

'Following our main course...'
'Oh, good I like puddings.'

'...John will now speak about your need to be born again.'

The Way to a Man's Heart

Contents

A four-page *Briefing* paper on how to use food and the chat show approach to reach men.

A *Discussion* sheet on men's invitation dinners written by Alan Smith, a vicar with vast experience on reaching men.

Two *Invitation* cards to a meal or event.

For an *Illustration* of what not to do at a men's supper see page 32.

Extras

An investment portfolio
- Invest some time in serious thinking about evangelism of men.
- Invest some money in good-quality publicity and presentation.
- Invest some effort in a realistic programme to reach the men outside your church.
- It will all be a worthwhile investment in the kingdom of God.

Truth and proof
Take a look at the work of mathematician Kurt Godel.

1. For every consistent formal theory of arithmetic, there are formulas such that neither they nor their negations are derivable as consequences of the axioms of the theory. (The famous Incompleteness Theorem)
2. Truth and provability are not the same thing.
3. The human mind is not like a digital computer.

Read *The Emperor's New Mind*, by Roger Penrose, Vintage Press 1990.

Useful addresses for evangelistic speakers:

CPAS,
Evangelism Division
Athena Drive,
Tachbrook Park,
WARWICK
CV34 6NG
(0926) 334242

Maranatha Ministries
Christian Teaching
Centre,
KIRKBY STEPHEN,
Cumbria
CA17 4ES

Christian Viewpoint for Men
Townsend Chambers,
Amherst Hill,
SEVENOAKS,
Kent
TN13 2EL
(0732) 460625

The 40:3 Trust
46 Asthill Grove,
COVENTRY,
West Midlands
CV3 6HP
(0203) 504792

Diocesan evangelists
Many dioceses employ evangelists or missioners. Contact your local diocesan office.

The Way to a Man's Heart

If we are to reach out with good news to men, we will have to think of different styles of activity from those we have used to reach women. We will have to re-examine our Christian vocabulary and throw out some of our Christian jargon. We will be involved in risk-taking, and we won't get everything right first time. But I believe that now is the time for some creative thinking concerning evangelism for men.

Food, glorious food

Any woman can tell you that the way to a man's heart is through his stomach. Whether or not you agree with that, my observations over the last fifteen years show that men will attend evangelistic events that are linked with food. My theory is that the food gives him three safety factors.

First, he has an excuse for why he is attending. If anyone challenges him about going to a Christian event he simply replies, 'I'm only going for the food.' That is a face-saving formula which silences all ridicule from unsympathetic or hostile friends.

Second, when he arrives he knows what will be expected of him. People will expect him to eat. Now he knows how to do that. He has been doing it all his life. He can relax and enjoy it.(By the way, the food at most Christian events is far better than at many secular events. I find that Christians rarely realize how high their standards are.)

Third, the man has something to do with his hands. A man almost always needs something to occupy his hands. A steering wheel, a spade, a video zapper or a newspaper would be usual. A plate of food is an ideal alternative. The food approach can vary from a set dinner with several courses to a finger buffet or something much simpler.

For a man-to-man event, I often use the title 'Just Men' because there is a nice play on words. You can have a one-course meal calling it a 'Hotpot Supper'(don't forget all the sauces and trimmings though). We once ran a 'Fish 'n Chip' night, ordering them in advance from the best chippie in town and eating them straight out of the newspaper. At a different venue the Kentucky Fried Chicken outlet was just around the corner. A whole crowd turned up and the talk was about being a 'Franchise of Heaven' (Philippians 4:20).

Younger men can be attracted to the 'Food Crawl'. The first course is in house number one and the host talks briefly about how he became a Christian. The main course is in house number two with another testimony. The sweet course is at house number three where the evangelist pulls the evening together by talking about how to get a testimony for yourself.

The food does need to be good. If what you give the men exceeds their expectations, they will listen far more carefully to what you have to say. If the food is cheap, they will assume that it represents the value and quality of the message.

Food for thought

We have run a 'Meal with a Meaning' not just for men but for couples. There are three rules to remember:

1 Don't invite too many uncommitted people; you want to have the opportunity for individual conversations afterwards.

2 Don't let church members all sit at the same table. Work out a seat-

The food approach can vary from a set dinner to a finger buffet

ing plan and prayerfully mix and match your guests. Make good use of those in the church who may not bring a guest but who are excellent communicators and have the gift of evangelism.

3 Don't ask a woman (who has contact with the church) to bring her partner (who is out on the fringe of things). Take your invitation tickets to the man and ask *him* to be your guest and to bring his wife or girlfriend as well if he'd like to.

Recently we have noticed that in suburban areas weekends are often heavily committed for fringe members of the church. As families are more mobile and as grandparents live longer, more time is involved in visiting them at a distance. As a result, we are seeing some success with a mid-week meal event. That might, of course, clash with Bible study or home group commitments. As a church you may need to agree to cancel the week's home groups.For which is more important: feeding the insider or feeding the outsider? You will also be offering more than a cup of cold water (see Matthew 10:42 and Matthew 25:35).

All of your food events can include, but not necessarily conclude, with a Christian comment. For a male audience it should be an uncomplicated, straightforward presentation of the claims of Christianity. Men, it would seem, need to hear clear words and strong opinions.

Go for the overview and the big scene. Take up the challenge of answering the objections which men present. Take the ground from under their feet and let them fall into eternity.

Your most effective speakers on these occasions will be men who have the gift of an evangelist. They have the God-given skill of putting themselves into the skin of someone who seldom — if ever — comes to church and looking at things from his perspective. Don't be shocked if they don't use all of your favourite religious words. They are aiming to communicate the message, not to impress fellow church goers.

Breakfast meetings

One of the most successful times of the week for getting men together is a Saturday morning breakfast. My latest one was served in the bar of a pub. We started at 8.30 a.m. and promised to be clear at 10 a.m. The pub opened half an hour later so the men knew that we had a fixed finishing time. It is amazing how many men ask, 'When will it end?' I say, 'At 10 a.m., although if you understand what we talk about you'll feel the effects for eternity.' We have cornflakes and orange juice, followed by bacon and egg, sausage, mushrooms and fried bread, then toast and more toast and coffee and more toast.

But the men haven't come just to eat. They have come to listen to the Christian challenge in a setting where they feel comfortable. The publicity made this element of the event quite clear. Remember to introduce your speaker and a trailer of his theme right at the start of the event. This means that men can be talking, or at least thinking, about the subject all the way through the food. You have given them some food for thought!

Getting the right man

Another lesson I've learned from experience: fix the date of the event around the availability of the right speaker. Don't fix it to fit in with some church anniversary date.

I have also come to the conclusion that you need to invite your speaker twice. The first time is to give the

Men need to hear clear words and strong opinions

The Way to a Man's Heart

Let a sense of humour show through

Christians enough confidence to invite their uncommitted friends the second time. 'If I'd known it was going to be so good, I would have invited my neighbour,' is a comment that I have heard time and time again.

It adds to the cost to have two meetings, but it makes a huge difference to the number of new people who are brought along. So have your speaker to enthuse the team on the first occasion and then come back for the second leg game a little while later. The first match can be on home ground at church, the second in a secular venue. Don't leave too long a gap between the two events because most have short memories.

The Christian Chat Show approach

Sue Lawley does it brilliantly on radio. Jonathan Ross is the smoothie on television. Breakfast TV features it all the time and local radio couldn't continue without it. They all rely upon interviews and chatting to people about present-day events and their experiences of life.

Every church ought to be using this style of presentation as one of its contemporary evangelistic approaches.

People will come because you are going to be talking about the issues of the day and the events in the newspapers. They are interested and aware of those things. Sunday's sermon about Moses, a man they never knew, living thousands of years ago in a land that they have never visited, doesn't grip them in quite the same way.

You can use a chat show spot in the middle of a church service. But you could also make it an event on it's own. The setting needs to be informal and relaxed. Get a few of those invited to help you create a sort of television studio. Others can help with the sound and the video production. You will need to turn it into a video so that all the partners who weren't allowed to attend can watch it. You will also find that the men who took part and the ones setting it up also want to watch a re-run or loan it out proudly to their friends in the month that follows.

Planning the programme

The aim of the programme is to present Christian testimony and truth through relaxed talking. For a one-hour programme you will need three special guests and a music break. If one of your guests has just been in the local news, then that is a bonus. Any man from the world of sport will do. He may not play for a leading team, but he is probably still a better player than those at the show. Add a man from the world of business or a policeman/probation officer/teacher, because the issues of law and order or educational matters are always relevant. A man from the world of entertainment would also be good, or one from the medical profession.

So choose any three from those six general areas: sport, commerce, law and order, education, entertainment, health. We have even used two men and a five- minute clip of a famous man's testimony using a large screen video presentation. Don't be gentle in your questioning. The audience will relish a bit of cut and thrust. You are not there, however, to attack or embarrass your guest. Do let a sense of humour show through.

While the general drift of the questions should be pre-arranged, covered beforehand with your special guests, don't give them a list of questions. That always kills spontaneity. Do give them details of how you will start. Arrive early enough to rehearse their entrance with them and where they will sit on stage in order to be

heard. Tell them what the first question will be and how you will end the interview.

Always have them welcomed by the audience with applause; it boosts the guests' confidence. Always thank them with applause as you finish; it enables them to walk off stage more easily.

Your music break should always be a performance. You are not getting everyone to sing; someone is singing the message of Christian faith. Don't choose an obscure song but one that puts the truth plainly for men.

We invite men who plan to attend to send in any questions which they want to have answered. The presenter needs these the day before and has total discretion on whether or not to use any or all of these questions. The opportunity for members of the audience to ask individual questions of your guests comes in the mixing time over refreshments. Never give an open invitation for questions from the floor. One man who likes the sound of his own voice and has a point to prove can ruin the evening. It is not a public debate; it is a Christian chat show.

Try it and see

As the presenter I seek to probe into how a man's Christian faith affects the way he does his job. I always conclude the evening with a clear closing challenge to men to find faith by discovering the truth of Christianity for themselves. We have seen some great conversions as a result.

Six more tips for effectiveness

1 Send the presenter on a course to improve his skill.

2 Get someone to do careful research on the background of each special guest and give that to the presenter a week before the event.

3 Keep right up to date with today's news, nationally and locally.

4 Get the facts right.

5 Expect someone to turn to Christ as a result of the chat show.

6 Have the publicity ready to give out at the end of the evening inviting people to the next special event.

Conclude the evening with a challenge

The Way to a Man's Heart

Alan Smith, an Incumbent in Northants., who has wide experience of men's work writes:

'I am sold on men's invitation dinners, i.e. 7 p.m. two-course meal plus a glass of wine, priced so that even the unemployed can afford to bring somebody with them. It takes a number of years for men to get over the 'embarrassment factor' i.e. they can invite friends to it because the meal is good and the speaker is good. They may not agree with the speaker, but he is good. We have self-confessed non-Christian men, atheists and agnostics asking for information of the next men's dinner because of this. Both must be right. A poor after-dinner speaker will kill the whole thing dead. For this reason I only have two or three men's dinners a year. I would expect (from a very ordinary, non-eclectic, parish church) 100 men to sit down for the meal (40% non-Christians) and for the men to enjoy a 45 minutes' after-dinner speech designed to be directly evangelistic, and no punches pulled.

'Christian Viewpoint for Men will provide a list of speakers to those who join the organization, together with a CV on each.

'I have a pioneer church on a housing estate, from where two men came to our last dinner. I asked one of my men to write up their stories (names have been changed).

'"Bill Bryant accompanied me to the men's dinner. He is generally quiet by nature, but obviously enjoyed the meal and the speaker. I feel that he is becoming more responsive to God in his life, but has yet to make a total commitment."

'"Roy and his father came to the men's dinner. To quote Roy's wife, 'they both chopsied about it all the way home afterwards.' It turned out that Roy's father and my father had some common interests. Both had thoroughly enjoyed the evening and are both looking forward to the next one. Roy's father worships at chapel: Roy was brought up at chapel, but has lapsed, and is now coming to Whitefriars (church plant) almost every week the exceptions being when he has to work a Sunday morning shift. Both were impressed by the speaker. I am convinced from Roy's comments since that he has been given something to think about. I have been able to follow this up with my own testimony."

'Whenever I do a mission, I insist on a men's dinner. Recently I conducted a mission, leading a faith-sharing team from Rushden to a country parish with five villages and churches. There were only a handful of men altogether in the church from the five villages. So when I asked for a men's dinner, I was told it was not on. I insisted. The outcome was that the hall of a local school was used. Seventy men came. The church provided a first-class meal, and wine was served. I spoke with no punches pulled. All but five or six men asked for a Journey into Life. No, I am not saying that sixty-five were saved. I am saying that all listened. Most were interested enough to take a booklet. The vast majority were complete outsiders.'

1 Are you surprised by the 'success' factor which Alan describes in having men's suppers?

2 Why do non-church men accept dinner invitations?

3 What steps could your church take in either starting regular dinner evenings or improving existing evenings?

Two invitation cards

Come and join us

for _____

on _____

at _____

_____

_____

Men's Supper

Come and join us

for _____

on _____

at _____

_____

Guest speaker

_____

CPAS
Athena Drive
Tachbrook Park
WARWICK
CV34 6NG

Tel: 0926 334242
24hr Orderline: 0926 335855

Booklist

Further Evangelism Resources from CPAS

1993 CPAS Code	Title	Author and Publisher
82001	**Creating Confidence in Evangelism**	John Young, CPAS
82002	**Practical Ideas in Evangelism**	John Young, CPAS
82003	**Creating a Church for the Unchurched**	Anne Hibbert, CPAS
82004	**Planning a Church Mission**	Paul Weston, CPAS
00351	**Christian Basics**	CPAS video-based course
03508	**A World Apart**	Martin Robinson, Monarch/CPAS
03512	**Reaching the Unchurched**	Paul Simmonds, Grove Booklet
02171/2	**A Stage Beyond the Fringe**	Five drama sketches, CPAS
03507	**Children and Evangelism**	Penny Frank, CPAS Handbook, Marshalls
03416	**Growing the Smaller Church**	Mike Breen, CPAS Handbook, Marshalls
02055	**Good News Down the Street**	Mike Wooderson, Grove Booklet
00081	**Good News Down the Street**	Grove Booklet with CPAS cassette-based course.
03497	**The Well Church Book**	John Finney, SU/CPAS
03490	**Evangelism Through the Local Church**	Michael Green, Hodder & Stoughton.
03491	**The Case Against Christ**	John Young, Hodder & Stoughton.
03423	**Why We Can't Believe**	Paul Weston, IVP
03484	**Under Fives and their Families**	Judith Wigley, CPAS Handbook, Marshalls.
03489	**Evangelism through Small Groups**	Paul Berg, Grove booklet
03527	**My God**	Michael Green, Eagle
03533	**Growing New Christians**	Steve Croft, CPAS Handbook, Marshalls.
03523	**Finding Faith Today**	John Finney, Bible Society.

Lion Pocketbooks:

03471	**What's the Point?**	Norman Warren
03470	**Ten Myths**	Michael Green
03473	**Resurrection – Fact or Fiction?**	Richard Bewes
03474	**A Certain Faith**	Norman Warren
03472	**A New Dimension**	Michael Green
03486	**What's the Point of Christmas**	J John
03498	**What Happens after Death?**	David Winter
03487	**Jesus the Verdict**	John Young

Other books by Derek Cook.

03514	**Men! – what's missing in today's church**	Marshall Pickering
	An Evangelism Cookbook	Paternoster Press
	Help! My Wife's got religion	Maranatha Ministries

© CPAS 1993

To: Geoff
Best wish...

GW01464009

To: Geoff
Best wish...

March 31, 2003

Tell Kosak Shamali

Vol. I

Published by
Oxbow Books, Park End Place, Oxford, OX1 1HN

in association with
The University Museum
The University of Tokyo

ISBN 1 84217 052X

This book is available directly from

Oxbow Books, Park End Place, Oxford, OX1 1HN
(Phone: 01865-241249; Fax: 01865-794449)

and

The David Brown Company
PO Box 511, Oakville, CT 06779, U.S.A
(Phone: 860-945-9328; Fax: 860-945-9468)

or from our website

www.oxbowbooks.com

UMUT Monograph 1

Printed in japan

UMUT Monograph 1

Tell Kosak Shamali

The Archaeological Investigations
on the Upper Euphrates, Syria

Vol. I

Chalcolithic Architecture and the Earlier Prehistoric Remains

Edited by

Yoshihiro Nishiaki and Toshio Matsutani

Oxbow Books
in association with
The University Museum
The University of Tokyo

2001

Yoshihiro Nishiaki and Toshio Matsutani (eds.) 2001

Tell Kosak Shamali

− The Archaeological Investigations on the Upper Euphrates, Syria

Vol. I Chalcolithic Architecture and the Earlier Prehistoric Remains

Tokyo: The University Museum, The University of Tokyo

Issued March 31, 2001

Designed by Yae Kosugi

Printed by Yoshida Printing Inc., Japan

ISBN 1 84217 052X

The general view of Tell Kosak Shamali
Top: Tell Kosak Shamali after the 1997 season (from the south)
Below: The distant view of Tell Kosak Shamali (from the southeast). The Nahar Sarine runs in front.

CONTRIBUTORS

Masashi Abe, Department of Archaeology, Graduate School
of Humanities and Sociology, the University of Tokyo, Tokyo, Japan

Masayuki Akahori, Institute of Asian Studies,
Sophia University, Tokyo, Japan

Laure Belmont, Maison de l'Orient Meditérranéen, Lyon, France

Fengjun Duan, Graduate School of Engineering,
the University of Tokyo, Tokyo, Japan

Honglin He, Center for Space Information Science,
the University of Tokyo, Tokyo, Japan

Seiji Kadowaki, Department of Anthropology,
Tulsa University, Tulsa, the United States

Tatsundo Koizumi, Department of Archaeology, Faculty of Letters,
Waseda University, Tokyo, Japan

Toshio Matsutani, professor emeritus,
the University of Tokyo, Tokyo, Japan

Marie Le Mière, Maison de l'Orient Meditérranéen, Lyon, France

Yumiko Miyazaki, Laboratory for Radiocarbon Dating,
the University Museum, the University of Tokyo, Tokyo, Japan

Yoshihiro Nishiaki, Department of Prehistory of West Asia,
the University Museum, the University of Tokyo, Tokyo, Japan

Takashi Oguchi, Center for Space Information Science,
the University of Tokyo, Tokyo, Japan

Hiroshi Sudo, Department of Archaeology, Faculty of Letters,
Waseda University, Tokyo, Japan

Hiroyuki Tano, Institute of Environmental Studies, Graduate School
of Frontier Sciences, the University of Tokyo, Tokyo, Japan

Masatoshi Tao, Department of Archaeology, Faculty of Letters,
Tokai University, Hiratsuka, Japan

Kunio Yoshida, Laboratory for Radiocarnon Dating,
the University Museum, the University of Tokyo, Tokyo, Japan

PREFACE

Tell Kosak Shamali is a prehistoric site situated on the east bank of the Euphrates, about 40km south of the Turkish border (Fig. 1). It is a small mound located in the area to be submerged by construction of the Tishreen dam on the Upper Euphrates, north of the Tabqa dam. Since the early 1980s, a series of salvage archaeological operations by both Syrian and international teams has taken place in this dam flood zone producing a rich realm of information on the past human activities and their developments in this particular region of Syria (del Omo Lete, G. and J.-L. Montero Fenollós, 1999. *Archaeology of the Upper Syrian Euphrates, the Tishreen Dam Area*. Barcelona: Universitat de Barcelona). The excavations at Tell Kosak Shamali were carried out in this context by the University of Tokyo team between 1994 and 1997 with an emphasis on investigating cultural deposits of the Chalcolithic period.

Prior to the onset of the Tishreen Dam project, the Upper Euphrates valley in Syria was already known as a promising field for prehistoric research. Apart from an aerial survey in the 1920s (I.F.E.A.D. 1988. *Une Mission du Reconnaissance de l'Euphrate en 1992*. Damascus: Institut Français de Damas), rescue excavations before the Tabqa dam construction in the early 1970s were one of the earliest scientific attempts to demonstrate the significance of the area to understand the beginning of the plant and animal domestication in the early Holocene. Many traces of human occupation in the late Epi-Palaeolithic to the earlier

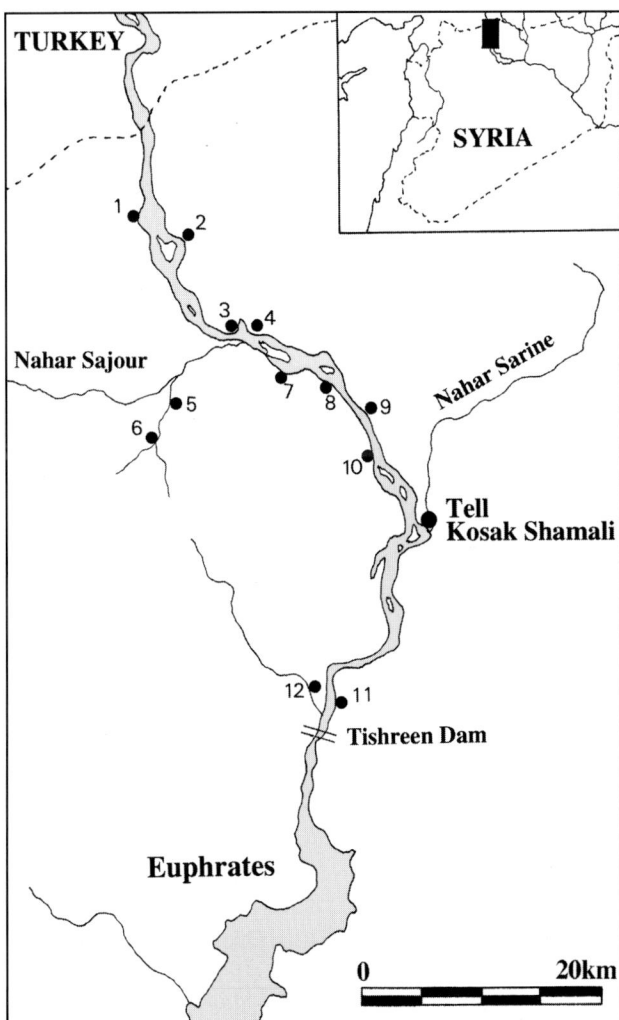

Fig. 1
Map showing the location of Tell Kosak Shamali and the related Ubaid and early Holocene settlements on the Upper Euphrates, Syria. *1: Tell Amarna, 2: Shioukh Tahtani, 3: Tell al-'Abr, 4: Tell Ahmar, 5: Molla Assad, 6: Tell Hudhud, 7: Hammam Seghir, 8: Hammam Kebir, 9: Ja'ade Mughara, 10: Qadahiye, 11: Jerf el-Ahmar, 12: Tell Halula. (Based on P. Sanlaville ed. 1985, and G. del Omo Lete and J.-L. Montero Fenollós eds. 1999).*

7

Neolithic periods were discovered at, for example, Tell Mureybet and Tell Abu Hureyra. In addition, the excavations at Habuba Kabira and Jabal Aruda, demonstrate the important role of this region in the urbanization processes that occurred in the late Chalcolithic in Syria.

In the following decades, a few surveys were undertaken in the north including parts of the Tishreen dam zone and the Sajour. Those by the British and the French teams in the late 1970s documented wide-ranging evidence of human occupation from Palaeolithic to historic times (Copeland, L., 1981. Chronology and distribution of the Middle Palaeolithic, as known in 1980, in Lebanon and Syria. In: *Préhistoire du Levant,* edited by J. Cauvin and P. Sanlaville, pp. 239-264. Paris: C.N.R.S.; Sanlaville, P., 1985. *Holocene Settlement in North Syria.* BAR i.s. 238. Oxford: B.A.R.). In the 1980s, the Tishreen dam area became once more the focus for intensive reconnaissance surveys in connection with construction of the dam. Tom McClellan's survey located over twenty Holocene settlements, many previously unrecognized, in the area to be flooded. Furthermore, the exploration by a French-Spanish team in 1989 confirmed several sites, including Tell Kosak Shamali, as having potentially rich Neolithic and Chalcolithic remains deserving serious study (Cauvin, M.-C. and M. Molist, 1987. Prospection néolithique sur le Haut Euphrate Syrien. *Annales Archéologique Arabes Syriennes* 38: 78-90). Excavations that followed at such major sites as Tell Halula and Jerf el-Ahmar indeed yielded valuable data enriching our understanding of the cultural processes of these periods.

With the information provided from these surveys and excavations, we visited the Tishreen area in 1993 and chose Tell Kosak Shamali as a place for our intensive archaeological operations. Our intention was to shed new light, through excavation, on cultural developments of the earlier Chalcolithic, namely the Ubaid period. Indeed, the surface materials indicated its obviously wealthy Ubaidian deposits. The Ubaidian, bridging the Neolithic and the late Chalcolithic, is a period that witnesses the development of Neolithic agrarian society into a more complex society. In comparison to earlier and later periods in this region, the Ubaid is underrepresented by previous research. Tell al-'Abr was the only site that had received substantial excavations at that time. The archaeological work at Tell Kosak Shamali was thus expected to fill an important gap in our information on Chalcolithic cultural developments leading to the emergence of urban society in northern Syria.

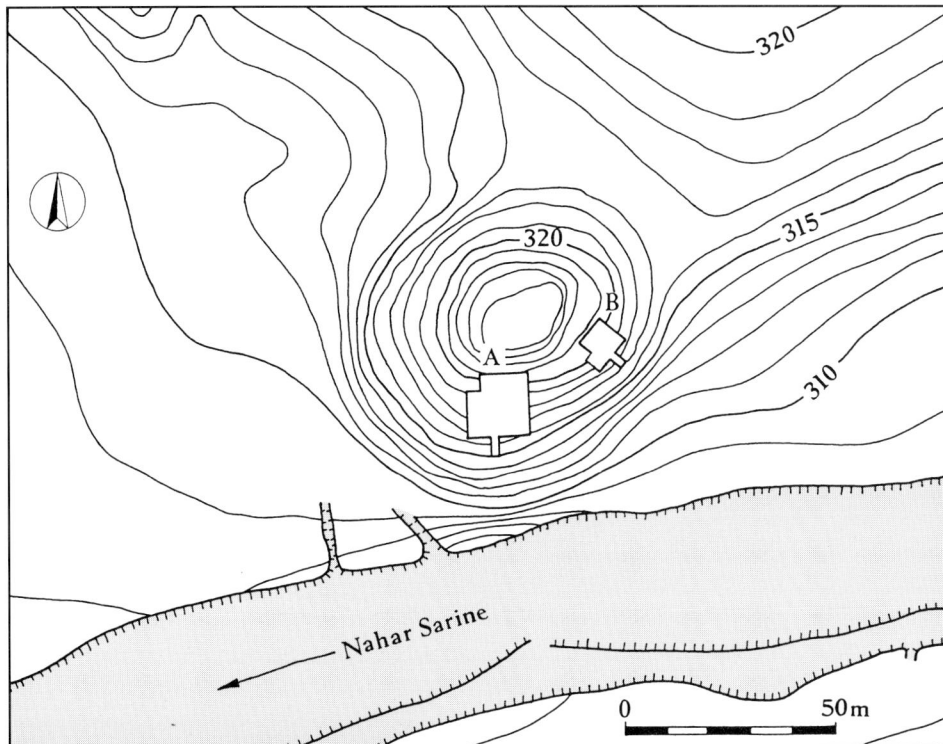

Fig. 2 The mound of Tell Kosak Shamali and the excavated areas.

Tell Kosak Shamali is a small oval mound of about 80m by 70m, rising approximately 9m above the surrounding terrain (Fig. 2). The southern side of the mound descends steeply toward the Nahar Sarine, a tributary of the Euphrates, which flows seasonally from the east. We chose the southern side for excavations mainly because heavy erosion appeared to have removed much of the later disturbed deposits. Following an initial sounding in 1994, more substantial fieldwork took place between 1995 and 1997, and two study seasons were designated in 1998 and 1999. These investigations revealed that in addition to the Ubaid period, the mound and surrounding area had evidence of occupation dating to the Palaeolithic, Neolithic and even Uruk periods. Therefore, we have a good set of stratified archaeological data for the size of the site.

The present volume is the first of reports to be published on the Tell Kosak Shamali project. Chapters 1 and 2 provide brief descriptions of the geographical and cultural settings of the site. These introductory chapters are followed by detailed descriptions of the architecture and stratigraphy in Chapters 3 and 4. Radiocarbon dates for the tell deposits are then presented and commented on in Chapter 5. Chapter 6 addresses the Palaeolithic remains discovered at the site, and the next three chapters (Chapters 7-9) furnish accounts on the Neolithic finds. The final chapter (Chapter 10) provides a summary of the present volume. While the architectural remains presented in Chapters 3 and 4 relate primarily to the Chalcolithic, more detailed reference to Chalcolithic discoveries will be presented in the following volumes.

The Tell Kosak Shamali project was made possible through with the most kind support of a number of individuals and institutions. It is our great pleasure to express our deepest gratitude to all of them.

First of all, we would like to thank Prof. Dr. Sultan Muhesen, the former Director-General, and Dr. Abudl Razack Mouaz, the current Director-General of the Directorate General of Antiquities and Museums, for their generous permit allowing us to undertake our investigations. We are also much indebted to Dr. Adnan Bounni, the former Director of the Department of Excavations, and the late Dr. Nasib Saliby and Dr. Bassam Jamous, the former Co-Directors of the Department of Excavations, who gave us help whenever we needed it. Dr. Mohamed Kadour, the former Director of Museums, also expressed his continued interest in our project. Practical support from Dr. Wahid Khayyata, Director of the Aleppo Department of Antiquities and Museums and his staff, Dr. Antoine Suleiman, Mr. Mohammed Muslim, Mr. Hamido Hammade and Mr. Mohammed Shabbane were most helpful to us both in the field and at the Aleppo Museum. The work of our Syrian representatives, Mr. Mahmud Shaqra (1994), Mr. Mohammed Ali (1995-1996, 1998), Mr. Mamon Showaf (1997), and Mr. Naser Sharf (1999), who carefully supervised our work, is deeply acknowledged. Mr. Adeeb Sbahe, an Aleppo-based surveyor, prepared an excellent contour map of the site for us. The wide ranging skills of Mr. Mustafa Shadi not only as chauffeur, but also in settling a variety of domestic matters helped us greatly. We are most grateful to all these people.

Our heartfelt thanks are also due to help from the Japanese in Syria. Mr. Takeshi Kagami, Japanese Ambassador to Syria, and his staff at the Embassy of Japan gave us encouragement as well as practical suppors. Dr. Giro Orita, ICARDA, and Ms. Yayoi Yamazaki, always welcomed us warmly. Mr. Ichiro Ogawa, Director of the Nippon Koei Co., Aleppo, provided us with the surveying equipment.

The project would never have been achieved without the backing from the University of Tokyo. Professors Akira Goto and Takeshi Hamashita, former Directors of the Institute of Oriental Culture, and their staff gave us unchanged encouragement, and the current director, Professor Yonosuke Hara very generously awarded us funding from the Mesopotamian Research Fund of the University of Tokyo for the present research. The former

Director of the University Museum, Professor Yoshihiro Hayashi, and the current Director, Professor Akihiko Kawaguchi graciously permitted us to use facilities for sample and data processing throughout the project. The museum staff, particularly Ms. Yayoi Ogawa and Ms. Hiroko Mikuni of the Department of Archaeology of Western Asia, have made a significant contribution in completing figures and photographs.

The cooperation and enthusiasm offered by the following members of our mission are also greatly appreciated: Tatsundo Koizumi (1994-1999), Takashi Oguchi (1995, 1996), Akiyo Maeda (1995), Seiji Kadowaki (1997, 1999), Masashi Abe (1997, 1999), Hiroyuki Tano (1997, 1999), Kosuke Yamagishi (1997), Masatsugu Nokubo (1998), the University of Tokyo; Marie Le Mière (1995-1998), Maison de l'Orient Meditérranéen; Manabu Furuyama (1994-1996), Nihon University; Masato Kurabayashi (1994), Josai International University; Takashi Tateno (1994), Tokyo Metropolitan Archaeological Center; Hiroshi Sudo (1995-1999), Ken Goto (1995), Takahiro Odaka (1996), Tae Makita (1996), Shogo Kume (1998), Waseda University; Masatoshi Tao (1996, 1997), Chizu Kanenaga (1995), Toshiaki Yanaida (1997, 1998), Tokai University; Hiroshi Kurosawa (1995, 1996), Meiji University; Masayuki Akahori (1996), Sophia University; Ryuji Shikaku (1996), Aoyama Gakuin University.

We would like to thank the following sources for financial support for the project: the Mitsubishi Foundation (1993-1996), the Monbusho Grant-in-Aid International Scientific Research Program (1994-1996, Grant No. 06041018), the Monbusho Scientific Research Program C(1) (1997-1999, Grant No. 09610401), the Mesopotamian Research Fund of the University of Tokyo (1997, 1998) and the Takanashi Foundation (1997).

Finally, our deep appreciation goes to Dr. Norah Moloney, the Institute of Archaeology, University College London, for her painstaking work in editing the English text of the present volume.

Toshio Matsutani   **Yoshihiro Nishiaki**
Professor Emeritus,   The University Museum,
The University of Tokyo   The University of Tokyo

CONTENTS

List of Figures

3

4

5

List of Tables

List of Plates

CHAPTER 1

Geomorphological and environmental settings of Tell Kosak Shamali, Syria

Takashi Oguchi

1.1 Site location

Tell Kosak Shamali is an archaeological site along the Upper Euphrates about 40 km south of the Syrian/Turkish border (Fig. 1.1). The site is located at the northern edge of the Syrian Desert, a wide arid lowland extending from the southern foothills of the Anatolian Highlands (Fig. 1.2). The site is about 80 km NNW of the Tabqa Dam, which forms the largest artificial reservoir along the Syrian Euphrates.

Tell Kosak Shamali is about 650 m from the east bank of the Euphrates and adjacent to a tributary called the Nahar Sarine (Figs. 1.3-1.6), a wadi with intermittent flow. The course of the Nahar Sarine by the tell is oriented ENE-WSW, but in the upper reaches it follows a meandering and incising course into the plateau-like landscape (Fig. 1.4).

The summit of the tell is about 26 m above the Euphrates and about 22 m above the Nahar Sarine (Fig. 1.6). The village of Kosak Shamali is on the gentle slopes behind the tell (Fig. 1.5). The tell is also close to the ruin of Qalaat Najm, a Medieval castle situated on the west bank of the Euphrates (Figs. 1.3 and 1.7).

Kosak Shamali has a climatic regime intermediate between desert and steppe. The mean annual precipitation is about 250 mm (Traboulsi 1981), with most rainfall occurring in the winter months between November and April. It is extremely dry in summer so that intensive farming is confined to the narrow zones along the perennial waters of the Euphrates.

The bedrock along the Upper Euphrates consists mainly of Tertiary sedimentary rocks, predominantly limestone and marl. Quaternary basaltic rocks also occur east of the Euphrates near the Syrian/Turkish border (Fig. 1.8). In addition to limestone and basalt, the Upper Euphrates carries Paleozoic/Mesozoic sedimentary and metamorphic rocks originating from the Turkish highlands.

Tertiary carbonate rocks widely occur along the Nahar Sarine near Tell Kosak Shamali (Fig. 1.9). Quaternary basaltic rocks also occur in hilly lands about a few kilometers ENE of the tell. Most gravel carried by the Nahar Sarine near the tell is carbonate, because the amount of water discharge in tributaries underlain by basaltic rocks is insufficient to flush gravel.

1.2 General characteristics of topography

Topographic characteristics in a ca. 7.5 x 9 km area around Kosak Shamali (Fig. 1.4) were analyzed using a digital elevation model (DEM) with a grid interval of 100 m (Fig. 1.10). The procedures of the DEM preparation and analyses are described in Appendix to this chapter. Figure 1.11 shows the relationship between the percentage of the area and the altitude calculated from the DEM. The altitude zones were classified into 5-m bins. Peaks at 295-300 m, 305-310 m, 345-355 m, and 370-400 m indicate the existence of low-relief surfaces at these altitudes.

The map of the slope angle derived from the DEM (Fig. 1.12) shows that steep slopes mainly occur 1) along the edges of the Euphrates flood plain, 2) along the Nahar Sarine, and 3) in the mountainous area to the east. The relationship between altitude and slope (Fig. 1.13) indicates that the average slope angle tends to be small for the altitude zone below 310 m and between 350 and 430 m, confirming the existence of low-relief surfaces within these altitudes (Fig. 1.11). The maximum slope for these altitude zones, however, is about 20 degrees (Fig. 1.13). Therefore,

DEM data with a slope angle of less than 3 degrees were selected from the four altitude zones corresponding to the peaks in Fig. 1.11, for the detailed mapping of the low-relief surfaces (Fig. 1.14). The lowest surface (295-300 m), Surface IV, corresponds to the present channel of the Euphrates. Surface III (305-315 m) corresponds to the floodplain and the lowest river terraces along the Euphrates. Surface II (345-355m) occurs mainly upstream of the Nahar Sarine and in Miliha Village southeast of Kosak Shamali (Figs. 1.14-1.16). Surface I broadly occurs in three zones: north, northeast, and southeast of Kosak Shamali (Figs. 1.14-1.16). The distribution of Surfaces I and II (Fig. 1.14) and topographic profiles across the surfaces (Figs. 1.17 and 1.18) indicate that these surfaces are dissected fluvial terraces formed by the Euphrates. In our previous report, Surfaces I and II were combined and called Q1 and the lower terraces were called Q2 to Q6 (Nishiaki *et al.* 1999). For consistency, Surface I and Surface II are hereafter referred to as Q1a and Q1b, respectively.

1.3 Field surveys

1.3.1 River terraces

River terraces lower than Q1b broadly occur along the lower and middle reaches of the Nahar Sarine (Figs. 1.16 and 1.19-1.21). The distribution of these terraces was investigated. However, because the terraces were small, the DEM and existing topographic maps were not useful for mapping them. Although stereo pairs of aerial photographs have often been used to classify river terraces, such photos for Kosak Shamali were unavailable. Therefore, field surveys on the river terraces were undertaken during the 1995 and 1996 seasons.

Well-developed terraces are confined to a 2-km reach of the Nahar Sarine near its junction with the Euphrates. Only the lowest terrace (Q6) occurs along the ca. 600-m reach between the junction and the tell, whereas, more terrace levels are observed upstream from the tell (Figs. 1.19 and 1.20). Thus, 16 topographic profiles, perpendicular to the reach, were constructed to investigate terrace distribution upstream from the tell (Figs. 1.22 and 1.23), with intervals between the adjacent

profiles of 100 m along the reach. The profiles were surveyed using a slope profiler with a 2-m span, manufactured by Tokyo Research Co. Ltd. (Fig. 1.24). Terrace surfaces were identified based on the visual inspection of profile shapes. The longitudinal profile of the Nahar Sarine was also surveyed in the field with a hand level and a measuring tape. Fig. 1.25 illustrates the longitudinal profiles of the river bed and terraces identified from profiles, permitting the classification of terraces from Q2 to Q6 according to height and continuity. The result of the terrace classification is shown in Figs. 1.22, 1.23 and 1.25. These figures illustrate that Q2 and Q3 have a spotty distribution but Q4, Q5, and Q6 occur more continuously. Q6 widens between 100 and 400 m from the tell and between 1000 and 1500 m. In contrast, Q4 is widest between 500 and 800 m from the tell (Figs. 1.22 and 1.23).

Two further profiles through the tell were surveyed: one across the Euphrates and the other across Kosak Shamali village. The first profile shows Q2 and Q6 along the Euphrates (Fig. 1.26), and the second shows the gentle slope behind the tell below a steeper slope of limestone bedrock (Fig. 1.27).

1.3.2 Fluvial and colluvial deposits

Deposits forming river terraces were investigated in the field. Q6 deposits are widely exposed on the channel bank of the Nahar Sarine. They consist mostly of fine bedded sediments with occasional gravel layers (Fig. 1.28). Higher terrace deposits tend to contain more gravel. The Q2 fluvial deposits behind the tell (Fig. 1.29) have been transported by the Euphrates, as in addition to limestone, they also contain basalt, sandstone and metamorphic rocks.

Fluvial gravel similar to the Q2 terrace deposits in Fig. 1.29 is exposed at the western slope of the tell (Fig. 1.30). The gravel is rounded and contains basalt, sandstone, and metamorphic rocks as well as limestone (Fig. 1.31). The top of the gravel layer is located about 12 m below the summit of the tell. Trenching survey at the southern slope of the tell (Fig. 1.32) also indicated the existence of the buried fluvial gravel. In addition, the fluvial gravel is overlain by a layer with angular gravel, which is further covered with human-related tell deposits (Figs. 1.32 and 1.33). On the basis of this stratigraphic information and the topographic profile in Fig. 1.27, a geological cross section through the tell was constructed (Fig. 1.34). The section indicates that the angular gravel layer is colluvial foot slope deposits. The top of the fluvial deposits below the tell, plotted in the river terrace longitudinal profile (Fig. 1.25), revealed that the Q4 terrace is buried below the tell. Figs. 1.22 and 1.23 show that along the Nahar Sarine upstream from the tell, Q4 often smoothly joins the gentle colluvial slopes behind the terraces, indicating that Q4 is partly covered with colluvial deposits. Therefore, shortly after Q4 was formed, conditions were probably favorable for the development for colluvial-slope at the tell and elsewhere.

1.4 Discussion

The ages of the river terraces were estimated based on terrace classification, stratigraphy of deposits, and relevant literature. Besançon and Sanlaville (1981) have classified river terraces along the Euphrates between Jerablus and Qara Qozaq, about 12 to 40 km upstream from Kosak Shamali. They concluded that the 50-55 m terrace is Middle Acheulean, and the 30 m terrace is Upper Acheulean corresponding to Oxygen Isotope Stage 6. On the basis of its height above the river bed, Q1b in the Kosak Shamali region can be correlated with the Middle Acheulean terrace, and Q2 with the Upper Achulean terrace (Table 1.1).

Besançon and Sanlaville (1981) identified two further river terrace levels. One is the highest terrace formed in the Lower Acheulean or preceding periods, with which Q1a in the Kosak Shamali region is equivalent. The other is located below the Upper Acheulean terrace (Q2) and is thought to have formed in the Last Glacial period. Q4 can be correlated with this Last Glacial terrace as the colluvial deposits below the tell contain abundant Middle Palaeolithic artifacts, while the deposits themselves are covered with sediments including Natufian materials (Nishiaki et al. 1999), indicating that the colluvial deposits accumulated during the Middle or Upper Palaeolithic. Previous research in the Levant inferred that angular gravel could have been produced by freeze-thaw action during the latter stage of the Last Glacial period, Oxygen Isotope Stage 2 (e.g., De Vaumas 1970; Koizumi 1978; Farrand 1979, 1980). This inference suggests that the colluvial slopes in Kosak Shamali were formed primarily in the Upper Palaeolithic due to freeze-thaw action. Because Q4 is directly covered with colluvial deposits, it probably formed in the Middle to Upper Palaeolithic during the Last Glacial age. Q3 appears to be close to Q4 in age, judging from the small differences in height between them along the lower reach of the Nahar Sarine (Fig. 1.25).

In summary, accumulation of the human-related sediments at Tell Kosak Shamali began around the Pleistocene-Holocene transition, covering the surface of the Last Glacial colluvial deposits (Table 1.1). The sloping surface of colluvial deposits did not restrict tell formation because deposition by freeze-thaw action on the flat Q4 terrace provided a gently inclined surface (Fig. 1.34). Rather, this small surface inclination may have facilitated human settlement, because it enabled quick water discharge during times of rainfall.

Q5 and Q6 were formed, after human settlement had occurred, by the downcutting of the Euphrates and the Nahar Sarine (Table 1.1). The great width of Q6 suggests that the height of the river bed was stable for a long time. Q6 can be correlated with the Qoa terrace along the Syrian Euphrates near the Turkish border, identified by Geyer and Besançon (1997) and Belmont (1999). The incision of the present channel into Q6 is distinct in the lower to middle reaches of the Nahar Sarine (Fig. 1.25). The existence of a knick point about 1300 m upstream of the tell (Figs. 1.25 and 1.35) suggests that future recession of the knick point will induce rapid channel incision in the upper reaches.

Table 1.1 Inferred chronological table for the Kosak Shamali region.

Geological age	Oxygen Isotope Stage	Landform	Tell	Archaeological age
Holocene	Stage 1	Q6		Ubaid
		Q5	Settlment	
				Natufian
Last Glacial age	Stage 2	Colluvial slope	Colluvial slope	Upper Palaeolithic
		Q4	Q4	Middle Palaeolithic
		Q3		
Middle Pleistocene	Stage 6	Q2		Upper Acheulean
		Q1b		Middle Acheulean
		Q1a		

References

Belmont, L. (1999) *Implantation géographique de trois sites néolithiques précéramiques dans la Vallée du Haut Euphrate Syrien: Jerf el Ahmar, Dja'dé, Halula.* Mémoire du DEA, Faculté de Géographie, Université Lumière Lyon 2. Lyon: Université Lumière Lyon 2.

Besançon, J. and P. Sanlaville (1981) Apercu Géomorphologique sur la vallée de l'Euphrate Syrien. *Paléorient* 7(2): 5-18.

De Vaumas, E. (1970): Phenomenes cryogeniques de la cote Libanaise. *Rev. Géogr. Phys. Géol. Dyn.* 12: 265-292.

Derry, D. R. (1980) *A Concise World Atlas of Geology and Mineral Deposits.* London: Mining Journal Books.

Farrand, W. R. (1979) Chronology and palaeoenvironment of Levantine prehistoric sites as seen from sediment studies. *Journal of Archaeological Science* 6: 369-392.

Farrand, W. R. (1980) Pluvial climate and frost action during the Last Glacial cycle in the easetern Mediterranean-evidence from archaeological sites. In: *Quaternary Paleoclimates. GEO Abstracts*, edited by W.C. Mahaney, pp. 393-410. Norwich.

Geyer, B. and J. Besançon (1997) Environnement et occupation du sol dans la vallée de l'Euphrate Syrien durant le Néolithique et le Chalcolithique. *Paléorient* 22(2): 5-15.

Koizumi, T. (1978) Climate-genetic landforms around Jabal and Douara and its surroundings. *Bulletin of the University Museum, the University of Tokyo* 14: 29-51.

Nishiaki, Y., T. Koizumi, M. Le Mière and T. Oguchi (1999) Prehistoric occupations at Tell Kosak Shamali, the Upper Euphrates, Syria. *Akkadica* 113: 13-68.

Ponikarov, V. P. (1966) *The Geologic Map of Syria, 1:200,000.* Ministry of Petroleum, Department of Geological and Mineral Research, Syrian Arab Republic.

Traboulsi, M. (1981) *Le Climat de la Syrie: Exemple de degradation vers l'aride du climat méditerranéen,* thèse 3e cycle. Lyon: Université Lumière Lyon 2.

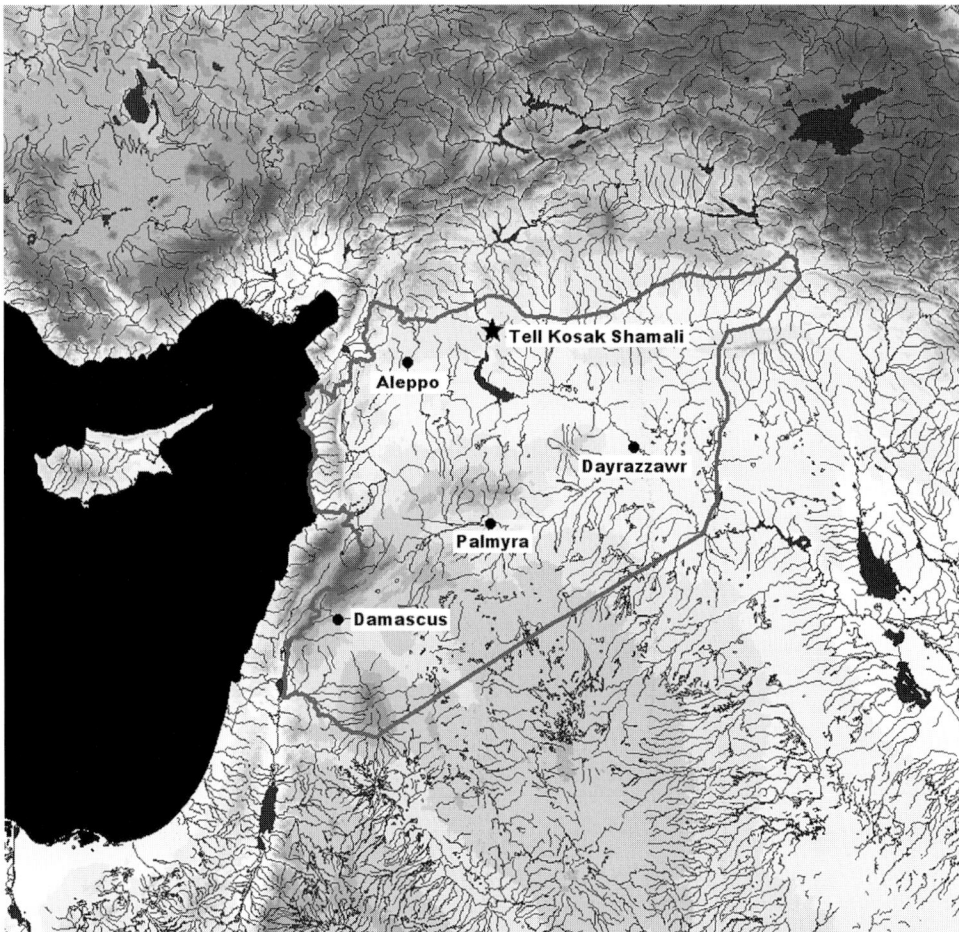

Fig. 1.1 Topography and drainage systems in and around Syria.
See Appendix for data sources and cartographic procedures.

0   200 km

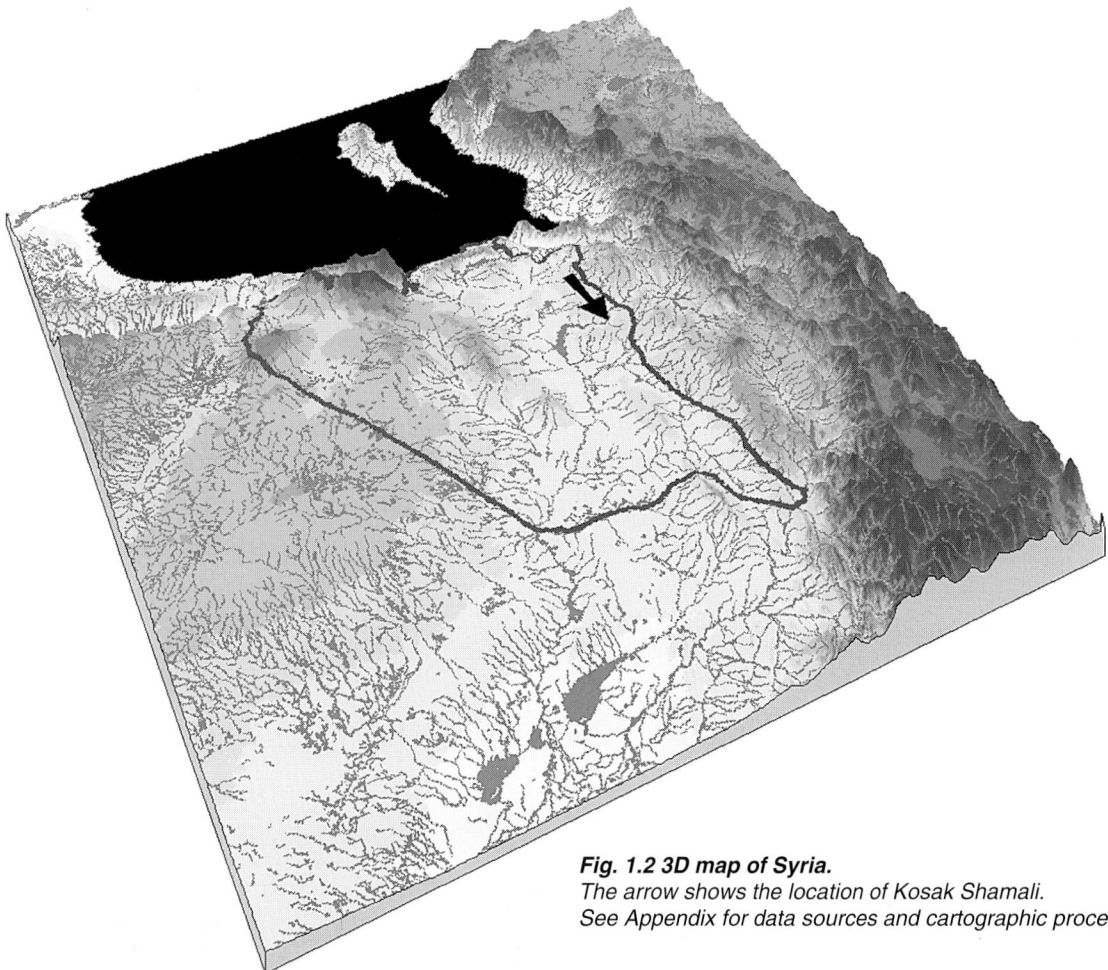

Fig. 1.2 3D map of Syria.
The arrow shows the location of Kosak Shamali.
See Appendix for data sources and cartographic procedures.

Fig. 1.3 Satellite image of the Upper Euphrates near Kosak Shamali.
The image was provided by the Corona Satellite Photography Library, US Geological Survey.

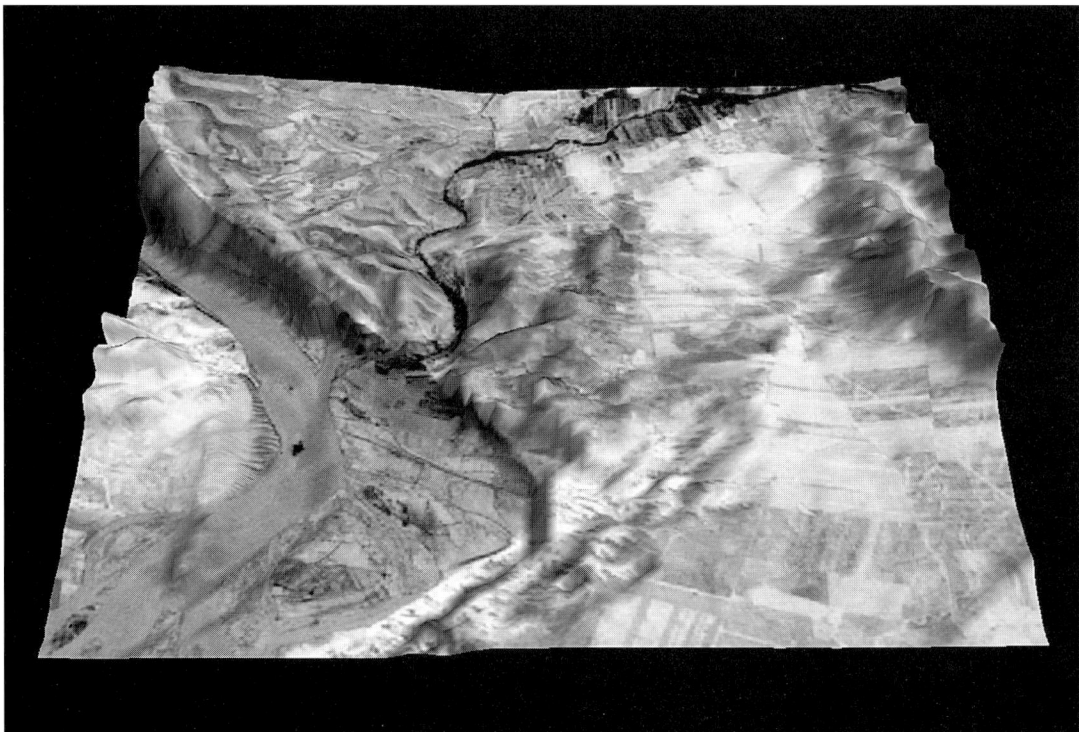

Fig. 1.4 3D image of the Upper Euphrates near Kosak Shamali.
See Appendix for data sources and cartographic procedures.

Fig. 1.5 Kosak Shamali seen from Qalaat Najm, a castle on the west bank of the Euphrates.

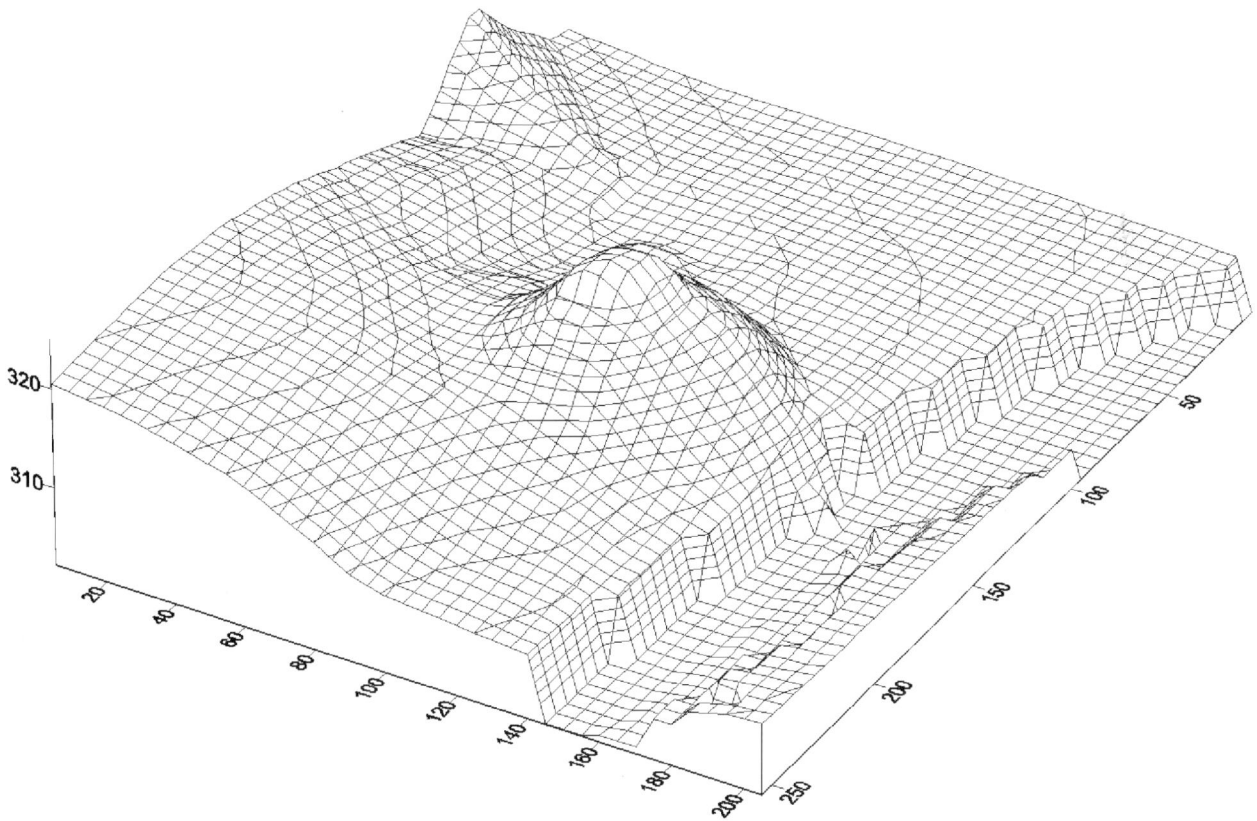

Fig. 1.6 3D wire-frame view of Tell Kosak Shamali and the Nahar Sarine.
Frame size is 5 m in both X and Y directions. Contour interval is 1 m.
See Appendix for data sources and cartographic procedures.

Fig. 1.7 Qalaat Najm, Tell Kosak Shamali and the Euphrates.

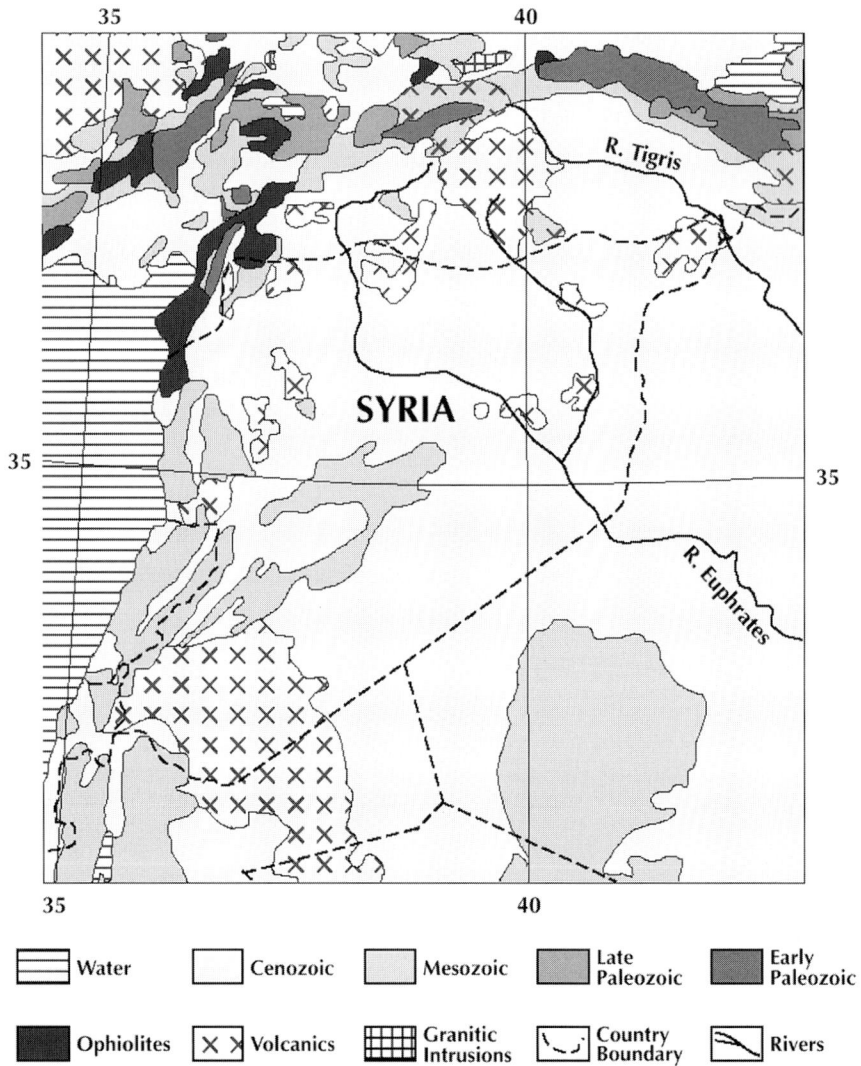

Fig. 1.8 Generalized geological map of Syria and surrounding areas (after Derry 1980).

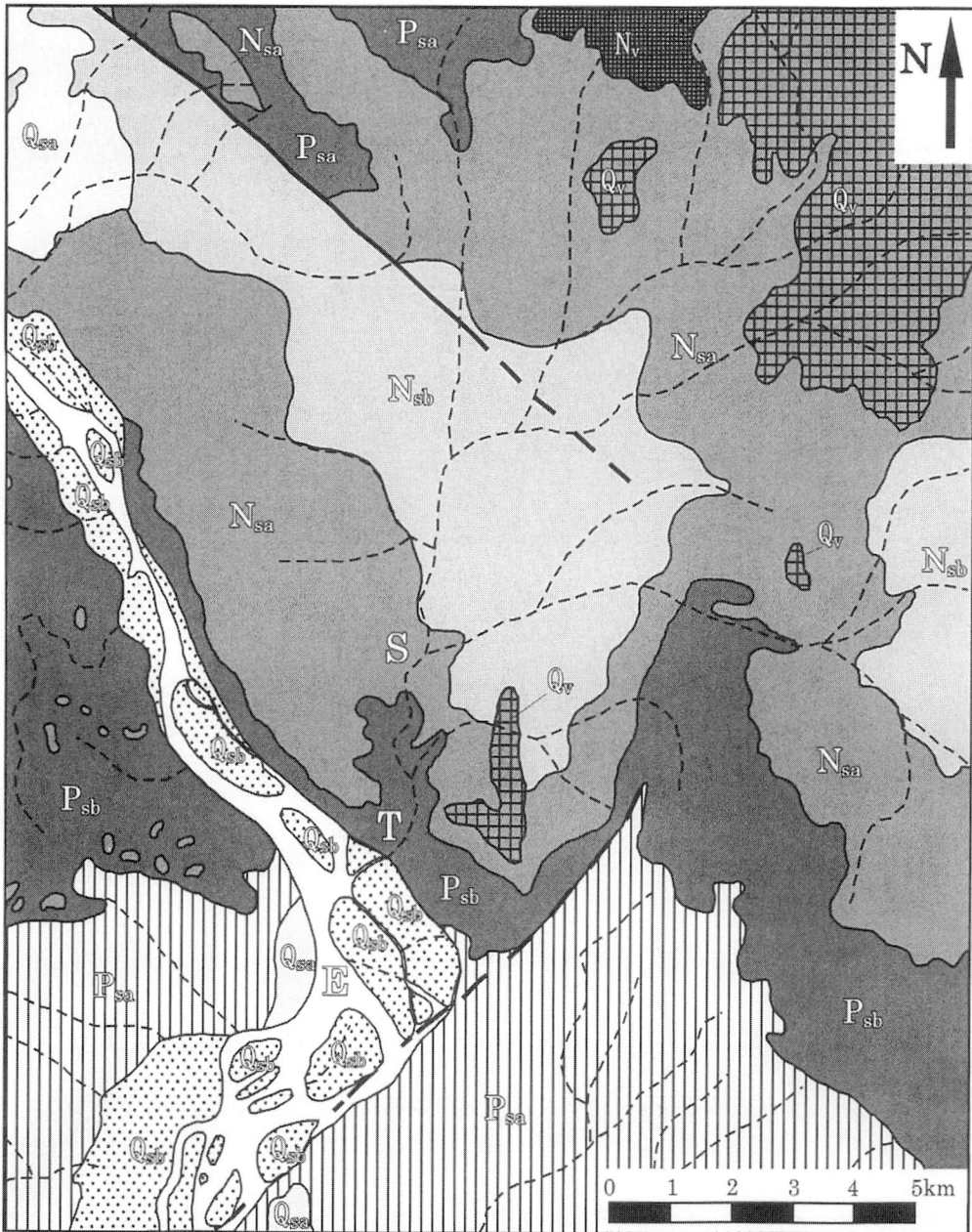

Fig. 1.9
Geological map in and around Kosak Shamali (after Ponikarov, 1966).

Psa: Paleogene (Eocene) calcareous sediments, Psb: Paleogene (Oligocene) calcareous sediments, Nsa: Neogene (Helvetian) calcareous sediments, Nsb: Neogene (Tortonian) calcareous sediments, Qsa: Middle Quaternary fluvial sediments, Qsb: Holocene fluvial sediments, Nv: Neogene volcanics (basalt), Qv: Quaternary volcanics (basalt and tuff).

E: The Euphrates, S: The Nahar Sarine, T: Tell Kosak Shamali.

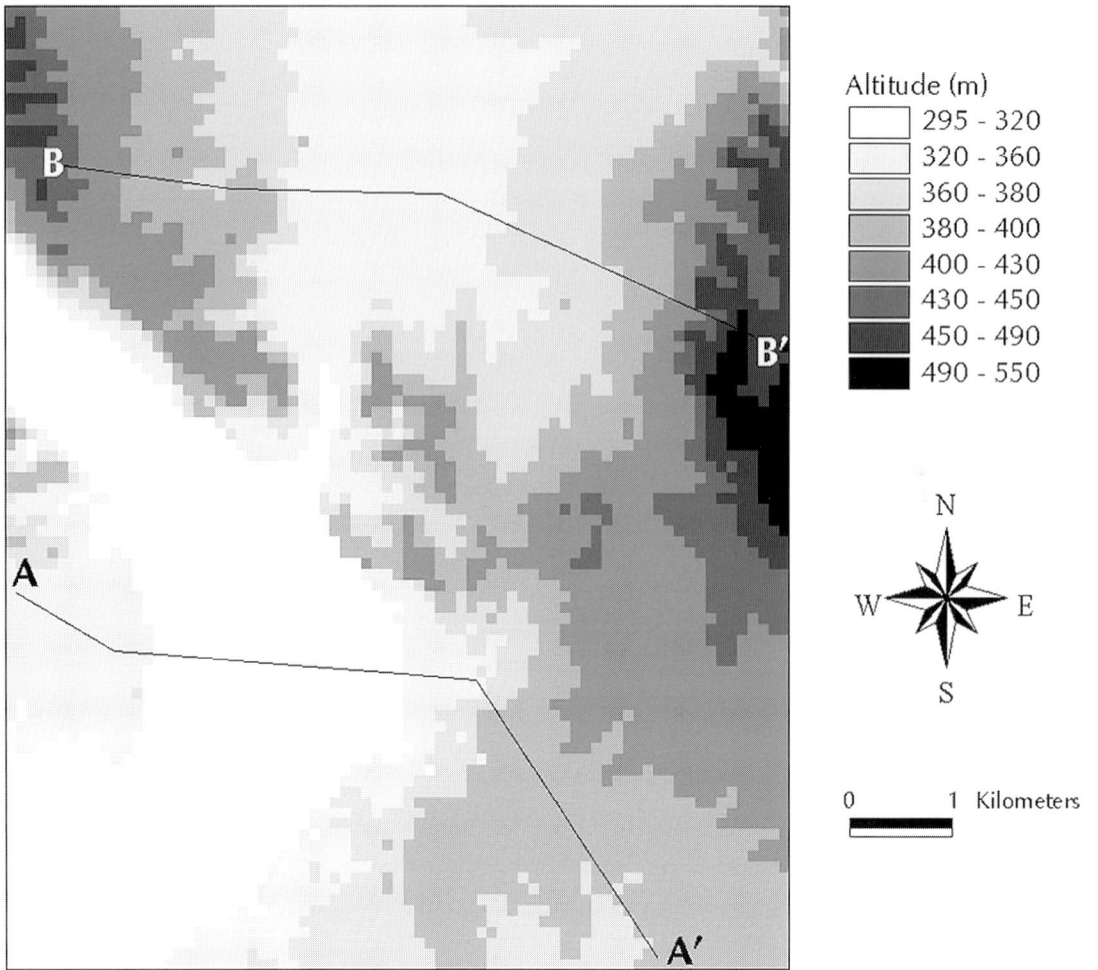

Fig. 1.10
**Altitude distribution for the Kosak
Shamali region based on the 100-m
DEM.**
*See Appendix for data sources and carto-
graphic procedures. A-A' and B-B' are the
locations of the topographic sections in
Figs. 1.17 and 1.18 respectively.*

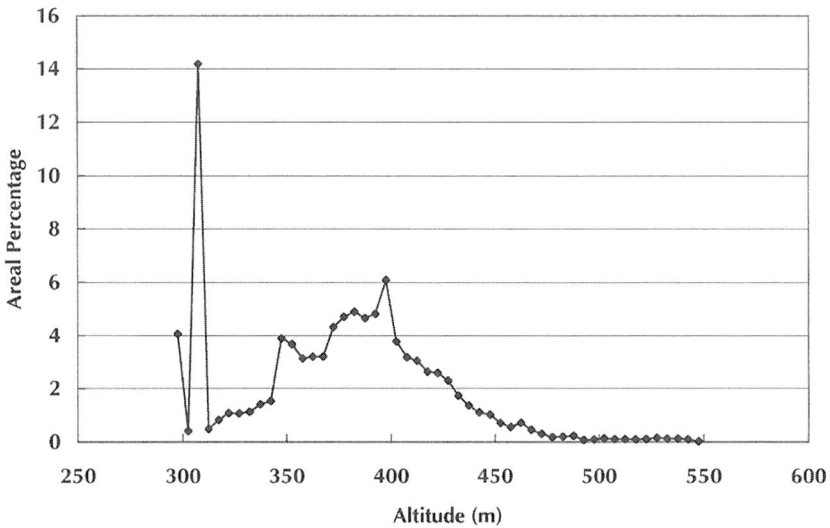

Fig. 1.11 The relationship between altitude and area for the Kosak Shamali region.
Altitude zones are classified using 5-m bins.

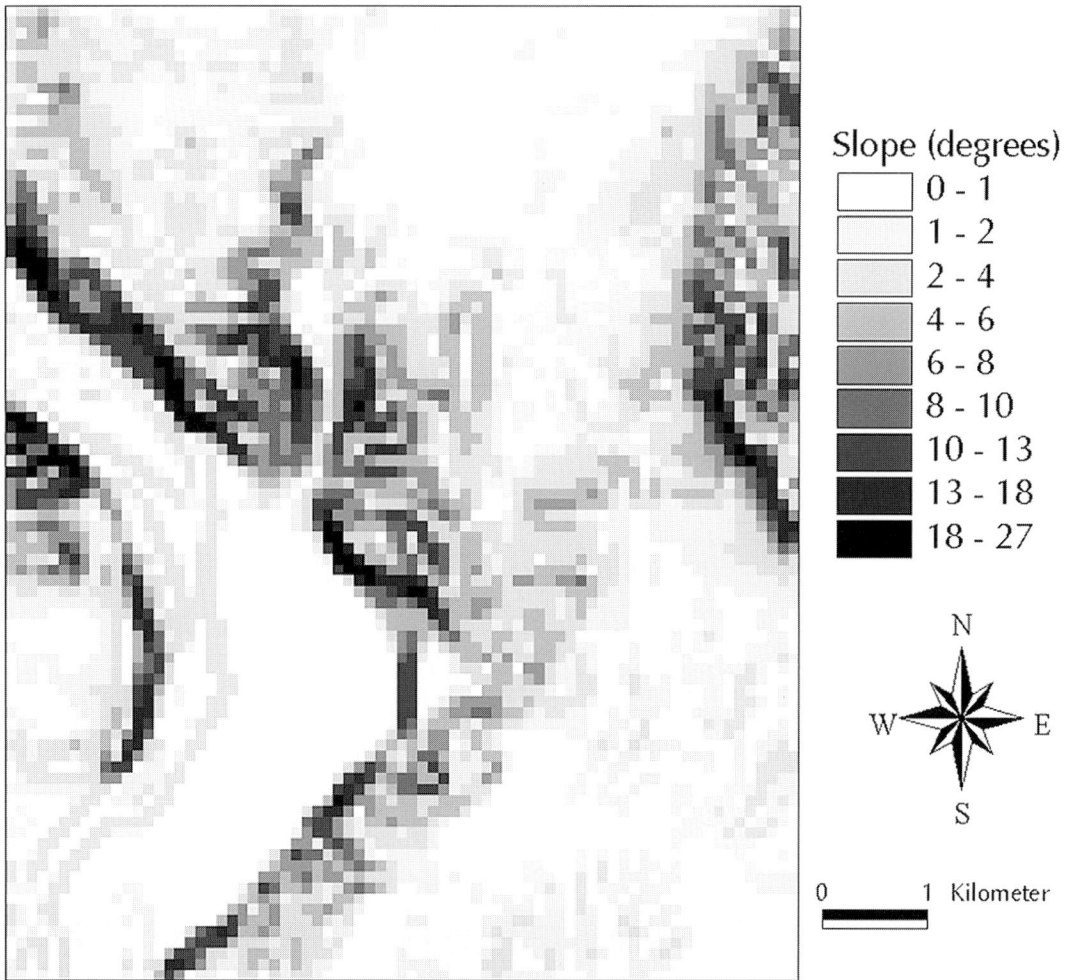

Fig. 1.12 Slope distribution for the Kosak Shamali region based on the 100-m DEM.
See Appendix for data sources and cartographic procedures.

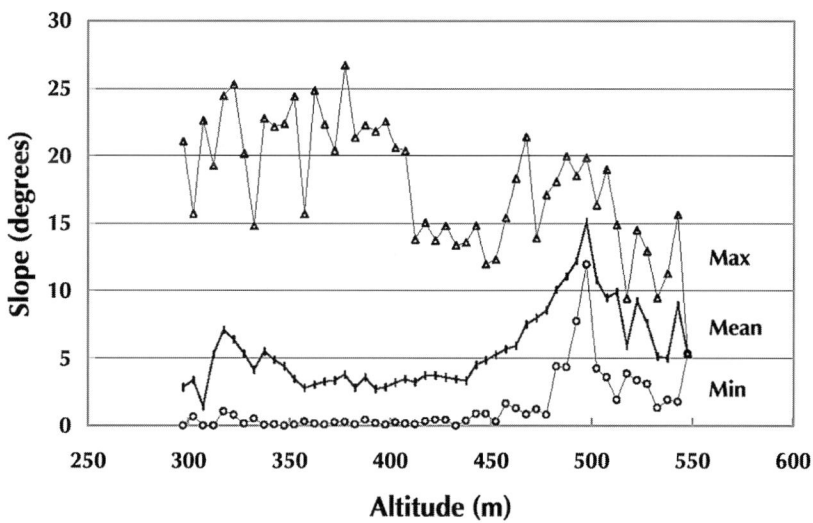

Fig. 1.13
The relationship between altitude and slope for the Kosak Shamali region.
Altitude zones are classified using 5-m bins. Mean, maximum, and minimum slopes are plotted for each bin.

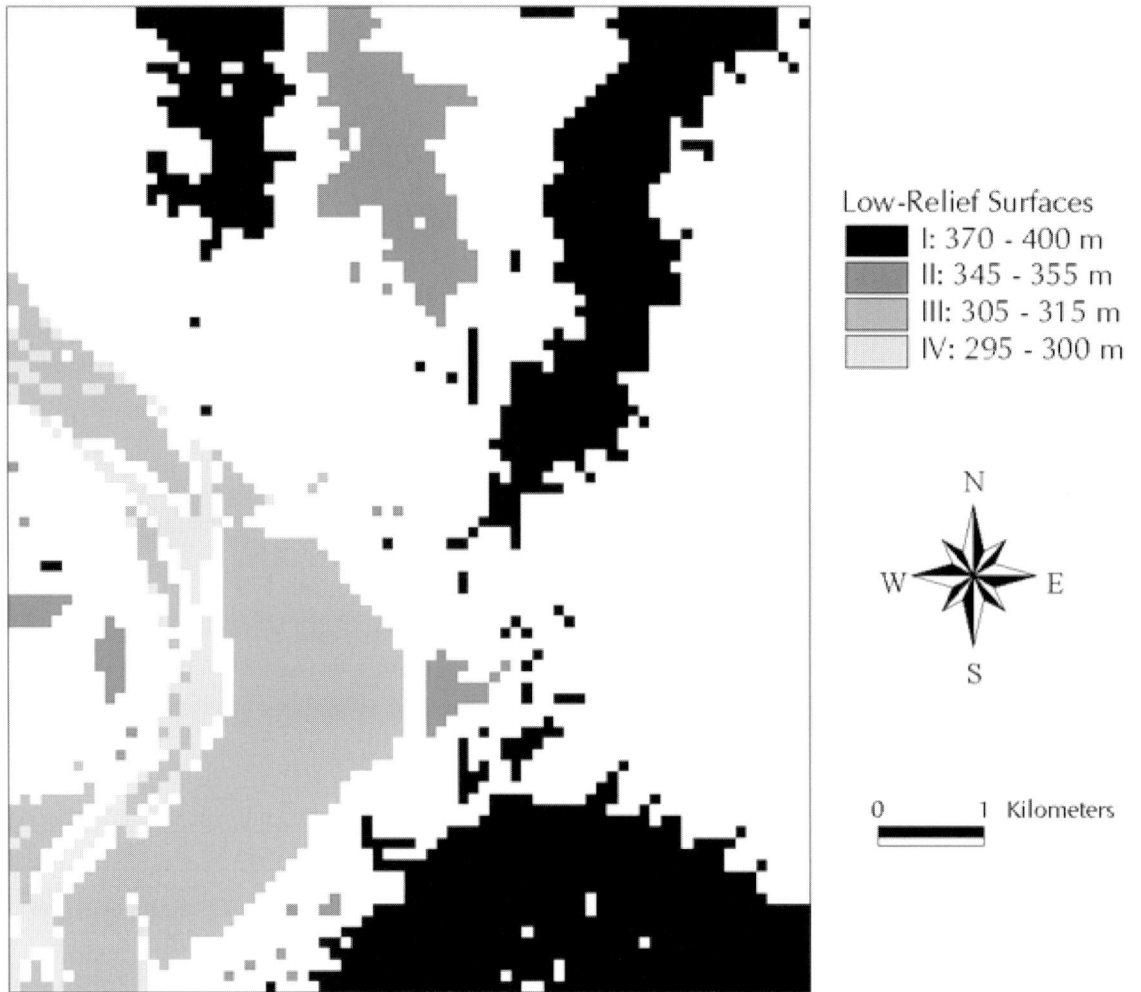

Fig. 1.14 Distribution of distinct low-relief surfaces in and around Kosak Shamali.

Low-Relief Surfaces

I: 370 - 400 m
II: 345 - 355 m
III: 305 - 315 m
IV: 295 - 300 m

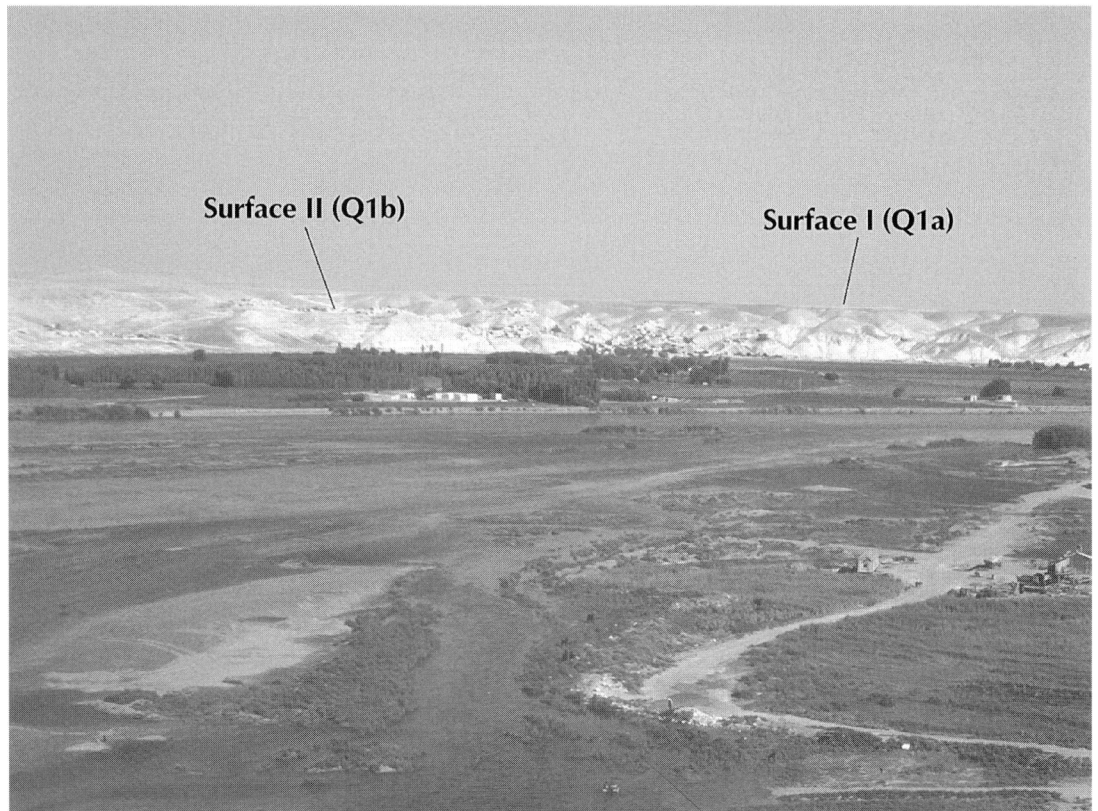

Fig. 1.15 Surface II (Q1b) in Miliha Village to the south of Kosak Shamali, and Surface I (Q1a) behind, seen from Qalaat Najm.

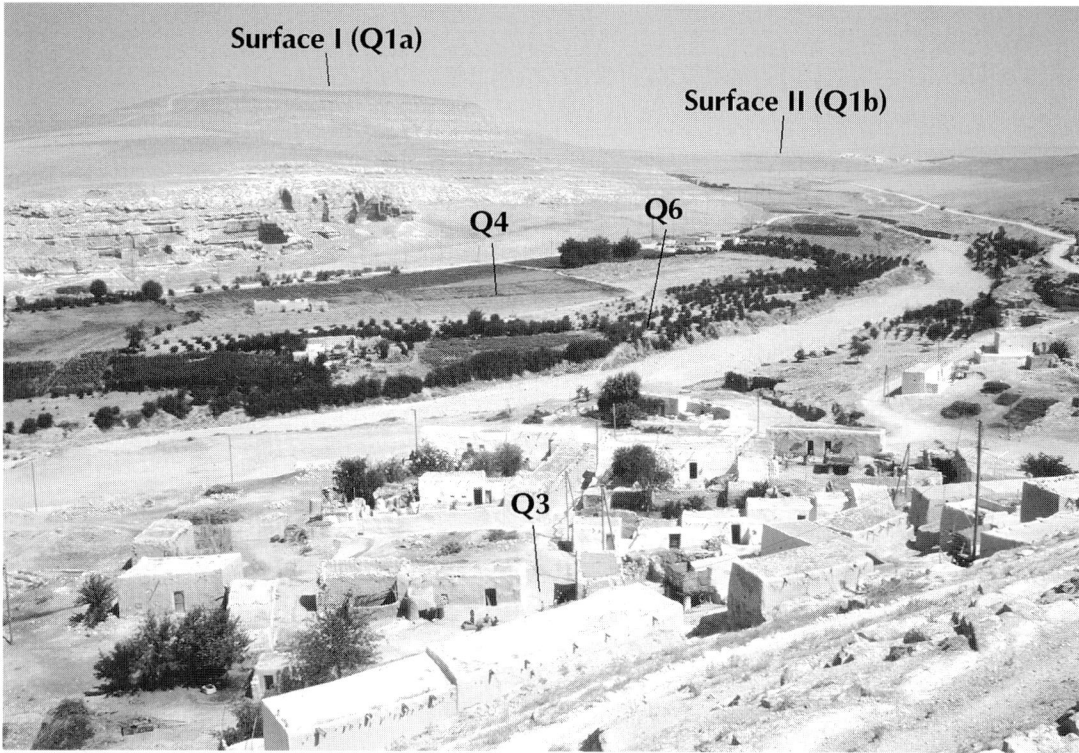

Fig. 1.16 Surface I (Q1a) and Surface II (Q1b) in the upstream area of the Nahar Sarine, seen from the lower reach.

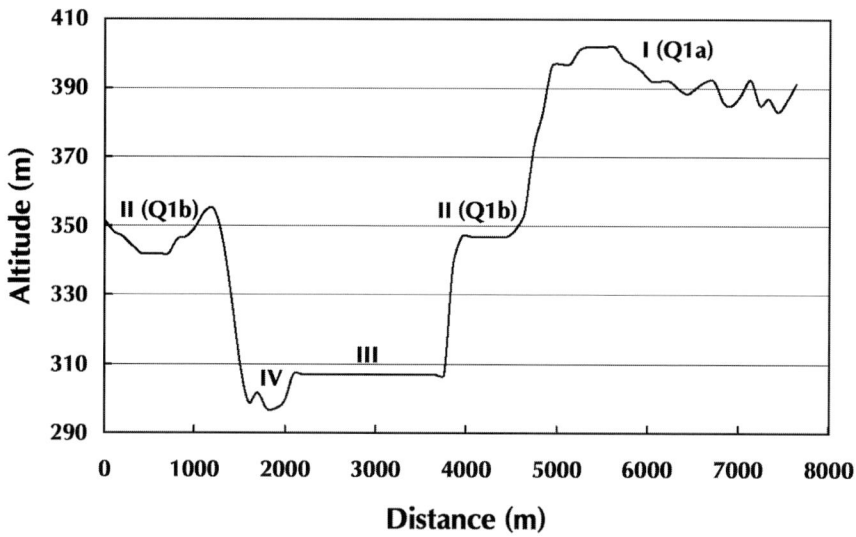

Fig. 1.17
Topographic cross section across the Euphrates constructed from the 100-m DEM. See Fig. 1.10 for the location of the section.

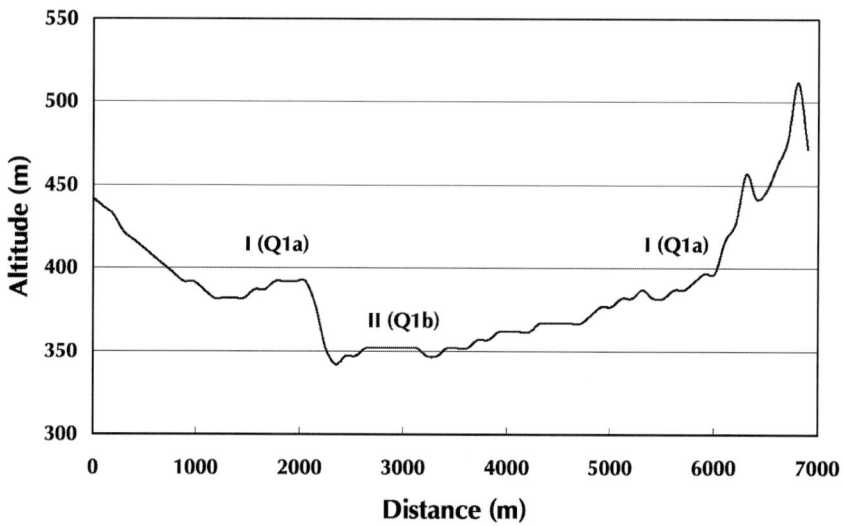

Fig. 1.18
Topographic cross section across the Nahar Sarine constructed from the 100-m DEM. See Fig. 1.10 for the location of the section.

Fig. 1.19 River terraces along the lowest reach of the Nahar Sarine.

Fig. 1.20 River terraces along the middle reach of the Nahar Sarine (1).
The center of the photo is about 600 m upstream from the tell.

Fig. 1.21 River terraces along the middle reach of the Nahar Sarine (2).
The center of the photo is about 1,200 m upstream from the tell.

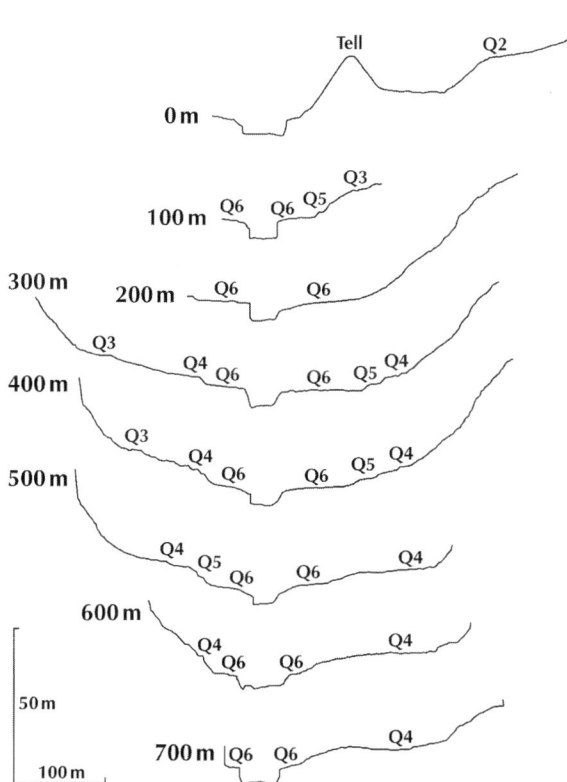

Fig. 1.22 Topographic cross sections along the Nahar Sarine, 0 to 700 m from the tell. *Distance from the tell is measured in an upstream direction. Sections are viewed from upstream.*

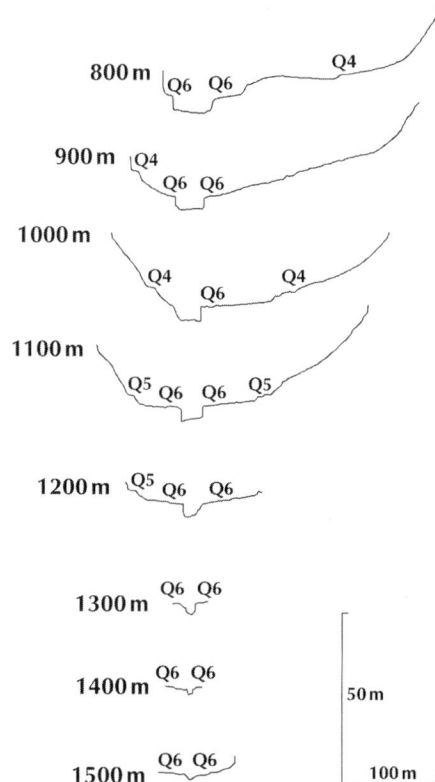

Fig. 1.23 Topographic cross sections along the Nahar Sarine, 800 to 1500 m from the tell. *Distance from the tell is measured in an upstream direction. Sections are viewed from upstream.*

Geomorphology – 33

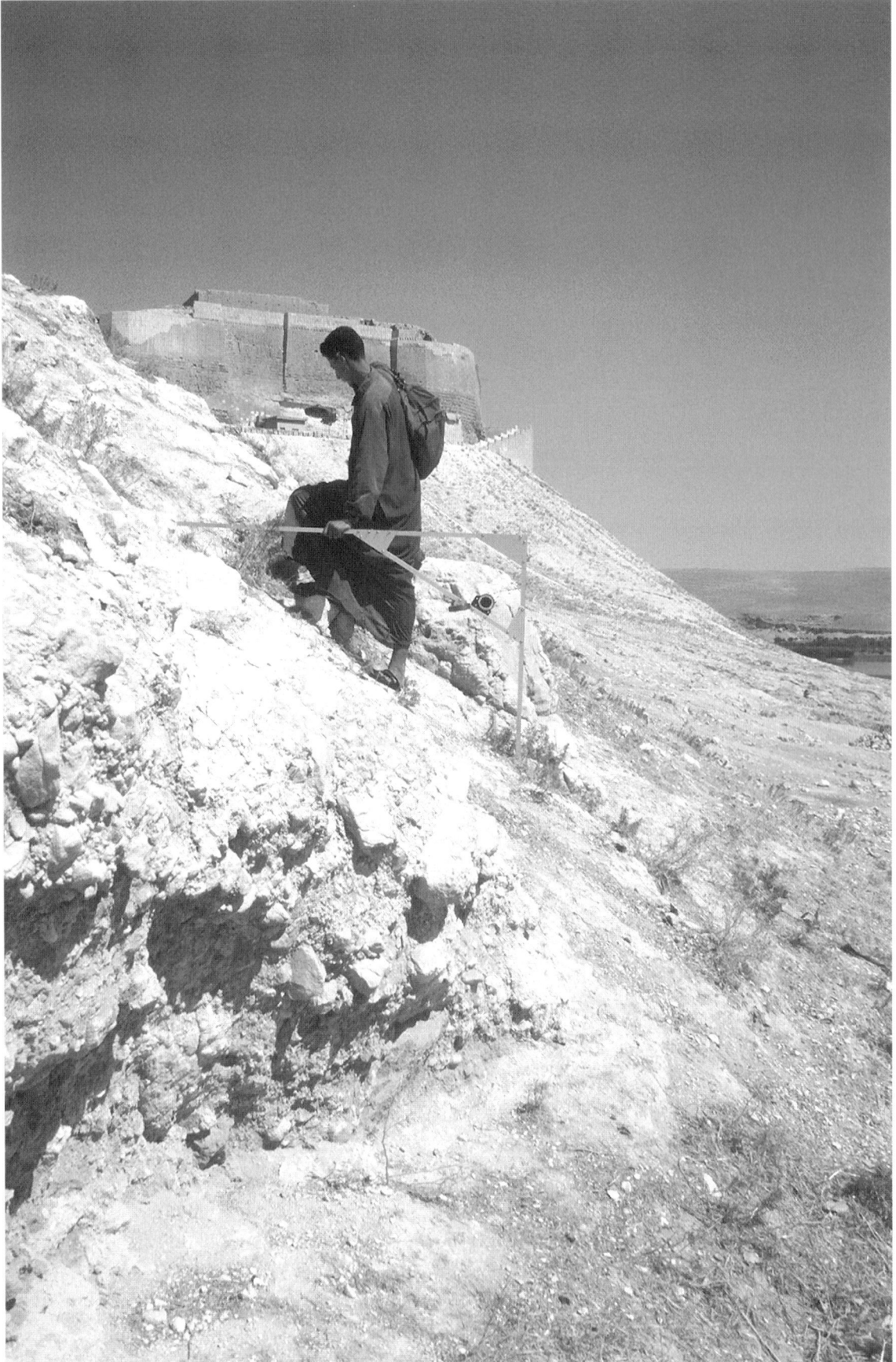

Fig. 1.24 Topographic survey near Qalaat Najm using the slope profiler.

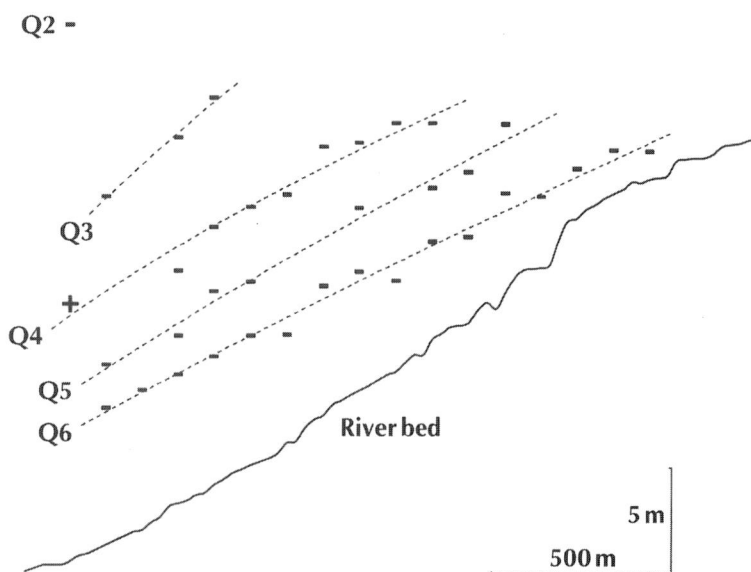

Fig. 1.25 Longitudinal profiles of river terraces and the present river bed along the Nahar Sarine.
The cross shows the top of buried fluvial deposits at the tell.

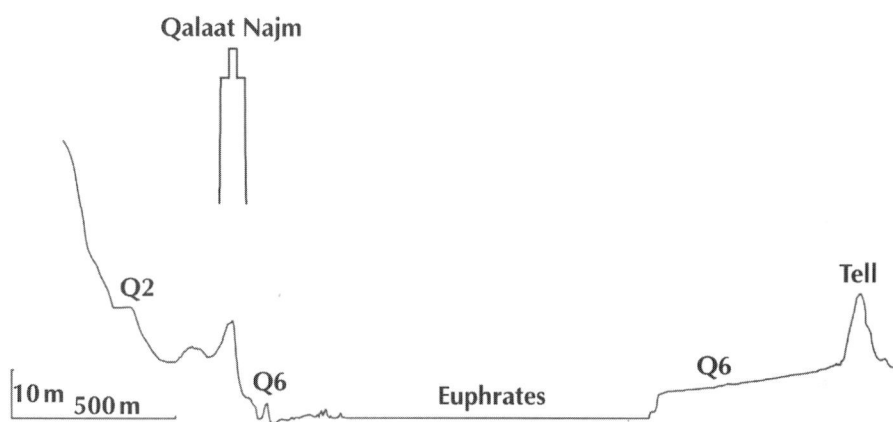

Fig. 1.26 Topographic profile across the Euphrates.

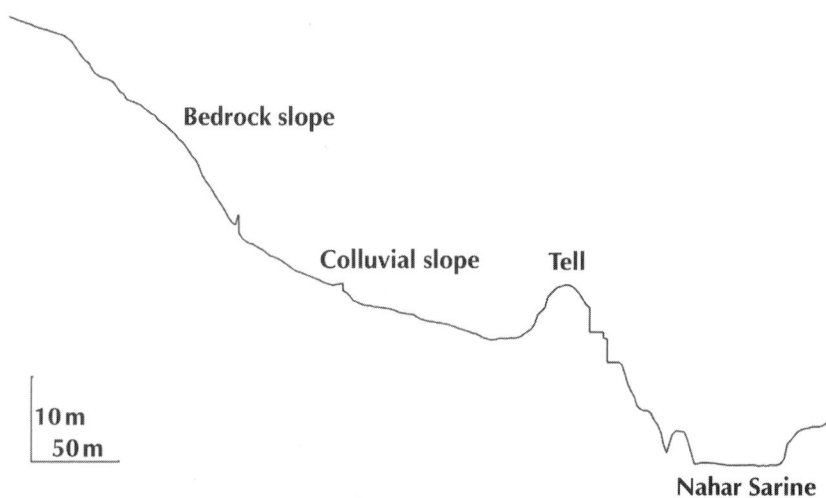

Fig. 1.27 Topographic profile through the tell and the colluvial foot slope.

Fig. 1.28 Deposits of Q6 exposed along the Nahar Sarine, about 1,100 upstream from the tell.

Fig. 1.29 Deposits of Q2 near the tell with rounded gravel.

Fig. 1.30 Fluvial deposits exposed on the westen slope of the tell.

Fig. 1.31 Rounded gravel collected from fluvial deposits exposed on the western slope of the tell.

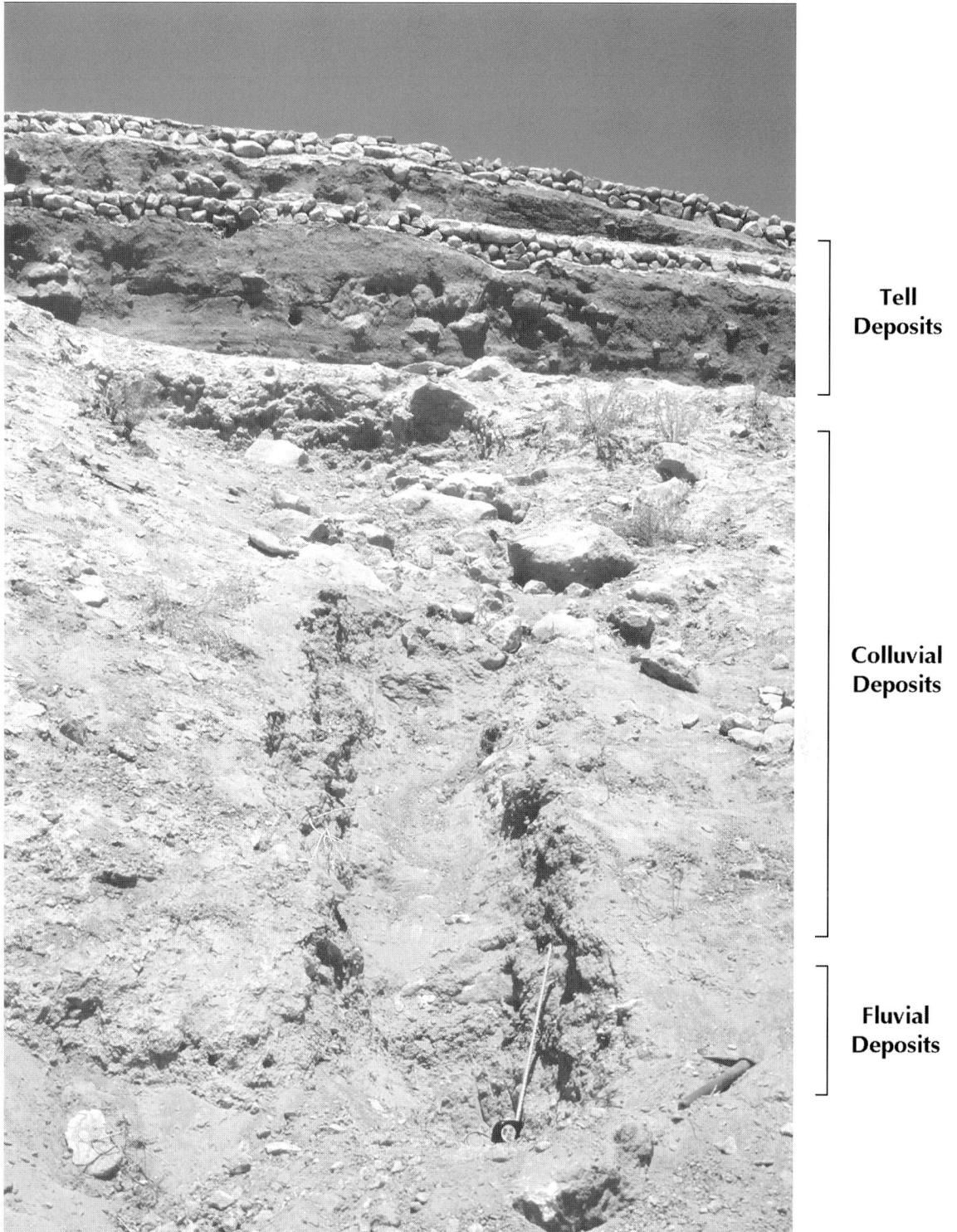

Tell Deposits

Colluvial Deposits

Fluvial Deposits

Fig. 1.32 Stratigraphy of deposits at the southern trenched slope of the tell.

Fig. 1.33 Angular gravel collected from colluvial deposits exposed on the sourthern slope of the tell.

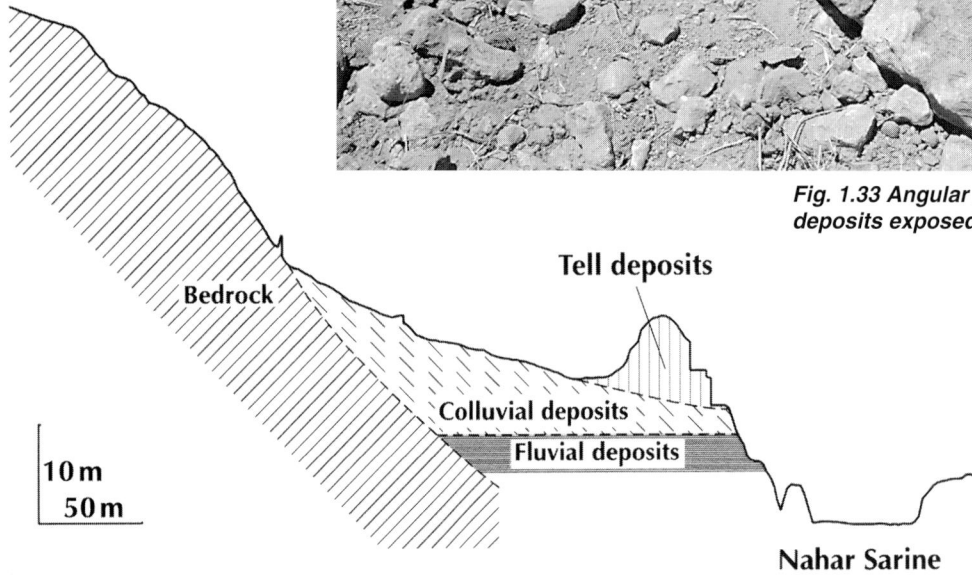

Fig. 1.34 Inferred geologic section through the tell.

Fig. 1.35 A knick point on the bed of the Nahar Sarine, about 1,300 m upstream from the tell.

APPENDIX | # Cartographic representation and data analyses using digital elevation models

Takashi Oguchi,
Fengjun Duan,
Laure Belmont and
Honglin He

The digital elevation model (DEM) is a data file of a topographic surface arranged as a set of regularly-spaced x, y, z locations where z represents surface elevation. DEMs permit the flexible cartographic representation of landscapes (Jones 1997) as well as quantitative landform analyses (Pike 1988). The recent development of Geographic Information Systems (GIS) has facilitated the various applications of DEMs including the creation of the bird's-eye view, a three-dimensional landscape image.

We examined three DEMs with different scales for cartographic representation and landform analyses for the Kosak Shamali region and surrounding area. We explain below the methods and technical background of the DEM preparation, cartographic presentation and data analyses, with a brief introduction to software packages used.

1-km DEM

The U.S. National Geophysical Data Center provided a DEM called GLOBE that covers the whole earth. Data for Syria and surrounding areas were taken from the DEM. The original DEM is projected on to the longitude/latitude coordinate system with a grid interval of 30 arc seconds, approximately 1 km in mid latitude regions. We converted the projection into the UTM (Universal Transverse Mercator) to provide a DEM with a grid interval of 1 km. The interpolation was performed using the PROJECT module of IDRISI32, GIS software from Clack Labs. The resultant 1-km DEM has 1,070 rows and 1,050 columns.

We loaded the DEM into ArcView, GIS software from ESRI. Vector data for drainage networks, lakes and oceans in and around Syria were compiled from the Digital Chart of the World CD-ROMs also supplied by ESRI. The data were overlain on the DEM using ArcView to create the map of Syria and surrounding area (Fig. 1.1). The DEM was also loaded to Visual Explorer, mapping software from WoolleySoft, to create a bird's-eye view on which the map image of Fig. 1.1 is superimposed (Fig. 1.2).

100-m DEM

A 100-m DEM for an area along the Upper Euphrates near Kosak Shamali was produced from various data sources: satellite images, existing maps, and height control points obtained from the GLOBE DEM. The resultant DEM has 75 columns and 89 rows. The DEM was loaded into Imagine, GIS and remote sensing software from ERDAS.

A satellite image for the Kosak Shamali region, purchased from the Corona Satellite Photography Library, US Geological Survey (Fig. 1.3), was scanned and rectified into an image which can be directly overlain on the 100-m DEM (Fig. 1.36). The rectification was performed with the Geometric Correction module of Imagine using 11 ground control points (GCPs). The image and the DEM were arranged with the Image Drape module of Imagine to create a 3D landscape view (Fig. 1.4).

The DEM was also loaded to ArcView to create altitude distribution and slope distribution maps (Figs. 1.10 and 1.12). ArcView calculates slope using eight neighboring points of a DEM (Horn, 1981). The DEM and slope data were summarized according to altitude zones and the results were exported to Microsoft Excel to produce graphs of area-altitude and slope-altitude relationships (Figs. 1.11 and 1.13). The low-relief surfaces mapped in Fig. 1.14 were identified from both the altitude and slope data by applying a query command of ArcView. Macro scripts of ArcView also aided in the construction of topographic profiles from the DEM (Figs. 1.17 and 1.18).

5-m DEM

A high-resolution 5-m DEM for a small area surrounding Tell Kosak Shamali was created from a 1:500 topographic map with a contour interval of 1 m. The map was surveyed in the field by our mission members and a Syrian surveyor. A mesh layer with a 5-m interval in X and Y directions was overlain on the map. Then the elevation of each lattice point of the mesh was read and typed into a Microsoft Excel spreadsheet to provide a DEM with 51 columns and 41 rows. The DEM was loaded to Surfer, a mapping package from Golden Software, to create the wireflame 3D view of Fig. 1.6.

References

Horn, B.K.P. (1981) Hill shading and the reflectance map. *Proceedings of the IEEE* 69: 14.

Jones, C. (1997) *Geographical Information Systems and Computer Cartography.* Singapore: Longman.

Pike, R. J. (1988) The geometry signature: quantifying landslide susceptibility terrain type from Digital Elevation Models. *Mathematical Geology* 20: 491-511.

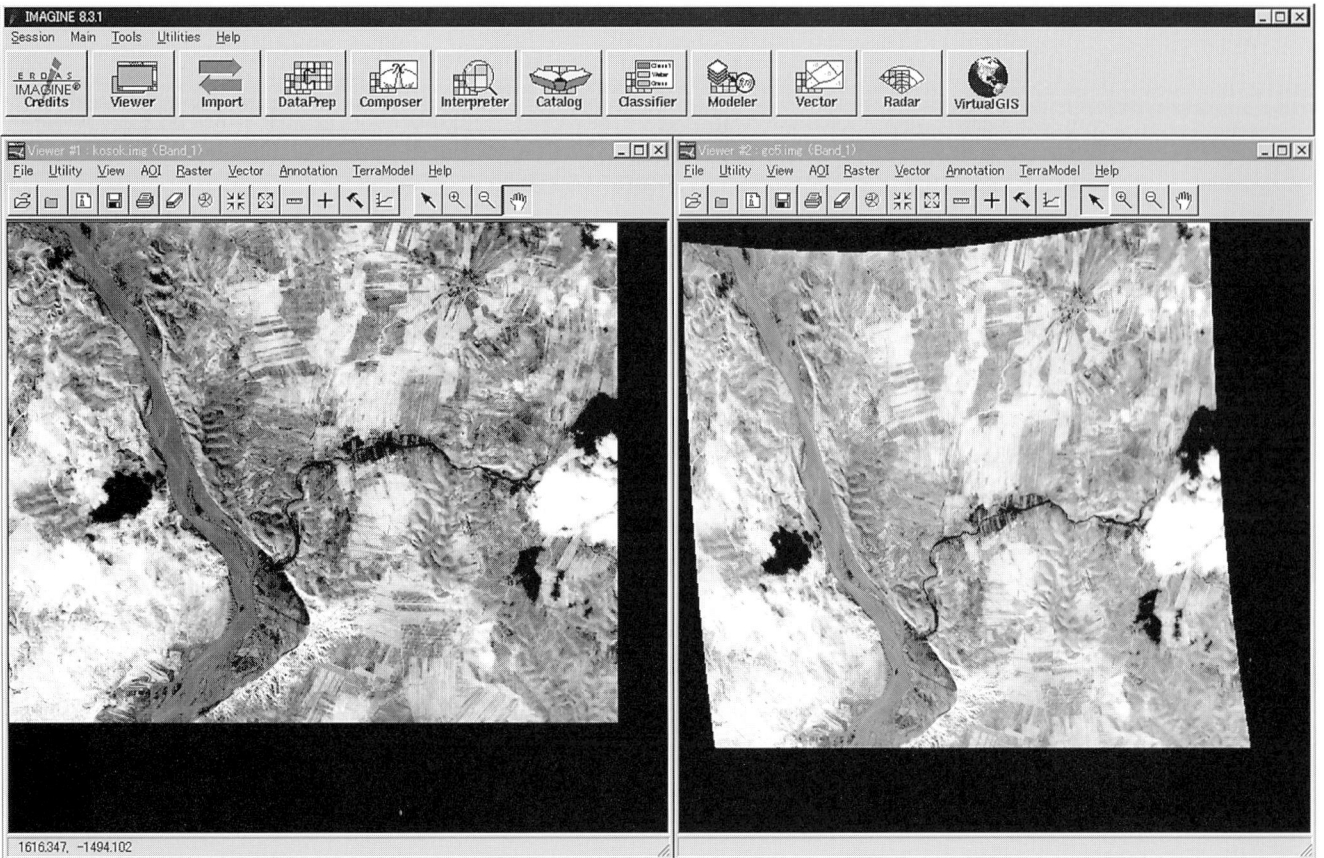

Fig. 1.36 Rectification of the Corona satellite image using ERDAS Imagine. *Left: original, right: rectified.*

2

The socio-historical setting of Kosak Shamali: A field report from a modern village on the Euphrates, Syria

Masayuki Akahori

2.1 Introduction

This is a report concerning the fieldwork under-taken in the Hamlet of Kosak Shamali, east of Aleppo in Syria. I conducted research there dur-ing the months of July and August, 1996, in coop-eration with the archaeological research team. While the team concentrated upon research of the Palaeolithic, Neolithic and Chalcolithic site of Tell Kosak Shamali at the village, I conducted interviews with the people of the village in order to clarify its history, to obtain information that could come in useful for archaeological research, and to explore the possibility of a general survey of the area on the basis of multi-disciplinary view-points. Even though this is merely a preliminary report, because the time spent on my research was not long enough, it may be useful for researches of other disciplines to understand the general socio-historical setting of the present vil-lage in that area.

Usually anthropologists use fictious names for persons and places under research so that they can avoid unexpected results in their description about them. However, that principle cannot be applied to the research of Kosak Shamali, because archae-ological research identifies the same factors clear-ly. Therefore, I used real names in many cases in this paper, while I refrained from mentioning matters of privacy. Consequently, I had to accept that such a method would limit the amount of data I could use. Its validity should be judged in the current of recent debates on anonymity of the field, which have been important issues in anthropological theories over the last two decades (cf. Clifford and Marcus 1986).

In this paper, transliteration of Arabic follows the normal dialect of the village. However, although the village name should be written as Qisq or Qosq, the name "Kosak" is used in accor-dance with other papers.

2.2 General information of the village

Leaving Aleppo east northeastward and crossing the Euphrates, we find the village of Kosak on its east bank where the river, Nahar Sarine joins the Euphrates. The village takes the form of a col-lected one with white-walled houses clinging onto slopes on both sides of the river valley. It is divided into two parts; one is Kosak Shamali (Qisq al-Shamali, Kosak of the North) and the other is Kosak Gibli (Qisq al-Gibli or Qisq al-Janubi, Kosak of the South). While the popula-tion of Kosak Gibli exceeds Shamali, the latter is older. The above-mentioned tell is along the Nahar Sarine, and the hamlet of Kosak Shamali spreads between that tell and the hill. There are 41 households in Kosak Shamali, whose popula-tion is about 250. It is estimated that the village as a whole has about 90 households and 600 inhab-itants. It may be much larger, if we adopt its administrative definition, whose census data of 1998 indicates that the total population is 966 and that the number of households is 157. The origin of the village name, Kosak, is unknown, but it is clearly not of Arabic origin.

As for the common facilities of the village, we can find a mosque, a meeting place, a pumping station and an elementary school. All except for the school are in the center of Kosak Gibli. There are three graveyards; the oldest one exists on the western outskirts of Kosak Shamali and the other two are placed on the eastern outskirts of the village, sand-wiching the Nahar Sarine. The old graveyard is still in use and epitaphs of the tombs indicate that two new graveyards have been used since the latter half of the 70s. There are no family tombs and no specific areas for particular descent lines, but some tendencies can be seen for descent lines according to which graveyard they usually use.

The village headman (*mukhtar,* which means a chosen person) is an elderly man of Kosak Gibli, and some others are elected as different officials. They do not have a specific building to function as an office. Some elders among the villagers are called *'arifa* (wise men), who take a large part in the decision making in village matters. In addition, a young man holds the position of *mu'azzin* and *imam* of the village mosque. He also works as a teacher at the school. There are three other teachers, two of whom were not born in this village.

The major industry of the village is agriculture as there are fertile arable lands on the banks of the Euphrates and the Nahar Sarine as well as on the hills behind the village. On the bank of the Euphrates, people cultivate cotton, maize, sesame, broad beans and lentils. In addition, various kinds of vegetables for family consumption are planted on both sides of the Nahar Sarine and pomegranates and almonds are also planted. The hills are the place for the cultivation of wheat and barley, and people also use them for grazing sheep and goats. Sharecropping is not rare, but it is usually done by landed farmers who have surplus manpower. Institutionalized landlordship has not developed in this village. People always try to diversify their way of living, and working as laborers at the archaeological site duly supplied them with such occasion.

Villagers say that the Nahar Sarine had an abundant quantity of flow in the past, and they installed pumping waterwheels and watermills along it. Their wrecks can still be seen now. Today, in addition to the above-mentioned village pumping station, some people possess small pumps to supply water to their fields.

In addition, large sandbanks (*jazira*) of the Euphrates are cultivated and cedars are planted there. However, it does not belong to Kosak but to a village on the opposite bank.

2.3 Position of the village in the wider local community

When one stands in the valley of the village of Kosak, the surrounding scenery may give the impression that the village is a small scaled closed society. It is not true. If he or she climbs one of the hills behind the village, one can easily see the village of Qal'a (Qarya al-Qal'a) on the opposite bank of the Euphrates, the village of Hawija (Jazira al-Hawija) on the sandbank far down the stream and the village of Miliha (Qarya Miliha) further away on the same side as Kosak. There is also a branch village of Kosak, Dhija (al-Dhija) upstream of the Euphrates. Qal'a is the nearest in a straight line, but the people of Kosak do not have strong social ties with the people of that village. One reason is of course that there is no bridge to cross the river near Kosak, but also that people of both villages belong to different descent lines, and this weakens social ties. Among the forty-seven couples that I knew the natal village names of wives, only one woman came from Qal'a while five came from Khawija and six from Miliha. There are eight endogamous couples, which is not so remarkable in number and is not considered normative among the villagers.

Going against the stream of the Nahar Sarine, one soon reaches the town, Sarine (Sarin or Sarin al-Shamaliya). It is the center of the social network, which includes farming villages like Kosak in the surrounding area. The town can be reached from Kosak on foot and many villagers are engaged in wage labor there. Besides a small permanent market (*suq*) vending vegetables and daily necessities, a Wednesday market (*bizar*) of livestock and other goods attracts many people. There is also a junior high school and government offices in Sarine. Bread or vegetable sellers who go daily or weekly to Kosak by car or cart are in most cases residents of Sarine.

The village people living around Sarine have strong ties of kinship and affinity with one another. There are some large descent groups encompassing villages, and their leaders are called *mukhtar* like village headmen. Elderly persons of the descent groups including those *mukhtars* are called *sheykhs* (chiefs) by the people. The largest descent category which includes most of the Arabs of this area is known as the 'Awn. A part of its descendants also live on the west bank of the Euphrates, but they do not have strong social ties with co-descendants of the east bank. People often explain this with the logic of descent segmentation, that is, an ancestor of the 'Awn of the west bank and an ancestor of the 'Awn of the east bank were brothers whose father was 'Awn. (cf. Zakariya 1983: 128ff. *et al.*)

Beyond the Euphrates and further west of Sarine is

a larger town, Monbij. Monbij is a town that provides the villagers of Kosak with goods and services not for daily use but sometimes necessary for their life. In Mobij there is a senior high school, a hospital and a medium scale roofed market where people can obtain luxury goods and industrial products. Five days a week, privately operated buses from Khawija or Miliha go via Kosak and Sarine to Monbij.

Sarine and Monbij are part of the weekly markets network. Though most villagers of Kosak do not go to weekly markets except for the ones at Sarine and Monbij, they know of the existence of the network. Some of them who sell goods at those markets told me the schedule of markets as follows:

Sunday: Jarniya, 'Ayn al-'Arab
Monday: Suluk
Tuesday: Monbij
Wednesday: Sarine
Thursday: Mas'udiya, Ashyukh
Friday: 'Ayn 'Isa
Saturday: Monbij

If we map those towns, we can easily see that there are at least two cycles of weekly markets in this region and that Sarine is the point of contact.

Small buses and taxies are available at Monbij, which can take villagers of Kosak to towns and cities further away. When going westward to Aleppo, they pass through another town named Bab (al-Bab). Though it is larger than Monbij, villagers do not stop in it, because the trip between Aleppo and Kosak takes just three hours. Usually people go directly to Aleppo when they have some business requirements that they are unable to satisfy in Monbij.

The social sphere of activity of the villagers of Kosak is summarized here; it is extended unilinearly from Aleppo via Monbij to Sarine, and spread in a limited area around Sarine. It, of course, belongs to the ordinary pattern of farming villages that have towns and cities in their reach (cf. Redfield 1941).

2.4 Language and religion

A young man from Kosak presented the following classification of the people living in their neighborhood.

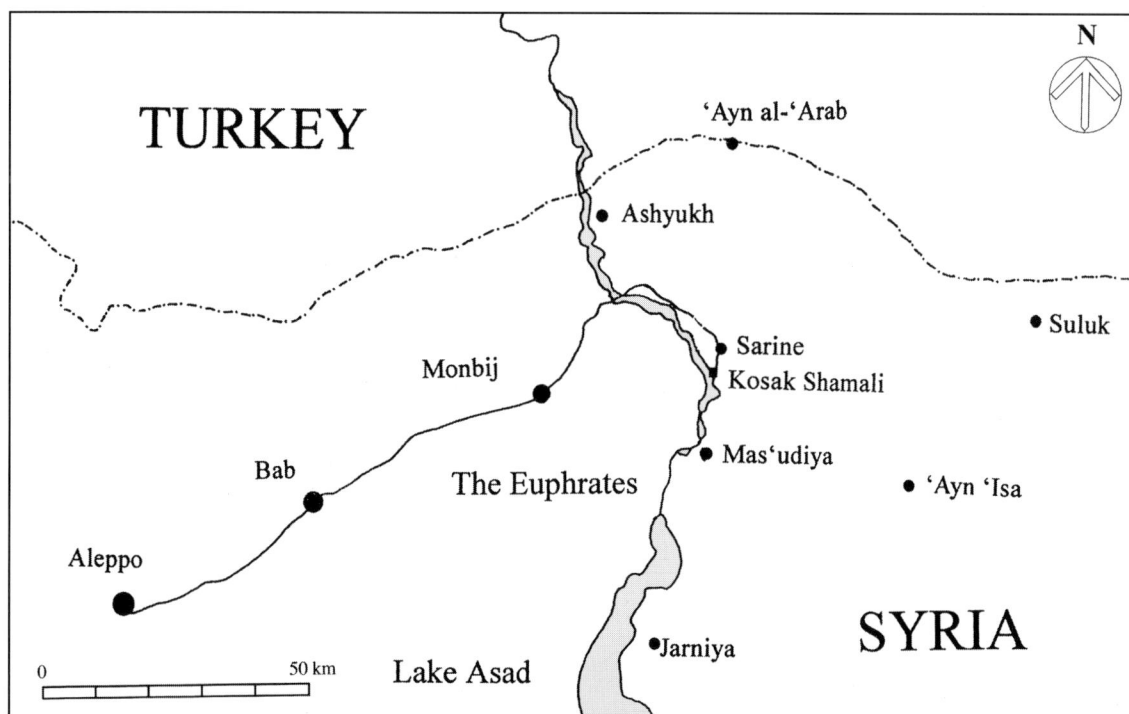

Fig. 2.1 Northern Syria including the village under study (Kosak Shamali).

Classification 1
    Others: Bedouins, Townsmen (*hadar*),
        Kurds and Turks
    Ourselves: Farmers (*shawaya*)
Classification 2
    Others: Christians, Armenian Orthodoxes
        (*Arman*) and Jews
    Ourselves: Muslims

The term, *shawaya*, comes from barley (*sha'ir*) and it means "people who cultivate barley."

Those classifications have some points that attract attention. In classification 1, distinction by language is mixed with that by livelihood and place of residence. In classification 2, Armenian Orthodoxes are distinguished from ordinary Christians (Here, ordinary Christians means Syrian Orthodoxes). As I have already taken up livelihood and residential patterns in the previous sections, some characteristics of language and religion will be explained here. As the young man stated, the villagers of Kosak are Arabs by language and Muslims by religion without any exception.

I do not have enough information about details of their Arabic dialect, because I collected only 500 basic nouns, adjectives and verbs, and there were only two informants who supplied systematic data. However, even such scarce data revealed some characteristics of their dialect. As for pronunciation, a change in the original sounds "k" and "q" is noticeable. Besides the change from "q" to "g," which is found in many dialects of Arabic, a change from "q" to "ch" (like from *haka*, to tell, to *hacha*) and a change from "q" to "j" (like *thaqil*, heavy, to *tijil*) often happen. Grammatically, use of the plural female form for the third person pronoun (*hun*) and the female plural form of verbs (e.g. *hun yiktibn* for "they (f. pl.) write") are unique. Compared with dialects of other regions, the dialect of the people in Kosak is clearly based on standard Syrian dialect, while it also seems to be strongly influenced by the Iraqi dialect. (cf. Cowell 1964; Woodhead and Beene 1967). In addition, they are familiar with various dialects in Syria and also with the Egyptian dialect through mass media such as television and radio.

As for religion, a lack in a very common factor in the popular belief and practice of Islam should be mentioned. That is, there is neither a shrine of saints nor a family that has brought up traditional intellectuals (*'ulama'*) in the village. As the villagers of Kosak know of saint veneration and have respect for traditional intellectuals, the fact that they do not have such institutions and families in their village is out of the ordinary.

2.5 Families and kinship

In the village of Kosak, a couple of houses share their walls with each other, which give them the appearance of compounds integrated by common kinship. However, the sharing of house walls is not related to kinship relations and there is no equipment used in common by those houses.

Houses have white walls, which are made of stones or bricks, plastered by materials mixed with cut barley stems. On the ridgepole and horizontal pillars, the roof is covered with shingles or bark. They usually consist of a guestroom, a bedroom, a living room and a kitchen. They also have various equipment in the front yard, among which are a lavatory, an open-air bed on a high floor used in the summer and a porch called *khowsh*. The *khowsh* is a place for various kinds of work, and is used for welcoming guests in the summer as well.

Households are called *beyt* rather than *usra* or *'a'ila*. They are formed according to patrilineal descent and viri-patrilocal residence, in each of which nuclear families or stem families (families including a couple, their son's couple and their unmarried children) usually live together. Joint families (families constituted of more than two couples whose husbands are brothers) are rare. This means that only one of the sons lives with their parents after he gets married, while daughters marry out to other families and other sons form a new household with their wives. Nuclear families are thus divided into two types; one is transitionally formed by the death of parents, and the other is newly formed by the sons who left the home of their parents. In the latter case, sons and their wives often set up a new residence near their parents' dwelling, so that correspondence can be found, not strictly but to some extent, between kinship and distribution of houses.

The words used to call or refer to other persons

also teaches us many things about the constitution of households and the spread of kinship (Akahori 1994a). In Kosak, when referring to each other in daily life, only a personal name is used for young persons and a personal name or the teknonym (*kunya* in Arabic) is used for adults if they are married and have children, where choice depends on the relationship between the referring person and the one referred to. On formal occasions, a personal name, his or her father's name and the title (or a family name) are sequentially mentioned. A combination of a personal name and the father's name or of a personal name and the title are possible. Terms like son (*bun*) or daughter (*bint*) are not put between a personal name and the father's name.

In most cases, the definite article (*al-*) is put before the title used as the third item of the formal call and reference, which means that the title plays a different role from the first and the second item. Among the forty-one households in Kosak Shamali, thirty-three households share the title with others.

> al-Sulayman: 6 households
> al-Hasan: 5 households
> al-Ahmad: 3 households
> Buzan: 3 households
> al-Mastaw: 3 households
> al-Milla: 3 households
> al-Hajji: 2 households
> al-Hamdi: 2 households
> al-Mahmud: 2 households
> al-Salih: 2 households
> al-Shawakh: 2 households
>
> Other households which do not share the title with others: al-'Abbas, al-Hamdush 1, al-Hamdush 2, al-Hammadi, al-Husayn, al-Ibrahim, al-Jazzar, al-Sheykh; The two Hamdush households are not kin though they have the same title for their family name.

The name that I give here as the title or family name is called *nisba* by the villagers themselves. They are taken from the personal names of the ancestors of families. Although it is usual to make a *nisba* from the ancestor's name and to use it as the family name, villagers of Kosak do not shape *nisbas* by transforming the original name of the ancestor (e.g. from the personal name, Farid to the *nisba*, al-Fardi). Instead, they simply put the definite article before the original name without

transformation, which is not *nisba* in its grammatical sense (Though al-Hamdi and al-Hammadi are *nisbas* in their forms, they themselves are ordinary personal names and they are not the transformed *nisbas* from other personal names of ancestors) (cf. Akahori 1994a: 329; Geertz 1983).

It should also be noted that the ancestors who originated those *nisbas* are direct agnates who died most recently. That is, they are usually fathers of the oldest members of families. As a result, we can expect that those family names change generation by generation and it does not seem reasonable to call them family names (At the same time, it means that people change their family names once or twice in their lifetime by the death of their direct agnates, though I could not collect examples in the research of 1996). Actually, five households use the name of Hasan, dead son of Sulayman as their family names, while six other households of their cousins call themselves al-Sulayman. This is because two brothers of Hasan (i.e. two other sons of Sulayman) are still alive.

This system of calling and referring to names is different from the prevalent one practiced widely in Egypt, where personal name, father's name and paternal grandfather's name are mentioned sequentially. In addition to putting the definite article before the third name, it differs in that the third person who should be mentioned is not a grandfather but a great-grandfather, if the grandfather is still alive. Therefore, it cannot be considered as a simple reference to personal names. On the other hand, it is difficult to consider the third names as a mark to indicate belonging to clear-cut descent groups (clans or tribes) because they are used for a short time - maybe less than thirty years or so. What we can say of that system is that the villagers of Kosak are conscious of the logic of patrilineal descent, which unifies some households into a larger one, but that they adapt the logic only to a limited extent so that they can make only small, unstable groups.

Data are insufficient to say much about marriage patterns, which anthropologists usually consider to be a significant factor in molding the basic social relations of the village in addition to descent. As in many regions of the Middle East, villagers of Kosak say that they prefer the paternal parallel cousin marriage (marriage with one's father's brother's child). Nevertheless, the number of marriages with the first paternal cousin was just one among the thirty-nine examples of which I knew the kinship ties between couples. Though we should take the range of classificatory cousins into consideration, it does not seem that preference for paternal parallel cousin marriage is widely put into practice in the village. Remarriage after divorce and bereavement is usual, but polygamous marriage is rare. I found among sixty-one couples just three polygamous couples, of which the husband is the same person. I also found six men among thirty nine that had married their sister's husband's sister, and this pattern of sister exchange is more remarkable than usual. As a whole, we could not find any definite pattern of marriage, which can make systematic marriage alliances among the households of Kosak Shamali.

2.6 Descent groups

Married women in most cases do not live with their agnates and thus the stem family (*beyt*) is not a descent group in its strict sense of the term. However, villagers usually consider the *beyt* as the smallest unit of patrilineal descent segmentation and that the aggregate of households sharing the common title or family name is a larger descent group which unifies some households. This larger segment is also called *beyt* in a classificatory sense. On the other hand, most of the people in the surrounding area of Sarine belong to the inclusive descent line (*'ashira*) named the 'Awn. Here we can expect as a link between smaller *beyts* and larger *'ashira* existence of intermediary descent categories. We can see such intermediary social categories, where social groups for daily life (villages and herding camps) and the wider political system beyond daily life (tribes or chiefdoms) are formed on the same logic of patrilineal descent (Akahori 1994b).

In the field under research, this category is called *fukhath* (thigh of sheep). One of the elderly men of Kosak said that there were eight major *fukhaths* in the village. The following are their names shown with the names of *beyts* in Kosak Shamali that belong to each *fukhath*.

al-Sheykh Khalil: al-Ahmad, Buzan, (al-Husayn)

al-Sulaymanat (or al-Sheykh Hasan): al-Sulayman, al-Hasan, al-Mahmud, (al-Mastaw)

al-Dhawahra: al-Hajji, al-Hamdush 1

al-Hawadra: al-Ibrahim, al-Hamdush 2, al-Shawakh

al-Lahamda: al-Hamdi

al-Shawahra: al-Milla, al-Sheykh

al-Hafut: no household in Kosak Shamali

al-Fayadat: no household in Kosak Shamali

Households which do not belong to the above *fukhaths*: al-Salih, al-'Abbas, al-Hammadi, al-Jazzar

If we consider that an *'ashira* is divided into *fukhaths*, a *fukhath* into classificatory *beyts* and then a classificatory *beyt* into individual households (*beyts*), it would be an oversimplification. The classificatory *beyt* is not a territorial unit because households belonging to the same classificatory *beyt* are often distributed in different villages. Even elderly men of Kosak cannot cover the names of classificatory *beyts*, which belong to their own *fukhath* if they are in other villages. Moreover, genealogical relations among the eponymous ancestors of classificatory *beyts* of the same *fukhath* are rarely remembered by people. Similarly they can neither explain the relations between ancestors of the *fukhaths* nor complete the genealogical chart of the 'Awn as a whole. Thus the list shown above is only a part of the segmentation of the 'Awn as a whole. Strictly speaking, it shows how individual households of Kosak Shamali unify and merge into larger units, rather than how the total population of the 'Awn is divided and segmented.

Moreover, the political relations among the *beyts* may possibly affect the above classification. If we see the names of *fukhaths*, we can easily find that the Sheykh Khalil and the Sheykh Hasan (another name of al-Sulaymanat) are names of eponymous ancestors themselves, while the other six names like al-Dhawahra are transformed from the original personal names to the form phonetically suitable as the name of the group. The name, al-Sulaymanat, is also a regular female plural form made easily from the ancestor's name, Sulayman. It is not so mature as a collective noun compared with other names like al-Dhawahra. The person who showed the above classification was an elderly man of the

Buzan family, and the people of the Sheykh Khalil, to which the Buzans belong, are proud of their being the oldest descent line of the village of Kosak. On the other hand, the Sulaymanat settled in Kosak in the later period, but they have larger manpower now and consider themselves as a rival of the Sheykh Khalil. The name, Sheykh Hasan, therefore, may indicate two points; one is that the Hasans are influential among the Sulaymanat and that the Sheykh Hasan are rivaling the Sheykh Khalil even in the form of their names. In addition, two *beyt* names bracketed in the above list, the Husayn and the Mastaw, are grafted onto the *fukhath* by affinal ties. All these points indicate that the above list does not express pure descent relations among the groups, but that it is influenced by the political relations among them. Because political relations in the village are often expressed in the idiom of kinship and descent, it is easy to misread such appearances.

One of the reasons for difficulty in showing a comprehensive descent segmentation is the shallow memory of villagers regarding genealogy. This is not general in this area. A *mukhtar* of the Sheykh Khalil, who live in another village, for example, could show the genealogical chain from himself via Muhammad, brother of Sheykh Khalil, to the eponymous ancestor of the *'ashira*, 'Awn. He even could go beyond that point and reached the ancestor of five *'ashiras* including the 'Awn and then ended his ancestry at the fourth caliph, 'Ali (ca. 596-661) (i.e. Jasim / Muhammad / Hefni / 'Abd-Allah / Muhammad / Zahir / Musa / 'Uthman / Salim / 'Awn / al-Sa'd / 'Ubayd / Karb al-Zabidi / Qa'd / 'Abd-Allah / 'Ali). He also narrated the legend about their ancestor 'Awn with that genealogy. In that tale, 'Awn was kidnapped and taken to Iraq by one of the slaves of his father, Sa'd. The slave held grudges against this famous chief (*amir*) of the Bedouins of eastern Syria because he was once harshly punished for his bad behavior to his master. After 'Awn grew up in Iraq, he distinguished himself there and then returned to Syria with his family and followers. Here, we can see the people in the area consider that they have some particular ties with Iraq as I have pointed out in the analysis of their Arabic dialect. Even in Kosak, people belonging to the Sheykh Khalil have more interest in genealogy than other villagers do and they are proud of being descendants of Sheykh Khalil, grandfather of grandfather of the oldest member of

the Buzans, whom they consider the very person who founded the village Kosak. Although people of the newly prospering family, the Sulaymanat, laughingly dismiss the legend of village foundation by Sheykh Khalil, they themselves do not remember even the name of the great-grandfather of their oldest. People of other descent lines are just about equal in their knowledge of genealogy.

Less memory regarding genealogy and lower interest in it may result mainly from the declining importance of descent affiliation in the daily life of the people of this area. Though this cannot be applied to influential families like the *mukhtars* and *sheykhs* of descent groups, there are no families of that rank in the village of Kosak. Generally speaking, loosely formed aggregates of about fifteen households seem to be the largest descent based unit that still has some meaning for ordinary villagers.

2.7 Conclusion: Past and future of the village of Kosak

What I learnt about Kosak in the short period of research in the summer of 1996 leads us to the conclusion that the present village was founded in the not so distant past.

It was presumably in the 19th century. If we believe the oral tradition of Sheykh Khalil, ascendants of five or six generations previously founded the village. There is no information to fix the year of the village's foundation directly, but we have a lot of circumstantial evidences here; corporate activities as a village are not so popular; landlordship has not been developed; sandbanks on the Euphrates are used by people of other villages; local saints and families of local intellectuals are lacking; household constitution is easy to change and its size is limited; people do not consider that affiliation to larger descent groups or categories plays an important role in their life. All of this tells us that the village of Kosak cannot be a village founded long before.

We should not overlook the possibility that social functions of traditional villages sometimes degenerate or disappear in the process of modernization. We must also admit that there are many uncertain factors before drawing a clear conclusion. So long as we get information through interviews with villagers, we can trace only history that exists in the form of people's memory. Usually such information is of much significance for learning about the past of small traditional communities, which do not inherit historical documents. However, what it clarifies is only a part of the history, which has been barely maintained in the memory of villagers. It does not refute the possibility that other people may have lived in the same place as the village of Kosak, but at different times. Actually, the archaeological research team knows that, after the settlement at Tell Kosak Shamali was once given up, another settlement appeared in the same place about 2000 years ago. Also they found more than ten graves of Muslims in the south slope of the same Tell, which tells us that there were people who used that mound as a graveyard of their village or hamlet in the Islamic period before Kosak was founded.

The village of Kosak is included in an area that would be submerged by the construction of a new dam at Lake Asad (Olmo Lete and Fenollós 1999). The people of the Sheykh Khalil have already begun to move to a new village, Dikan, founded by one of their members near Sarine. What surprised me when I was talking with the villagers of Kosak was that they showed neither grief for the extinction of their village nor deep attachment to their homes. It contrasts highly with the case of the Nubians of Egypt, with some of whom I conducted interviews in 1989 (It was a part of the joint research with students of Department of Anthropology, Alexandria University. No paper has been yet published.). They had to move to the surrounding area of Kom Ombo, one of the major towns in Upper Egypt, in the 1960s due to the construction of the Aswan High Dam. Most of them expressed in interview an irresistible desire to return to their homeland (As for the Nubians after the 1960s, see Fernea and Fernea 1990; Jennings 1995). To explain with certainty the reason for villagers' lack of attachment is difficult. It may be because the village does not have a long history, or it may be purely because the research period was too short to get in touch with their deep emotions. However, if possible, I would like to consider it as an expression of their indomitableness, which gives them the strength to live their daily lives under the most difficult conditions.

References

Akahori, M. (1994a) *Asl*: The expression of ancestry among the Bedouin of the Mediterranean coast of Egypt (in Japanese). *Japanese Journal of Ethnology* 58(4): 307-33.

Akahori, M. (1994b) The Movement of nomads of the Mediterranean coast of the Libyan Desert (in Japanese). In: *The Mechanism of Cultural Contacts in the Islamic World, Vol. 3: The Dynamic Movement of People and Information.* Tokyo: Institute for the Study of Languages and Cultures of Asia and Africa, Tokyo University for Foreign Studies.

Clifford, J. and G. E. Marcus (eds.) (1986) *Writing Culture: The Poetics and Politics of Ethnography.* Berkeley: University of California Press.

Cowell, M. W. (1964) *A Reference Grammar of Syrian Arabic.* Washington, D. C.: Georgetown University Press.

Fernea, E. W. and R. A. Fernea (1990) *Nubian Ethnographies.* Chicago: Waveland Press.

Geertz, C. (1983) "From the native's point of view": On the nature of anthropological understanding. In: *Local Knowledge,* edited by C. Geertz. New York: Basic Books.

Jennings, A. M. (1995) *The Nubians of West Aswan: Village Women in the Midst of Change.* Boulder: Lynne Rienner.

Olmo Lete, G. del and J.-L. Montero Fenollós (eds.) (1999) *Archaeology of the Upper Syrian Euphrates: The Tishrin Dam Area.* Barcelona: Universitat de Barcelona.

Redfield, R. (1941) *Folk Culture of Yucatan.* Chicago: University of Chicago Press.

Woodhead, D. R. and W. Beene (eds.) (1967) *A Dictionary of Iraqi Arabic: Arabic-English.* Washington, D. C.: Georgetown University Press.

Zakariya, A.W. (1983) *'Asha'ir al-Sham.* (in Arabic) Damascus: Dar al-Fikr.

CHAPTER 3

Excavations in Sector A of Tell Kosak Shamali: The stratigraphy and architectures

Yoshihiro Nishiaki, Masatoshi Tao,
Seiji Kadowaki, Masashi Abe and Hiroyuki Tano

3.1 The method of excavations

The excavation in 1994 started by opening four stepped trenches on the southern slope of the mound (Matsutani and Nishiaki 1995). The four trenches (A, B, C and D) were all 2m in width, but varied in length from 4m to 20m (Fig. 3.1). Trenches A, C and D ran parallel in a north-south direction, while Trench B was rotated 45 degrees anti-clockwise to run northwest-southeast. Each trench was excavated in 2m x 2m squares, with numbering starting from the north. The longest, Trench A, stretched 20m from the top downwards, in which Squares A6 to A15 were excavated. The lowest two squares contained virtually no cultural deposits; the virgin soil was exposed just below the topsoil. Trench B was set up on the southeastern part of the mound, about 30m east of Trench A. It was 10m long and included Squares B5 to B9. Trench C, consisting of only two Squares C10 and C11, was located 4m west of Trench A, and the 6m-long Trench D, with Squares D8 to D10, was opened 4m east of Trench A.

Investigations of these trenches revealed the presence of two major occupational sequences at Tell Kosak Shamali: a Neolithic to Ubaid sequence in the southwestern part of the mound, and a series of Post-Ubaidian and Urukian levels accumulated in the southeast. The former area was designated in the following seasons as Sector A, and the latter as Sector B. Thus Trenches of A, C and D of the 1994 season were incorporated into Sector A, and Trench B was merged in Sector B. Each sector was excavated more extensively between 1995 and 1997 under two different 4m x 4m grid systems (Nishiaki 1998, 1999, in press b and c; Fig. 3.1; also see Chapter 4).

Sector A covered the southwestern area of the mound. We set up a 4m x 4m grid system in a north-south / west-east direction, and named each square with a combination of alphabetical and cardinal numbers, from north to south, AA, AB, AC, and from west to east, 1, 2, 3... A total of fifteen squares were wholly excavated, i.e. AD4 to AD6, AE3 to AE6, AF3 to AF6, and AG3 to AG6, and the eastern half of Square AH4 (Squares A14 and A15 of Trench A) was also excavated as a sounding in the initial season. The total area excavated was 248m². Squares AF3 to AF5, AG3 to AG5, and AH4, all located close to the southern edge of the mound, were exposed to the virgin soil. As Square AH4 was almost sterile, the present report describes the architecture and the stratigraphy of the other squares.

The archaeological contexts of features, constructions, deposits, artifacts and other discoveries were carefully recorded during the excavations. When encountered, every meaningful context was given a separate code to help specify its locus with reference to the overall stratigraphic and spatial positioning system. The codes, representing the smallest unit of excavation, were defined with the square name and a cardinal number, for example, AD4-25, which represents the 25th context discovered in Square AD4. Another number was added to the last in some cases, such as AD5-99-10, to indicate the precise spatial position of objects in the mapped context. Many such codes were produced during the excavations. Through stratigraphic analysis in the field and laboratory, they were then compiled and related to a particular layer, feature or level. The features were designated with the level number first; 804, for instance, denotes the fourth feature defined in Level 8. The following descriptions refer to such feature numbers in principle, but in the catalogue of artifacts they are also accompanied by the original context codes to allow more detailed examination of their locus in the future.

The deposits were removed with small iron trowels and picks as well as paint brushes and dustpans. All the *in situ* remains discovered on a room floor or ancient surface were mapped three

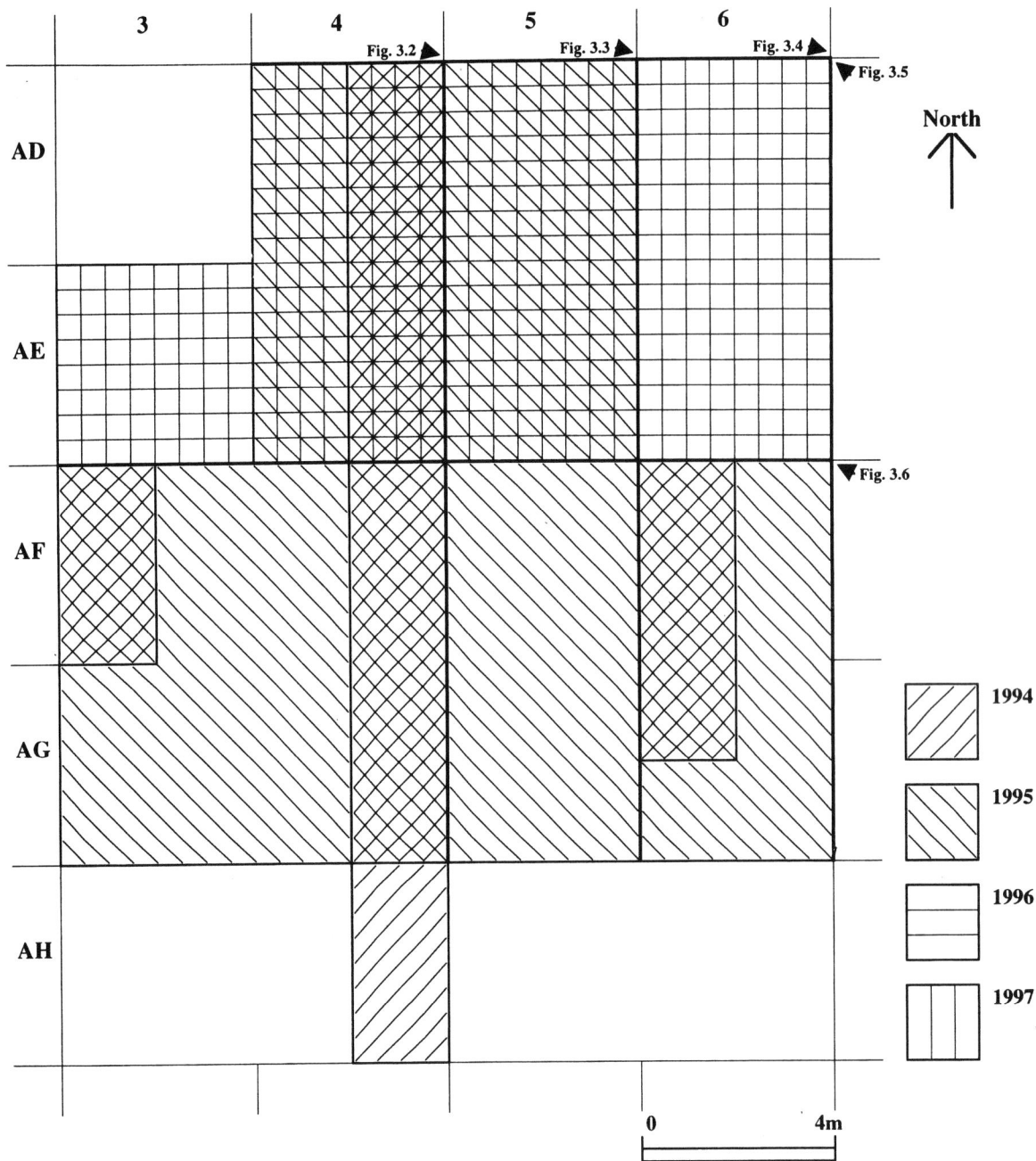

Fig. 3.1 Excavation squares of Sector A, 1994-1997.

dimensionally. In selected contexts of particular importance, such as the well-preserved room floors of Level 10 and enigmatic basal pits of Level 18, smaller items were recovered through dry-sieving, using sieves with a ca. 2.5mm mesh. Ash and charcoal remains were sampled as blocks so that they could be sent to the laboratory in their original condition.

Despite our attempts, we failed to locate an official asl control point in the vicinity of the site. Therefore we placed the datum point for measurement on top of the mound, using a 1/200,000 geographical map prepared by the Russians in

1940s. Its height, 325m asl, and other heights mentioned in the section drawings of this report should be thus understood as merely provisional until the control point measurement comes into use.

3.2 The stratigraphy (Figs. 3.2-3.6)

The excavations exposed a long, 5m-thick sequence of deposits spanning the Neolithic to Ubaid periods in its 18 occupation levels (Figs. 3.2-3.6). Virgin soil, consisting of hard reddish brown soils containing numerous limestone cobbles and

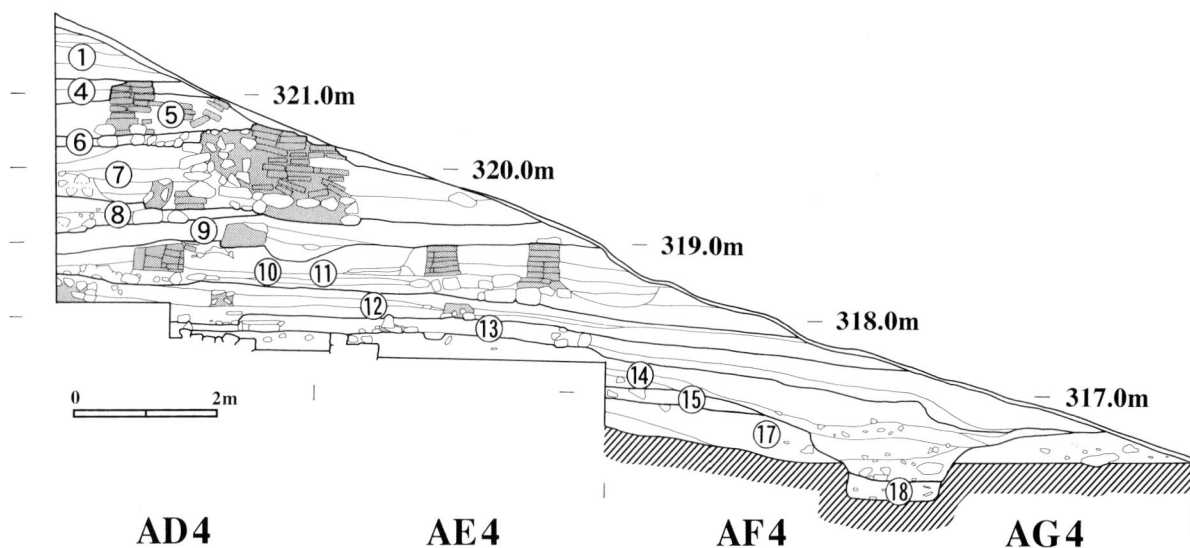

Fig. 3.2 Stratigraphy of the eastern wall of Squares AD4 to AG4.

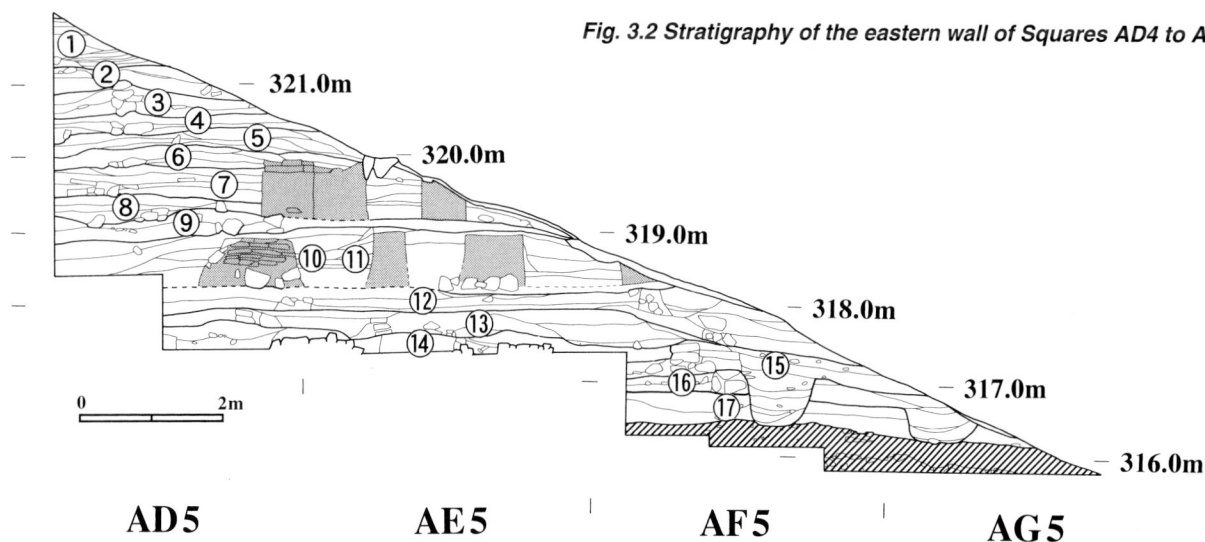

Fig. 3.3 Stratigraphy of the eastern wall of Squares AD5 to AG5.

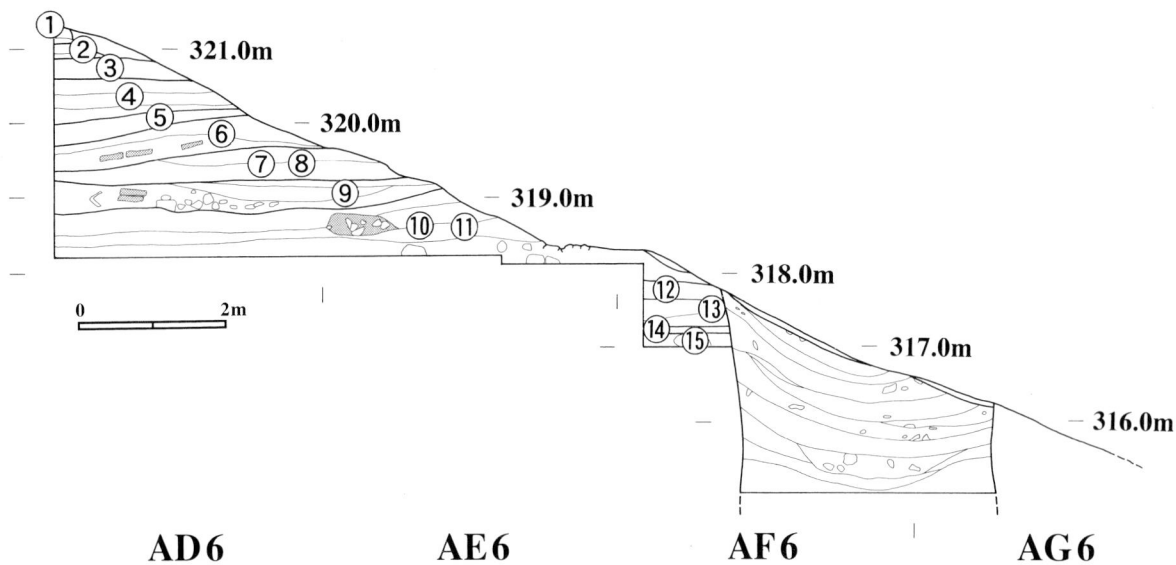

Fig. 3.4 Stratigraphy of the eastern wall of Squares AD6 to AG6.

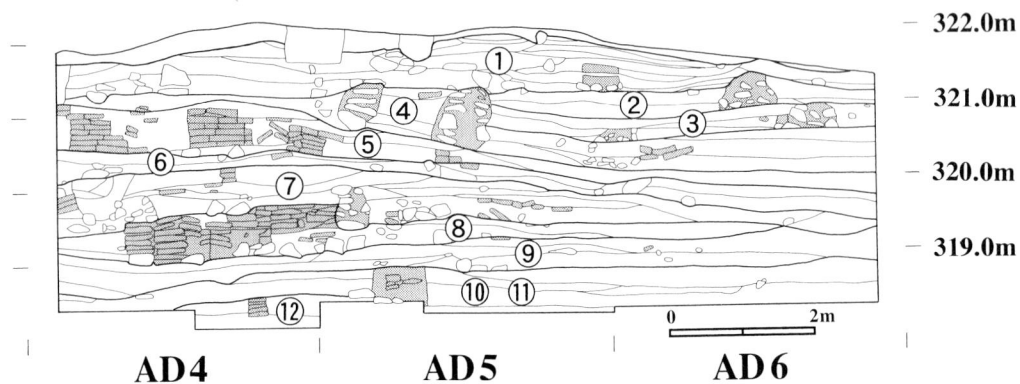

Fig. 3.5 Stratigraphy of the northern wall of Squares AD4 to AD6.

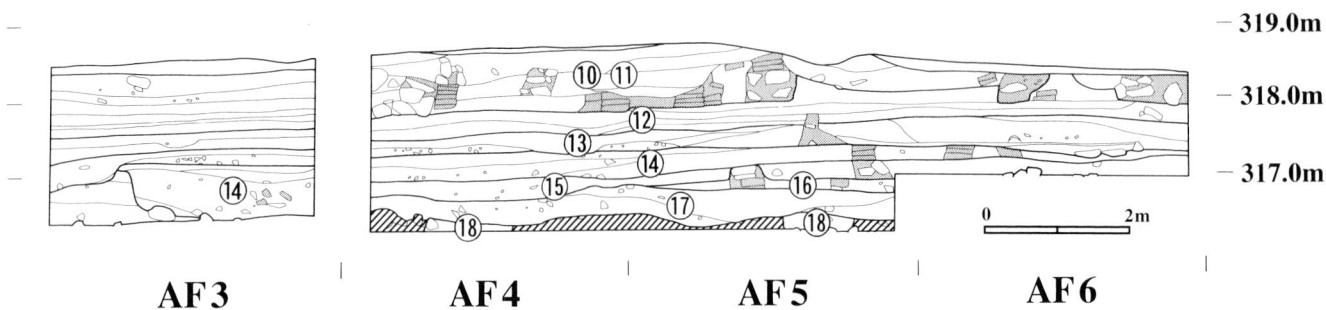

Fig. 3.6 Stratigraphy of the northern wall of Squares AF3 to AF6.

pebbles, was reached in the southern squares. Apart from a few Palaeolithic artifacts (see Chapter 6), it was virtually sterile, hence the term "virgin soil". It is possible that more extensive excavation might have located the original provenance of these secondary finds somewhere within the mound. The earliest occupation level, Level 18, was directly on virgin soil. An occupational gap of over at least several hundred years is evident after the abandonment of Level 18, during which serious erosion occurred, resulting in the accumulation of Level 17, composed of mixed deposits from various periods but without architecture. The overlying sixteen levels were all well stratified, although unevenly distributed in the excavation area. Distribution of the higher levels was confined to the north, as heavy erosion had caused the excavated area to slope steeply to the south.

The periodization of these occupation levels was determined by ceramic typology (Nishiaki *et al*. 1999). Level 18 was assigned to the Late Neolithic (Pre-Halaf), Levels 17-10 the Early Northern Ubaid, Levels 9-4 the Late Northern Ubaid, and Levels 3-1 the Terminal Northern Ubaid. This small area was thus repeatedly occupied, resulting in a dense accumulation of architectural debris relative to the volume of the entire deposits. Each level was, therefore, rather thin, with an average thickness of about 30cm. Consequently, besides a few exceptions (e.g. Levels 6-8 and 10), it is only the base of the structures that remained. At best these consisted of stone foundations and/or small patches of mudbrick/*tauf* remnants. The plans that appear in this chapter are thus two-fold: 1) to illustrate full details of the stone foundations/walls and their collapsed remnants, and 2) to show the arrangement of mudbrick walls, reconstructed using information from the mudbrick and/or *tauf* patches associated with them.

3.3 Architecture

3.3.1 Level 18 (Figs. 3.7 & 3.8; Pl. 3.1: 1 & 2)

Level 18 was exposed in six squares forming a rectangular area of 12m x 8m at the southern edge of Sector A (Figs. 3.7 and 3.8). Architectural remains were poorly preserved due to serious destruction by later building activities and erosion that occurred during the break in occupation. Features of interest included a few round pits and an elongated shallow depression dug into virgin soil. Standing structures were virtually non-existent, but the large number of limestone cobbles distributed in the level might have originally been part of some building structures. Artifactual remains from these features were mainly from the late Pottery Neolithic, occasionally mixed with a small number of Ubaid materials intruding from later levels.

Pit 1801 was a pit located at the northern edge of Square AF4. It had a diameter of around 105cm, and was at least 40cm deep although the bottom was not reached during excavation because of its location on the wall of the square and the large limestone cobbles in it. A similar pit, 1802, was found at the northeastern corner of Square AF5. Slightly larger than 1801, about 120cm in diameter, it was also filled with numerous limestone cobbles.

An elongated shallow depression, designated as 1803, extended from northwest to southeast in Square AF5. The top part was heavily eroded, and it was unclear whether or not it formed a kind of ditch or the base of some other construction. That which remained was about 2.8m long and 40cm wide, and some 15cm deep.

An oval pit (1804), 105cm x 70cm, filled with loose reddish brown soils, was located just south of 1803. The pit which showed isolated signs of animal burrows, was around 35cm deep when excavated, but the upper part had been completely removed by an Ubaidian ditch from Level 14 (1408). The pit slightly overlapped Pit 1805, an irregular oval pit of 150cm x 110cm. Again its upper part had been fully removed by the Ubaidian ditch (see Fig. 3.2; Pl. 3.1: 1 and 2), and its remaining depth was about 40cm. The fill characteristically consisted of loose reddish brown soils, containing much charcoal and small lime-

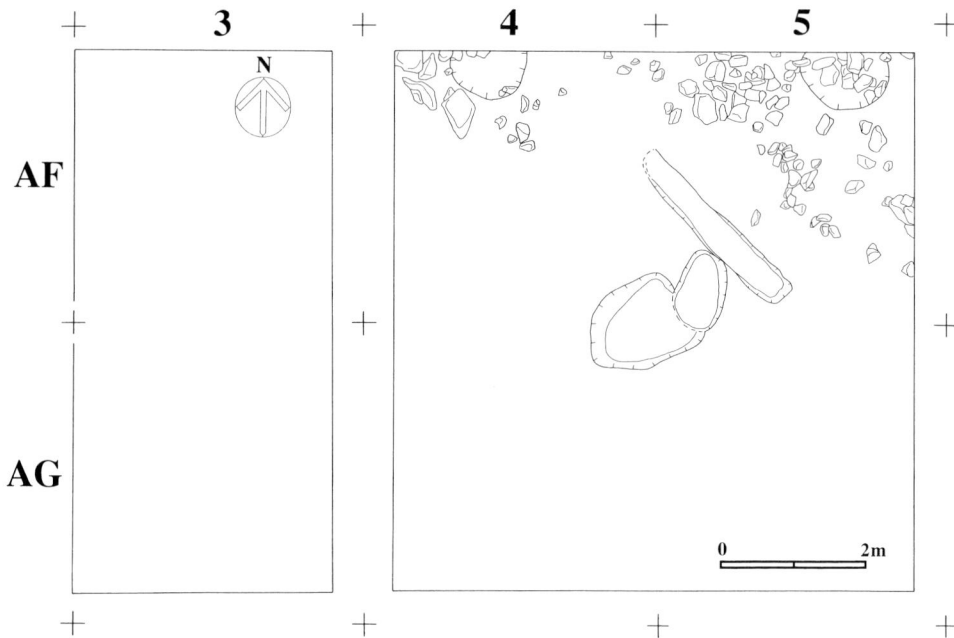

Fig. 3.7 Plan of Level 18 features.

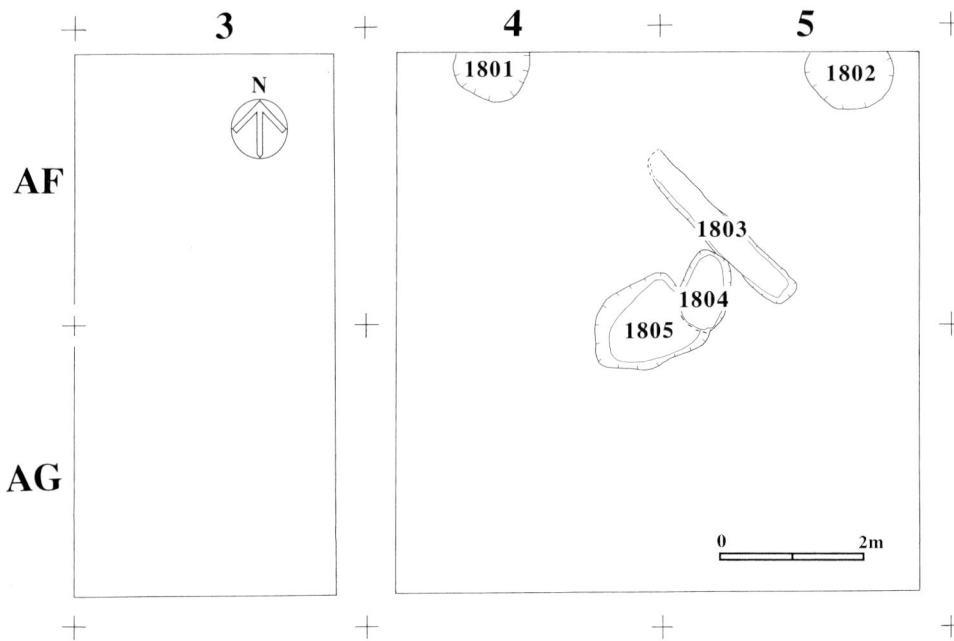

Fig. 3.8 Reconstruction of Level 18 features.

stone cobbles. The function of these pits is as yet uncertain, but their overall similarity in shape and depositional contexts to the pits of Level 8 of Sector B (see Chapter 4) is striking. Pits of this kind were apparently quite commonly distributed in the Neolithic settlement at Tell Kosak Shamali.

3.3.2 Level 17

This level, varying in thickness from 50 to 70cm (Figs. 3.2, 3.3 and 3.6), was distributed in all the squares excavated to virgin soil. It contained no definite architectural remains. The deposits consisted of compact cream to reddish brown soils and a considerable quantity of limestone cobbles. These cobbles were particularly numerous in the lower layers of Squares AF3 and AF4, where angular shapes of 5 - 60cm long were widely scattered. It is presently unknown whether or not they formed part of a specific structure or its collapsed remnants as their distribution showed no particular patterning.

The artifacts from this level included Ubaidian, Neolithic and even some Epi-Palaeolithic pieces, obviously reflecting the secondary nature of the level.

3.3.3 Level 16 (Figs. 3.9 & 3.10)

Deposits from this level were limited to the eastern part of the excavation area (Fig. 3.6) attaining a maximum thickness of about 30cm. The few architectural remains revealed in Squares AF5, AF6, AG5 and AG6, consisted of fragments of stone foundations and a small round pit (Figs. 3.9 and 3.10).

The stone foundations or walls of limestone cobbles, located primarily in Square AF5, were badly preserved. Mudbrick walls that once must have stood on them were detected in places. The main axes of the buildings were oriented WSW-ENE. Construction details are unknown due to the complete erosion of the western and southern areas. Nevertheless, remnants of mudbrick walls enabled us to reconstruct at least three rectangular spatial units, 1601-1603 (Fig. 3.10). A concentration of limestone cobbles (Feature 1605), was discovered south of these units which must also have formed part of the same architectural complex as indicated by patches of mudbrick walls on the cobbles. However, the original form has been altered by substantial distur-

bance caused by a small pit from Level 15 (1505) and a very large pit from historic levels.

South of this poorly preserved architectural complex was a circular, round bottomed pit of approximately 90cm in diameter and 50cm in depth (1604), filled with dark grayish ash.

3.3.4 Level 15 (Figs. 3.11-3.13; Pl. 3.1: 3)

The compact light brown soil deposits of Level 15 (averaging 20 - 30cm thick) were distributed mainly in the eastern part of the excavation area. Architectural remains, very similar to those in Level 16, were confined to Squares AF5, AF6 and AG6 (Figs. 3.11 and 3.12).

Remnants of stone foundations, covered with compact mud on which poorly preserved mudbrick walls had been set, were detected in Squares AF5 and AF6. As in Level 16, the axes of the walls were oriented WSW-ENE. Two spatial units (1501 and 1502) were identified on both sides of the main wall (Fig. 3.12). A scattering of limestone cobbles (1504) suggested another wall extending at a right angle WSW and ENE, but the precise plan could not be determined due to disturbance by the huge historic pit.

Two round pits of a similar size (1503 and 1505) were recognized south of this architectural complex. 1503 was about 90cm in diameter, nearly 80cm in depth with a fill of blackish gray ash, similar to Pit 1604 in Level 16. Pit 1505, slightly eroded in the southwestern part, was flask-shaped, with a diameter of about 80cm at top, 100cm at bottom, and a depth of around 80cm (Fig. 3.13; Pl. 3.1: 3). The inner surface showed clear traces of fire, and was filled with a lot of dark brown ash, charcoal and reddish brown burnt soils. It was probably a kiln.

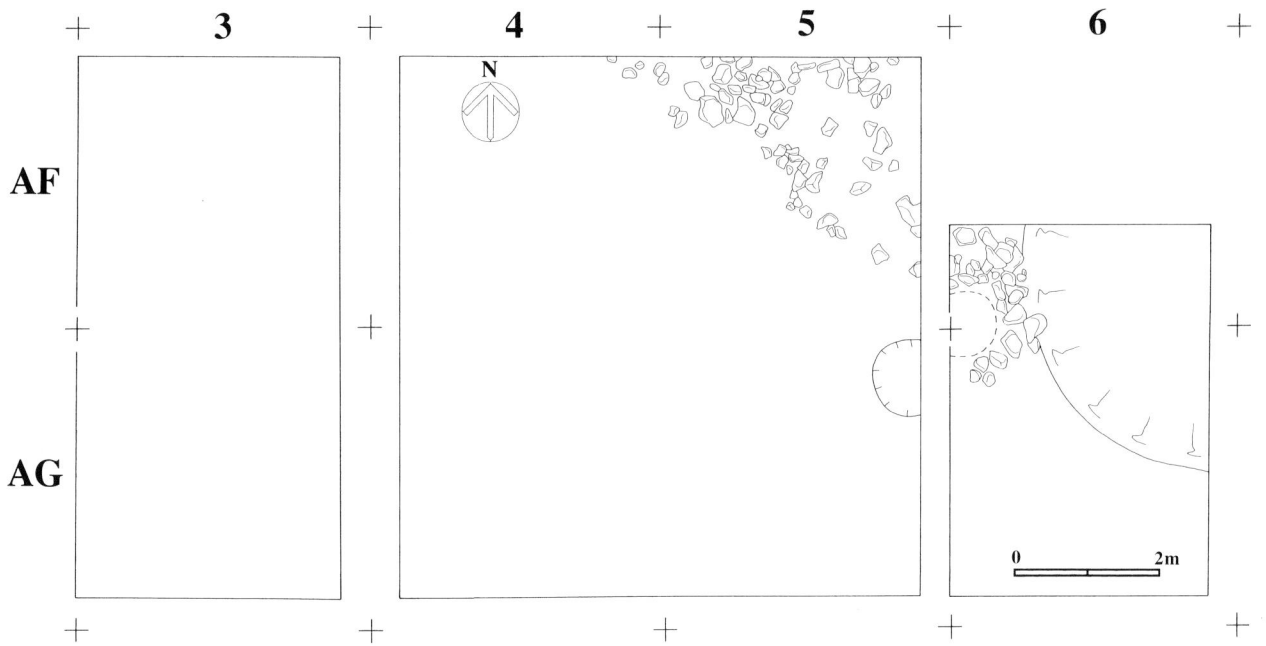

Fig. 3.9 Plan of Level 16 structures.

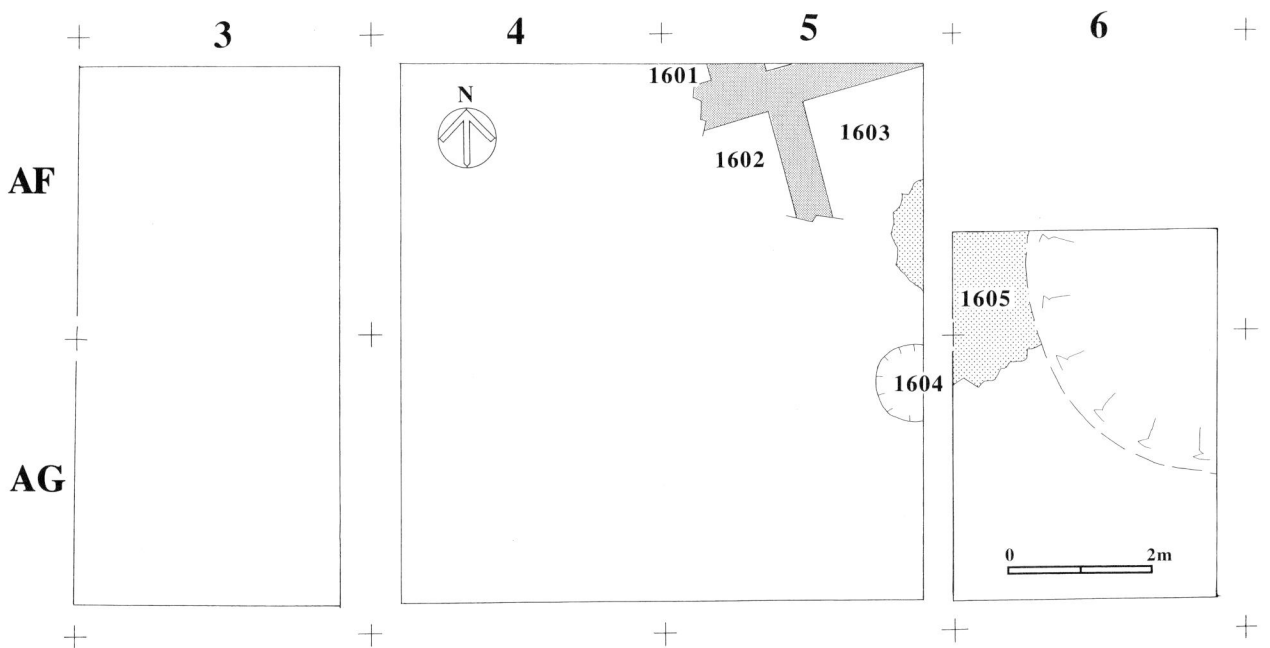

Fig. 3.10 Reconstruction of Level 16 structures.

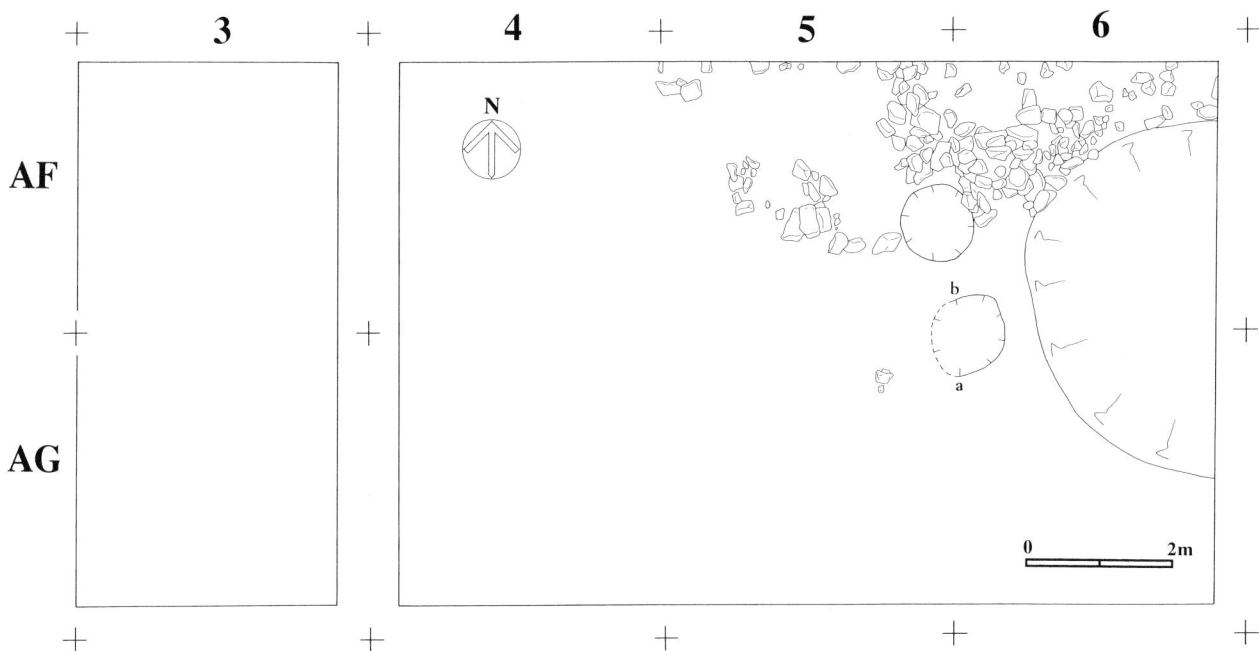

Fig. 3.11 Plan of Level 15 structures.

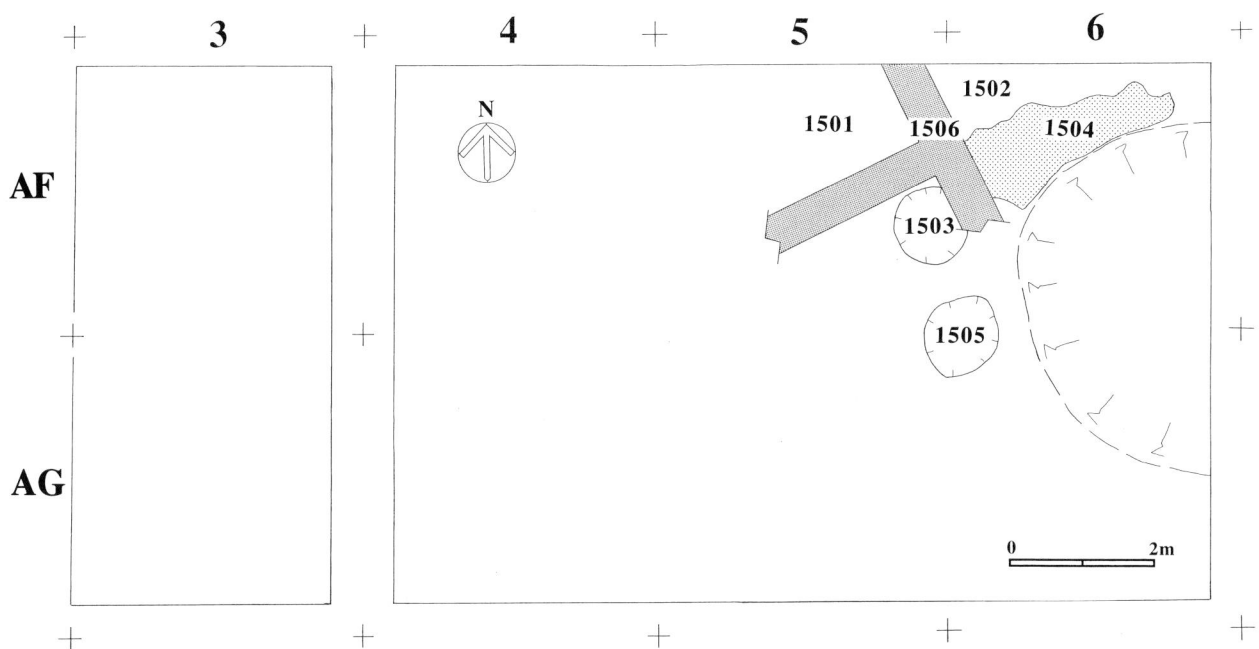

Fig. 3.12 Reconstruction of Level 15 structures.

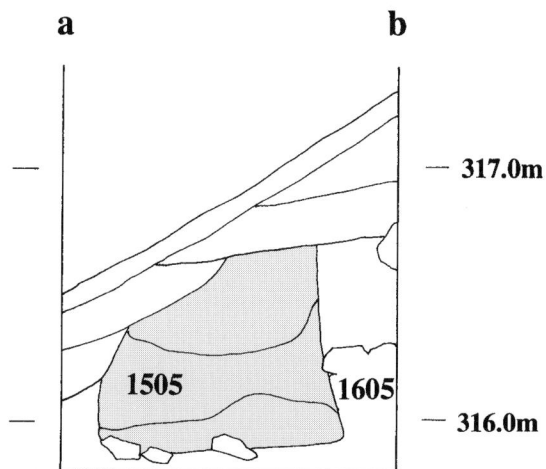

Fig. 3.13 North-south section of Pit 1505 (Level 15).

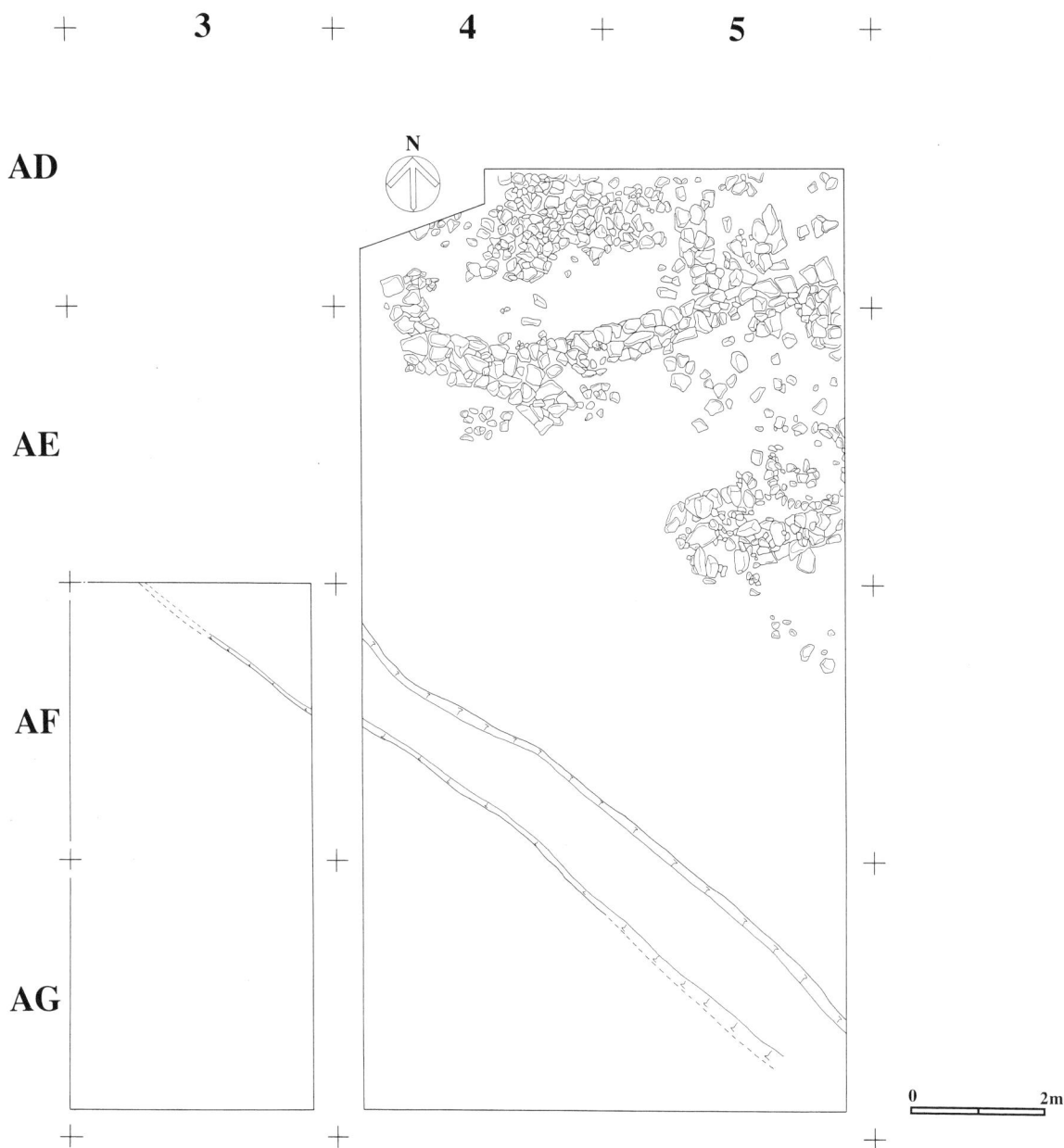

Fig. 3.14 Plan of Level 14 structures.

3.3.5 Level 14 (Figs. 3.14-3.16; Pl. 3.2)

From this level on a larger area was exposed. Level 14 was excavated in ten squares and was about 70cm thick. Mudbrick walls on stone foundations, oriented on the same axes as in earlier levels, were revealed in the northern part of the excavation area (Figs. 3.14 and 3.15; Pl. 3.2: 1). At least four rectangular rooms or spatial units were recognized (1402, 1403, 1405 and 1406). A dense concentration of limestone cobbles (1401) was discovered close to the northern edge of Squares AD4 and AD5 which might also represent a collapsed wall, although no associated mudbrick construction was discovered.

A rectangular space of about 1.3m by 3.8m (Unit 1402) was located in the northwest sector of the excavation area. Two walls joined a curved wall made of larger stone cobbles (1409) at the southwest corner. The curved wall stood about 40 cm high when discovered. It reminds us of part of a Halafian tholos, but its extensions towards the south and the west were missing. Located to the east, Unit 1403 was filled with large limestone cobbles probably derived from the collapse of surrounding walls. Unit 1405, south of 1402, appears to be an open, rectangular area of at least 1.4m by 2.2m, with a passage to 1406, and on its eastern side a rectangular room of 1.6m by 2.6m. Remains of a round oven, reaching 15 cm high at most, were revealed at the southeastern corner of Unit 1406 (Fig. 3.16). The oven (1407), with an opening of about 40cm wide towards the northwest, consisted of a neatly made limestone cobble wall, about 16cm thick, covered with substantial mudplaster (Pl. 3.2: 2). The inside diameter of the oven was about 100cm. The floor was also mud-plastered and hardened black by fire.

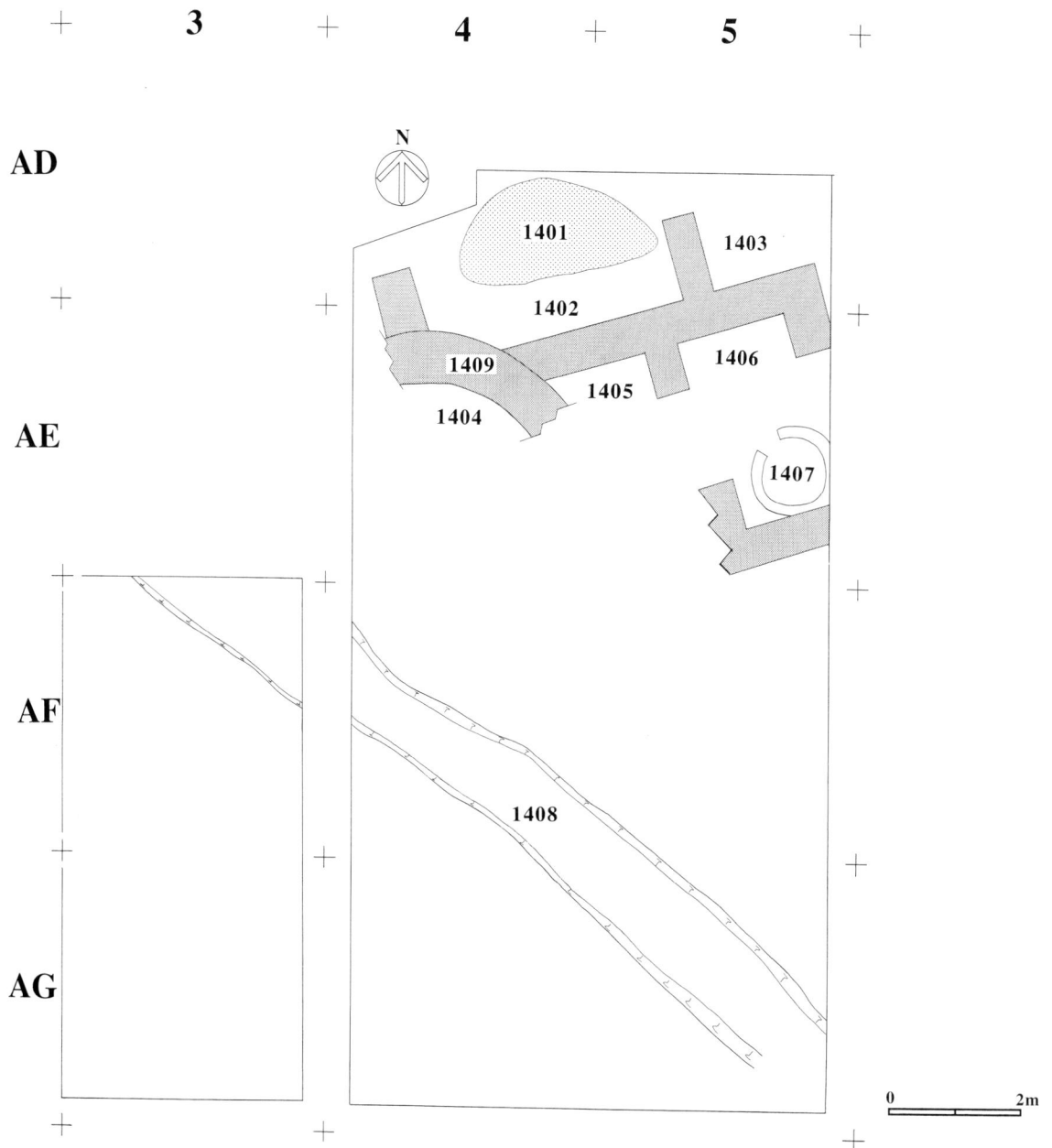

Fig. 3.15 Reconstruction of Level 14 structures.

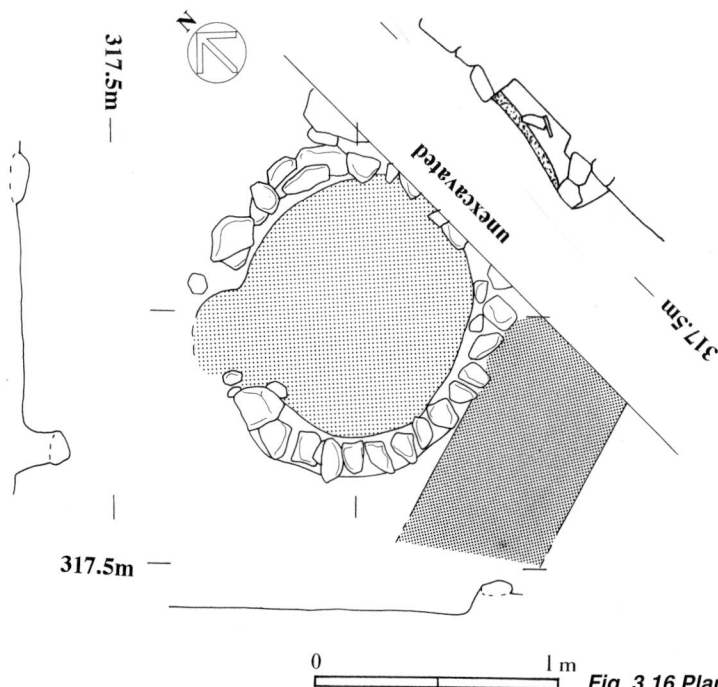

Numerous objects were discovered in primary context from this building complex. They included pottery production tools such as grinding stones and palettes, as well as pottery sherds, and flint tools such as sickle elements. An important *in situ* discovery was that of a stone bar lying on a stone palette (Pl. 3.2: 3), probably used for pigment preparation.

Among the features of this level was Ditch 1408 extending at least 12m northwest / southeast at the edge of the mound (AF3 to AG5). The ditch was about 3m wide at the top, 1- 1.2m deep, with a flattish bottom about 1.2m wide. The fill consisted of a series of gray sands, or yellowish brown soils containing plenty of charcoal. Since no architectural remains were discovered further to the south, this ditch appears to have bordered the settlement area.

Fig. 3.16 Plan and sections of Oven 1407 (Level 14).

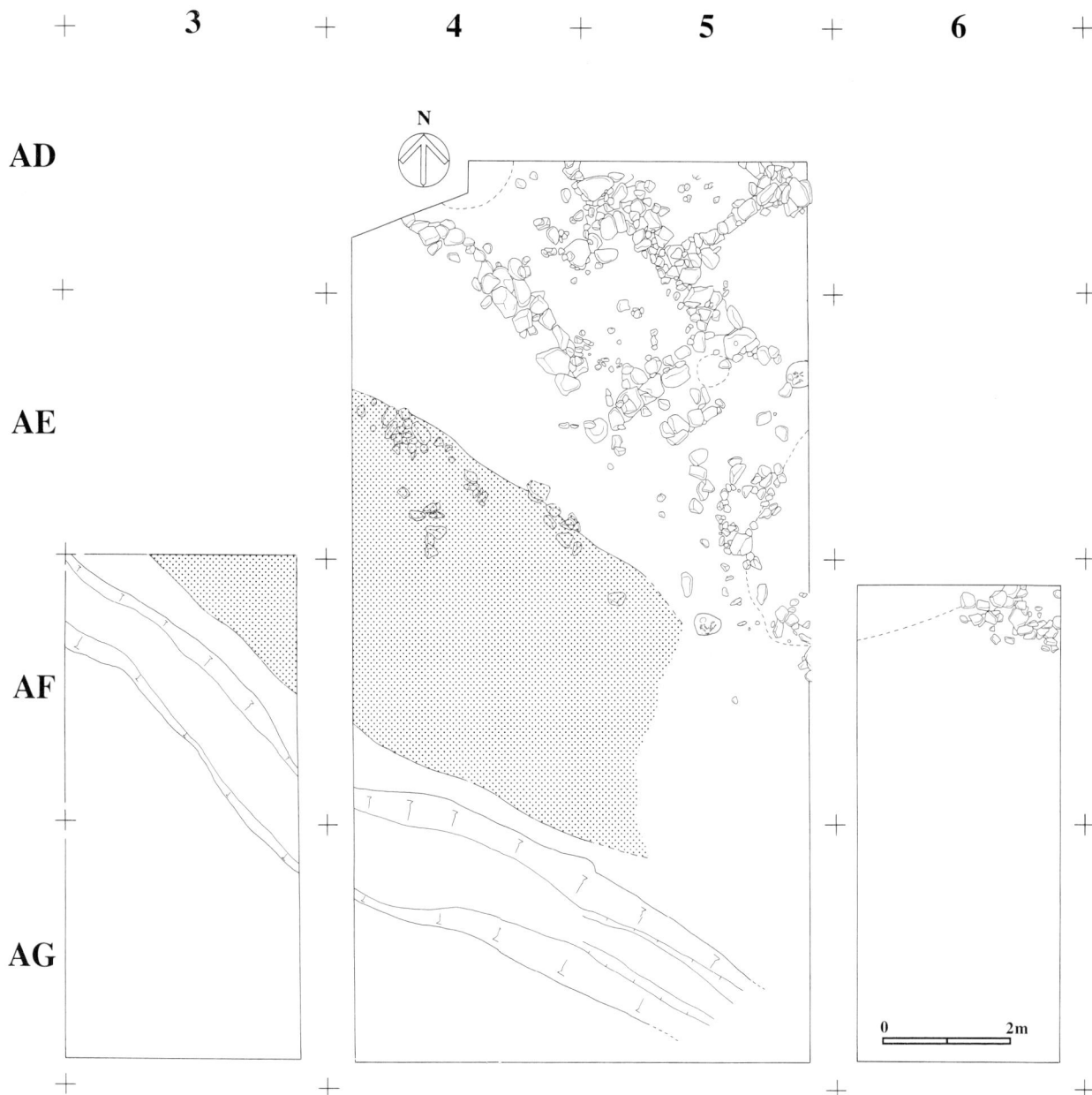

+ 3 + 4 + 5 + 6 +

Fig. 3.17 Plan of Level 13 structures.

3.3.6 Level 13 (Figs. 3.17-3.19; Pls. 3.3 & 3.4)

Level 13 was also exposed over a relatively large area covering 12 squares. In architectural plan it is completely different from the lower levels (Figs. 3.17 and 3.18; Pl. 3.3: 1). The buildings, composed of several rectangular units partitioned by mudbrick walls on stone foundations, were oriented in a NW-SE direction, a pattern seen in all the upper levels. The deposits of this level also displayed notable differences from the underlying ones. They were basically compact light brown soils alternating with thin layers of black ash, while the layers of Levels 14 to 17 were generally composed of compact reddish brown soils associated with numerous limestone cobbles. These differences may suggest the presence of an occupational break after Level 14, although it was difficult to identify a layer separating the architecture of the two levels.

The building complex, partitioned by mudbrick walls constructed on stone foundations, consisted of at least five spatial units (1301 to 1305). Each unit was represented by a small square or rectangular room/open space about 1.6m long. Units 1302 and 1303 had thick ash deposits in parts. There was an 80cm-wide passage between 1303 and 1304, and 1304 had a 65cm-wide opening toward the southwest. A passage, at least 1m wide, extended between 1302 and 1305, below which an infant burial pit (1318), about 42cm by 35cm and 20cm deep, was discovered. Another notable discovery from this complex was a very well preserved, 32cm-long curved sickle, composed of five flint elements fixed with bitumen to a bone handle. This rather exceptional piece was discovered *in situ* on the floor of Room 1301, partly inserted into a crack of Wall 1315 (Pl. 3.4: 1 and 2).

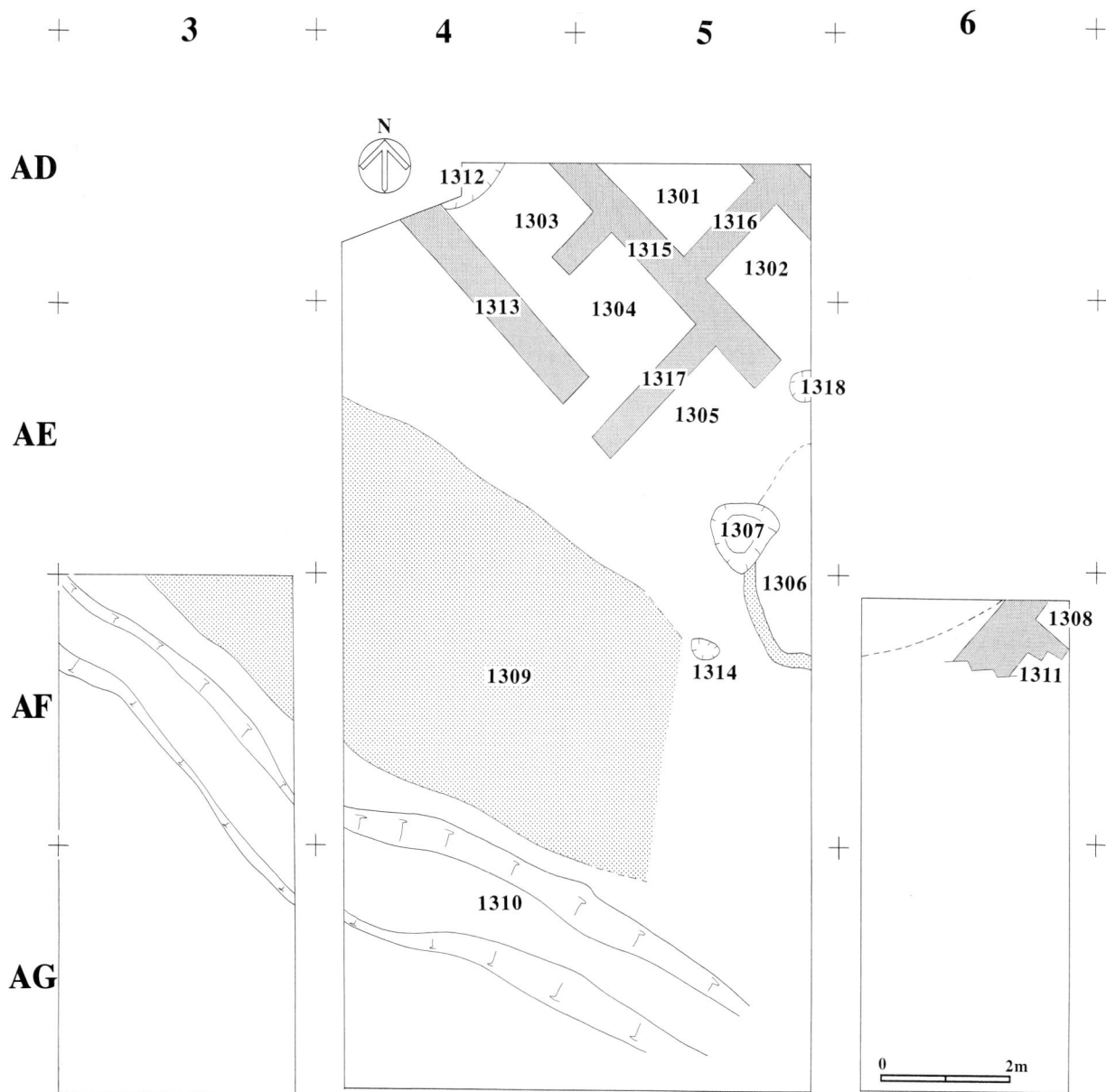

Fig. 3.18 Reconstruction of Level 13 structures.

In the southeast were some remnants of a stone foundation that may have been part of the construction (1308 and 1311), but heavy erosion and disturbance by the historic pit prevented reliable identification.

Between these architectural complexes was a space with no linear mudbrick walls or stone constructions. A thick accumulation of reddish brown to blackish brown ash (1306) was the major feature in this space. The southwestern end (AF5) was partly encircled by a curved *tauf* wall with a core of limestone cobbles. The wall was about 30cm thick and 40cm high but its extent was only traced to a quadrant some 120cm long. It had been eroded at the southeastern end and was connected to a round mud and limestone cobble feature (1307) in the north. The overall shape of

1306 was unknown but it apparently continued into the unexcavated area of Square AE6, where it may have been oval in plan and over 2m long. As shown in Fig. 3.19, the base of the WE section of this feature had been burnt and had an accumulation of black ash about 120cm in diameter (Pl. 3.3: 2). The fill consisted mainly of burnt soil of an orange brown color close to the encircling wall and a reddish brown color away from it. While deflation seems to have affected the eastern area, evidence of fire was also apparent on the bottom. Our current interpretation of this feature is that it is related to a pottery kiln. This interpretation is supported by the *in situ* discovery of a kit of potters' tools on the floor just by the encircling wall in Square AF5. These consisted of six ground stones made of river pebbles (Pl. 3.3: 2), probably used as palettes or polishing tools for pot-

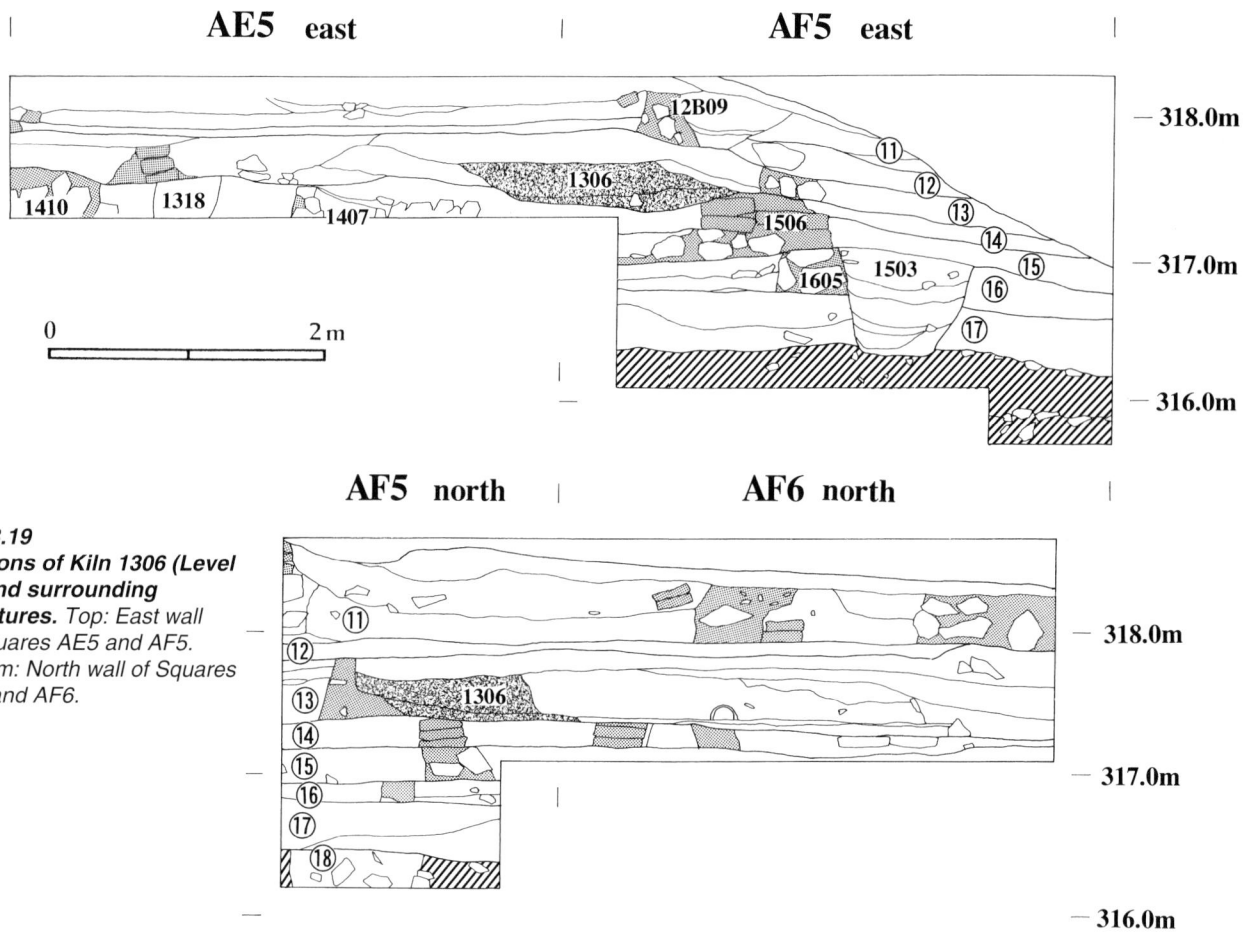

AE5 east   **AF5** east

AF5 north   **AF6** north

Fig. 3.19
Sections of Kiln 1306 (Level 13) and surrounding structures. *Top: East wall of Squares AE5 and AF5. Bottom: North wall of Squares AF5 and AF6.*

tery production. Similar sets of ground tools were also uncovered in 1304 and 1305, not far from 1306.

Other features characterizing Level 13 were an open area paved with limestone and river pebbles, and a ditch, both situated close to the southern edge of the mound. The pavement (1309), 4.5m wide and at least 9m long, extended along the southwestern edge of the settlement area. It was a very hard layer about 15cm thick, with numerous pebbles (some 5 to 10cm long) but very few sherds and flint artifacts.

The Level 13 ditch (1310) was about 3m wide at the top, nearly 1m deep and contained a lot of hard silts, sands and charcoal (Pl. 3.3: 3). The bottom of the ditch was rather flat, with the result that it resembled an inverted trapezoidal cross section. The size and shape of the ditch was very similar to the Level 14 ditch (1408).

3.3.7 *Level 12* (Figs. 3.20-3.24; Pl. 3.5: 1 & 2)

Level 12 corresponds to a compact light brown soil layer about 40cm thick on average. It contained a rectangular structure of mudbricks on stone foundations about 9m by 4.5m, in Squares AD4, AD5, AE4 and AE5 (Figs. 3.20-3.23; Pl. 3.5: 1). The longer axis of the structure was oriented

basically in the same direction as the previous level. General construction techniques also remained the same, but the limestone cobbles used for the foundation were much smaller (about 15cm to 20cm at maximum) than those in Level 13. Mudbricks were preserved sporadically suggesting the original walls were also insubstantial. This was particularly the case for the interior walls and their form was difficult to clearly determine.

Evidence of re-flooring at least twice was noted for this building complex. The basic plan of the buildings remained the same (Figs. 3.22 and 3.23), but some modification was noted, hence each was defined as 12A and 12B. There were probably six rooms in both levels or floors, but the partitioning walls were unclear. The architectural differences between 12A and 12B are as follows. In the earlier Level 12B, Room 12B06 had a 1.4m-wide opening to the south, that had been closed by a wall in Level 12A (12A05). There was an oven (12B05) set into the floor of 12B06 at the west corner of the main room (Fig. 3.24; Pl. 3.5: 2); it was U-shaped in plan, about 110cm by 90cm, with a 45cm-wide opening to the northeast. The 20cm-thick wall was made of *tauf* with a core of a few mudbricks. The mudbricks were made of an extremely fine textured, whitish gray clay. The floor, hardened with fire, was neatly plas-

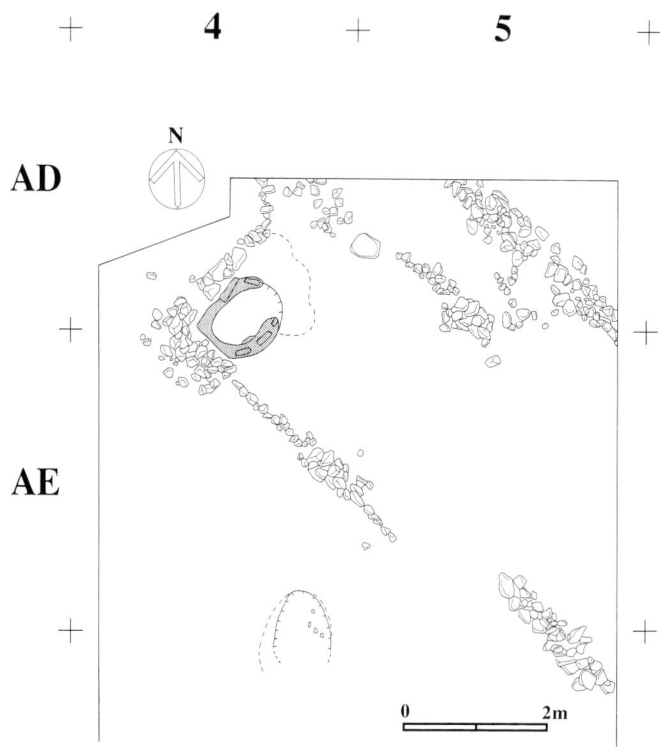

Fig. 3.20 Plan of Level 12B structures.

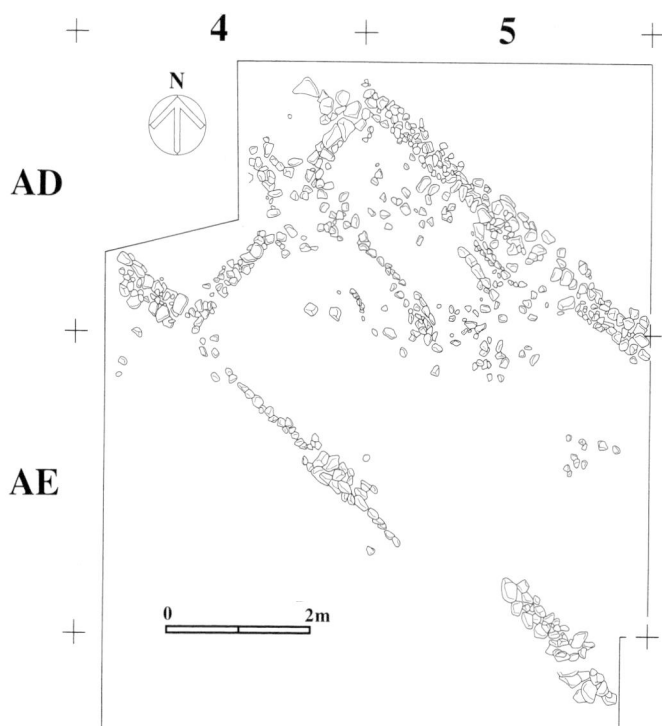

Fig. 3.21 Plan of Level 12A structures.

tered and sloped downward on the inside about 14cm below the room floor. A layer of ash extended about 130cm by 70cm near the opening.

In addition to this building complex, a few pits were noted close to the edge of the settlement. Pit 12B08 was a round, flat-bottomed pit with a diameter of 80cm at the top and 105cm at the bottom, and a depth of about 45cm. It was flask-shaped in section, similar to Pit 1505 of Level 15. The pit was filled with dark grayish brown ash. Three further pits (12B11 to 12B13) were revealed in Square AG3. Their size and shape varied, but they were all full of ash.

3.3.8 Level 11 (Figs. 3.25 & 3.26; Pl.3.5: 3)

This level was fully exposed in seven squares in the northern half of the excavation area, and partly exposed in the four southern squares (Figs. 3.25 and 3.26; Pl. 3.5: 3). The architectural plan showed continuity from the underlying level. Level 11 walls either overlapped or were next to those of Level 12. However, for the most part, the remains from Level 11 were confined mainly to foundation stones, as the upper structures had been almost completely removed by later levels. These stone foundations extended over an area 11.5m by 11m. The size and arrangement of the foundation stones suggests that this architectural complex may have consisted of at least two perhaps three different building units.

Four rather thick foundation walls (1114, 1120, 1121 and 1118) ran parallel in a NW-SE direction. A similar thick wall (1113) was set at a right angle to these walls. While the thick walls were composed of two rows of limestone cobbles, about 70 to 80cm wide, the thinner wall was a single row of limestone cobbles of a similar size. Although no mudbrick walls were detected, remnants of mudbrick and the presence of a similar complex in Level 10 (see below) suggest that some partitioning walls had been laid to connect Walls 1114, 1120 and 1121. Thus several rooms or spaces could be defined: 1101-1107, 1109 and 1111. There seemed to be narrow passages between 1101 and 1102, and between 1102 and 1105. The structures between 1121 and 1118 were difficult to understand fully as they had been badly damaged by a large pit from the overlying level (10B12) and a smaller, subsequent pit to the north. The remain-

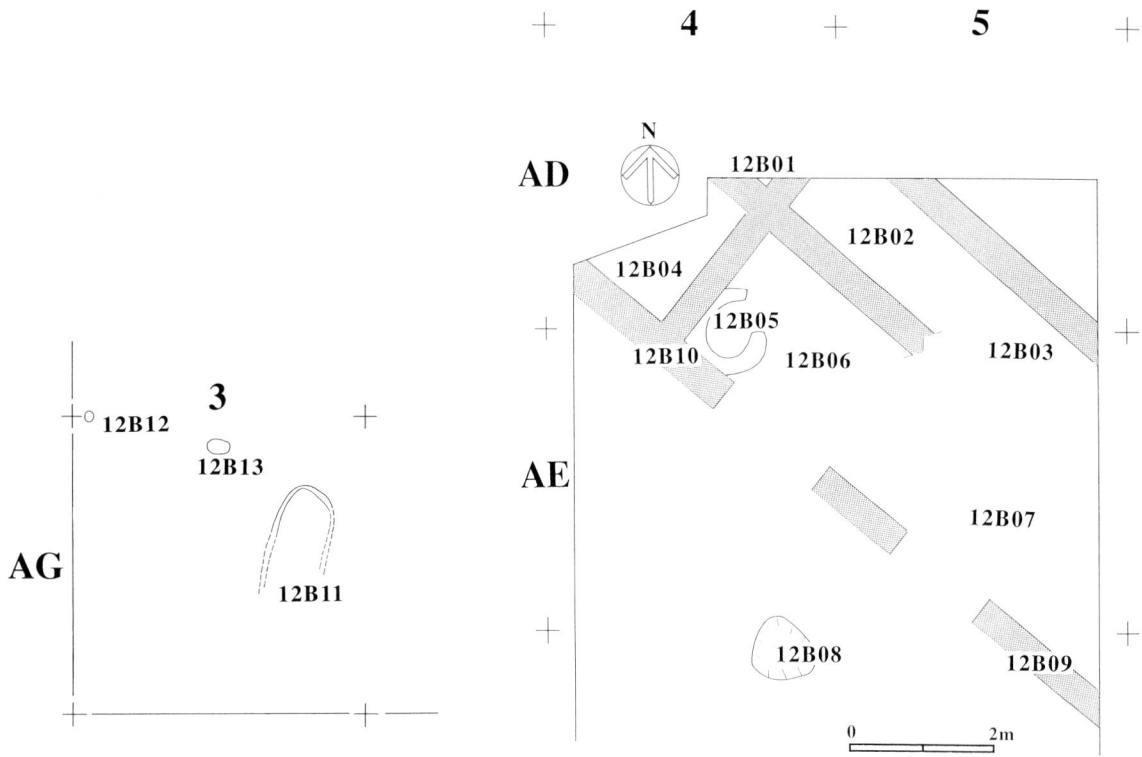

Fig. 3.22 Reconstruction of Level 12B structures.

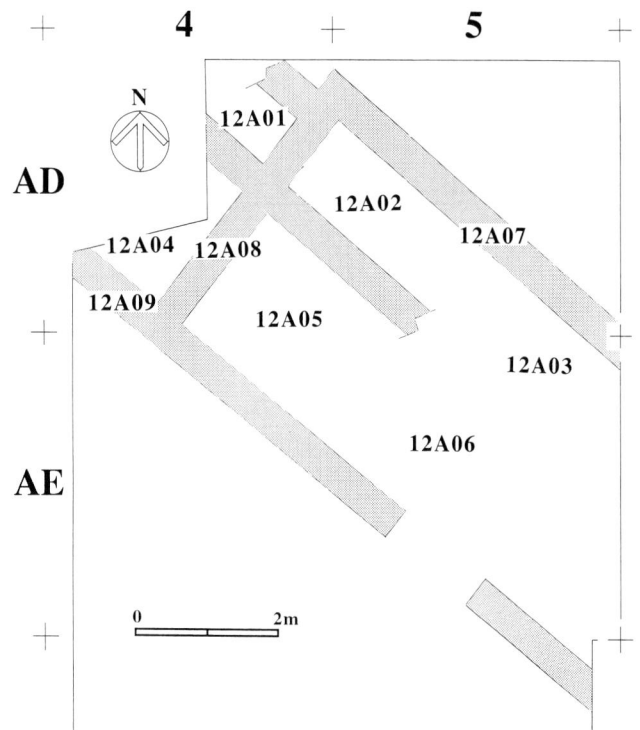

Fig. 3.23 Reconstruction of Level 12A structures.

ing stone foundation walls, all devoid of mudbrick remnants, may indicate the presence of two compartments inside (1108 and 1110).

The limestone foundations in Square AE6 consisted of smaller cobbles mostly less than 10cm in diameter. Although connected to Walls 1114 and 1120, the foundations of 1122 and 1123 had been shifted slightly SES, and may have been a later addition. Similarly the stone row running parallel southwest of 1121, also of smaller limestone cobbles, can be considered another addition (1117).

3.3.9 Level 10 (Figs. 3.27-3.42; Pls. 3.6-3.12)

This level produced a remarkable building complex consisting of a well-preserved burnt building and additional structures (Nishiaki in press a). The burning resulted in the exceptional preservation of room floors, on which numerous ceramics, stone tools and other objects were discovered *in situ* (Fig.

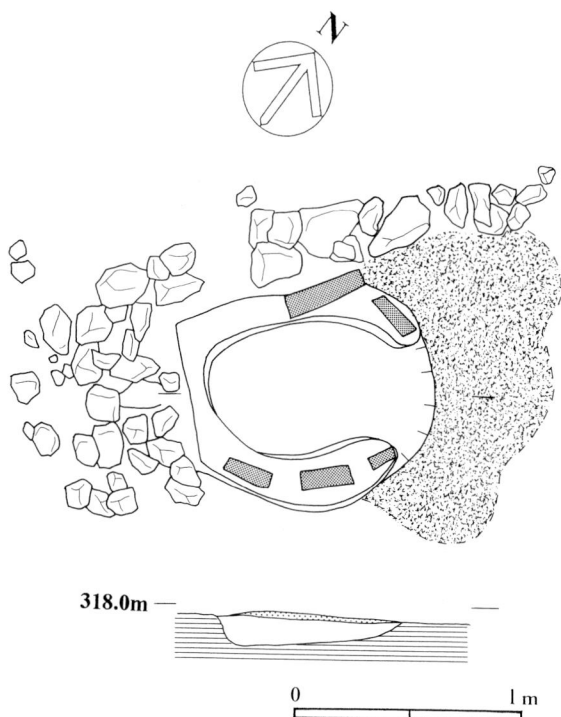

318.0m —

0   1 m

Fig. 3.24 Plan and section of Oven 12B05 (Level 12).

3.27; Pl. 3.6: 1 and 2). The building, oriented northwest-southeast, covered an area of approximately 9.5m by 6.5m, although the southern area had been destroyed by erosion. The basic structure resembled that of Level 11; in fact most of the mudbrick structures of Level 10 had been built using the stone walls of Level 11 as a foundation. While it might be argued that Levels 11 and 10 merely represented different parts of the same building, there are reasons to suggest that these two levels belonged to different phases of a rebuilding process that occurred almost in the same place. Firstly, the plan of Level 11 stone walls differs from that of the mudbrick walls of Level 10, and the difference was particularly evident in the southwestern area. It can be seen in Level 10 that the complex arrangement of the Level 11 stone walls had been fully filled in to create the flat well plastered floor of Room 10B08, and that the passage between Rooms 1105 and 1102 had been blocked with a mudbrick wall. Furthermore, parts of the Level 11 structure had been destroyed by the Level 10 structures. The disturbance between Walls 1121 and 1118 by Pit 10B12 has already been mentioned. In addition, some limestone cobbles of Wall 1121 were missing from Room 1105, due to the digging of Pit 10B13 (see below).

Level 10 itself was also divisible into two re-building or re-flooring phases. The earlier phase (10B) was distinguished by the presence of two pits, 10B12 and 10B13 (Figs. 3.28 and 3.30), which were both fully filled and covered with the well-made mud-plastered floor of Level 10A. Pit 10B12 was irregularly shaped, some 340cm long and 170cm wide and dug to a depth of 30 to 40cm, which had clearly destroyed the underlying stone and mudbrick structures (Fig. 3.32). Its fill was mostly ash, containing mudbrick fragments and limestone cobbles perhaps deriving from Level 11. Pit 10B13, on the other hand, was a regular circular pit of 150cm by 136cm and around 40cm deep, with a fill basically composed of four strata, the second of which was especially rich in ash (Fig. 3.33). The function or use of these pits, which show no trace of plastering on the inner surface had contain much ash in their fills, is as yet unknown.

The burnt building of Level 10A was so well preserved that it deserves more detailed description. The walls of Level 10A stood about 60cm high when discovered. The outer walls on the northwest

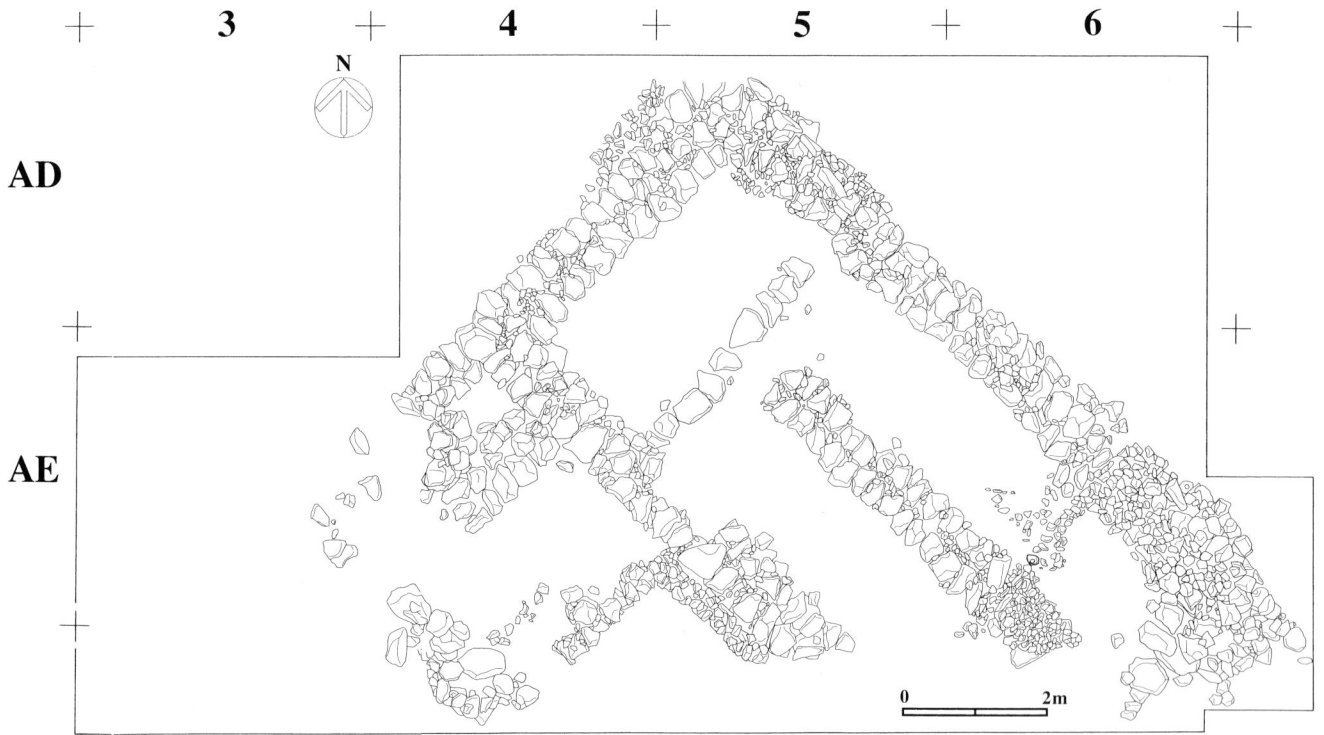

Fig. 3.25 Plan of Level 11 structures.

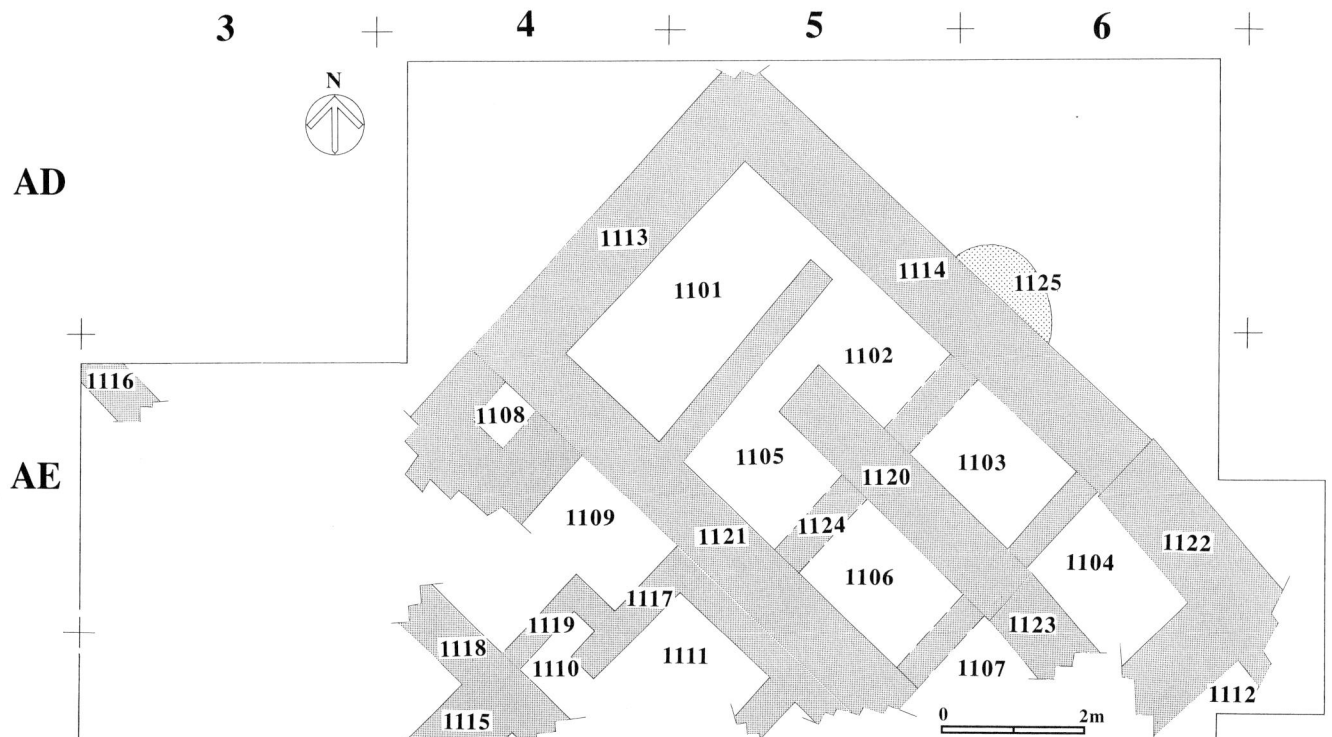

Fig. 3.26 Reconstruction of Level 11 structures.

(10A19) and northeast (10A23), and the two inner walls (10A20 and 10A25) along the longer axis were rather thick. They were formed of one and a half rows of mudbricks set lengthwise, together about 60cm wide. These walls were built on a foundation of large limestone cobbles of up to 65cm in maximum length. The thinner partitioning walls that were perpendicular to the main walls were formed of only one row of mudbricks and lacked a stone foundation. It is reasonable to assume that thicker ones on massive stone foundation were load-bearing walls that supported the ceilings (Kubba 1998: 55). The beams, made of poplar as demonstrated by the analysis of charred remains (George Willcox, pers. com.), were probably laid in the NE-SW for the small rooms. On the other hand, the absence of a load-bearing wall to be paired with Wall 10A19 and the rarity of associated charcoal remains suggest that Room 10A01 had no substantial ceiling.

Close examination revealed the building procedure of the walls as follows (Fig. 3.34): the foundation stones were usually laid in two, occasionally three rows and were covered with fine-textured gray clay to create a flat platform on which rectangular mudbrick walls were laid. At the northwestern wall of Room 10A01, the core portion of the wall was made with *tauf* instead of mudbricks (Section A-A' in Fig. 3.34; Pl. 3.7: 3).

Mudbricks varied in size greatly. While the thickness is concentrating at around 7 to 10 cm, the length and the width display a considerable variation. Fig. 3.35 shows histograms based on measurements of the seventy eight samples of mudbricks from the burnt building. The width, ranging from 14 to 38 cm, clearly follows a bimodal distribution, with two concentrations around at 18-19 cm and at 30 cm. These widths seem to correspond to the lengths of men's hand and forearm respectively. On the other hand the range of the length is far larger, which may partly reflect intentional segmentation of complete bricks by the Ubaidian architects to fill narrow gaps in a wall, or our inaccurate identification of bricks during the fieldwork. Nevertheless it obviously has a single peak at 48-49 cm, i.e. the sum of the above two widths. These measurements show that the mudbricks were manufactured at Tell Kosak Shamali following a cubit system based on the human body, as suggested at other Ubaidian sites in Iraq (Kubba 1998: 47). Mudbrick work with this system resulted in producing two distinct forms of mudbricks, i.e. those of 18-19 cm x 48-49 cm and 30 cm x 48-49 cm, the prevalent use of which can be easily recognized on the wall of 10A19.

The building in the excavation area consisted of at least nine spatial units, defined as 10A01 to 10A09.

10A01

This is the largest room (4.2 x 2.4 m) located in the northwest. Rectangular in plan, it had two entrances, one in the southwest from 10A08 and the second in the east from 10A02. The floor was plastered with very hard fine clay. In the northern corner there was a small, semi-circular shaped container-like structure (10A13) enclosed by a hard clay wall about 8cm thick (Fig. 3.36; Pl. 3.8: 1). The wall was only 15cm high when discovered, and the upper part was missing. Part of the wall, closer to Wall 10A23, was also missing. The structure appears originally hook-shaped (see below). While the bottom of this structure was full of ash and charcoal suggesting evidence of fire, it could have been caused by the burning of the entire building. It seems more likely that this structure was a container, rather than an oven or a kiln.

At the southern corner there was a larger clay plate (10A17) (Fig. 3.37; Pl. 3.8: 2). The plate, 115cm by 113cm at its base, probably represented the lowest part of a kiln whose superstructure was completely missing. It was horseshoe-shaped with an opening toward the interior of the room. The kiln wall (about 15 to 20cm thick) and floor were of plastered with mud. The plastered floor (up to 8cm thick) sloped gradually downward toward the inside. The upper 3 to 5cm layers of the plaster had been hardened red by fire suggesting this kiln had a relatively long life. Its size and the shape closely resembled those of the clay constructions claimed as pottery kilns at Tell al-'Abr, a similar Ubaidian site about 20 km north of Tell Kosak Shamali (Hammade and Yamazaki 1995).

Feature10A29 was next to 10A17 (Fig. 3.38). Like 10A13 it was a hook-shaped structure with a yellowish gray clay tauf wall, about 10cm thick enclosing a shallow oval pit of 55 x 36 x 10cm. A few

Fig. 3.27 Plan of Level 10 structures with the floor remains.

sherds, river pebbles and an obsidian blade were recovered from the pit. This hook-shaped structure was so close to Kiln 10A17 that these had probably been in use together.

Tens of thousands of sherds and other artifacts were discovered on the floor of 10A01 (Pl. 3.7: 1, 2). Meticulous refitting strongly indicates the main function of this room as pottery storage, in which over 150 complete pots had originally been stored (Nishiaki in press a). Other objects were also recovered in quantity, among them flaked and ground stone artifacts, pigments and horns, indicating that other activities had also occurred. Stone artifacts were particularly numerous in a narrow space between Kiln 10A17 and Wall 10A20.

10A02

A series of smaller square rooms was situated southeast of 10A01. Their size (about 1.8m x 1.8m) reminds us of the basic unit of measurement proposed for the Ubaidian buildings of Iraq by Forrest (1991). Room 10A02 was connected to 10A01 by an 80cm-wide passage. The floor was covered with a great deal of charcoal, particularly rich in the southern corner. A group of flint cores, a horn and a ceramic scraper were found along the northeastern wall (Pl. 3.9: 1 and 2). Of particular interest was a bowl revealed at the northern edge of the passage to 10A01 (Pl. 3.8: 3). It contained two crescent-shaped clay scrapers and a flint flake, considered to be a potter's tool kit. A limestone cobble (70cm x 38cm x 15cm) was near the center of the room. It is unlikely that it had been part of the wall or the ceiling because of its rather isolated location. Similar stones often discovered at other workshop rooms were probably anvils for craft activities, perhaps related to pottery production.

10A03

Room 10A03 was also a square room the same size as 10A02. As with other small rooms (with the exception of 10A02) it had no entrance at the base. Access must have been through higher parts of the walls or from the ceiling. Much charcoal, including carbonized grain and wood, was found on the floor. The largest piece of wood perhaps derived from roof beams was 105cm long with a diameter of nearly 20cm (Pl. 3.9: 3). A crushed

clay structure (10A24) was situated at the eastern corner of the room. Roughly U-shaped in outline, the structure (measuring 50 x 28cm) which opened into the inside room, showed no trace of intentional firing. The *tauf* wall of the structure was about 8cm thick. The upper part of the structure was missing, but a ground slab of basalt (35 x 34 x 7cm) was discovered on it, although in a secondary context. It is assumed that this structure was used for storage as it contained a lot of charred grain.

Refitting of a group of pottery sherds, discovered *in situ* in the southwestern half of the floor, indicated the presence of over twenty complete pots (Pl. 3.10: 1). It is evident that, as with Room 10A01, this room also functioned as a pottery storage area.

10A04

The southern part of this room was missing. Along the northwestern wall a clay structure (10A27), consisting of 2 - 3cm-thick clay plate fragments, was revealed (Fig. 3.39; Pl. 3.10: 2). Although crushed too badly to enable reconstruction of the original shape, it was apparently longer and narrower than 10A13. Fragments of a clay wall and the possible ceiling were discovered, extending along the room wall over an area of 120cm by 25cm. Much carbonized grain was discovered in association with this structure. A few jars were located along Wall 10A25, which also contained abundant carbonized grain. The jars, as well as the clay structure, were probably grain containers.

10A05

There was also much carbonized grain and charcoal on the floor of this room (Pl. 3.10: 3). The grain was especially abundant near the northeastern wall forming an accumulation up to 8cm thick (Pl. 3.11: 1). The available evidence suggests that it was originally stored in a clay structure or container, whose remnants were found at the northern corner (10A26). The container was a shallow depression of about 50cm by 35cm, partly encircled with an 8cm-thick *tauf* wall (Fig. 3.40). Again it was hook-shaped. A clay disk of the similar thickness was discovered inside, perhaps part of its collapsed ceiling.

A limestone cobble situated near the center of the

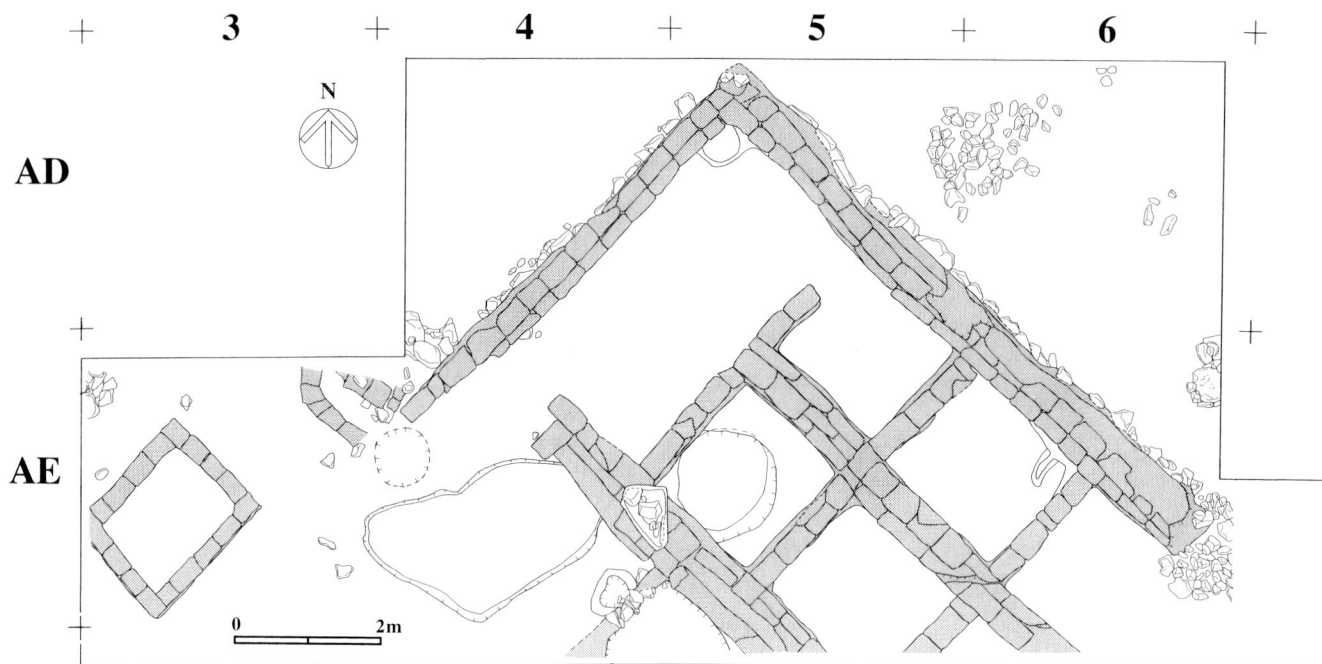

Fig. 3.28 Plan of Level 10B structures.

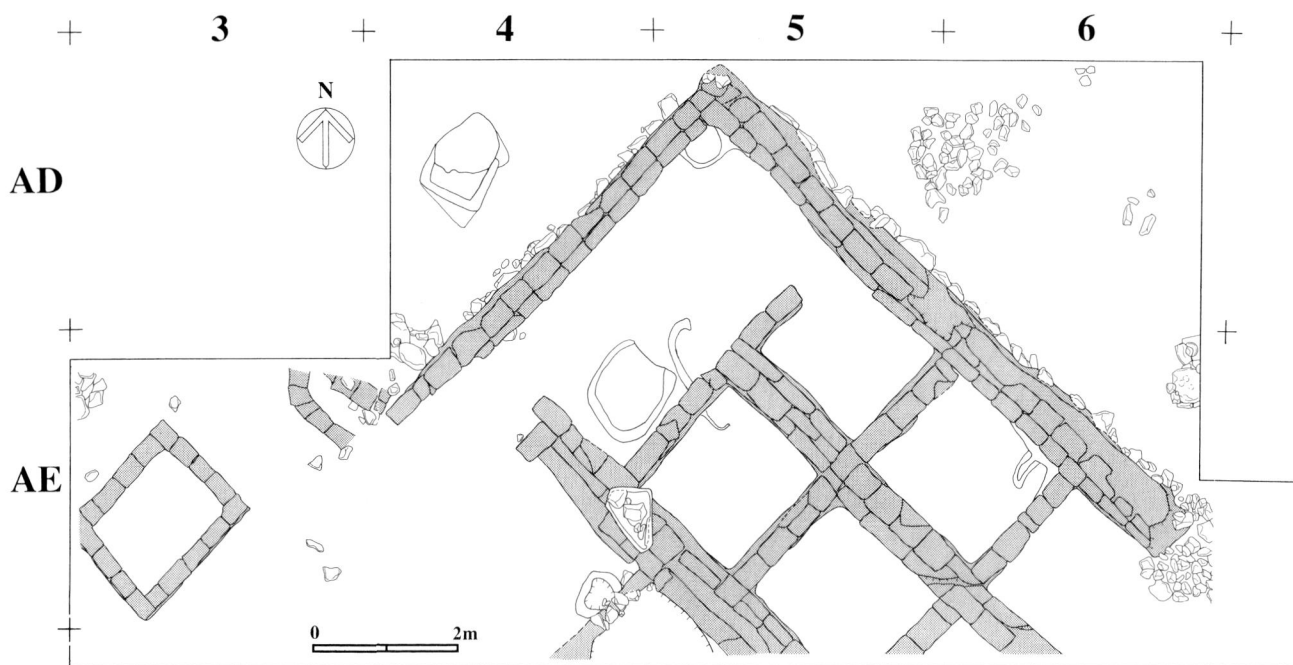

Fig. 3.29 Plan of Level 10A structures.

room seems to have functioned as an anvil. It was rather flat, 35cm x 25cm and about 15cm thick, with a shallow depression about 8cm in diameter on the top surface.

10A06

Erosion had removed the southern part of this room. Carbonized grain was distributed on the floor, with dense accumulations at the northern and the western corners (Pl. 3.11: 2). A crushed jar at the northern corner was a grain container. Several charred wood branches, nearly 40cm long and about 2 to 3cm in diameter, were discovered along the northeastern wall .

10A07

Only the northern corner of this room remained. No *in situ* objects were discovered in this small area of the room floor.

10A08

This spatial unit, situated south of 10A01, extended 3.9m in a northwest-southeast direction, but its extension toward the south was unclear due to erosion. It appeared to have been an open space because, in contrast to other rooms, the fill rarely yielded charcoal or wood beams. Instead, it usually contained blocks of burnt soil and mudbrick fragments, presumably the result of collapsed walls.

The floor was covered with a hard plaster of fine whitish gray clay. The floor was relatively free of objects except for the area close to the passage to Room 10A01, where numerous pottery sherds were distributed. The distribution of sherds represented an obvious continuation from 10A01. A thick accumulation of fine whitish brown clay in the center of the room suggested the space may have been used mainly as a place for clay storage.

10A09

Only the northern half of this unit was mapped. During the 1994 sounding (Trench A), a narrow mudbrick wall running perpendicular to 10A20 had been encountered in the south. The wall was obviously a part of this unit so that 10A09 must have originally formed a room the same size as other small rooms in this building complex. The

inner surface of the walls and the floor were heavily burnt and covered with a thick accumulation of reddish brown soil and charcoal. The charcoal was sampled for radiocarbon dating. The floor produced few other *in situ* finds.

A rectangular-walled compartment of about 1.6m by 1.2m was revealed in the southwest of the building complex (10A11; Pl. 3.11: 3). It is unknown whether this small structure belonged to Level 10A or 10B. The mudbricks were set lengthwise in one row directly on the ground. The function of this structure is as yet unknown as the floor was almost devoid of artifacts. To the north a construction made of one row of mudbricks (10A10) joined Wall 10A19, but poor preservation prevented identification of the complete plan and features. A square-shaped clay structure (90 x 90cm) was discovered further to the north (10A28; Fig. 3.41; Pl. 3.12: 1). It had a 15cm thick *tauf* wall and an opening to the north. The bottom was heavily burnt and contained much black ash which was also distributed in front of the opening. This feature is most likely a kiln.

A couple of structures with stones were recovered in the eastern area. Two concentrations of irregular limestone cobbles were among them, a large one of 2m by 1.4m (10A14) and a smaller patch to its east (10A15). An interesting feature (10A12), consisting of a circular pierced stone and a flat stone plate, was located at the eastern wall of Square AE6 (Fig. 3.42; Pl. 3.12: 2 and 3). The pierced stone resembles a door socket, but there were no room walls nearby. The stone had been set on a flat limestone and several small limestone pebbles had been inserted between the two. Another flat limestone (46 cm in diameter), with a polished or well rubbed surface was situated to the south within a circle of small angular limestone pebbles. This feature may have been related to pottery manufacture although it is difficult to determine how it was used. Could the pierced stone be a lower part of a turning divice to shape pottery?

3.3.10 Level 9 (Figs. 3.43 & 3.44)

The poorly preserved building in this level consisted of a few intermittently arranged stone foundations and remnants of mudbrick walls (Figs. 3.43 and 3.44). The basic room plan and the architectural axes of the structures, however, closely resembled those of Level 10. In fact, the long

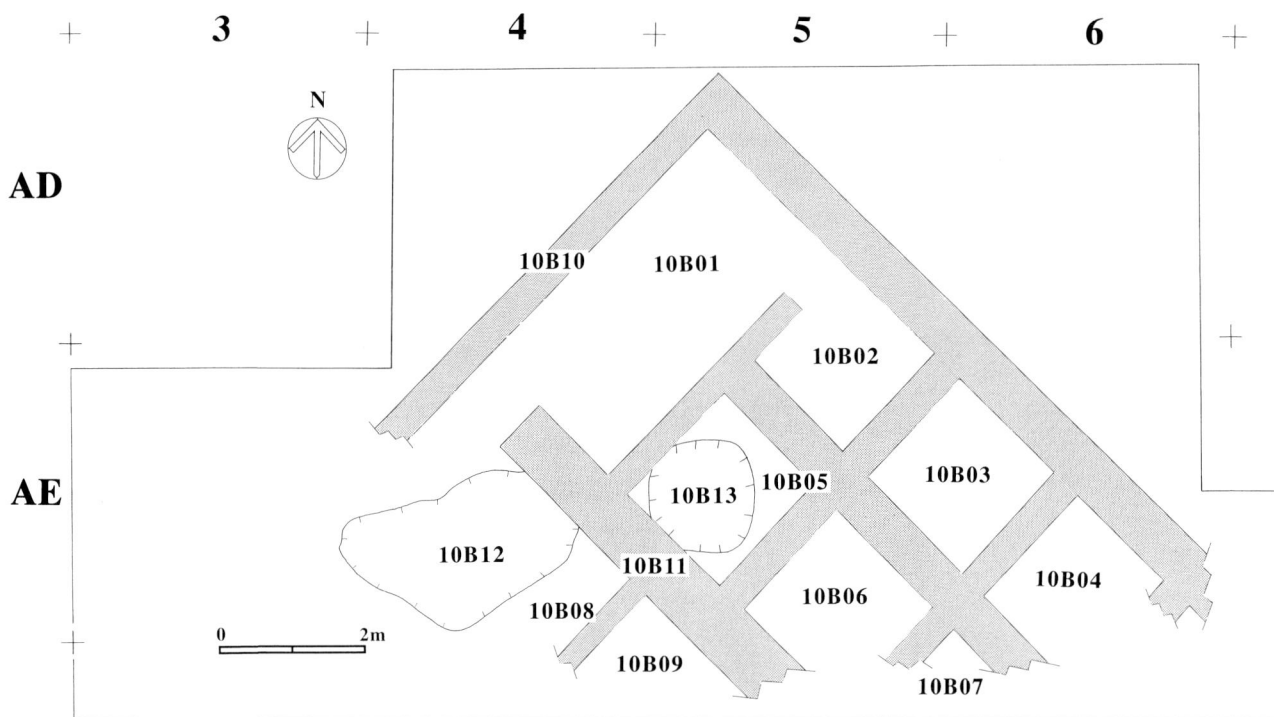

Fig. 3.30 Reconstruction of Level 10B structures.

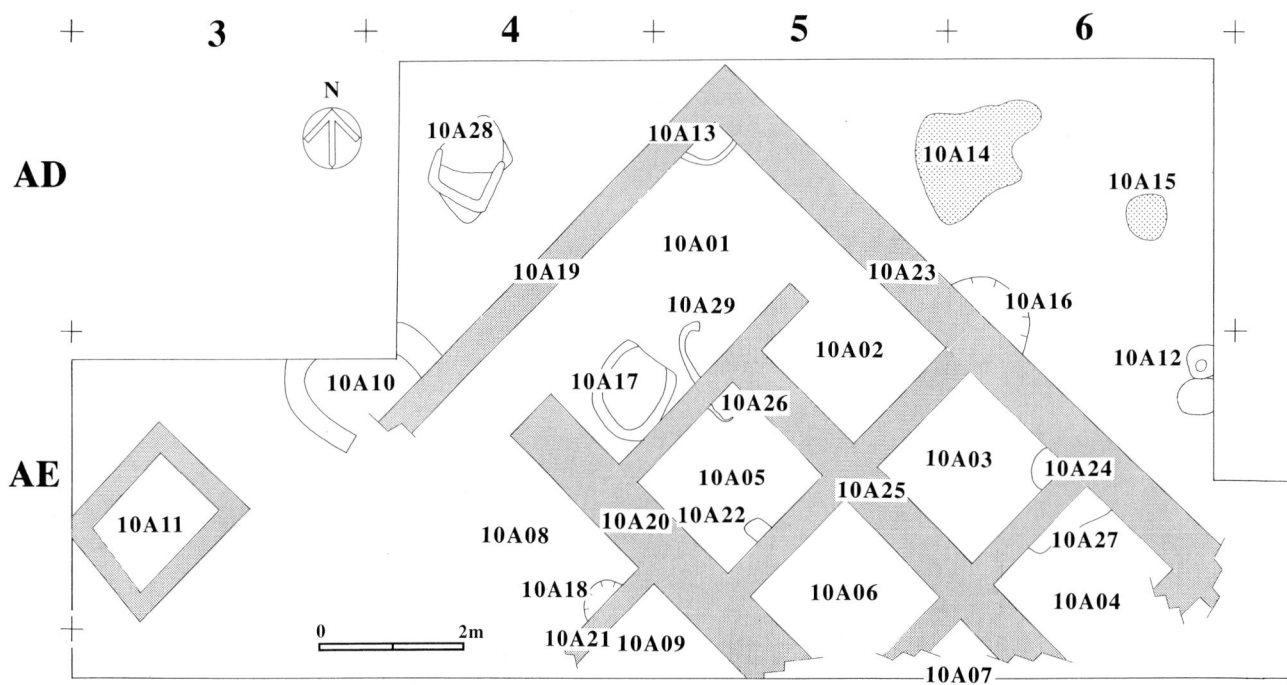

Fig. 3.31 Reconstruction of Level 10A structures.

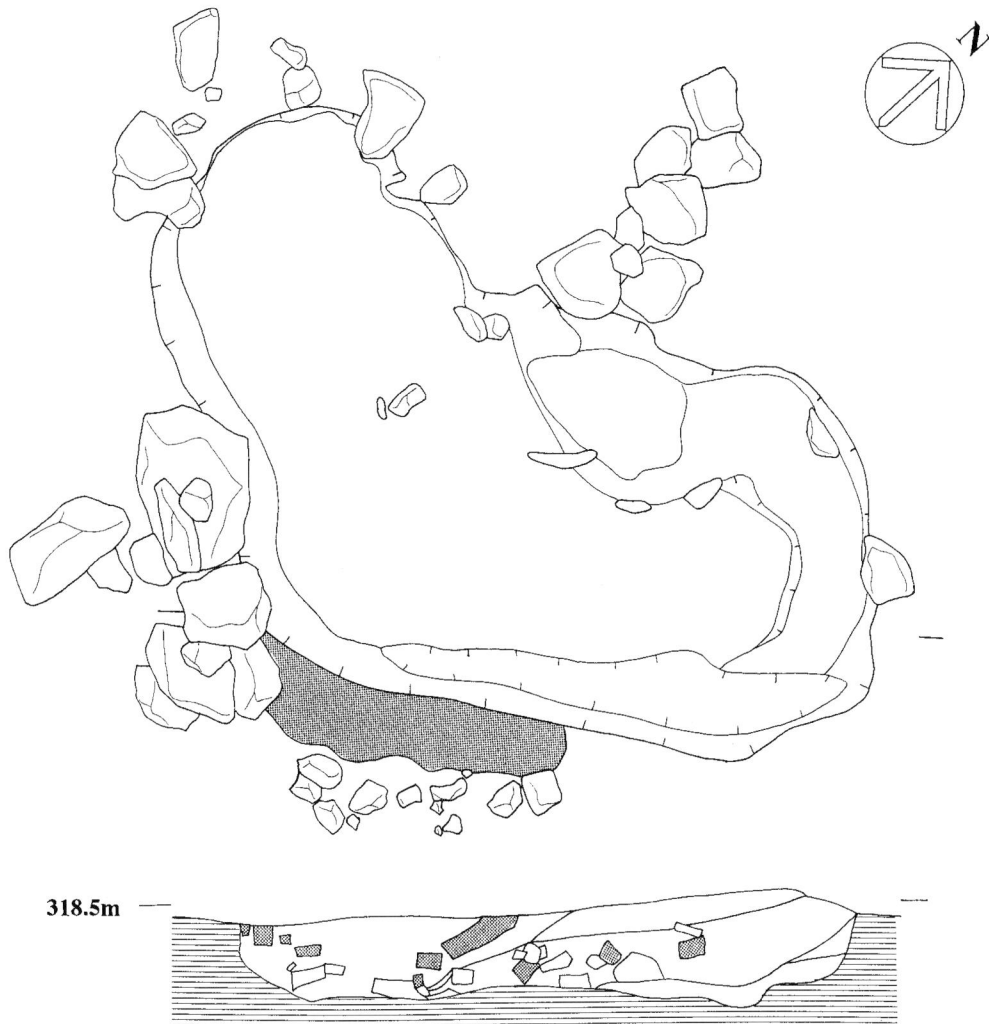

318.5m —

Fig. 3.32 Plan and section of Pit 10B12 (Level 10B).

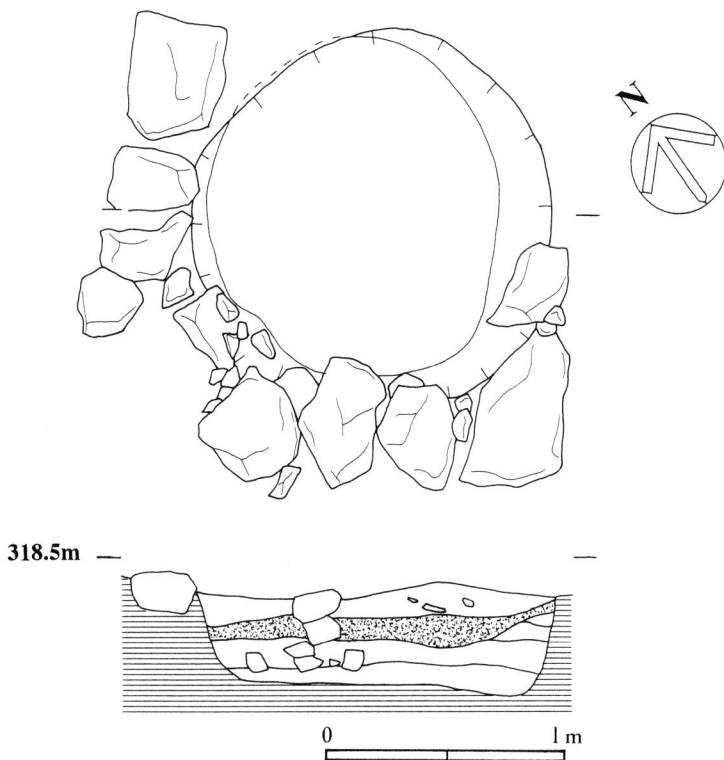

318.5m —

Fig. 3.33 Plan and section of Pit 10B13 (Level 10B).

wall running from Squares AD5 to AE6 directly overlapped Wall 10A23 in places, although it was located slightly to the north. The other walls also ran in parallel to those of Level 10, but were in slightly different locations. They had probably been partitioned by mudbrick walls, remnants of which were detected in places (903).

Collapsed walls of limestone cobbles (5 - 35cm in size) (904) were discovered in the eastern area. A crushed jar found *in situ* in the north should be mentioned.

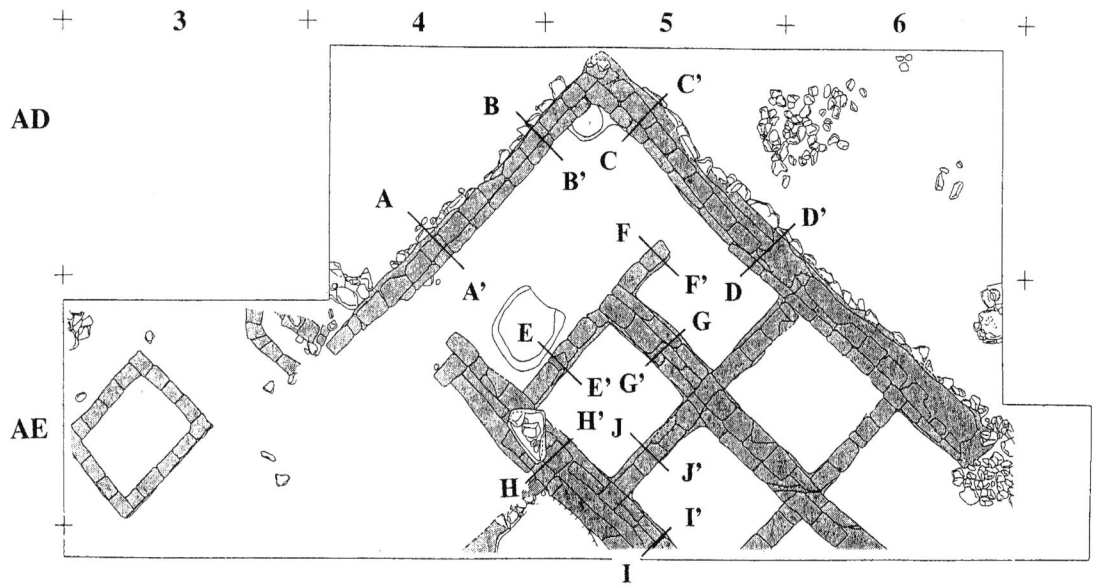

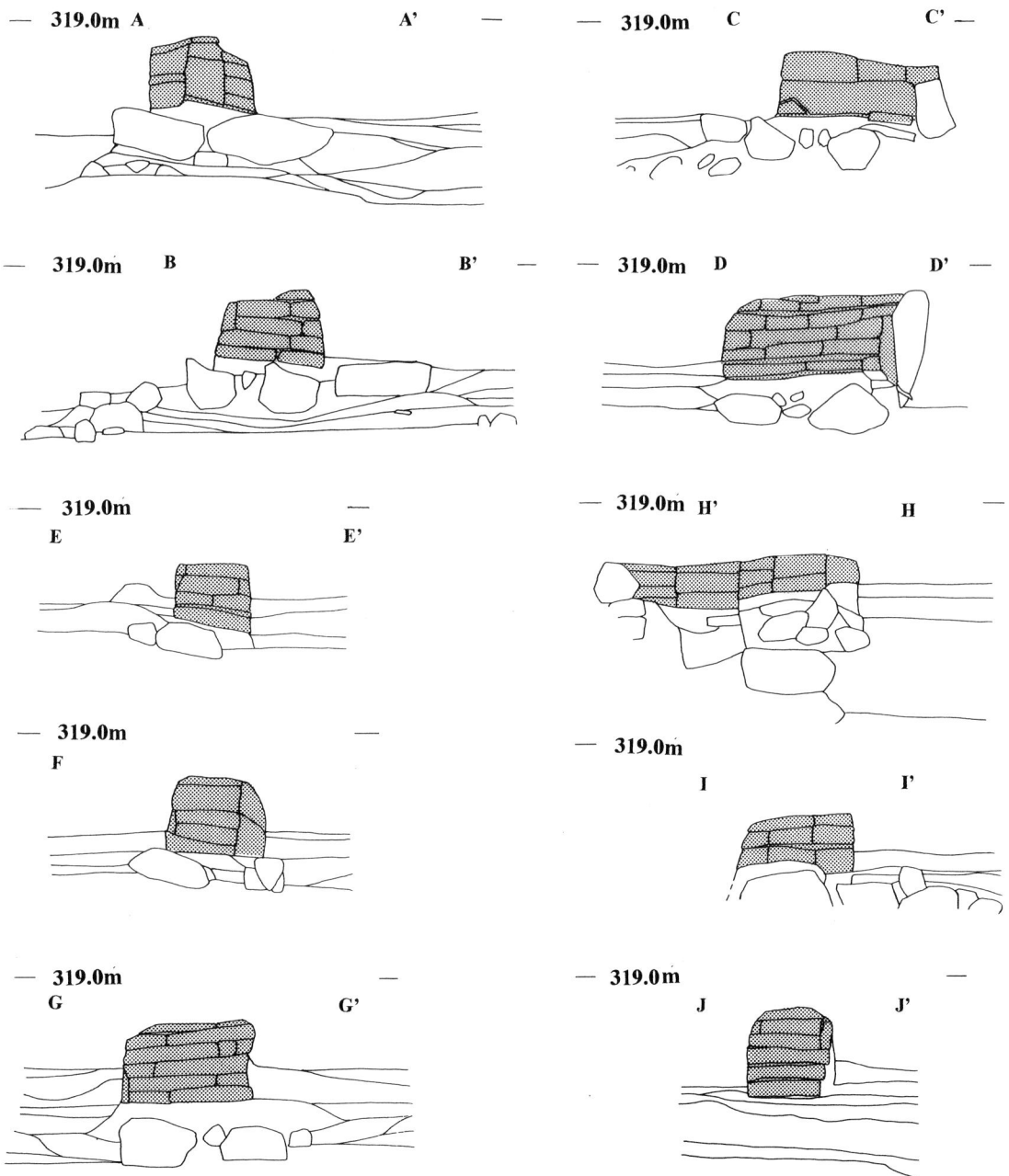

Fig. 3.34 Sections of the walls of Level 10A.

0   1 m

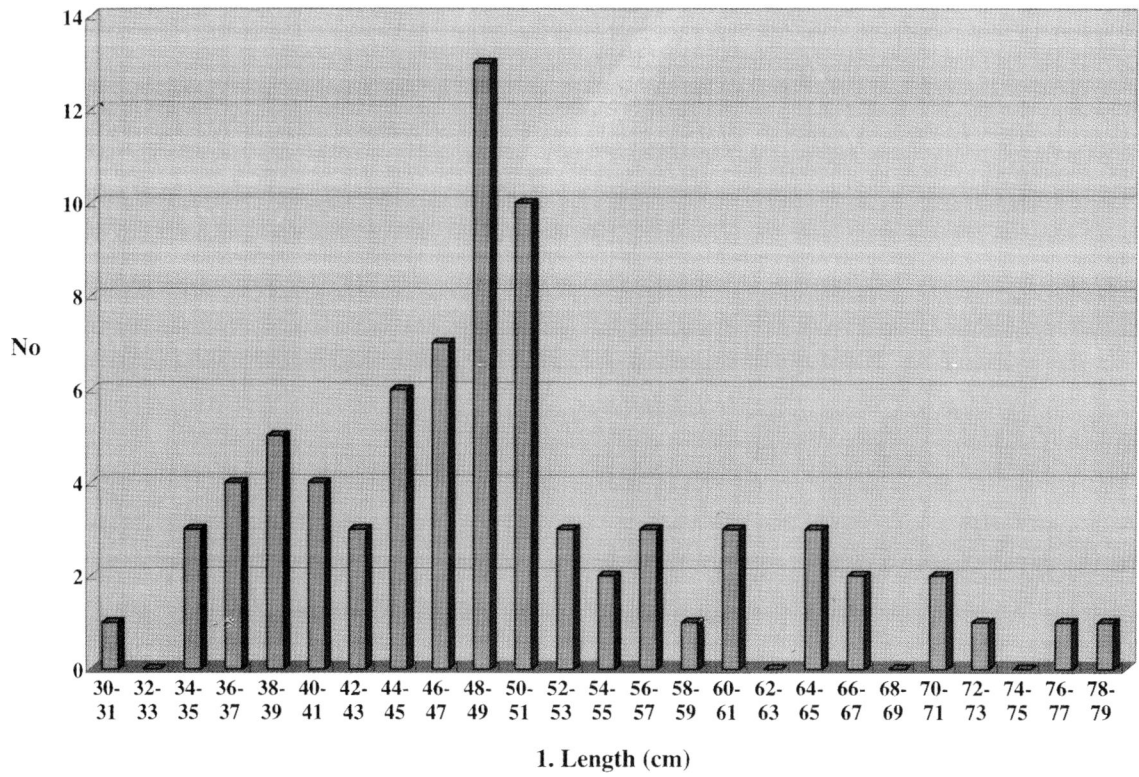

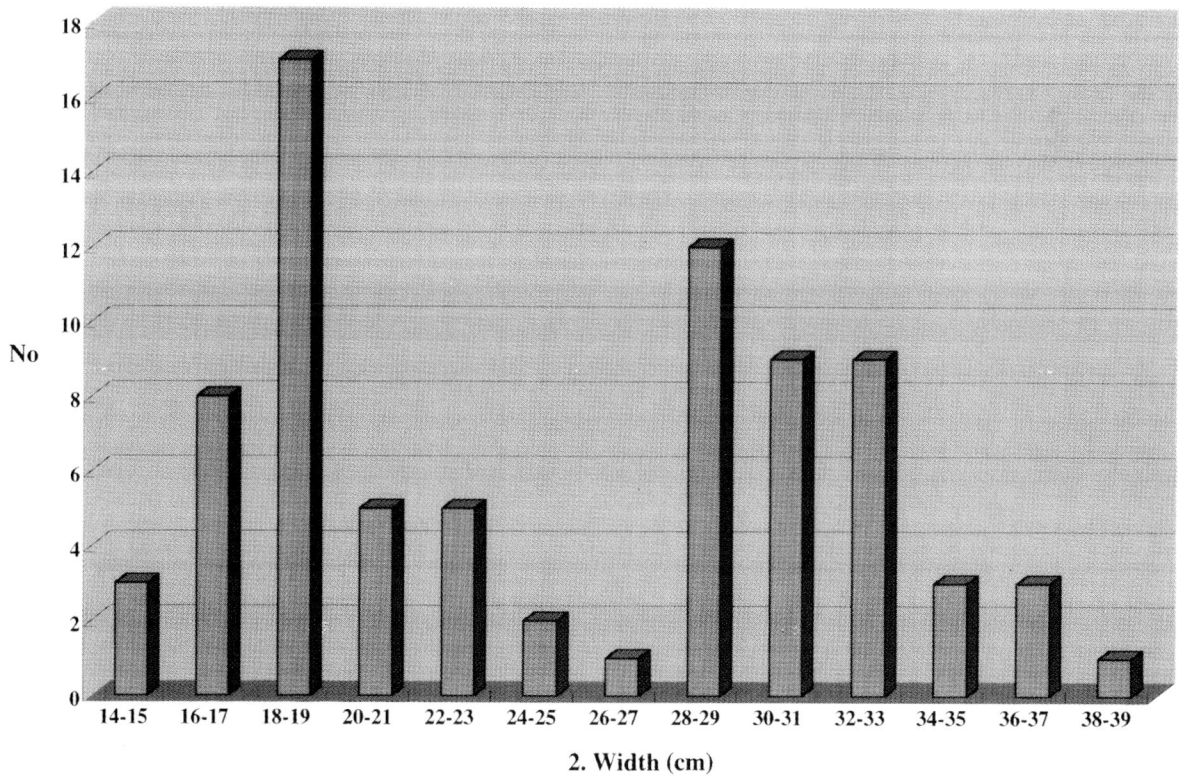

Fig. 3.35 Length and width of mudbricks used for the burnt building (Level 10A).
The sample size is 78.

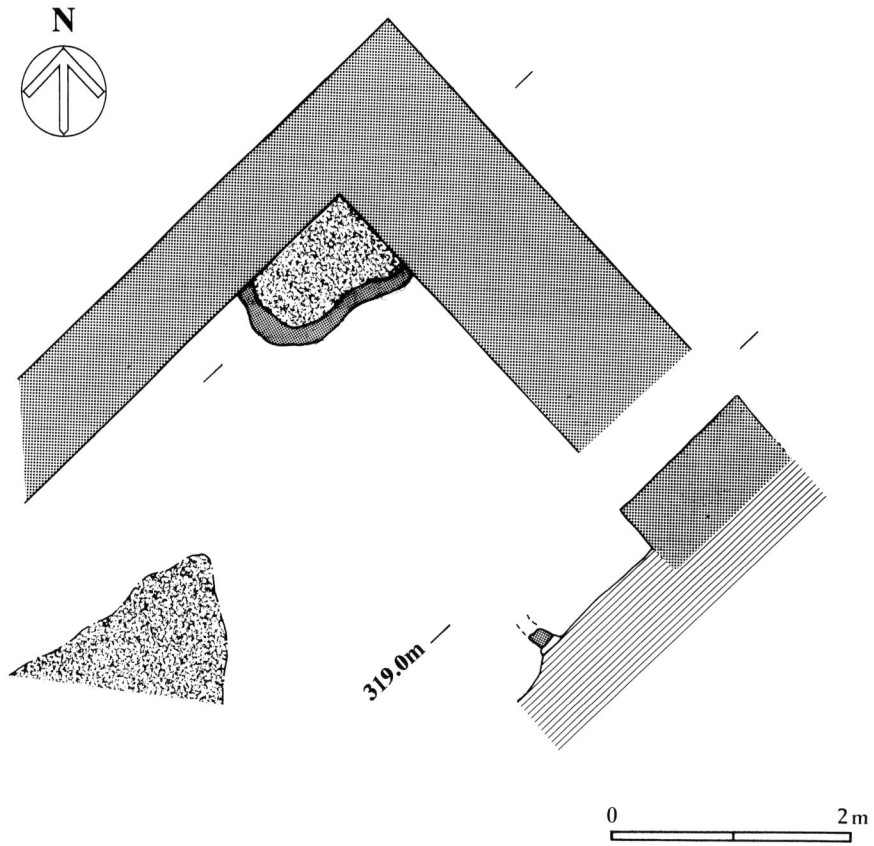

Fig. 3.36 Plan and section of Feature 10A13 (Level 10A).

0 2 m

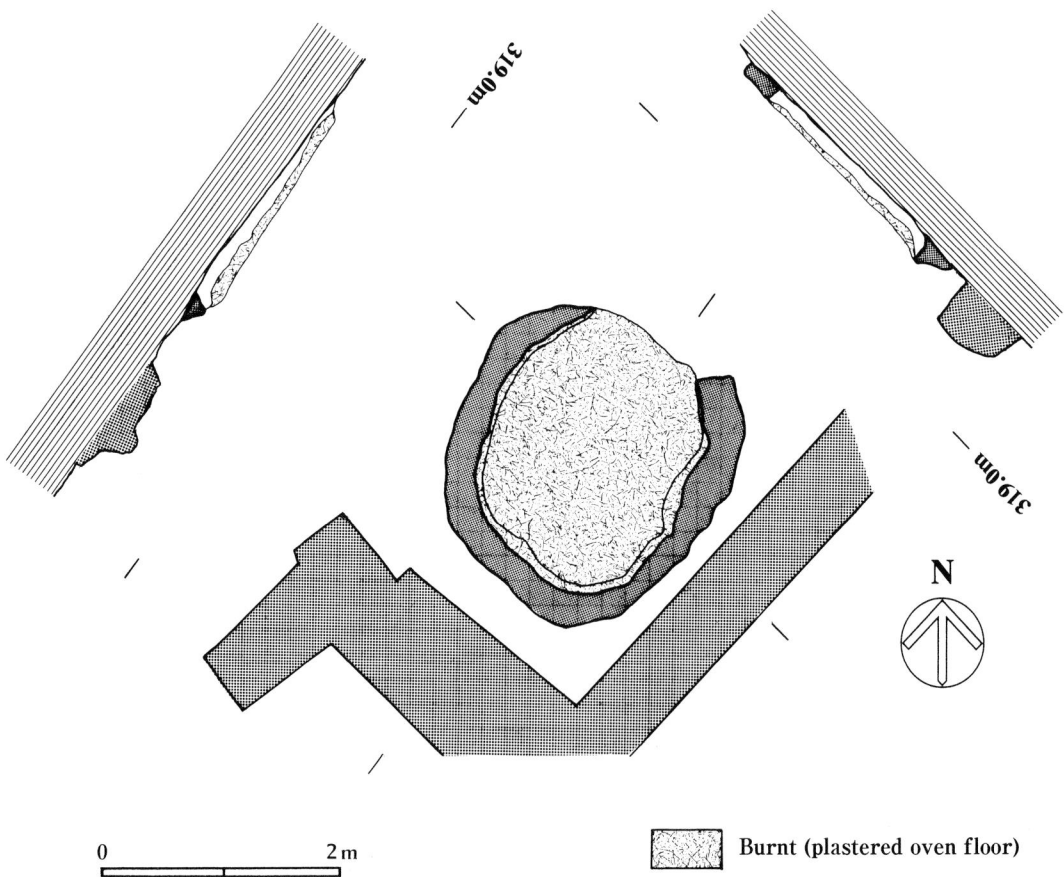

319.0m

319.0m

▨ Burnt (plastered oven floor)

0 2 m

Fig. 3.37 Plan and section of Kiln 10A17 (Level 10A).

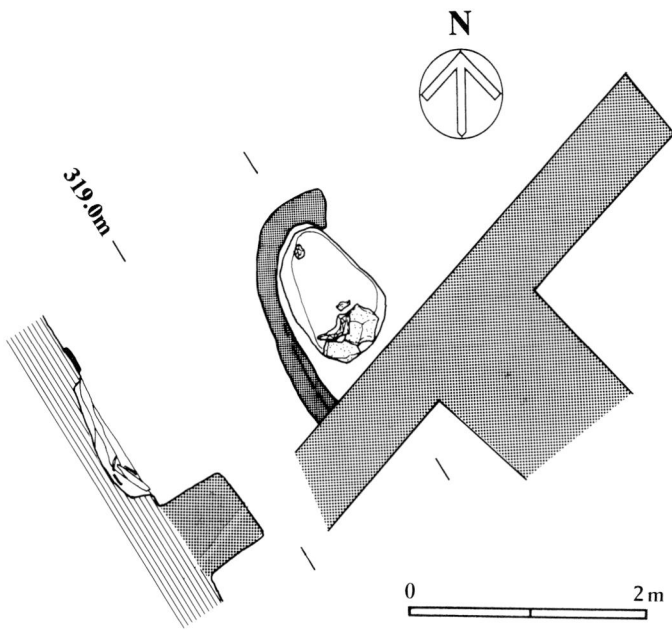

Fig. 3.38 Plan and section of Feature 10A29 (Level 10A).

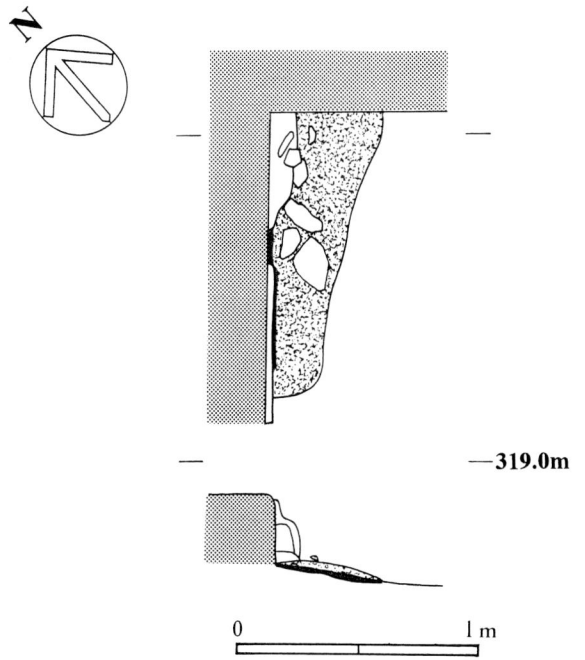

Fig. 3.39 Plan and section of Feature 10A27 (Level 10A).

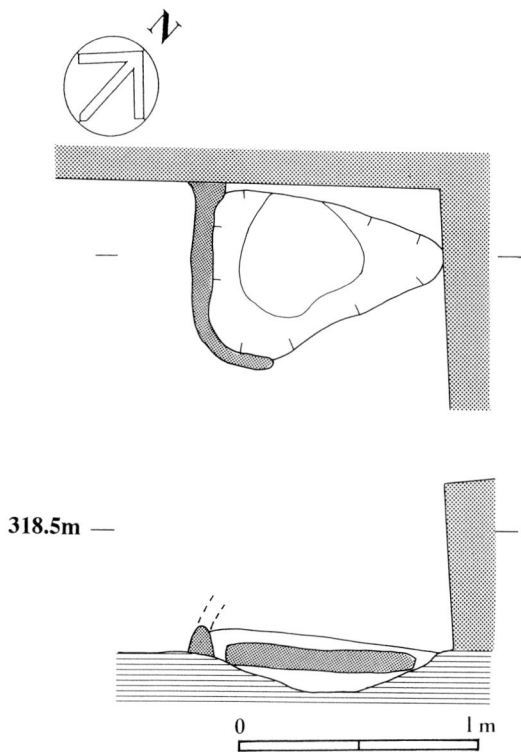

Fig. 3.40 Plan and section of Feature 10A26 (Level 10A).

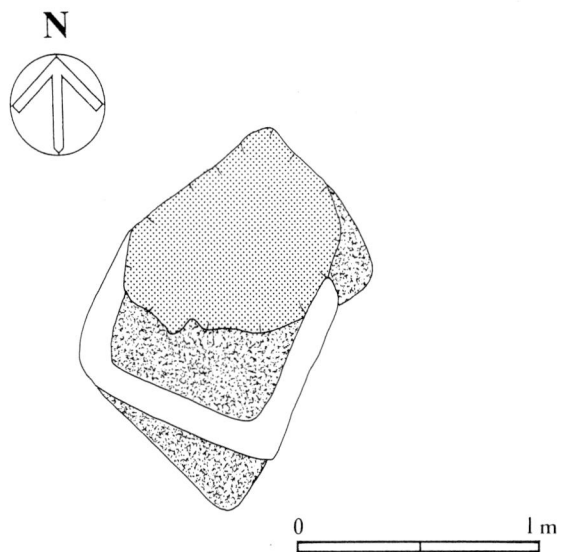

Fig. 3.41 Plan and section of Kiln 10A28 (Level 10A).

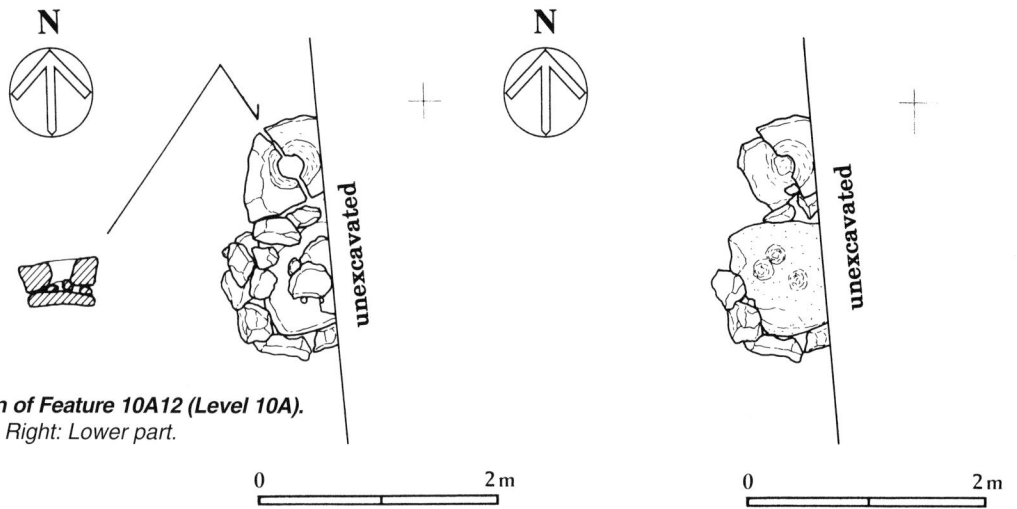

Fig. 3.42 Plan and section of Feature 10A12 (Level 10A).
Left: Upper part, Right: Lower part.

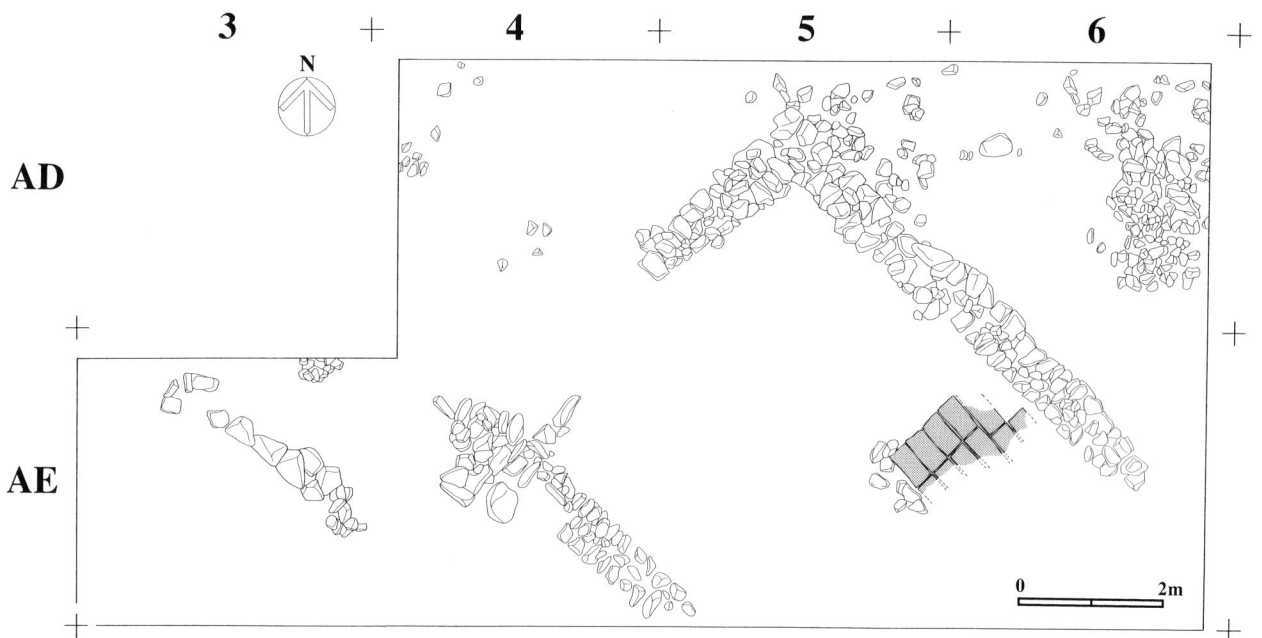

Fig. 3.43 Plan of Level 9 structures.

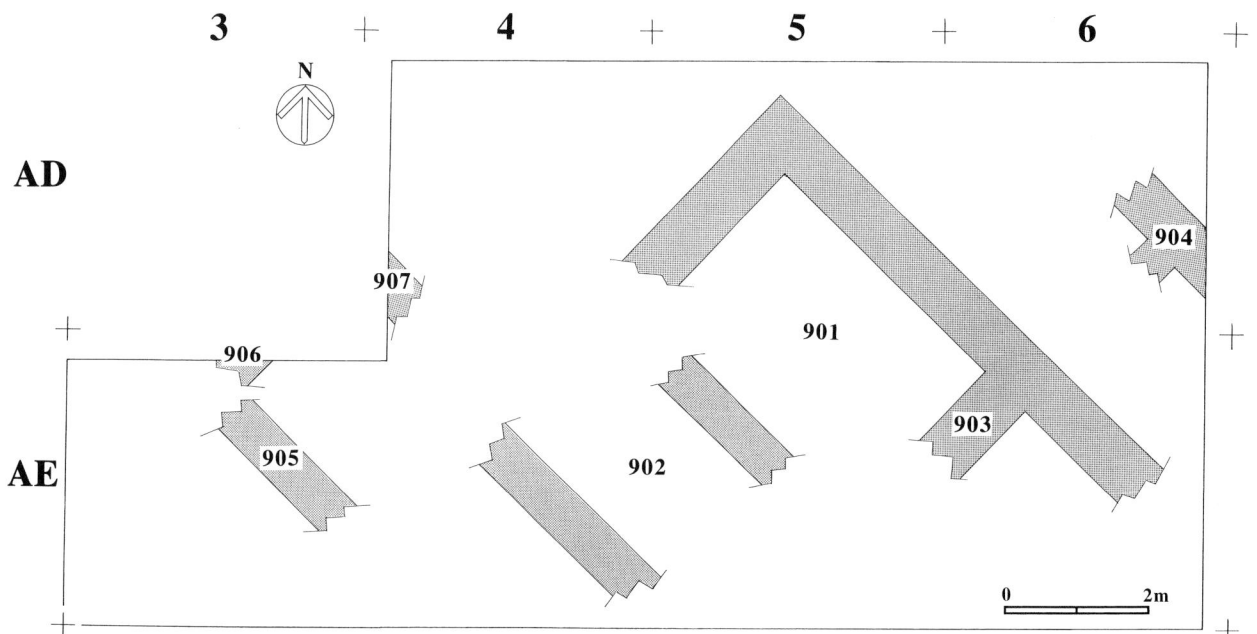

Fig. 3.44 Reconstruction of Level 9 structures.

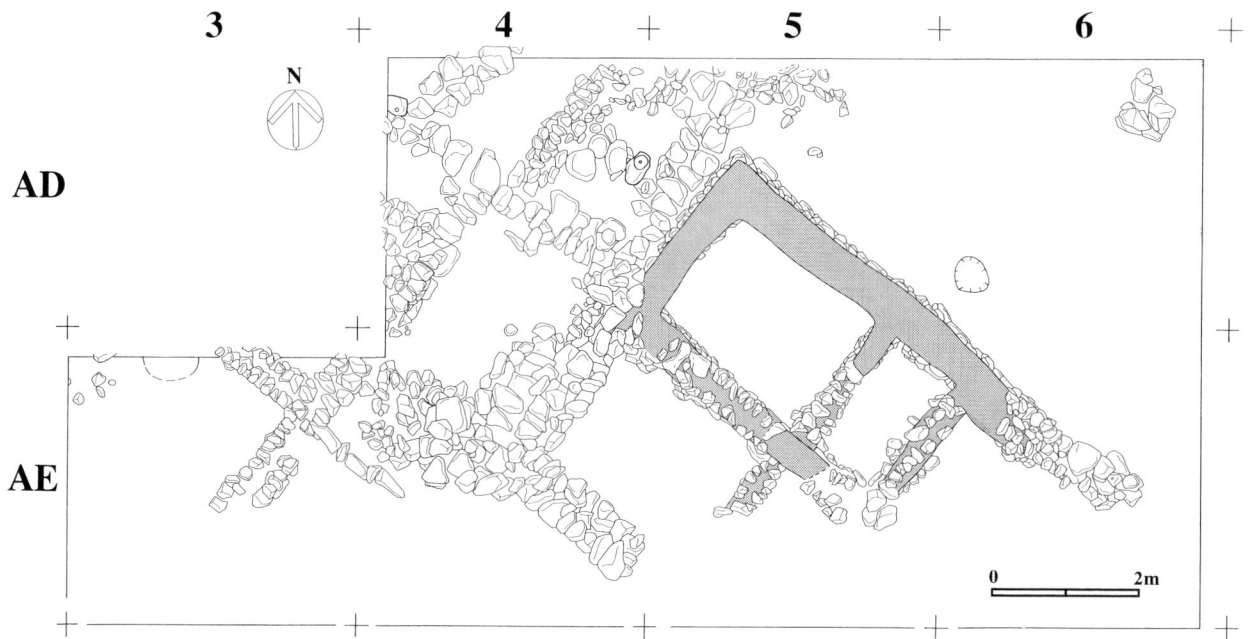

Fig. 3.45 Plan of Level 8 structures.

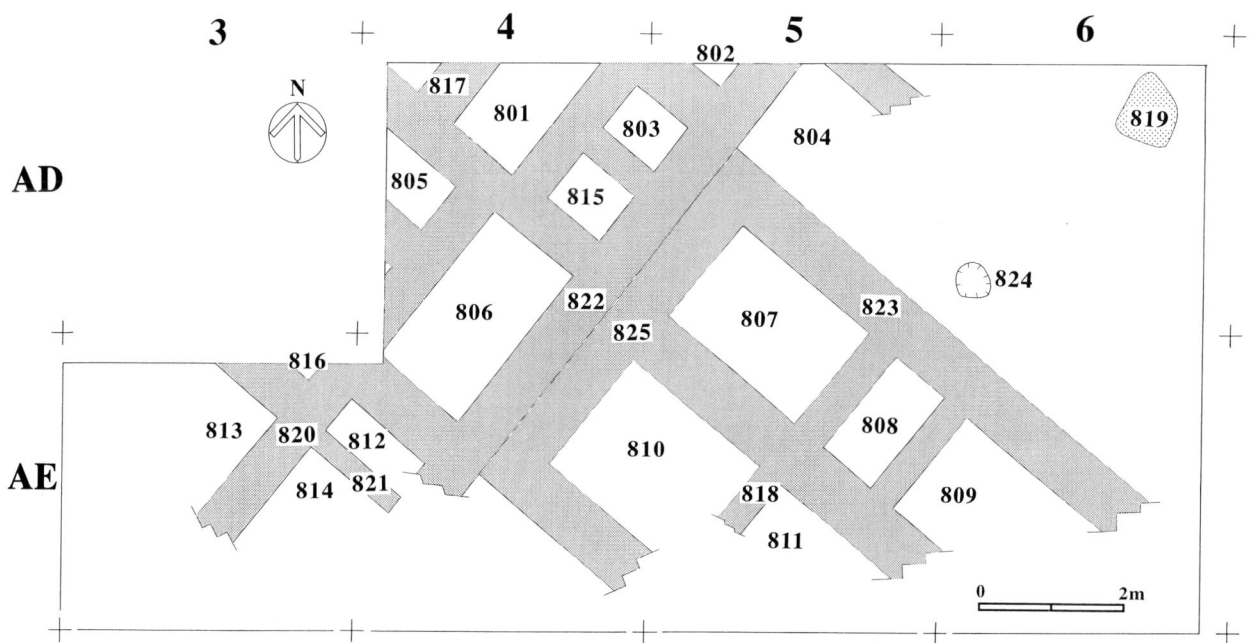

Fig. 3.46 Reconstruction of Level 8 structures.

3.3.11 Level 8 (Figs. 3.45-3.47; Pl. 3.13)

This level and the overlying two levels probably represent a short occupation period. All levels shared a well preserved rectangular building in the southeast, to which a group of small rooms of mudbrick walls on stone foundations was attached in the northwest. The longer axis of the whole building complex in the southeast was oriented NW-SE, as in the lower levels, and construction techniques were also the same (Figs. 3.45 and 3.46; Pl. 3.13: 1 and 2). Most parts of the main wall (823), standing 70cm high from the foundation level, overlapped that of Level 9. The earlier standing structures had clearly been reused by later inhabitants and showed uninterrupted occupation from lower levels.

The architectural complex, consisting of two separate buildings in the northwest and southeast, included over ten rectangular or square rooms. The southeast complex consisted of at least five small rooms (807-811), the smallest measuring about 0.8 x 1.2m (808), and the largest 1.2 x 2m (807). Room interiors were all quite tidy, almost without objects, in striking contrast to the rooms of Level 10 mentioned earlier. The same holds true for the rooms in the northwest. There were at least ten units, (801-803, 805, 806, and 812-816) each separated by short walls and all rarely containing objects *in situ*. The Level 8 building appeared to have been abandoned and refilled intentionally, an interpretation supported by the nature of the fill of Room 807. As shown in the stratigraphy of the northern wall of Squares AE4 and AE5 (Fig. 3.47), the fill contained blocks of mudbricks probably thrown in from the east over a short period of time. The top was then neatly leveled in order to construct the buildings of Level 7.

No definite trace of standing buildings was identified in the northeastern corner of the excavated area. However, some buildings are likely to have been present in this area as well, as suggested by a concentration of limestone cobbles (819) probably representing part of a collapsed building, and an infant burial (824) discovered close to Wall 823.

3.3.12 Level 7 (Figs. 3.48-3.50; Pl. 3.14: 1 & 2)

The building in the southeast of this level is part of that in Level 8. The building, consisting of five small rooms (706-710), had been rebuilt with mudbricks using the walls of Level 8 as its foundation (Figs. 3.48 and 3.49). Ubaidian artifacts were found *in situ* on the floor. Of particular interest was a potstand located in the center of room 706 (Fig. 3.50; Pl. 3.14: 1 and 2), which was a reused broken jar with a collared rim that had been placed upside down. A square limestone anvil (27x 27cm), around which sherds, flint cores, pounding / grinding stones and a gazelle horn were scattered, was next to the pot-stand. This combination of objects, most likely related to pottery production, is

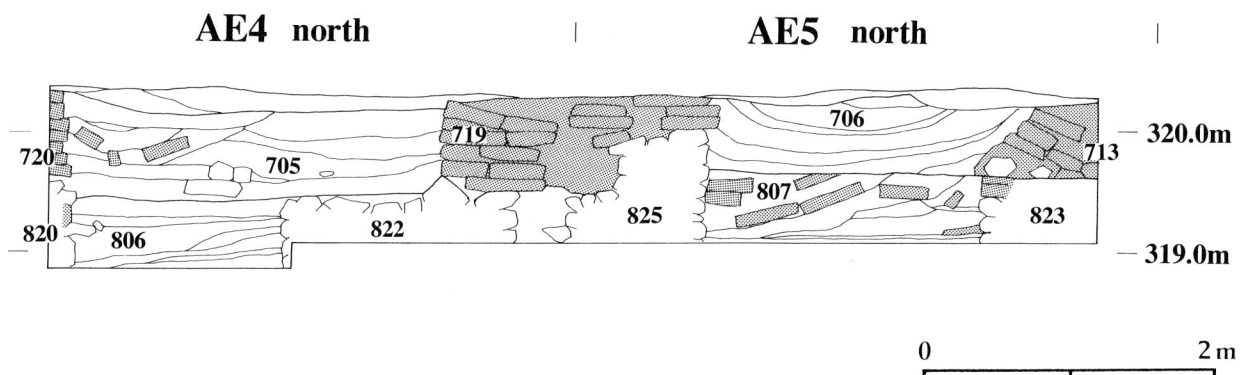

Fig. 3.47 North section of Squares AE4 and AE5 (Levels 7 and 8).

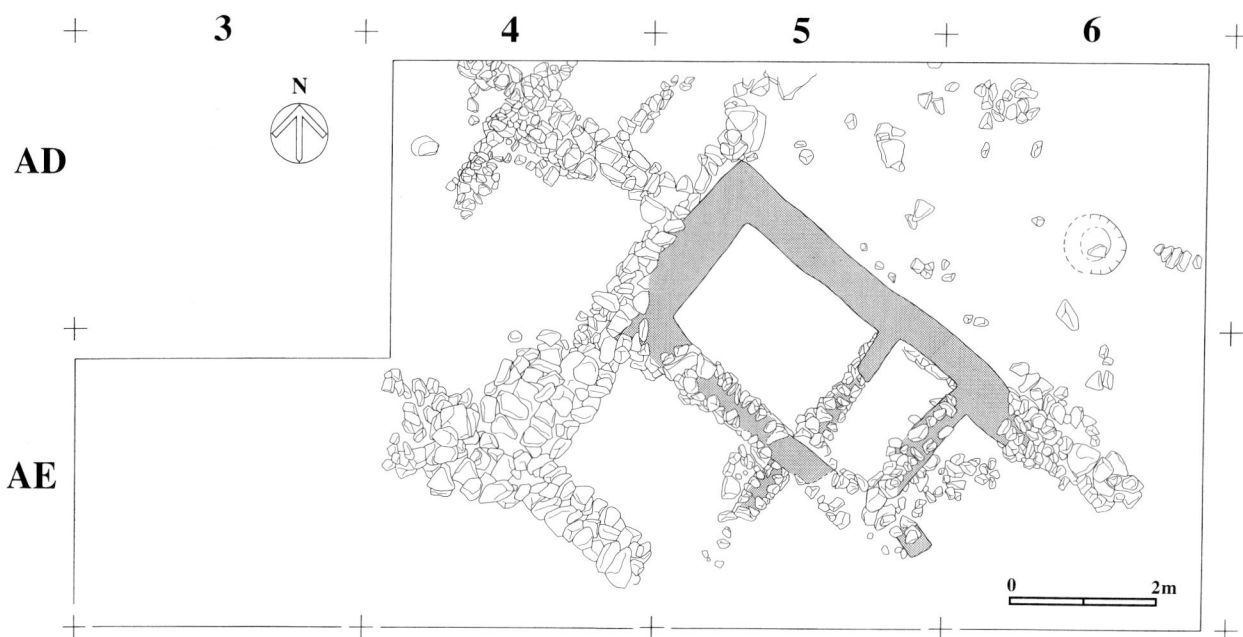

Fig. 3.48 Plan of Level 7 structures.

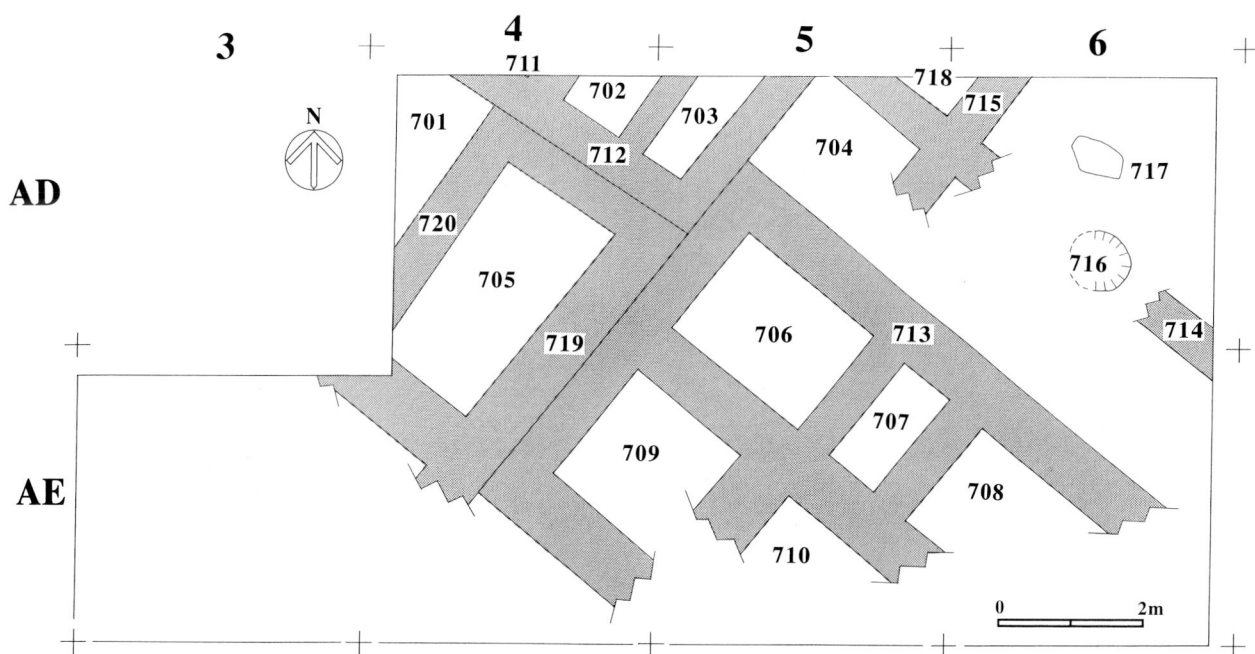

Fig. 3.49 Reconstruction of Level 7 structures.

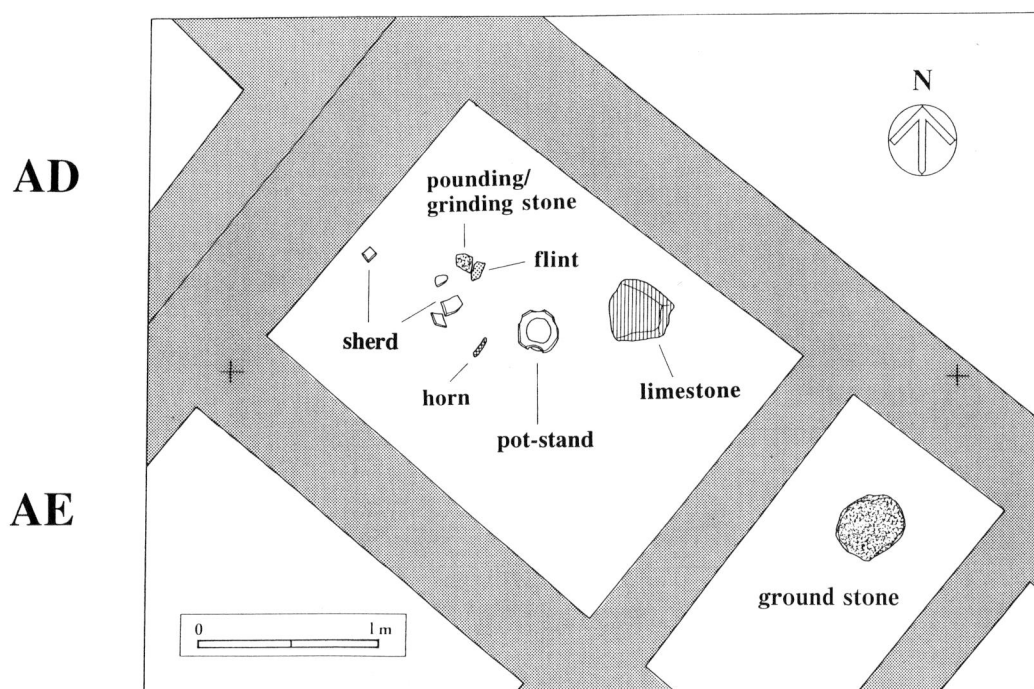

Fig. 3.50 The floor remains of Rooms 706 and 707 (Level 7).

remarkably similar to that from the upper levels (see below). A basalt ground stone (30 x 22cm) was found in Room 707 (Fig. 3.50). A group of almost 40 small river pebbles, was found near Wall 719 of Room 705. All similar in size, averaging about 5cm in length, these river pebbles showed little sign of use, and may have been stored for future use. There was no evidence to indicate that the fill in these rooms had resulted from intentional action, as seen in the section drawing (Fig. 3.47) that indicates a gradual accumulation of fill.

Several walls of at least 5 rooms, were annexed to this building in the northwest (701-703, 705 and 711). Another group of rooms was situated in the northeast (704 and 718). A block of fine whitish gray clay (80 x 75 x 12cm thick) was found in Square AD6 (717) where it had been probably stored for future use.

3.3.13 Level 6 (Figs. 3.51 & 3.52)

From this level upwards the deposits were excavated only in the northern part of the excavation area because of the steep slope of the mound. The building recorded in Levels 8 and 7 in the southeastern area was still standing, but the southern part had

been completely eroded (Figs. 3.51 and 3.52). To the north some stone foundations, constituting several rooms (601, 602, 604 and 605), were revealed. Rooms 601 and 605 were connected by a 40cm-wide passage. Mudbrick walls which had been laid directly on the ground created two more rooms (603 and 604) in Squares AD5 to AD6.

3.3.14 Level 5 (Figs. 3.53-3.55; Pl. 3.14: 3)

Level 5, poorly preserved, produced fragments of stone foundation and mudbrick walls (Figs. 3.53 and 3.54). A limestone cobble and *tauf* wall about 70cm wide, extended in a NW-SE direction (503), and annexed to it in the north and the west were mudbricks walls, built directly on the ground (502 and 504). A further remnant of mudbrick wall (506) running in the same direction as the other walls, was located in the east, in Square AD6.

An infant burial (505) was revealed to the south of these wall remnants (Fig. 3.55; Pl. 3.14: 3). It was a rather well-made feature, consisting of an oval pit (60 cm in diameter and about 30cm in depth), enclosed by small limestone cobbles. The inner surface of the stone enclosure was plastered with 2 to 2.5cm thick mud.

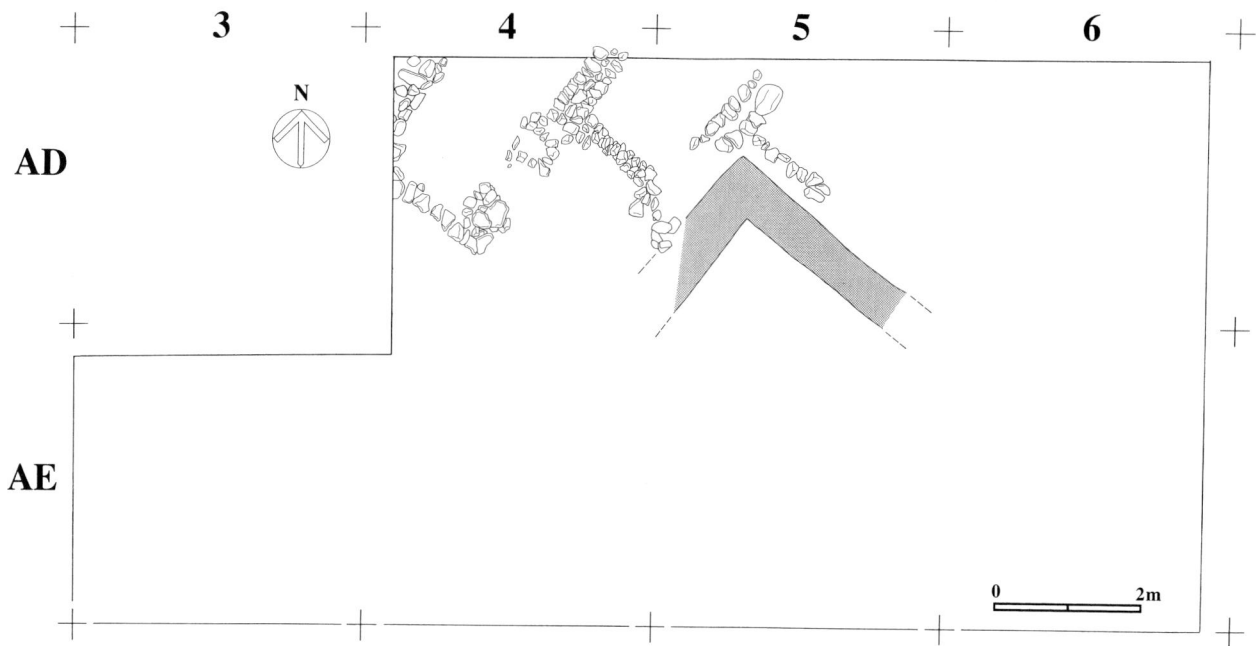

Fig. 3.51 Plan of Level 6 structures.

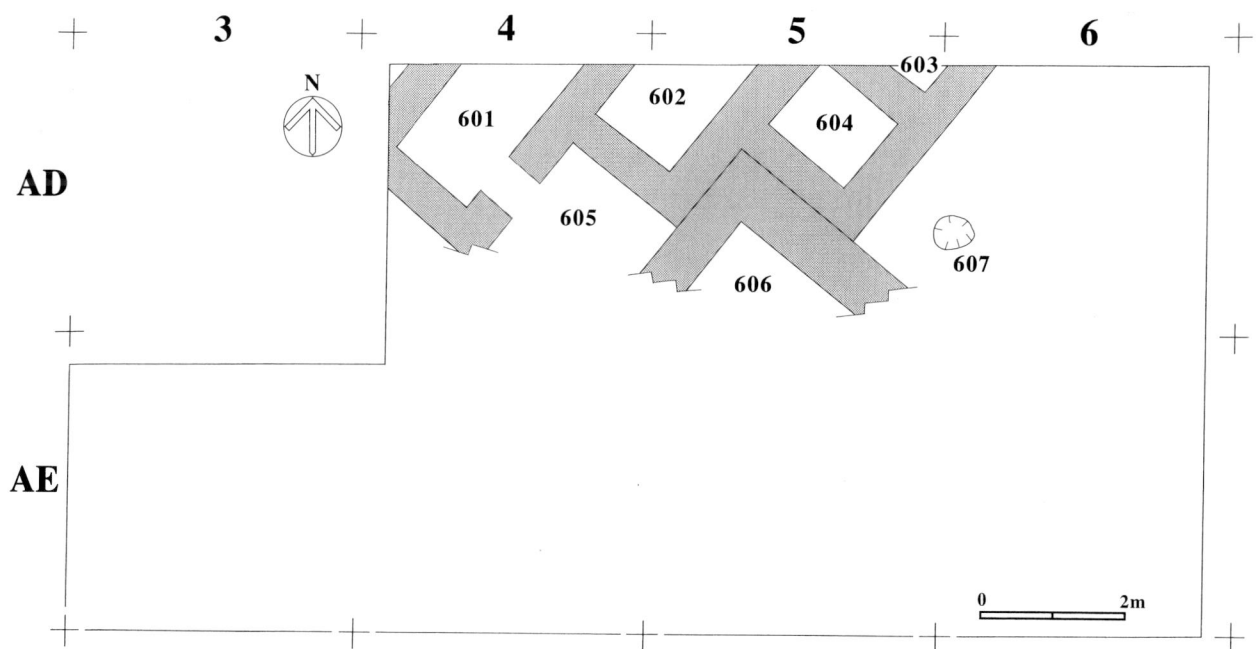

Fig. 3.52 Reconstruction of Level 6 structures.

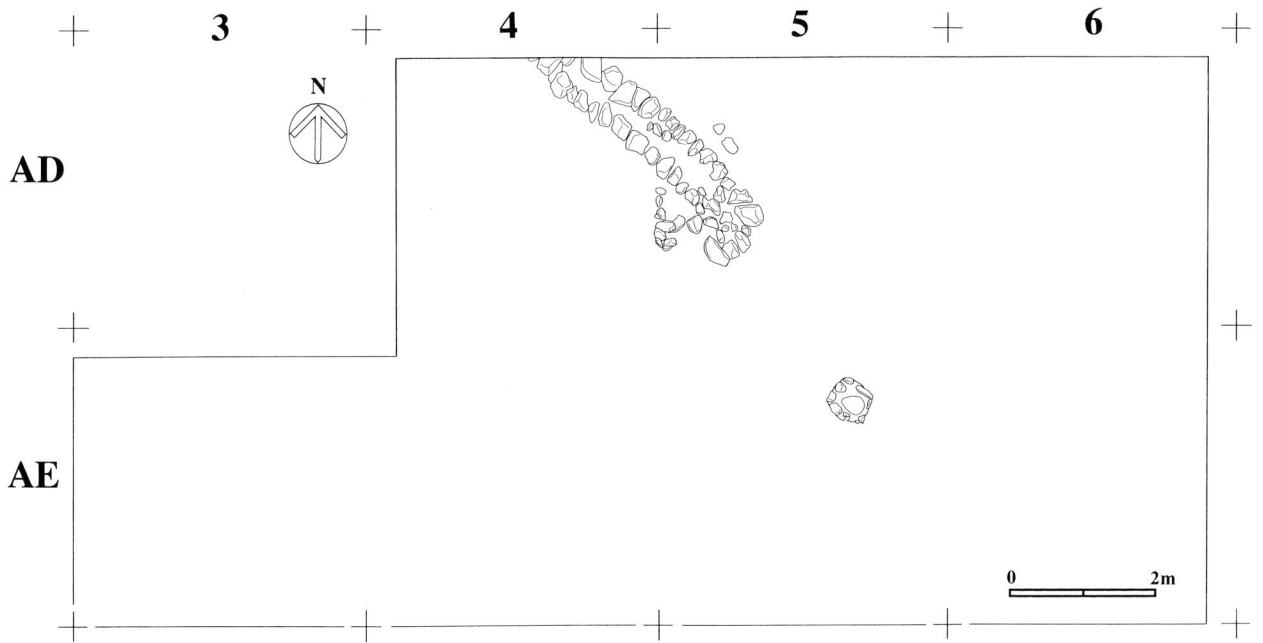

Fig. 3.53 Plan of Level 5 structures.

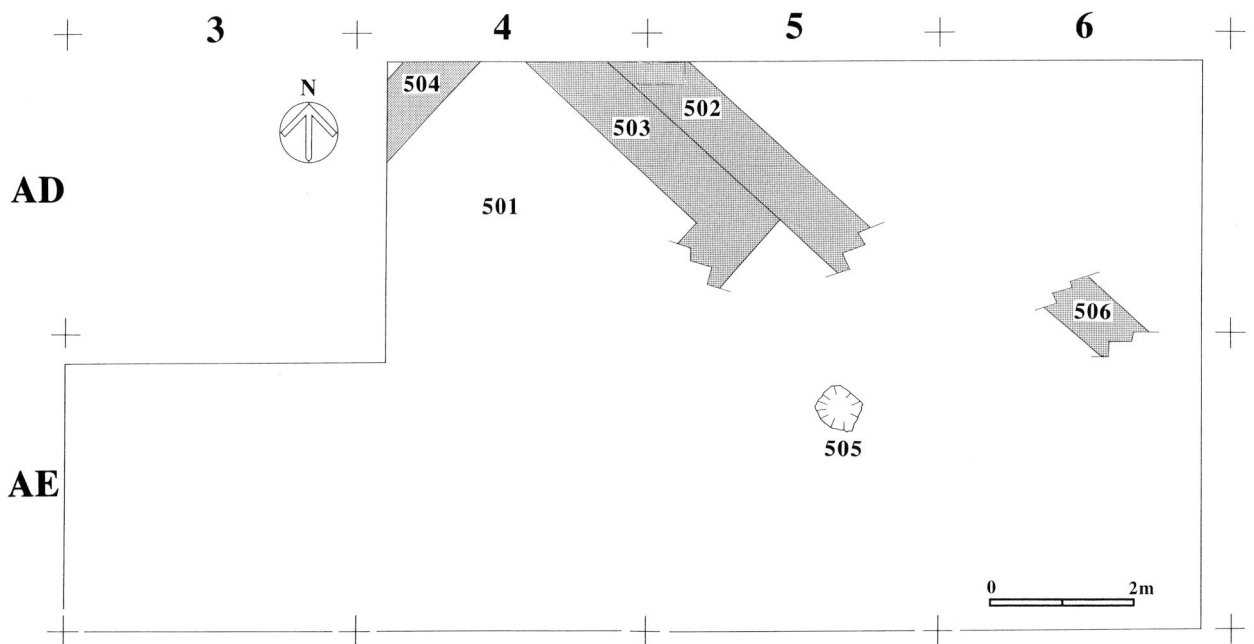

Fig. 3.54 Reconstruction of Level 5 structures.

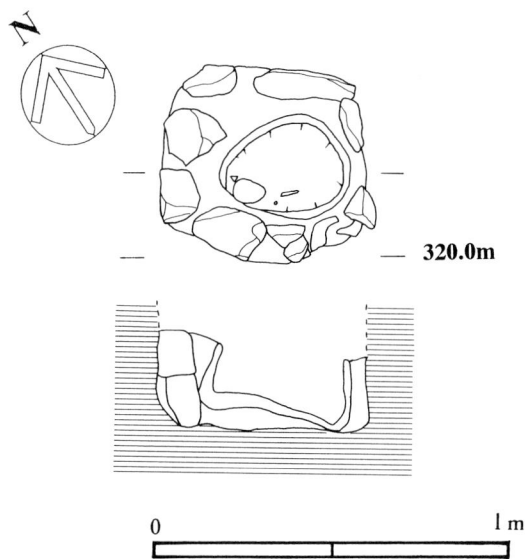

320.0m

0   1 m

Fig. 3.55 Plan and section of Burial 505 (Level 5).

3.3.15 Level 4 (Figs. 3.56-3.59; Pls. 3.15 & 3.16: 1 & 2)

Part of a rectangular building consisting of at least seven small rooms (401-404, and 409-411) was excavated from this level (Figs. 3.56 and 3.57). The direction and the construction methods of the walls remained the same as in the previous levels. The rooms were all rectangular-shaped, each 1.3 x 1.4 m. Room 403 was paved with mudbricks each about 54 x 24 x 8 cm. The wall between 403 and 404 had a limestone door socket.

The building had been re-floored at least three times and many artifacts were excavated *in situ* on each floor. Room 402 had the best preserved floors. Fig. 3.58:1 shows the earliest floor plan on which a scattering of pounding/grinding stones, sherds, and a few flat limestone cobbles lay (Pl. 3.15: 1). The second floor, illustrated in Fig. 3.58: 2, also produced a similar set of objects: sherds, flint cores, pounding / grinding stones, a stone palette, and a horn-shaped limestone object (Pl. 3.15: 2). These objects were scattered around two rather flat limestone cobbles (48 x 42 cm and 25 x 21 cm respectively). The latest floor (Fig.

3.58:3; Pl. 3.16: 1) again had the same combination of *in situ* objects which included a scattering of pounding / grinding stones, flint cores, sherds, and two gazelle horns. At the center was a round limestone cobble (around 50 x 42cm) with several small hollows on the surface. The cobble appears to have been used as an anvil for craft activities. This repeated pattern of finds suggests that the function of the room, probably related to pottery production, remained unchanged throughout years of occupation.

An infant burial (412) was discovered in Wall 407 (Fig. 3.59; Pl. 3.16: 2). The body was in a jar (diameter of 25cm), which had been buried in a pit of 40 by 35 cm. The pit had been dug through part of a Level 4 wall, but was covered by another wall of the same level. This interesting pattern indicates that the burial had been dug from the first or second floor mentioned above and was completely covered when the last floor was in use.

3.3.16 Level 3 (Figs. 3.60 & 3.61; Pl. 3.16: 3)

Architectural remains from Level 3 and upwards were distributed mainly in the eastern part of the excavated area (Figs. 3.60 and 3.61). Apparently the settlement began to move to the east, as shown in the section drawing (Fig. 3.5). This trend continued afterwards, with the result that the Post-Ubaid structures are in the southeastern part of the mound (Sector B; Chapter 4).

Structures of Level 3 were revealed in a small area only, along the northern edges of Squares AD5 to AD6. A corner of a room (301), made with mudbrick walls on stone foundations, was detected in Square AD6 (Pl. 3.16: 3). The axis and the construction methods were the same as in lower levels.

3.3.17 Level 2 (Figs. 3.62 & 3.63)

This level also produced a very limited amount of information on structures (Figs. 3.62 and 3.63). A corner of a mudbrick-walled room (201) was found in Square AD6. It almost overlapped Room 301 of the previous level, but was situated slightly to the north. A small round pit (202) (40cm in diameter and 25cm in depth) was located to the east. Its fill contained loose brown soil with ash.

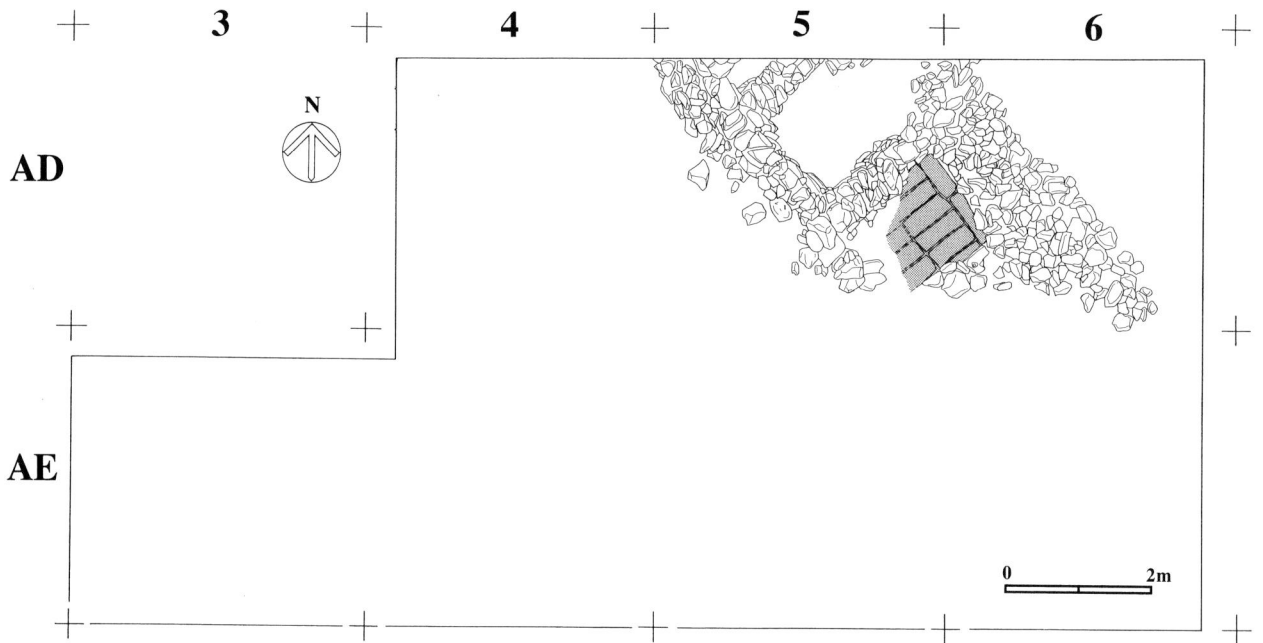

Fig. 3.56 Plan of Level 4 structures.

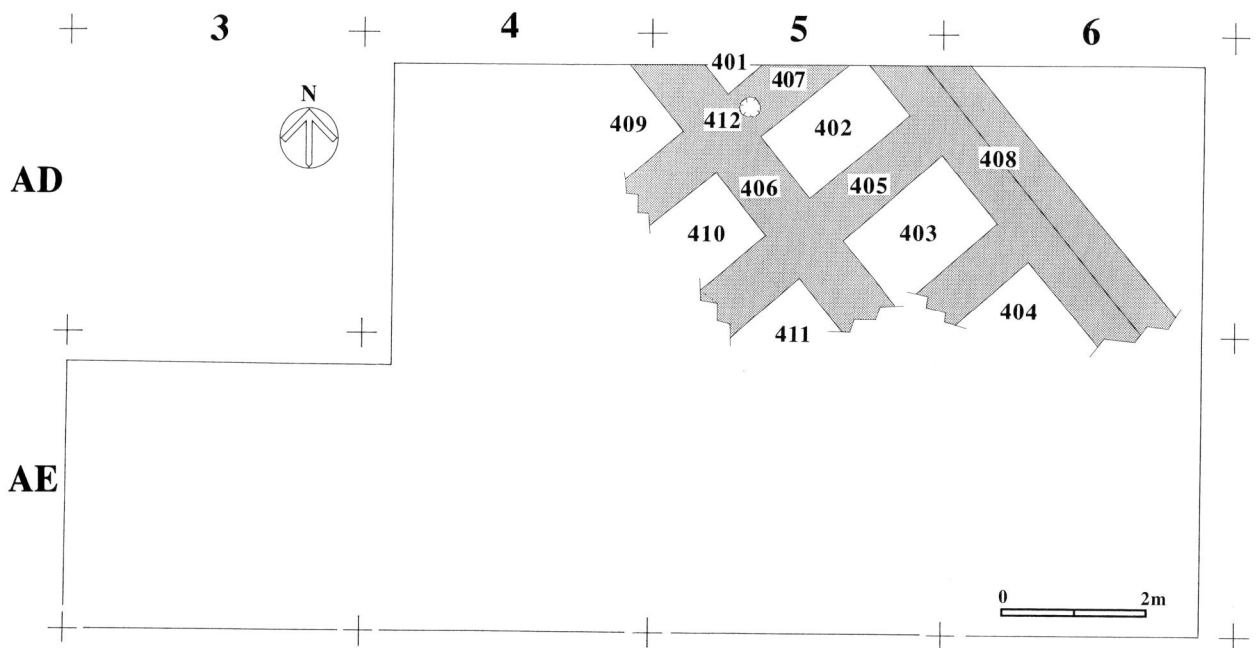

Fig. 3.57 Reconstruction of Level 4 structures.

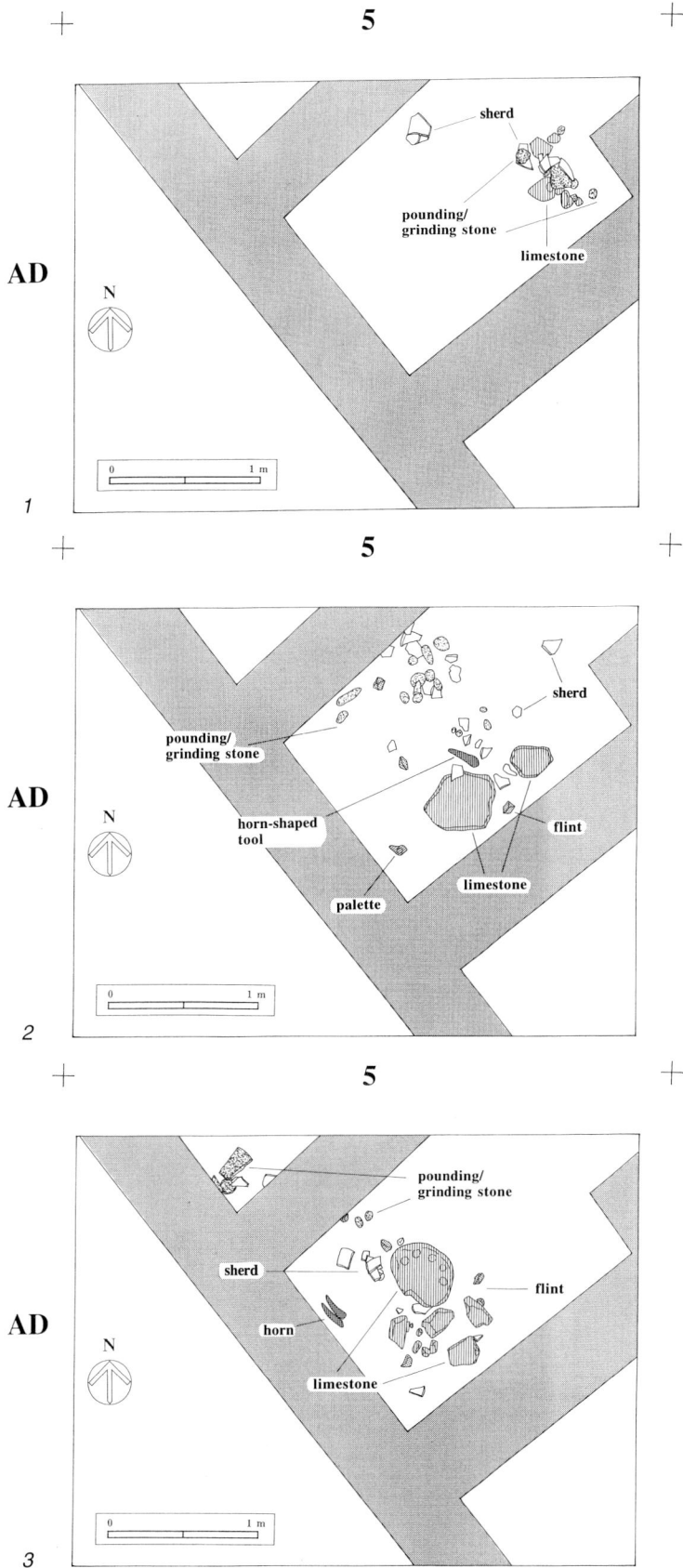

Fig. 3.58 The floor remains of Room 402 (Level 4).
1: The earliest floor, 2: The second floor, and 3: The latest floor.

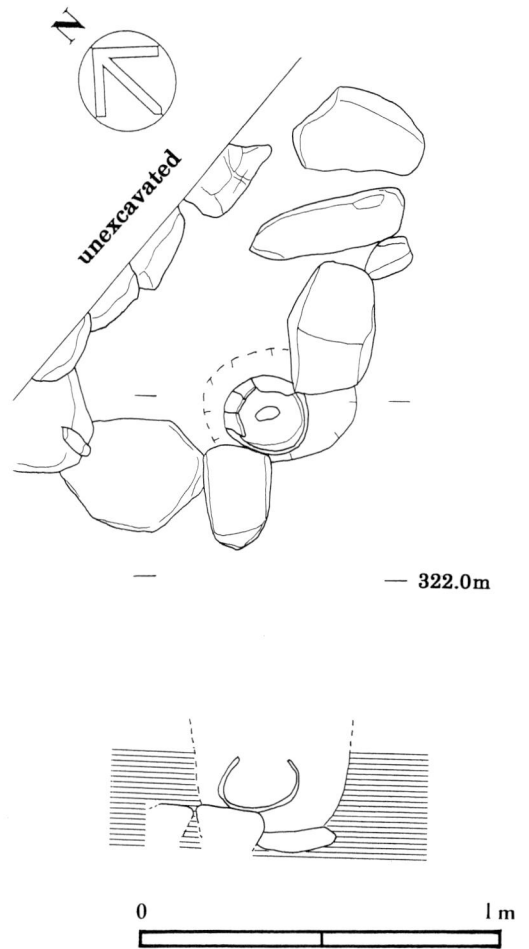

Fig. 3.59 Plan and section of Burial 412 (Level 4).

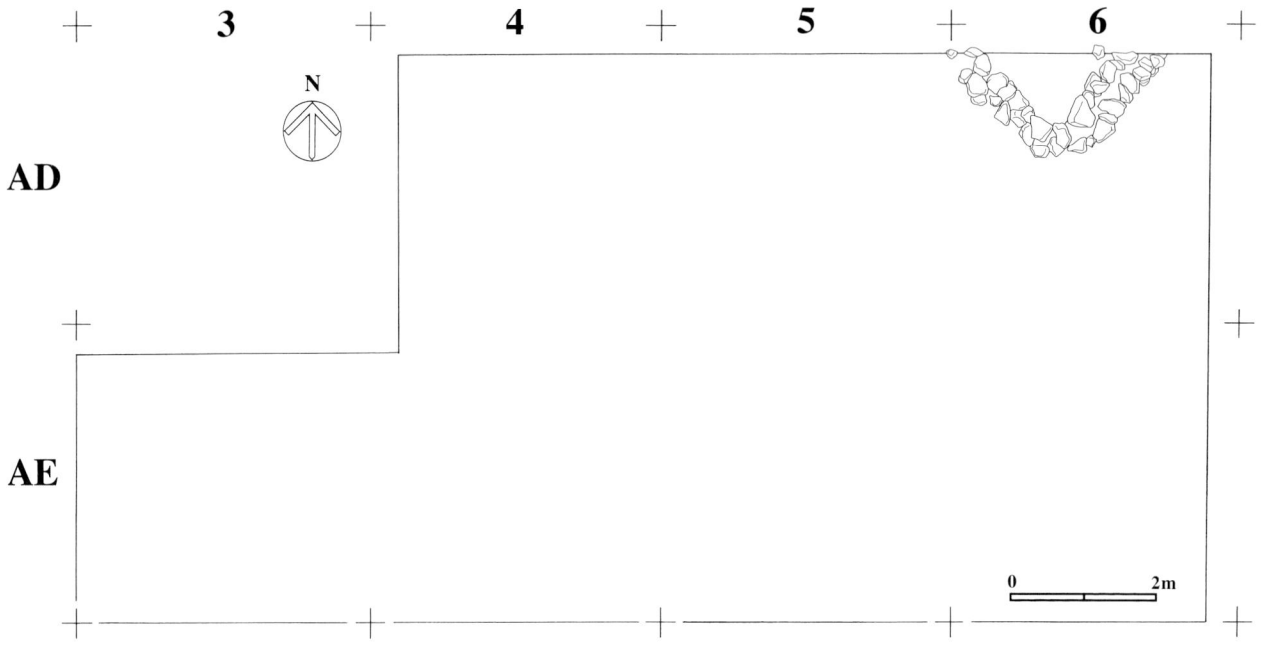

Fig. 3.60 Plan of Level 3 structures.

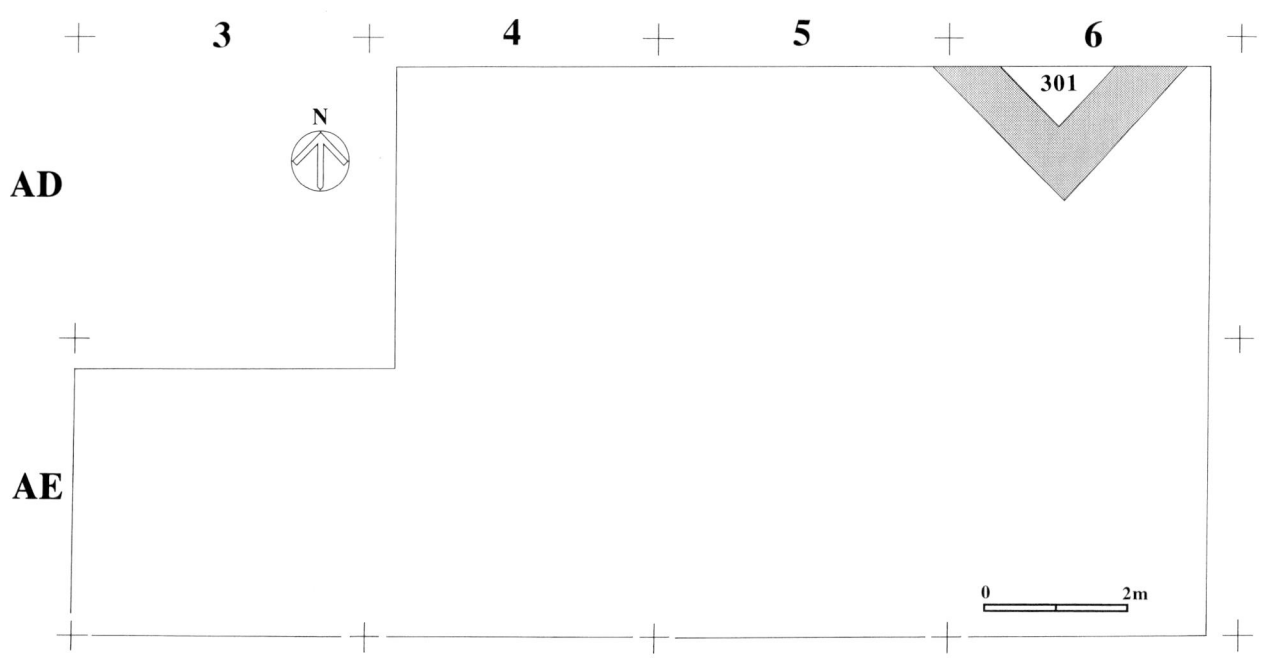

Fig. 3.61 Reconstruction of Level 3 structures.

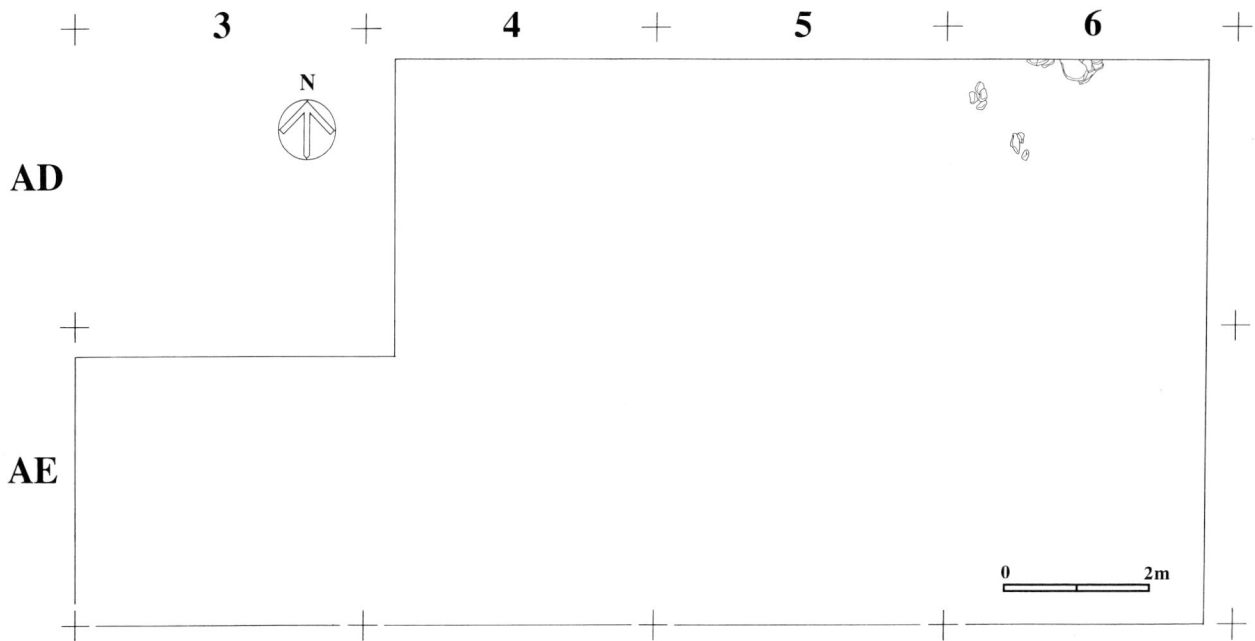

Fig. 3.62 Plan of Level 2 structures.

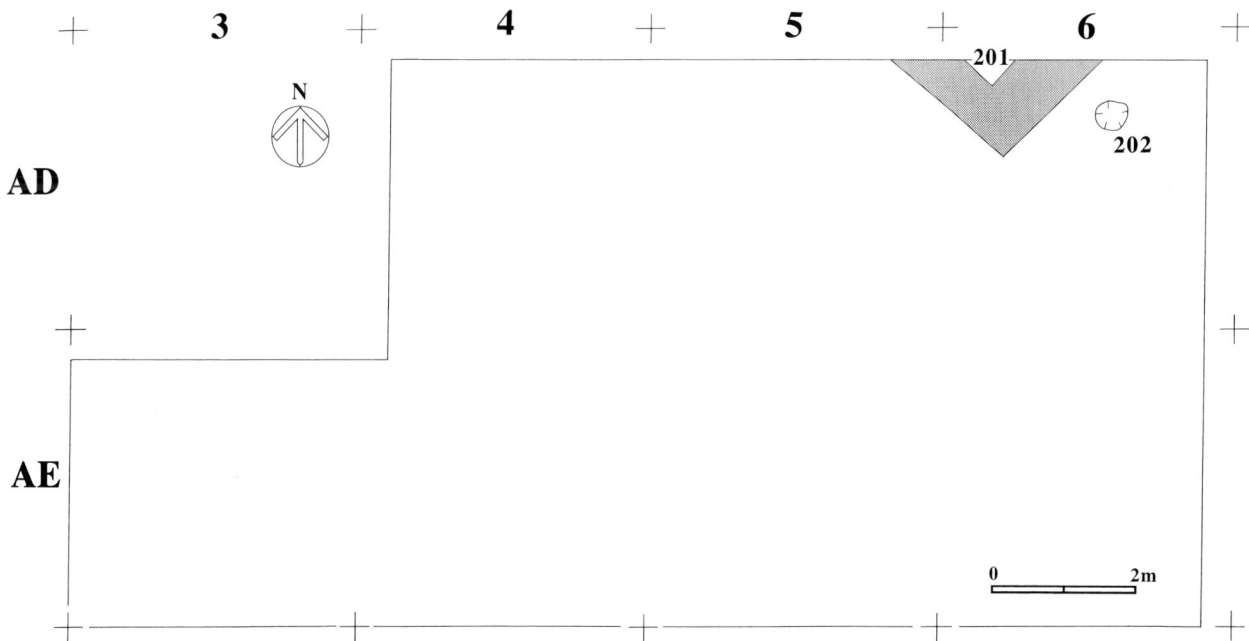

Fig. 3.63 Reconstruction of Level 2 structures.

3.3.18 Level 1 (Figs. 3.64 & 3.65)

As in Levels 2 and 3, only small parts of the buildings were uncovered (Figs. 3.64 and 3.65). They included two corners of mudbrick-walled rooms, one in Square AD4 (101) and the other in Square AD5 (102). The eastern corner of Room 101 had been partially destroyed by an Islamic tomb. A concentration of stone artifacts and ceramics were discovered in Room 102. Many relatively large flint cores and a possible hammer stone were on the floor at the eastern corner, probably representing a set of stone workers' tools.

3.4 Conclusions

Figs. 3.66-3.68 and Table 3.1 summarize by level a comparison of architectural and stratigraphic features in which building axis, stratigraphic relationship to earlier levels and other notable structures were examined. The results are shown with periodization based on ceramic typology. On the basis of this information the eighteen levels can be divided into several stratigraphic units. Level 18 contains only a few pits, and Level 17 represents erosional processes, yielding no identifiable building remains. Levels 16-14 can be grouped together in that the main building axis is aligned in the same direction. A break is indicated between Levels 14 and 13 by a change in the main axis of structures and a different soil composition. Level 13 is comparable to Level 12, in size as well as having their main walls aligned along the same directional axis. The buildings of Levels 11-9 had been clearly constructed following the same plan and technique. The structures of Level 8 had been built using the walls of the previous level, but were located slightly to the north. The basic architectural plan was maintained in Levels 7 and 6. Level 5 was insufficiently preserved to provide adequate data, but may have been similar in plan to Level 4. The deposits and buildings of Levels 3-1 had accumulated east of the previous levels.

The above summary emphasizes a continuity rather than interruption or break throughout the sequence. Exceptions are noted only in the lower levels. Level 18 produced only pits which had been scraped and covered with the secondary deposits of Level 17 after a gap of about a thousand years.

Another possible gap between Levels 14 and 13 requires a careful examination because it accompanies an evident change of the architectural tradition. Level 14 contained a curious structure with the curved wall (1409), a kind of architecture that never appeared again in upper levels. While buildings with curved walls are not uncommon at Ubaid settlements (e.g. Jasim 1985; Sono 1970), the wall in question seems somewhat different from the reported ones. It was a thick wall made with larger limestone cobbles packed tight with mud, and had a regular curvature that could have formed a round plan like a Halafian tholos. If indeed so, it would have originally been a circular structure with the inner diameter of about 3.7m. The size and the wall thickness (about 70cm), as well as the construction methods, are all within the range of Halafian examples documented at many sites in North Syria and Iraq (cf. Tsuneki 1998). The possible use of a tholos in the earliest stage of the Northern Ubaid, if confirmed, would encourage an intriguing discussion on the Halaf-Ubaid transition on the Upper Euphrates (Nishiaki *et al.* 1999: 31). However this interpretation faces a difficulty in stratigraphy. There was a ditch (1408) apparently too close to its southwest. Therefore the supposed "circular structure" would not have been in use when the ditch was made. Nevertheless the structure and the ditch belong to the same level, definitely earlier than Level 13, as evidenced by the stone pavement (1309) of Level 13 that covered them, and later than Level 15, as the ditch partly destroyed the Level 15 buildings. One possible explanation for this inconsistency would be that Level 14 in fact represents at least two occupational episodes, put into a single level by subsequent erosion.

This consideration will not make sense before the above interpretation of the structure 1409, badly damaged, gets demonstrated valid. In the meantime it is perhaps safer to emphasize the stratigraphic gap only. The gap is shown not only by the change of architecture but also by that of the sediments (see Section 3.3.6). The fact that the ditch of Level 14 (1408), about 1.2 m deep, was already full by the time the younger ditch (1310; Level 13) was dug may also be added to the list of supporting evidence.

The overlying thirteen levels are all dense accumulations with no sterile deposits or notable geological

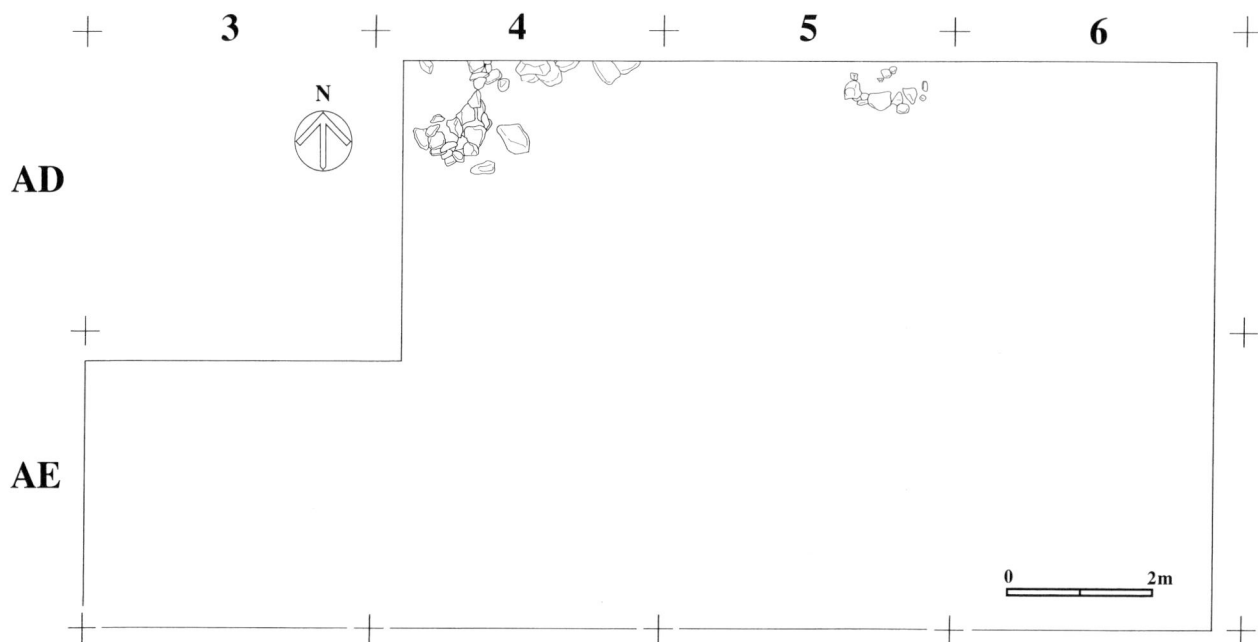

Fig. 3.64 Plan of Level 1 structures.

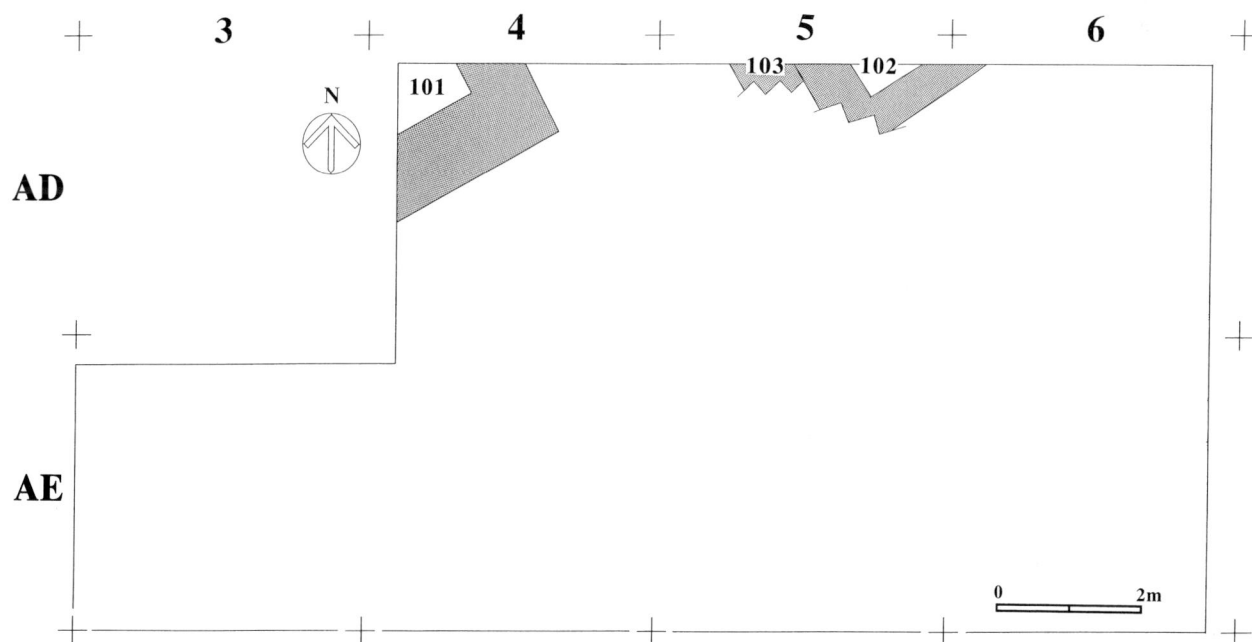

Fig. 3.65 Reconstruction of Level 1 structures.

events separating them. In fact, the basic architectural techniques remained much the same throughout these levels. The buildings had been constructed using a combination of mudbrick wall on stone foundations and *tauf* wall, often with a stone core. The stratigraphic division does not always correspond to the periodization indicated by ceramic typology although at times it is somewhat valid. This discrepancy is also considered a reflection of the strong continuity in occupation.

Attempts to interpret the structure of the Ubaidian settlement at Tell Kosak Shamali are limited by the small excavated area. However, some informative evidence exists for the earlier sequence. The structures from Levels 13 and 14, exposed over a relatively large area, suggest the southwestern area be at the edge of the settlement and bordered by ditches. In both levels, ditches of a similar size extending to the southeast were discovered. They are perhaps related to water drainage, as proposed for comparable ditches from Level XIV of Telul eth-Thalathat (Sono 1970) and Level I of Tell Songor B (Matsumoto and Yokoyama 1995). At Kosak Shamali, deposits within the ditches were overwhelmingly composed of layers of mud with gray sands and charcoal, reminiscent of flooding sediments (Matsutani and Nishiaki 1995). Water appeared to be a particular concern in this part of the settlement. The stone pavement (1309) constructed between the ditch and buildings in Level 13 further supports this inference.

The best evidence of the plan and technique of Ubaid architecture at Tell Kosak Shamali, comes from the burnt building of Level 10 (Figs. 3.27 and 3.31). The structure consists of a rectangular room (10A01), a series of small square rooms at an angle to it (10A02-10A07), some pottery kilns and other smaller structures. Similar structures are known from Level 6 of Tell al-'Abr (Fig. 11 in Hammade and Koike 1992), a site comparable to Tell Kosak Shamali in a number of ways. The architecture of Tell al-'Abr, considered to be a pottery workshop by the excavators, includes a rectangular room on the west and a few smaller square rooms on the east. Two kilns, with diameters of 80 -100 cm, were discovered along the northern wall of the rectangular room. Unlike Tell Kosak Shamali, the rectangular room is set lengthwise to the square rooms, and it contains a small square room at the northeastern corner. However, the architectural

pattern, the presence of nearly identical pottery kilns inside, and the location of the doorway to the rectangular room, closely resemble those of Level 10 of Tell Kosak Shamali. Furthermore, our Room 10A02 is comparable to the small room at the northeastern corner of Level 6 of Tell al-'Abr that has an opening to the west. Similarities exist in architectural techniques too: the load-bearing walls were built with a combination of two types of mudbricks of the same size as used at Tell Kosak Shamali (see Section 3.3.9), and the square rooms were also similar in size, about 1.8 m each side.

An isolated square room (10A11) and a kiln (10A10) were located in the southwest of the Level 10 building complex. Similar structures have been reported from a workshop in Level 4 at Tell al-'Abr (Hammade and Koike 1992). Although our kiln was not fully excavated as it was too close to the excavation limits, it also seems to be more or less octagonal in shape as at Tell al-'Abr. It is evident, then, that the inhabitants at these two settlements shared the same architectural tradition, which probably typifies Ubaidian pottery workshop structures on the Upper Euphrates. Tell al-'Abr is the only site at present which has produced sufficient data on Ubaidian architecture in North Syria. Although the sequence at Tell Hammam et-Turkman in the Balikh valley is good, the sounding trenches are not very informative in terms of architectural evidence (Meijer 1988). Detailed accounts of the more extensive excavations at Tell Ziyadah (Hole 1999) and Tell Mashnaqa (Thuesen 2000) must be published before we can place the Level 10 building of Tell Kosak Shamali in the regional context.

When viewed in the broader framework, the combination of a rectangular room and a series of small square rooms standing at an angle to it, is reminiscent of a wing of the "tripartite plan" buildings common in the Ubaid of North Mesopotamia. One finds similar complexes notably at Tepe Gawra (Tobler 1950) and Tell Abada (Jasim 1985). If this is so, a central hall should be located at either the northern or southern side of the Level 10 building. However, it is unlikely to be the area in the north for a number of reasons. Firstly, it extends over 4 m to the north without reaching the other wing. Central halls of fully excavated buildings from Tell Abada and Tepe Gawra, which are similar in length (ca. 7 to 11 m), are all narrower than 4 m (Kubba 1998: 86).

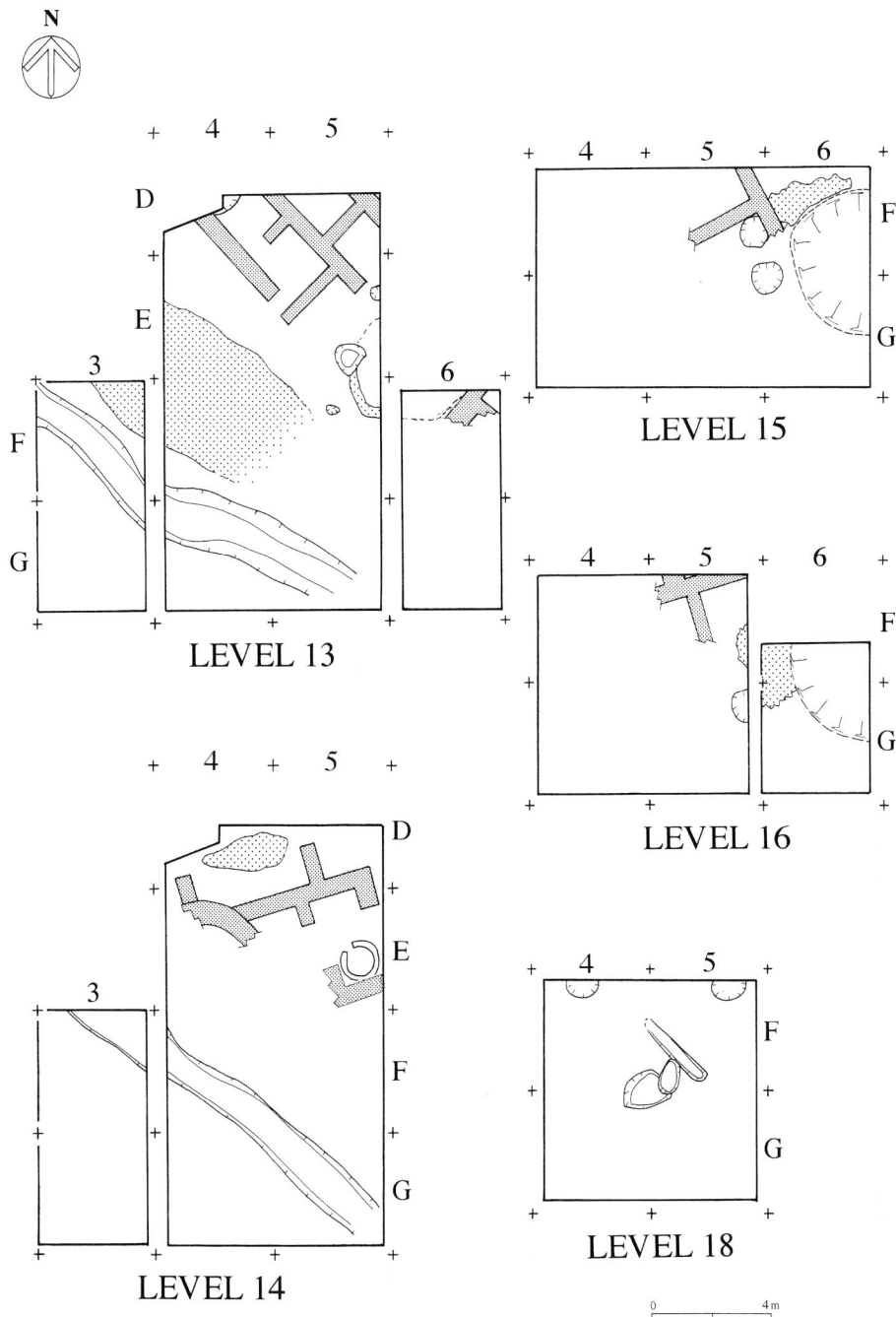

Fig. 3.66 A schematic sequence of building levels of Sector A (Levels 18-13).
Level 17 yielded no recognizable structure.

Secondly, the major wall (10A23) of the Tell Kosak Shamali building is supported by thick standing stones on its north side (Sections C-C' and D-D' in Fig. 3.34), probably indicating that it faced outwards. Thirdly the area in the north had no clear evidence of plastering as seen in the rooms. These observations indicate it was an open area, and that the central hall, if present, should be on the southern side. The area defined as 10A09 may represent it, but could also have been part of a small room as in Level 11 (Figs. 3.25 and 3.26). Heavy erosion in the south further weakens this interpretation. Therefore, it is wise, perhaps, not to interpret this complex as part of a tripartite planned building. Workshop structures

that did not follow the tripartite plan can be found in the literature. One such secure example is Building B of Level III of Tell Abada, which is also composed of a rectangular room and neatly arranged small square rooms (Jasim 1985).

The excavations at Tell Kosak Shamali revealed potters' workshops from other levels too. The bottom of a kiln (1306) was found in association with a set of pottery production tools in Level 13. The floor of Room 706 in Level 7 was well preserved and had similar tools *in situ*. Equivalent discoveries were also made in Room 402 of Level 4. The Level 15 pit (1505) may be added to this list as represent-

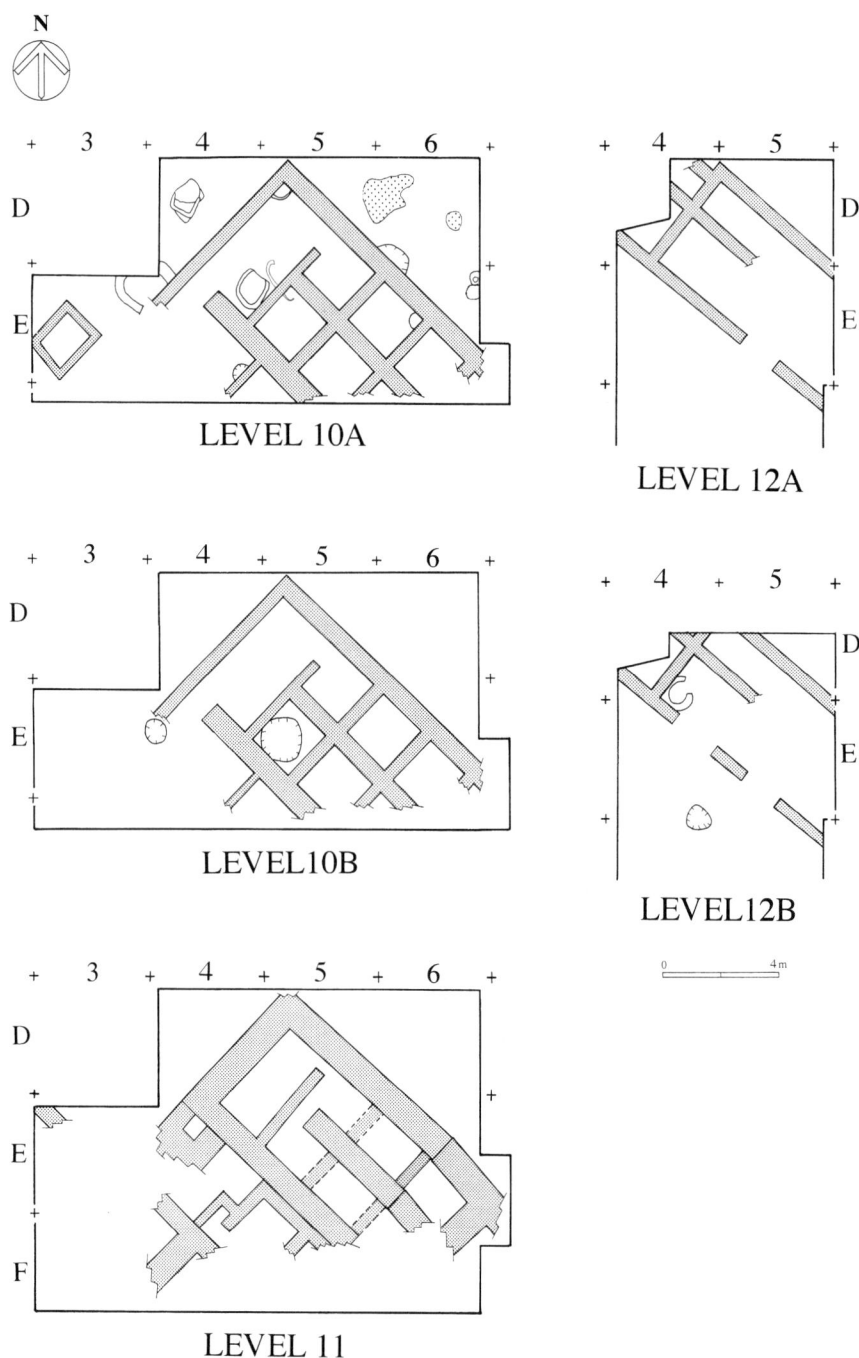

N

+ 3 + 4 + 5 + 6 +

D

E

LEVEL 10A

+ 4 + 5 +

D

E

LEVEL 12A

+ 3 + 4 + 5 + 6 +

D

E

LEVEL10B

+ 4 + 5 +

D

E

LEVEL12B

0   4m

+ 3 + 4 + 5 + 6 +

D

E

F

LEVEL 11

Fig. 3.67 A schematic sequence of building levels of Sector A (Levels 12-10).

ing a pottery kiln, but its use for pottery production has not been attested. These intermittent but repeated occurrences suggest that this part of the mound, located perhaps at the edge of the settlement, might have been an industrial area. In fact, structures from levels with no definite evidence for potters' workshop do not differ greatly from those of identified workshops. Interestingly, the excavators of Tell al-'Abr also reported evidence suggesting the repeated use of the same areas for pottery production in the Ubaid period (Hammade and Yamazaki 1995; Yamazaki 1999).

At the same time, caution is required not to overemphasize the industrial character of Tell Kosak Shamali. Domestic features were also identified, for example, ovens and infant burials as well as quantities of daily utensils such as sickle elements and clay spindle whorls. Circular ovens made of *tauf* with a core of either stones (1407; Level 14) or mudbricks and with an opening at the side (12B05; Level 12) were smaller than kilns. Both ovens were in a corner of a rectangular mudbrick-walled room. No adult burials were discovered within the excavation areas but infant

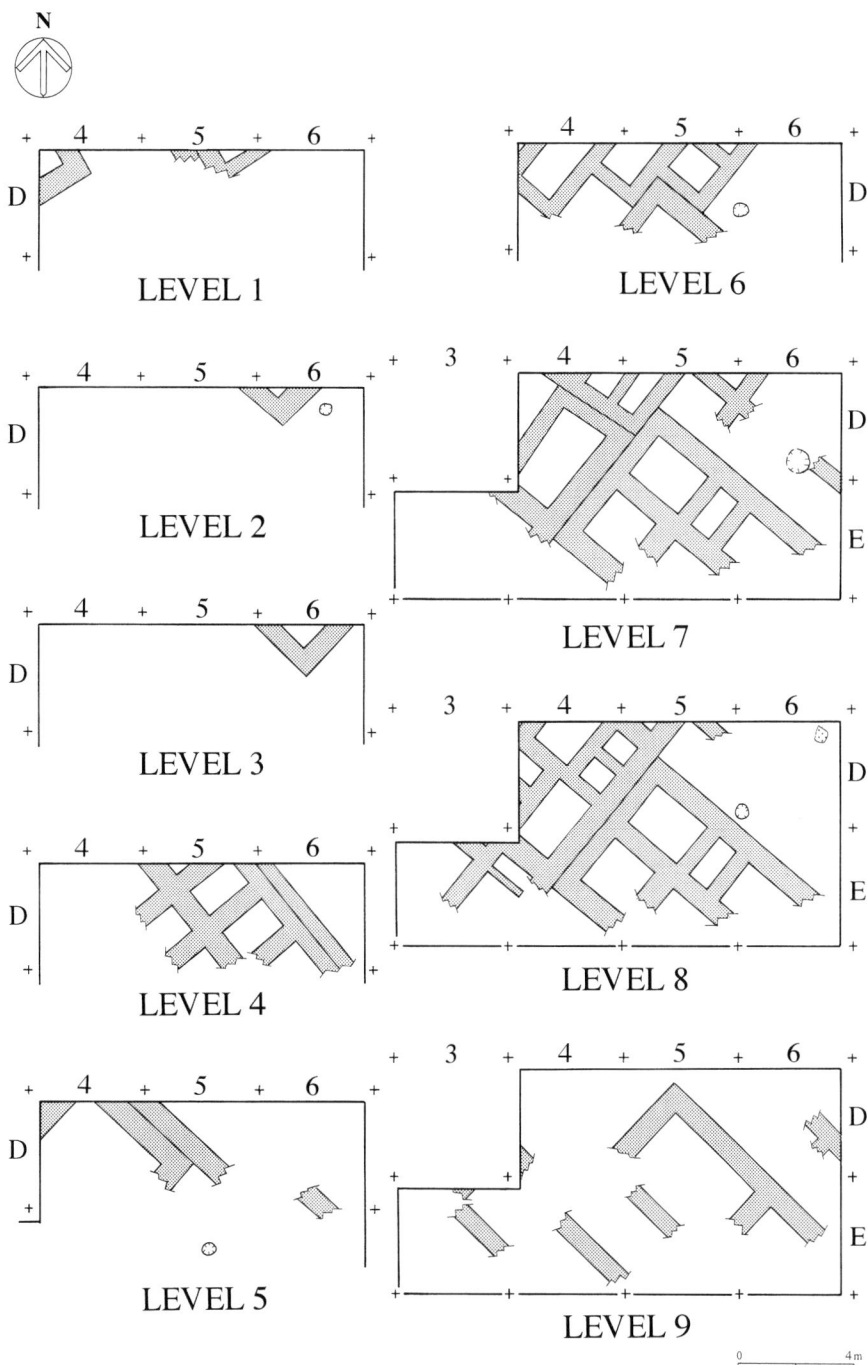

Fig. 3.68 A schematic sequence of building levels of Sector A (Levels 9-1).

burials were recorded in Levels 13, 8, 5 and 4. These four infant burials varied in construction methods as is common at other Ubaidian settlements: simple pits (1318 and 824), a pit lined with mud and stone (505), and a pottery urn (412) respectively. However consistency was apparent in the basic mortuary practice, bodies in a flexed position with no burial goods. The occurrence of these domestic features clearly overlapped with the above-mentioned workshop features in the same levels. This undifferentiated use of similar structures for different purposes may character-ize the use of space in the Ubaidian levels of Tell Kosak Shamali, in clear contrast with that in later levels. In the Post-Ubaid levels, a fully fledged pottery workshop was separated from the domestic quarter (see Chapter 4). In order to fully clarify this change, detailed spatial analyses are needed to identify specific activity areas or particular functions for each building. Such analyses will be attempted in separate chapters of this series of volumes for the Tell Kosak Shamali project.

Table 3.1 Summary of the stratigraphy and structures of Sector A.

Ceramic periodization	Level	The axis of architectures	Stratigraphic relationship to the earlier level	Remarks
Terminal Northern Ubaid	Level 1	NW-SE	Built directly on Level 2	
	Level 2	NW-SE	Built directly on Level 3	
	Level 3	NW-SE	Settlement moved to the east	
Late Northern Ubaid	Level 4	NW-SE	Built directly on Level 5	Infant burial
	Level 5	NW-SE	Built silghtly north of the previous buildings	Infant burial
	Level 6	NW-SE	Built directly on Level 7, sharing parts of the existent building	
	Level 7	NW-SE	Built directly on Level 8, sharing parts of the existent building	
	Level 8	NW-SE	Built directly on Level 9, but with some modifications	Infant burial
Early Northern Ubaid (Late)	Level 9	NW-SE	Built directly on Level 10	
	Level 10	NW-SE	Built directly on Level 11	The burnt building; kilns
	Level 11	NW-SE	Built directly on Level 12, but slightly in the north	
	Level 12	NW-SE	Built directly on Level 13	Oven
Early Northern Ubaid (Early)	Level 13	NW-SE	The main axis of building changed	Ditch; kiln; infant burial
	Level 14	WSW-ENE	Built in the same direction of Level 15	Ditch; oven
	Level 15	WSW-ENE	Built directly on Level 16	Kiln
	Level 16	WSW-ENE	Stone foundation remnants of a rectangular building	
	Level 17	None	No architectural remains	Mixed/disturbed deposits
Late Neolithic	Level 18	None	Constructed on "the virgin soil"	Bedrock pits

References

Forrest, J. D. (1991) Le système de mesures de longuers obeidien, sa mise en oeuvre, sa signification. *Paléorient* 17(2): 161-172.

Hammade, H. and Y. Koike (1992) Syrian archaeological expedition in the Tishreen dam basin: Excavations at Tell al-'Abr 1990 and 1991. *Damaszner Mitteilungen* 6: 109-175.

Hammade, H. and Y. Koike (1993) Some Remarks on the Uruk Levels at Tell al-'Abr on the Euphrates. *Akkadica* 84/85: 53-62.

Hammade, H. and Y. Yamazaki (1995) A preliminary report on the excavations at Tell al-'Abr on the Upper Euphrates, 1992. *Akkadica* 93: 4-10.

Hole, F. (ed.) (1999) *Miscellaneous Papers of the Yale University Khabur Basin Project, Northeast Syria, 1986-1997.* Unpublished manuscript. New Haven: Yale University.

Jasim, A.A. (1985) *The Ubaid Period in Iraq: Recent Excavations in the Hamrin Region.* BAR International Series 267. Oxford: Archaeopress.

Kubba, S.A.A. (1998) *Architecture and Linear Measurement during the Ubaid Period in Mesopotamia.* BAR International Series 707. Oxford: Archaeopress.

Matsumoto, K. and S. Yokoyama (1995) Excavations at Tell Songor B. *Al-Rafidan* 16: 1-273.

Matsutani, T. and Y. Nishiaki (1995) Preliminary report on the archaeological investigations at Tell Kosak Shamali, the Upper Euphrates, Syria: The 1994 season. *Akkadica* 93: 11-20.

Meijer, D.J. (1988) Tell Hammam: Architectures and stratigraphy. In: *Hammam et-Turkman I, Report on the University of Amsterdam's 1981-1984 Excavations in Syria, Vol. I,* edited by M. N. van Loon, pp. 69-127. Istanbul: Nederlands Historisch-Archaeologisch Instituut.

Nishiaki, Y. (1998) Tell Kosak Shamali 1997. *Chronique Archéologique en Syrie* 2: 143-148.

Nishiaki, Y. (1999) Tell Kosak Shamali: Preliminary Report on the Excavations (1994-1997). In: *Archaeology of the Upper Syrian Euphrates, the Tishreen Dam Area,* edited by G. del Omo Lete and J.-L. Montero Fenollós, pp. 71-82. Barcelona: Universitat de Barcelona.

Nishiaki, Y. (in press a) An Ubaidian burnt building from Tell Kosak Shamali, North Syria. *Proceedings of The First International Congress on the Archaeology of the Ancient Near East,* edited by P. Matthiae. Rome: University of Rome.

Nishiaki, Y. (in press b) Tell Kosak Shamali, 1998: The fifth season. *Chronique Archéologique en Syrie.*

Nishiaki, Y. (in press c) Tell Kosak Shamali, 1999. *Chronique Archéologique en Syrie.*

Nishiaki, Y., T. Koizumi, M. Le Mière and T. Oguchi (1999) Prehistoric occupations at Tell Kosak Shamali, the Upper Euphrates, Syria. *Akkadica* 113: 13-68.

Sono, T. (1970) Stratum and construction. In: *Telul eth-Thalathat, Vol. II, The Excavations of Tell II, The Third Season (1964),* edited by S. Fukai, K. Horiuchi and T. Matsutani, pp. 8-17. Tokyo: The Institute of Oriental Culture, The University of Tokyo.

Thuesen, I. (2000) Ubaid expansion in the Khabur: new evidence from Tell Mashnaqa. *Subartu* VII: .71-89.

Tobler, A. J. (1950) *Excavations at Tepe Gawra, Vol. II.* Philadelphia: University of Pennsylvania Press.

Tsuneki, A. (1998) Tholoi: Their socio-economic aspects. In: *Excavations at Tell Umm Qseir in Middle Khabur Valley, North Syria: Report of the 1996 Season,* edited by A. Tsuneki and Y. Miyake, pp. 164-176. Al-Shark 1. Tsukuba: University of Tsukuba.

Yamazaki, Y. (1999) Excavations at Tell al-'Abr. In: *Archaeology of the Upper Syrian Euphrates, the Tishreen Dam Area,* edited by G. del Omo Lete and J.-L. Montero Fenollós, pp. 83-96. Barcelona: Universitat de Barcelona.

Pl. 3.1 Architectural remains of Sector A (Levels 18 and 15).
1. Pit 1805 of Level 18 (from the north). Note Ditch 1408 (Level 14) overlying the pit.
2. N-S section of Pit 1805 of Level 18 (from the west).
3. N-S section of Pit 1505 of Level 15 (from the east).

Pl. 3.2 Architectural remains and artifacts of Sector A (Level 14).
1. General view of the stone walls of Level 14 (from the west).
2. Oven 1407 of Level 14 (from the east).
3. Stone bar on palette in situ from Room 1405, Level 14 (from the west).

Pl. 3.3 Architectural remains of Sector A (Level 13).
1. *General view of stone foundation walls of Level 13 (from the north).*
2. *W-E section of Feature 1306 of Level 13 (from the south).*
   A set of potters' tools was discovered in situ.
3. *Ditch 1310 of Level 13 (from the north). Ditch 1408 (Level 14) in front.*

Pl. 3.4 Flint sickle from Sector A (Level 13).
1. Flint sickle in situ *from Room 1301, Level 13 (from the northeast).*
   The left part was inserted in a crack of stone wall.
2. Close view of the flint sickle.

Pl. 3.5 Architectural remains of Sector A (Levels 12 and 11).
1. General view of stone foundation walls of Level 12 (from the northwest).
2. Oven 12B05 of Level 12B (from the north).
3. General view of stone foundation walls of Level 11 (from the northwest).

Pl. 3.6 Architectural remains of Sector A (Level 10).
1. *General view of the burnt building of Level 10 (from the north).*
   Note crushed ceramics in Room 10A01.
2. *General view of the burnt building of Level 10 (from the north).*
   The crushed ceramics were removed.

Pl. 3.7 Architectural remains of Sector A (Level 10).
1. Close view of Room 10A01 of Level 10 (from the northeast).
2. Close view of Rooms 10A01 and 10A08 of Level 10 (from the southwest).
3. Section of the northwest wall of Room 10A01 of Level 10 (from the southwest).
   Note the tauf embedded within the mud-brick wall.

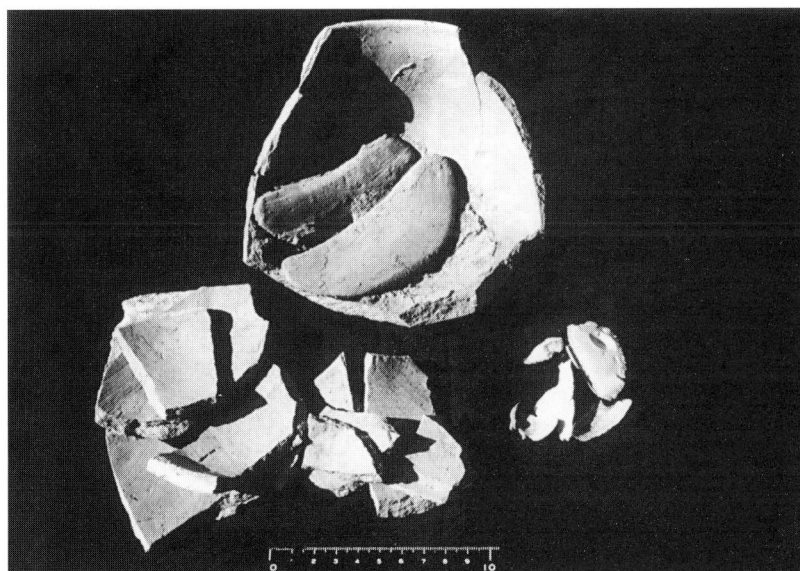

Pl. 3.8 Architectural remains and artifacts of Sector A (Level 10).
1. Feature 10A13 of Level 10 (from the southeast).
2. Features 10A17 and 10A29 (left) of Level 10 (from the north).
3. Jar containing two ceramic scrapers and flint flakes (front right) inside,
   discovered from the passage of Rooms 10A01 to 10A02.
   The sherds (front left) are conjoinable.

Pl. 3.9 Architectural remains and artifacts of Sector A (Level 10).
1. Close view of Room 10A02 (from the north).
2. Floor remains of Room 10A02 (from the west). Note the ceramic scraper and a horn.
3. Close view of Room 10A03 (from the northwest).
   Note the burnt wood remains on right.

Pl. 3.10 Architectural remains of Sector A (Level 10).
1. Crushed ceramics from Room 10A03 (from the north).
   The wood remains were removed.
2. Close view of Room 10A04 (from the southeast).
   Note the carbonized cereal grain covered with a crushed clay structure.
3. Close view of Room 10A05 (from the northwest).
   Note the carbonized cereal grain (front left).

Pl. 3.11 Architectural remains of Sector A (Level 10).
1. Carbonized woods and the accumulation of cereal grain from Room 10A05 (from the southwest).
2. Close view of Room 10A06 (from the southeast).
   The dark area represents a distribution of carbonized cereal grain.
3. Close view of Structure 10A11 (from the north).

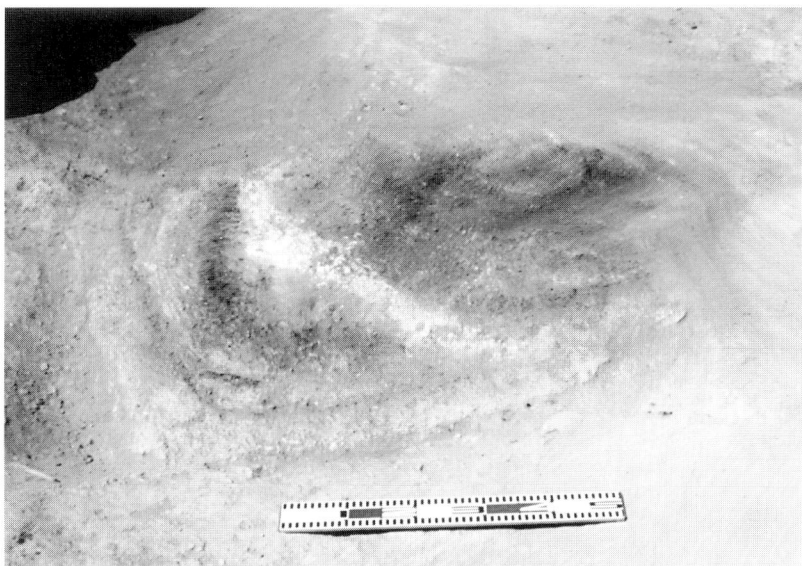

Pl. 3.12 Architectural remains of Sector A (Level 10).
1. Feature 10A28 of Level 10 (from the southeast).
2. Feature 10A12 of Level 10 (from the west).
3. Section of Feature 10A12 of Level 10 (from the west).

Pl. 3.13 Architectural remains of Sector A (Level 8).
1. General view of stone foundation walls of Level 8 (from the north).
2. General view of stone foundation walls of Level 8 (from the northwest).

Pl. 3.14 Architectural remains of Sector A (Levels 7-5).
1. General view of Room 706 of Level 7 (from the north).
2. Close view of the floor of Room 706 of Level 7 (from the east).
   Note a pot-stand, a bone spatula and a flat limestone.
3. Infant burial 505 of Level 5 (from the northeast).

Pl. 3.15 Architectural remains of Sector A (Level 4).
1. The earliest floor of Room 402 of Level 4 (from the north).
2. The second floor of Room 402 of Level 4 (from the northeast).
Note a horn-shaped limestone object in the center.

Pl. 3.16 Architectural remains of Sector A (Levels 4 and 3).
1. The latest floor of Room 402 of Level 4 (from the north).
2. Infant jar burial 412 of Level 4 (from the southwest).
3. Stone foundation walls of Level 3 (from the southwest).
   Parts of the stone walls of Level 2 are visible on the section.

CHAPTER 4

The stratigraphy and architectures of Sector B of Tell Kosak Shamali

Tatsundo Koizumi and Hiroshi Sudo

4.1 Introduction

Excavation of Sector A and B trenches began in 1994. Sector B trench is on the southeastern slope of Tell Kosak Shamali (see Chapter 3). In 1994 a 10 m-long trial step trench of five 2 x 2 m squares was excavated from the middle of the slope to close to base, with 50 cm-balk separating each square. We found a pottery kiln and other evidence of a pottery workshop in the first season. During the 1995 to 1997 campaigns, we investigated areas surrounding the kiln in order to reveal the rest of the pottery workshop. New 4 x 4 m squares were placed over the 1994-season grid ensuring that balks between squares did not straddle the grid lines. The squares were designated by capital letters from the upper of the mound to the lower, southeast by cardinal numbers, and from the left, southwest of the mound on the site map, to the right, northeast. Each square thus has a grid point at the west corner: for example, the grid point BD6 designates Square BD6 east of that point. We excavated a total of around 70 m² of the Sector B trench, a very small part of the entire tell. The Levels of Sector B are indicated by cardinal numbers from upper to lower (Figs. 4.1-4.5; Pl. 4.1): Level 1 is the latest, Level 8 the earliest. Features are designated with a combination of level and serial numbers. In order to avoid confusion with the numbering of Sector A, a capital B is added to the first. Thus B702, for example, refers to a feature No. 2 of Level 7 of Sector B.

4.2 Stratigraphy and architecture

4.2.1 Level 8 (Figs. 4.6 & 4.7; Pls. 4.2 & 4.3)

The 40-60 cm-thick Neolithic layer consisted of reddish brown soils on virgin soil (Pl. 4.3: 4). Most part of the Neolithic deposit in Sector B was very thin, and we were able to reveal only partial evidence of several architectural remains,

possibly due to the slope of the ground and the leveling preparations by upper level occupations. A relatively thick deposit and concentration of features were revealed in Squares BE5 and BE6.

At the eastern corner of Square BD6, we found a shallow, oval pit dug into virgin soil (B801), about 96 cm long, 64 cm wide and 15 cm deep with a fill of gray ash covered with small stones (Pl. 4.2: 1). This shallow pit was probably a hearth.

A late Neolithic pit (B802), with a diameter of about 114 cm at the top and 80 cm at the bottom, was discovered between Squares BE6 and BE7. The pit contained many limestone cobbles (about 30-35 cm long and 15-20 cm wide). The most impressive find of B802 was a "truncated conical stone", upright in the upper part of the fill (Pl. 4.3: 2). Stratigraphically, Pit B702 of the upper Level 7 cut Pit B802, indicating that B802 was older than B702. Not much was found in B802 except some late Neolithic pottery, so that it must be associated with the lower Level 8 of Sector B, that is, Pottery Neolithic.

At the western corner of Square BE6, a roughly 2m-long row of limestone foundation stones (B806) extended from North to South (Pl. 4.3: 3). Each foundation stone in the northern part measured about 30 cm x 20 cm x 10 cm. The stones in the southern half were arranged in a random pattern. Below this row of limestones, were two irregularly shaped Neolithic pits, B803 and B804 (Fig. 4.3; Pl. 4.2: 3).

Pit B803 was 80 cm in diameter at its mouth while B804 was about 120 cm. Both pits contained many limestone cobbles (30 x 20 x 10 cm) (Pl. 4.2: 2). Because these two pits had been dug side by side and were wider at the bottom than the mouth, the southern wall of B803 and the northern wall of B804 had been broken by each other (Fig. 4.7). It was impossible to distinguish which

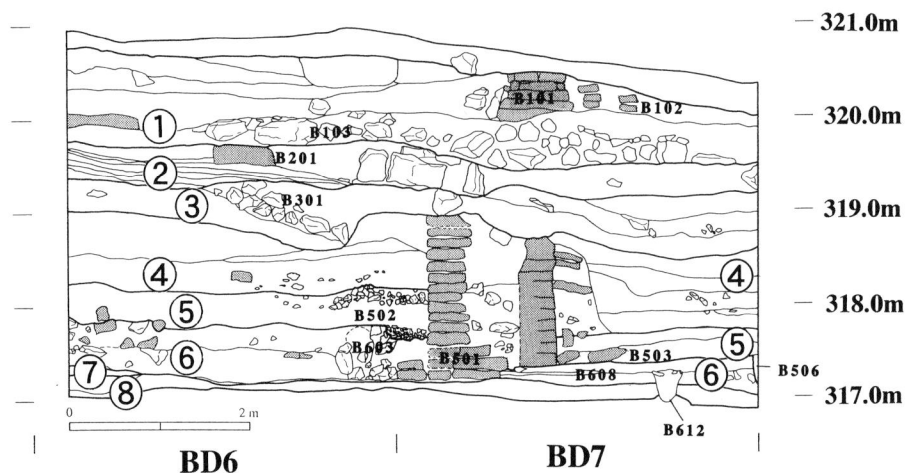

Fig.4.1 Northwest section of Squares BD6-BD7 in Sector B.

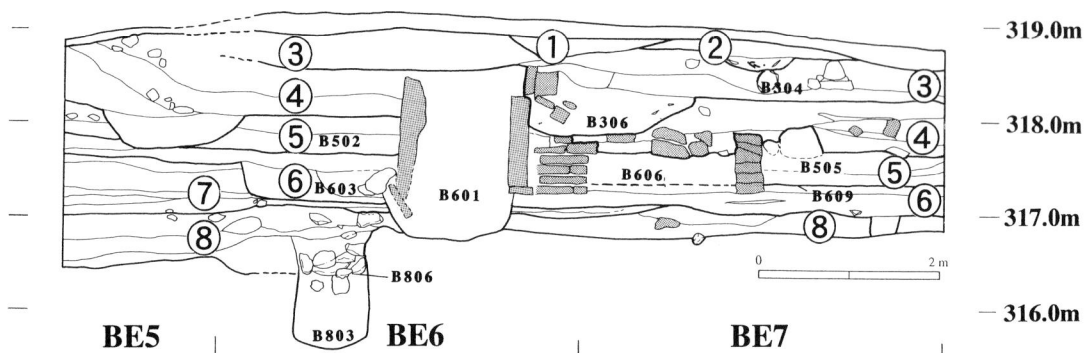

Fig.4.2 Northwest section of Squares BE5-BE7 in Sector B.

was earlier as the section could not be observed due to the dense fill of limestone in the pits. However, the similarity of finds from both pits suggested that they had been constructed within a short interval of each other.

Many late Neolithic potsherds were found in both pits. In addition, a complete jar was recovered from B804 (Pl. 4.3: 1), and a side-blow blade-flake from B803 (see Chapter 8).

In Square BE5, south of B804, another oval pit (B805), with an almost vertical wall was revealed, dug into virgin soil. It was about 110 cm along the long axis, about 80 cm on the short and about 70 cm deep. This pit contained many potsherds.

In sum, we found one hearth (B801) and three pits containing many limestone cobbles (B802, 803, and 804). These resembled those reported as *fosse-foyers* at Tell Halula, about 17 km south of Kosak Shamali (Molist 1998: Fig. 5). But at Kosak Shamali, there were no traces of fire, such as burnt soil and ash, except for B801. We suggest that these pits were for debris. They contained many limestone cobbles and potsherds, especially B803 and B804, and were in the lower part of Sector B which seems to indicate that B803 and B804 were not used at the same time. When one pit was full of stones, potsherds and debris, another had been constructed.

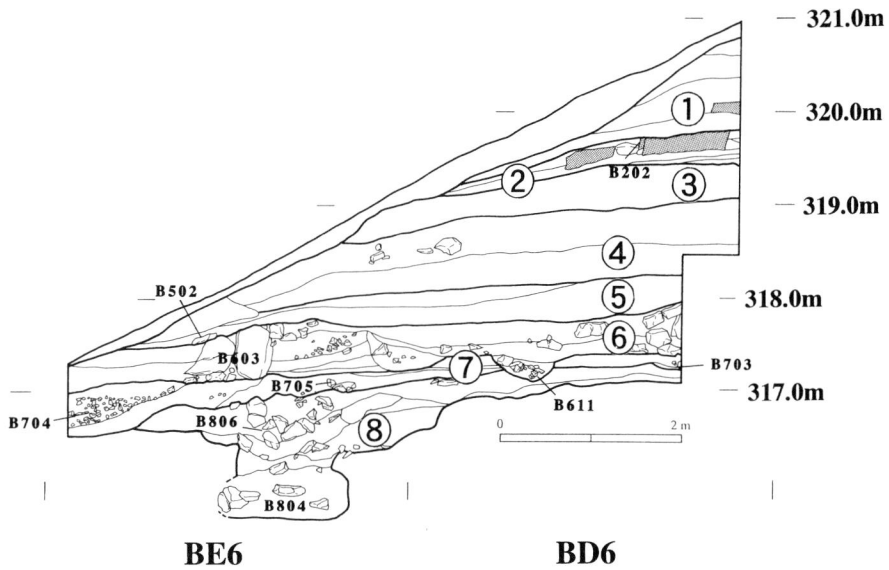

Fig.4.3 Southwest section of Squares BD6-BE6 in Sector B.

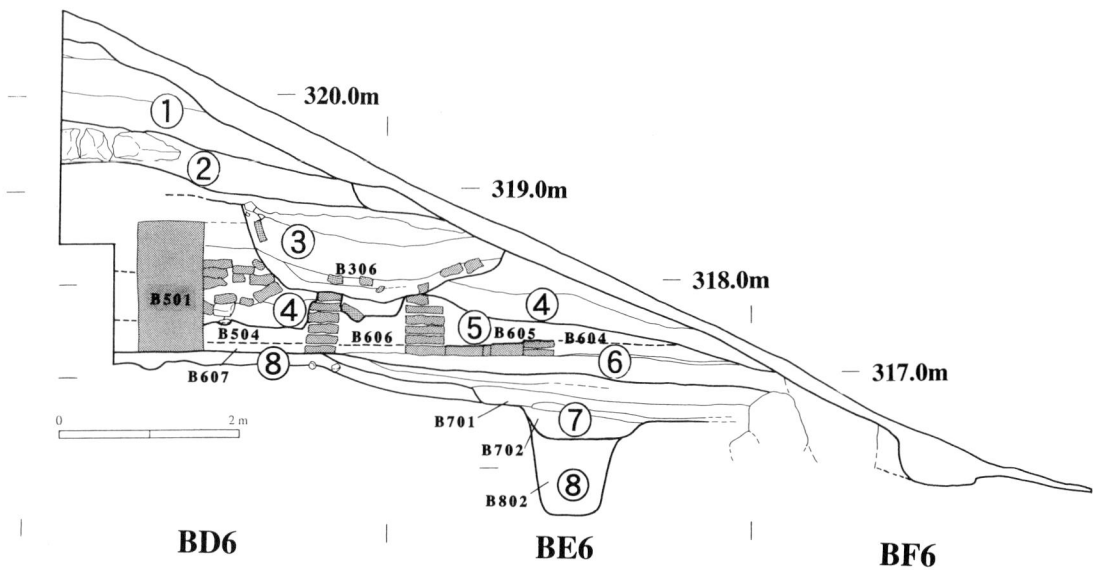

Fig.4.4 Northeast section of Squares BD6-BF6 in Sector B.

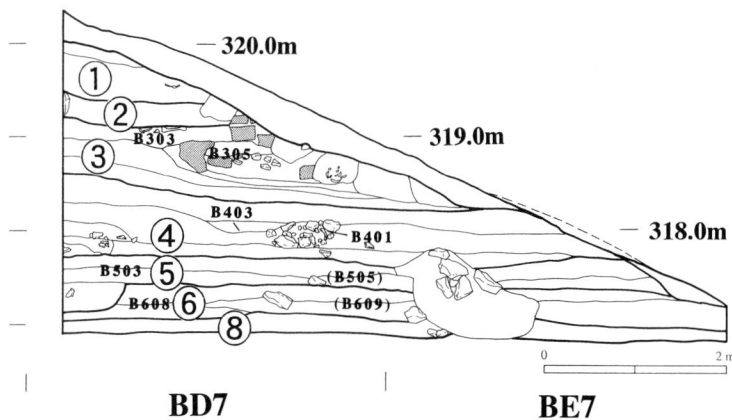

Fig.4.5 Northeast section of Squares BD7-BE7 in Sector B.

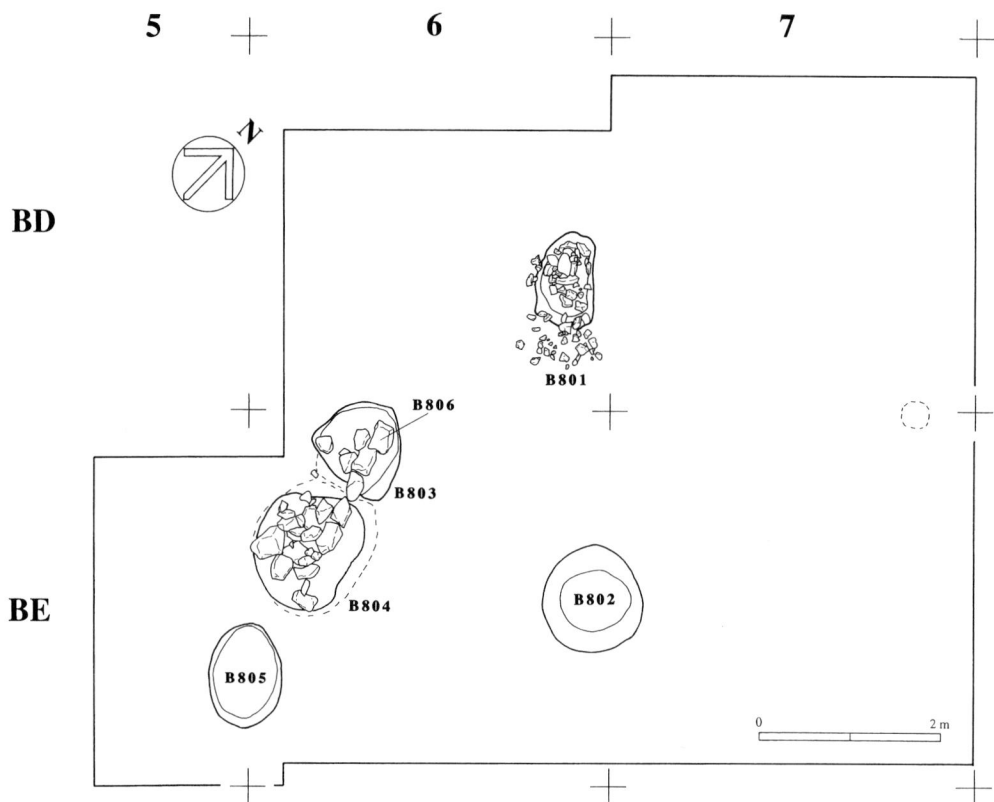

Fig.4.6 Level 8 plans of Sector B.

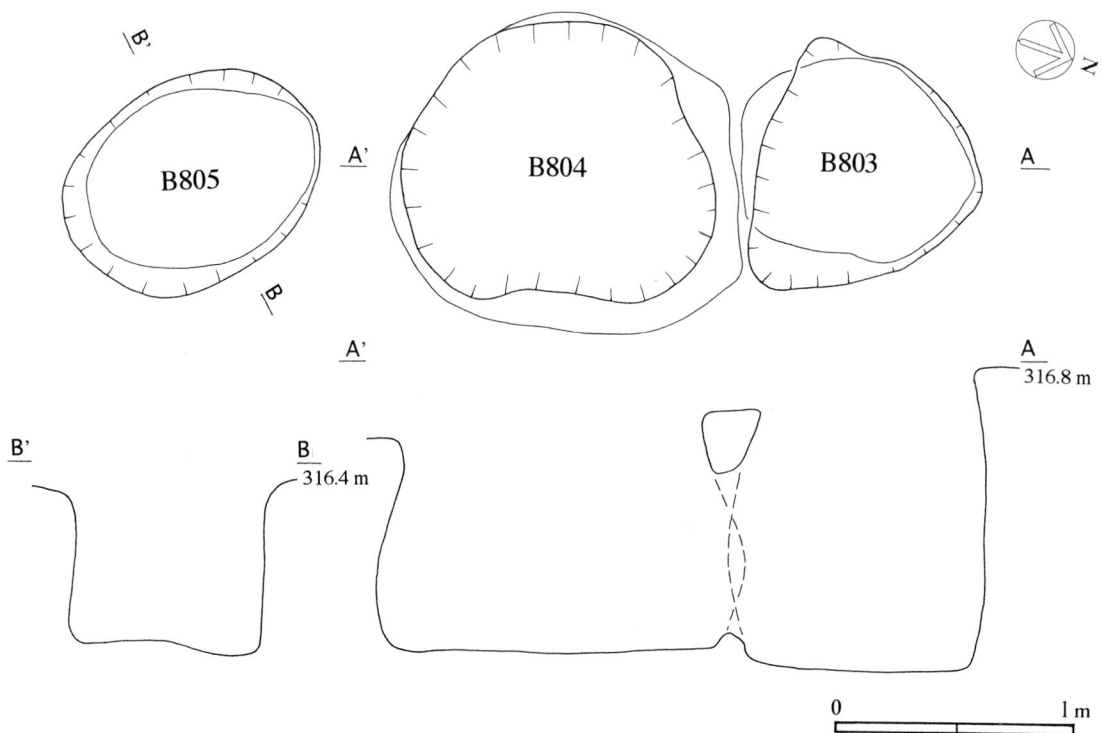

Fig.4.7 Pits B803-B805.

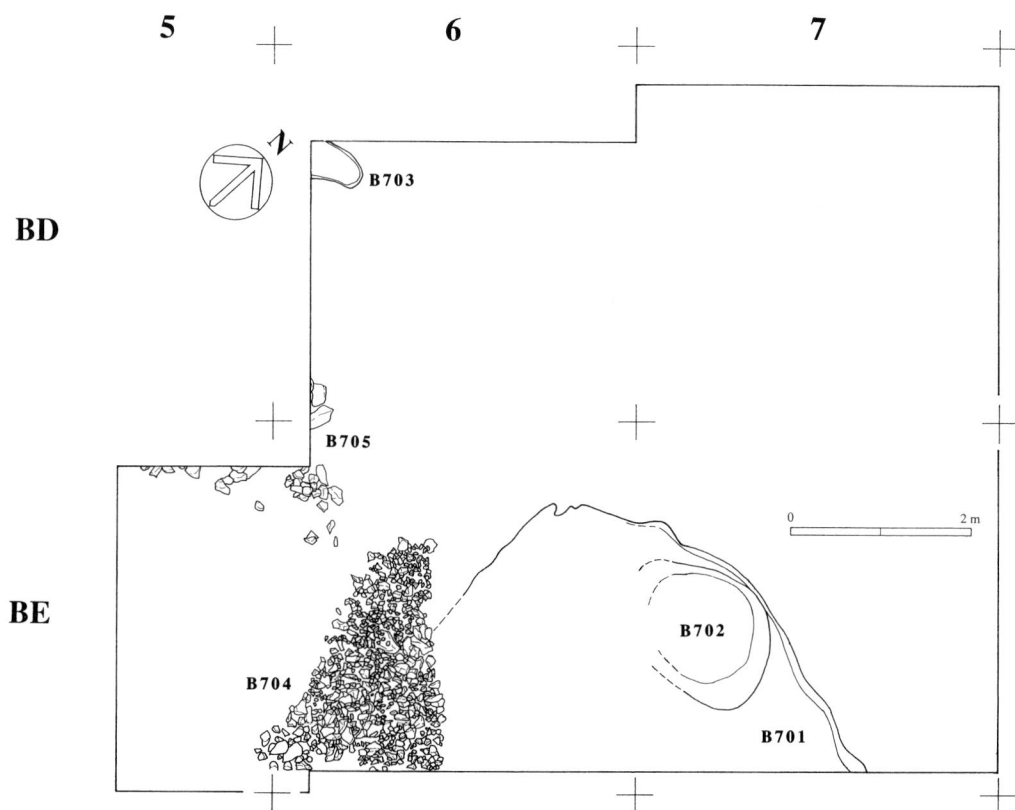

Fig.4.8 Level 7 plans of Sector B.

4.2.2 Level 7 (Fig. 4.8; Pl.4.4)

Level 7 is a thin layer of deposits directly overlying the Neolithic Level 8. The layer is restricted in distribution to the southern part of Sector B, where a cobble pavement including sherds, a stone concentration, a depression, and small pits were discovered, although no building complex was found.

B701 is a large shallow depression (4.5 m long x 3.5 m wide x 10-20 cm deep) dug into the slope of virgin soil (Fig. 4.4; Pl. 4.4: 1). The depression was filled with burnt clay, ashy debris, cobbles (greater than 5 cm in diameter) and overfired sherds. The bottom of depression had a grayish yellow floor hardened by firing.

Pit B702 (maximum diameter 2.0 m and 30 cm deep), dug from the bottom of B701, had a loose, dull yellowish brown fill with many small cobbles (1 to 3 cm in diameter), some ash and charcoal (Fig. 4.4).

B703 is a small shallow pit (40-70 cm diameter and less than 10 cm deep) dug from the western corner of Sector B. It was filled with charcoal, cobbles (5-10 cm in diameter) and a few artifacts.

B704 is a cobble pavement, more than 2.5 m long and more 2.1 m wide, on the southern slope of Sector B (Fig. 4.3; Pl. 4.4: 2). The pavement was composed of cobbles (5-20 cm in diameter), many sherds and lithic artifacts. These artifacts must have been washed down in refuse from the upper areas of the mound.

B705 is a stone concentration compiled of limestone cobbles, (about 10-20 cm in diameter), extending westwards following the contour of the surface (Fig. 4.3; Pl. 4.4: 3). The stone complex was probably located on the southeastern limit of the occupation areas in Level 7, although its function has not yet been determined.

4.2.3 Level 6 (Figs. 4.9-4.11; Pls. 4.5-4.9)

Level 6 was a Post-Ubaid pottery workshop complex, originally extending more than 10 m by 6 m. The pottery production and firing complex consisted of mudbrick walls set on well-leveled ground in the southwestern end of the mound, separated by a ditch from occupational areas (Pl. 4.5). The walls, parts of which were preserved up to a height of fifteen brick courses, were generally built of single rows of mudbricks (each brick usually 50 x 30 x 10 cm). Many nearly complete vessels or large sherds were found *in situ* on the floor of the pottery workshop.

B601 was a mudbrick pottery kiln in the workshop complex (Fig. 4.10; Pl. 4.6: 1). The kiln which was oval in plan and measured 1.6 x 1.5 m at the base and 1.5 x 1.4 m at the top, was preserved up to a height of 1.4 m. The floor of the complex was a closely packed foundation of dull yellow fill with many small sherds, flint flakes, and broken pieces of burnt- and/or mud-bricks. The kiln was an updraught type with the upper chamber for firing pottery and the lower for combustion. The combustion chamber, much of which was preserved, had its base set into a 40 cm-deep oval pit, 1.6 m x 1.3 m x 40 cm deep. The sunken structure would, then, have stood more than 2 m above its base (Fig. 4.11).

There were three openings in the combustion chamber (Fig. 4.11). The first, in the form of an equilateral triangle with 40 cm sides, faced Room B606 in the workshop and was definitely used for fuel supply (Fig. 4.10). The second opening just below the first, was oblong in shape (50 x 15 cm), and would likely have been almost square, with 50 cm sides, when open. This opening was probably used for the removal of ash: the four to five brick courses used to seal it during firing, would have been removed for the disposal of ash once firing had been completed. This is further suggested by the accumulation of ash in B601 that sloped towards the opposite side of the opening, possibly as a result of ash removal. The third, semicircular opening (80 cm in diameter) was also used for ash removal, and could have been made by cutting near bottom of the west wall of the kiln once the second opening began to function less efficiently (Pl. 4.6: 2).

The firing chamber was not as well preserved as the combustion chamber, and is seen mainly to the surviving, lower portions of the chamber walls (Fig. 4.11; Pl. 4.7: 1). The upper firing chamber may have been covered with a temporary dome of mudbricks and other materials, as indicated by the many fragments of burnt bricks in the fill of the lower chamber. A perforated clay grate on which pottery vessels were fired would have been placed on inner ledges of the kiln wall. However, as there was no evidence of the grate in the workshop, it could have been removed from the kiln when it was abandoned. We also observed that some parts of kiln wall had been carefully plastered several times during kiln maintenance (Pl. 4.7: 2).

B602 is a circular structure (1.6 m in diameter and 50 cm high) used for clay levigation in the preparation of finer clay (Pl. 4.8: 1). This feature had been built behind B601 in Room B604, the most southerly structure in the pottery workshop. The remaining circular wall of B602 consisted of a single row of mudbricks set in two vertical courses along the short axis. The very hard, dull yellowish brown fill of B602 consisted of gravel and clay blocks. Gravel and hard unfired clay blocks, which are generally unsuitable for pottery manufacture, would have been deposited on the floor as a result of the clay levigation process.

B603, another notable structure of the pottery workshop, consisted of a ditch and limestone cobble pavement to the west of B601 (Pl. 4.8: 2 and 3). Originally it had extended north-south for more than 8 m across open space with no conspicuous structures. The ditch (8.2 m long x 1.4 m wide x 60 cm deep) had been dug along the western wall of the pottery workshop, and the stone pavement (of cobbles 10 - 15 cm in diameter) had been built adjacent to the ditch on the slope (50 cm / 3 m). The northwestern part of the ditch had been obscured by later activity or disturbance. The fill which had accumulated on the 50 cm wide base consisted of tightly packed soil and contained few artifacts. Although this stone complex of ditch and pavement was contemporary, the ditch had been constructed earlier than the pavement. B611, a shallow pit (80 x 45 cm diameter) of uncertain use was located in an open area farther from the pottery workshop.

B604, B605, and B606 were a series of rooms in the

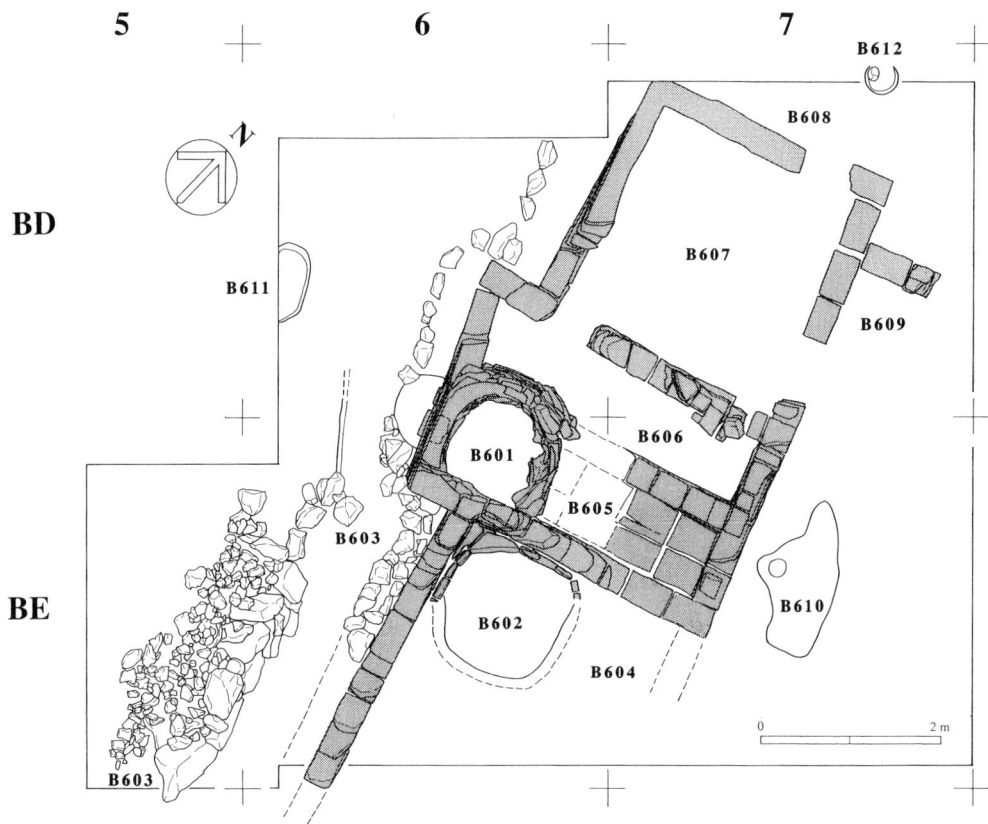

Fig.4.9 Level 6 plans of Sector B.

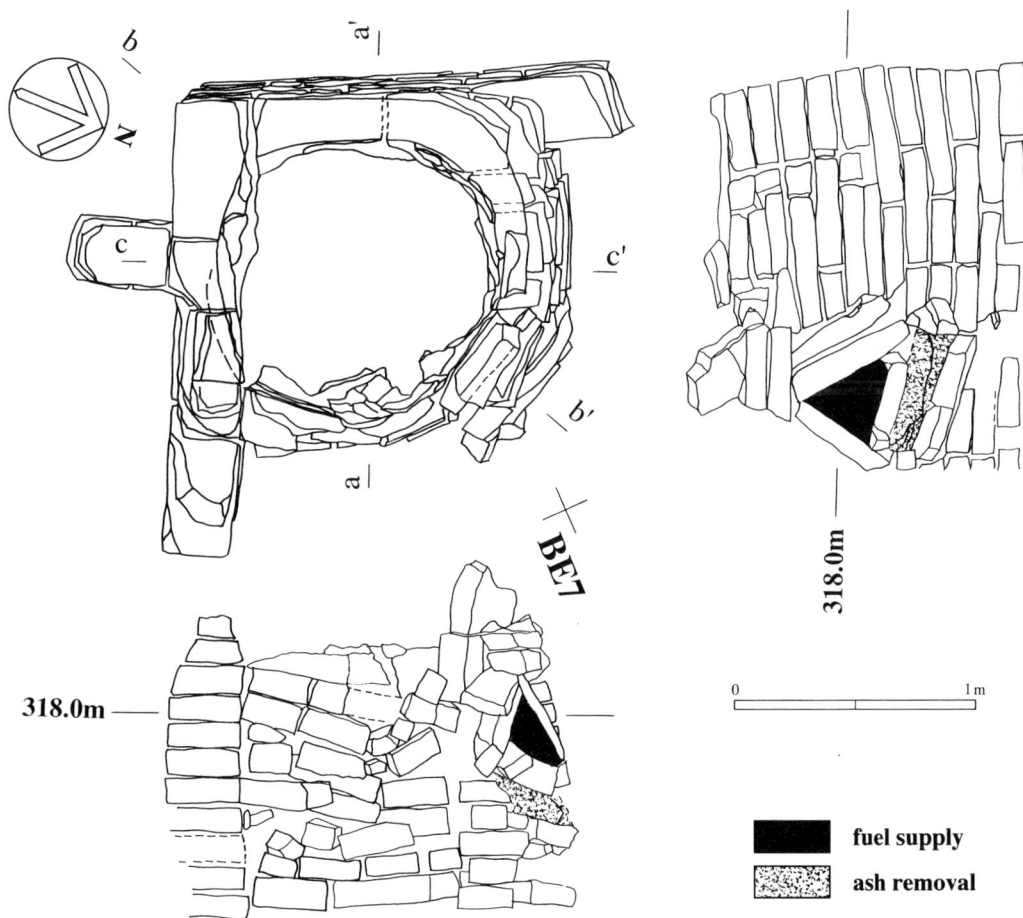

Fig.4.10 Pottery kiln B601.

fuel supply

ash removal

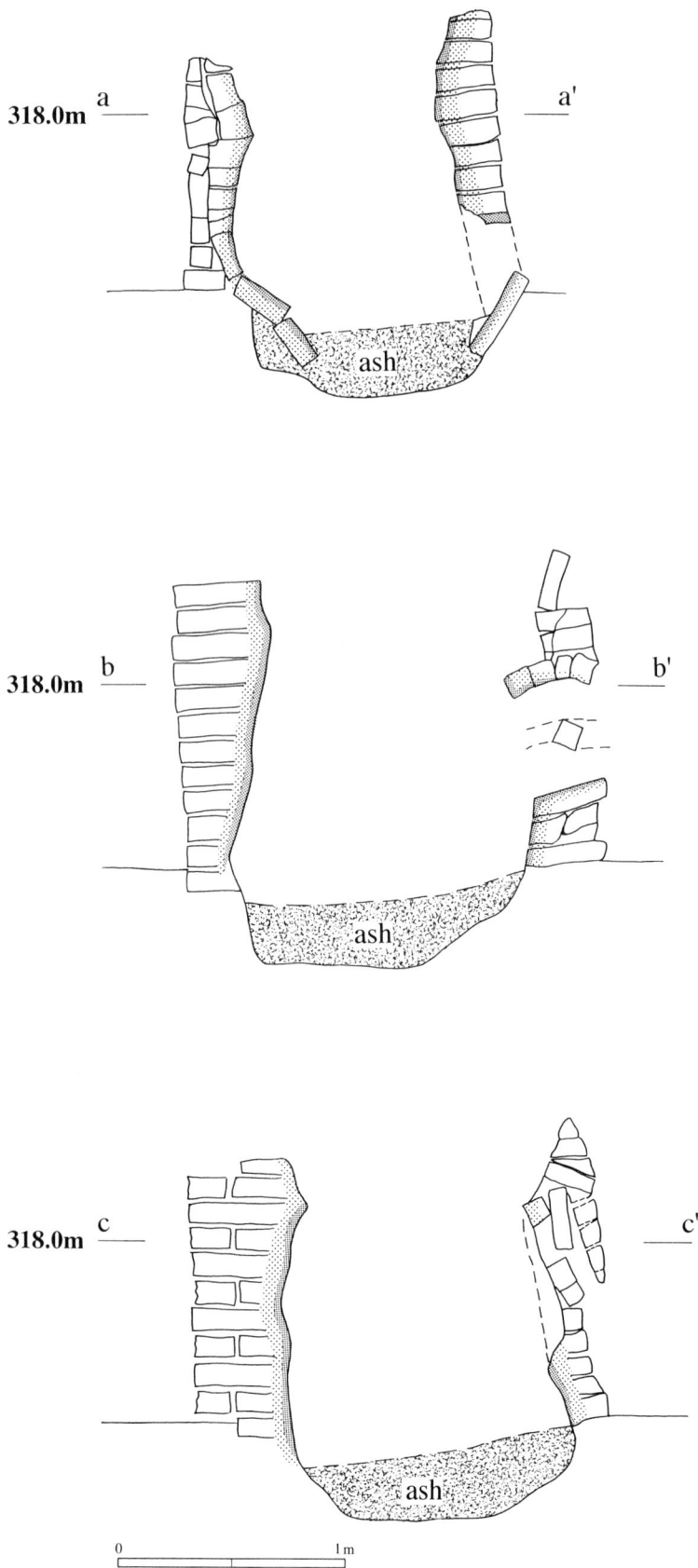

318.0m a ──   ── a'

ash

318.0m b ──   ── b'

ash

318.0m c ──   ── c'

ash

0   1 m

Fig.4.11 Sections of B601. *For the locations, see Fig. 4.10.*

pottery workshop with particular functions. The floors of B604 - B606 bore little trace of plaster. As B604 included the clay levigation structure (B602), B604 was probably used for vessel manufacture using the fine levigated clay produced in B602, although most of B604 had been destroyed by intrusive erosion in later periods. A distinctive feature of Room B605 is its paved, mudbrick floor that would have been extended to the eastern wall of B601. The northern wall of B605 was preserved up to a height of 60 cm, making entry between B605 and B606 difficult, but movement eastwards to B610 was easy (Pl. 4.7: 3). B605 seems, then, to have been a platform for loading unfired pottery vessels, taken from their temporary storage area through B610, into the firing chamber of B601, and removing the fired vessels. Few artifacts were recovered from B606 located to the northeast of B601. As B606 is nearest to the fuel supply opening (B601), B606 appears to have been used as a fuel supply preparation and storage area used during the firing process.

Rooms B607, B608, and B609, also used for pottery production, can be related to Rooms B604-B606. B607 was a square room, measuring 2.4 x 2.4 m in plan, adjacent to the northern side of B606. Room B607 had three entrances, one of which had well preserved, mudbrick walls up to a height of 1.6 m. No plaster was evident on its tightly packed floor. It was filled with larger pottery sherds than those found in other rooms such as B604-B606. Little remained of the upper fill of B607 due to the flooring of B501 and B504 in Level 5.

B608 was a room or space, more than 3 m in length and width, although the limit of the excavation prevented the original plan from being fully revealed. An infant burial (B612) was found in a small pit (35 cm in diameter and 35 cm deep) without any grave goods. The fill of B608 was far less compact than that of B607, but contained more charcoal fragments of about 1 - 1.5 cm in diameter. B609 was also a room or space of uncertain size. Many more sherds and unfired clay blocks were found in B609 than in other rooms. The ash assemblage from B610 was on the hard fired floor in B609, in the loose fill with a concentration of flint chips (Pl. 4.9: 3).

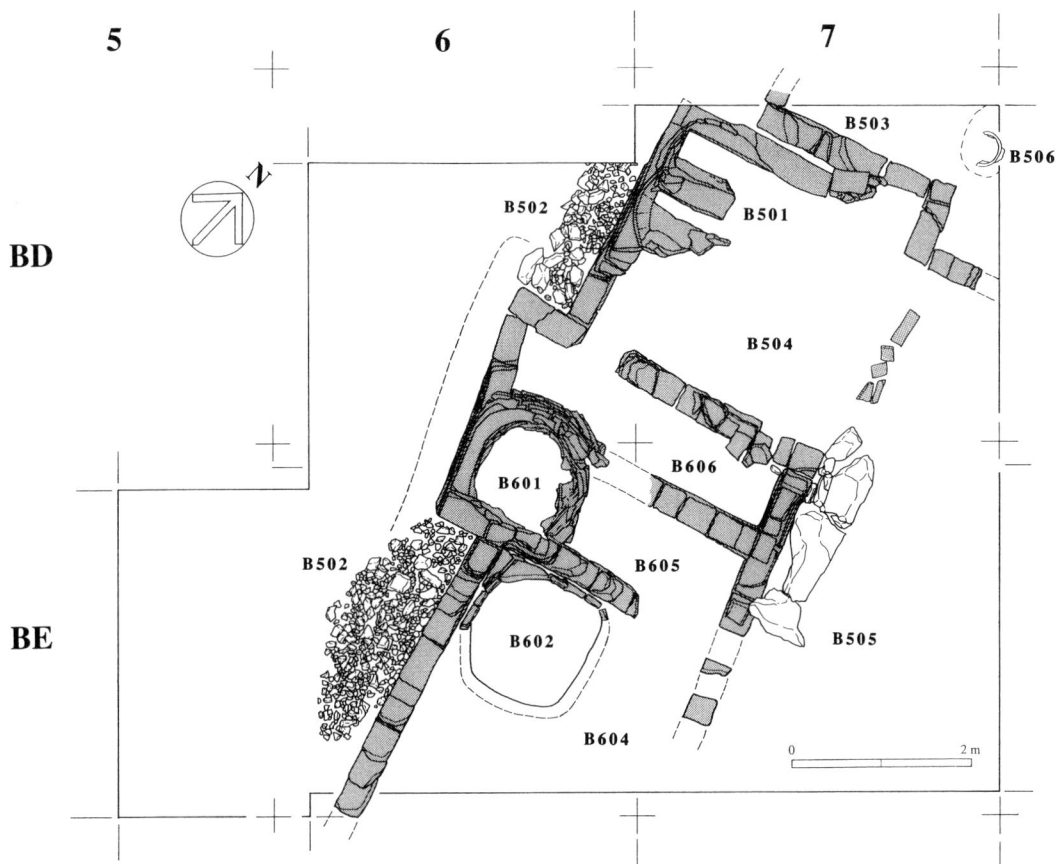

Fig.4.12 Level 5 plans of Sector B.

4.2.4 Level 5 (Figs. 4.12-4.15; Pls.4.10-4.13)

The Post-Ubaid building complex of this level covers an area of more than 9 m by 5 m, and is virtually the same as the pottery workshop in Level 6 described above. The complex consisted of several rooms, some showing continuous use from the previous level, with a stone pavement (B502) extending along the western wall of the complex dividing the pottery workshop from residential areas. The workshop walls were made of mudbrick, the same size as those in Level 6 (50 x 30 x 10 cm). Many complete or nearly complete pottery vessels were found on the floor of the Level 5 workshop.

B501 was another Post-Ubaid pottery kiln measuring about 1.2 m in length, 1.6 m in width, and 1.4 m in height. Its basic structure was quite different from that of B601 as it had been built using the pre-existing main walls of the workshop. Once the stratum had been leveled, several large sherds were laid down horizontally, after which a wall of a single row of eleven mudbrick courses (each 30 cm wide and 10 cm thick) had been erected on the closely packed foundation (Fig. 4.13; Pls. 4.10: 2 and 3; 4.11: 1 and 2). This wall resembled a partition, added to the main work-

shop wall, dividing the area into two combustion chambers. It was preserved up to a height of 1.2 m.

The base of B501 was rectangular in plan measuring 1.2 m x 0.9 m, but the upper area inside the walls had been scraped and mud-plastered to form two semi-circles for the combustion chamber (Fig. 4.13). The surface of these walls had been vitrified by high temperature firings; most parts had been overfired to a dark olive color while the lower part was reddish brown. Although no pieces of clay grate were found during the excavations, one could have been placed above the combustion chamber, probably supported by the wall. A number of factors support this hypothesis: the top surface of the supporting wall (1 m long x 30 cm wide), was not as vitrified as the rest of the wall (Fig. 4.13; Pl. 4.11: 3); many burnt mudbrick fragments, loose ash, charcoal, and sherds had accumulated on the bottom of the combustion chamber. These mudbricks had likely been used to make a temporary dome during firing as mentioned for B601 above.

B502 was a pavement of cobbles (diameter 5 - 15 cm) and sherds extending over the open area by the main walls of the pottery workshop (Pl. 4.13:

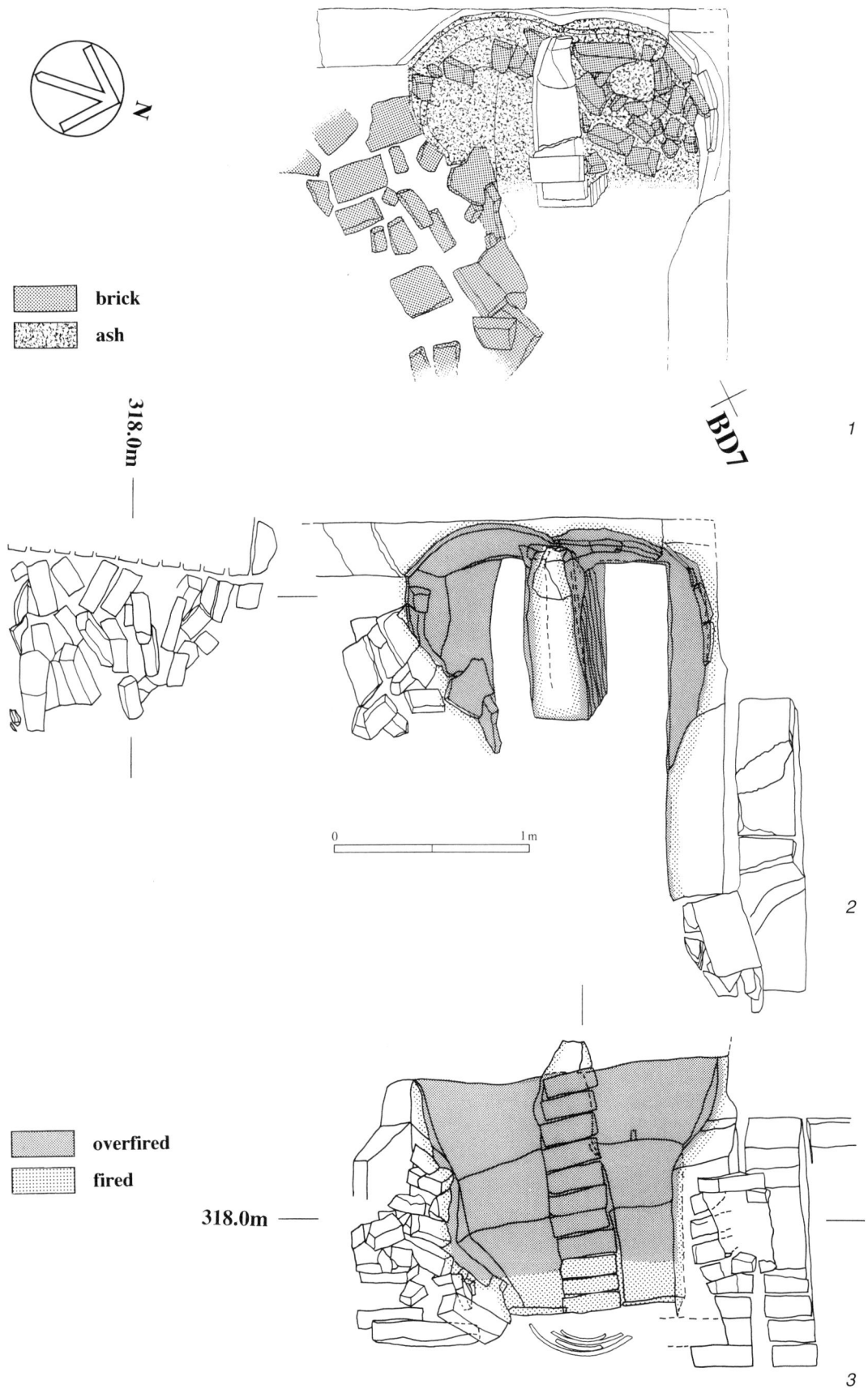

Fig.4.13 Pottery kiln B501. *1: Top view. Note the collapsed mudbricks inside. 2: Top and side views. The collapsed mudbricks were removed. 3: Front view.*

BD7

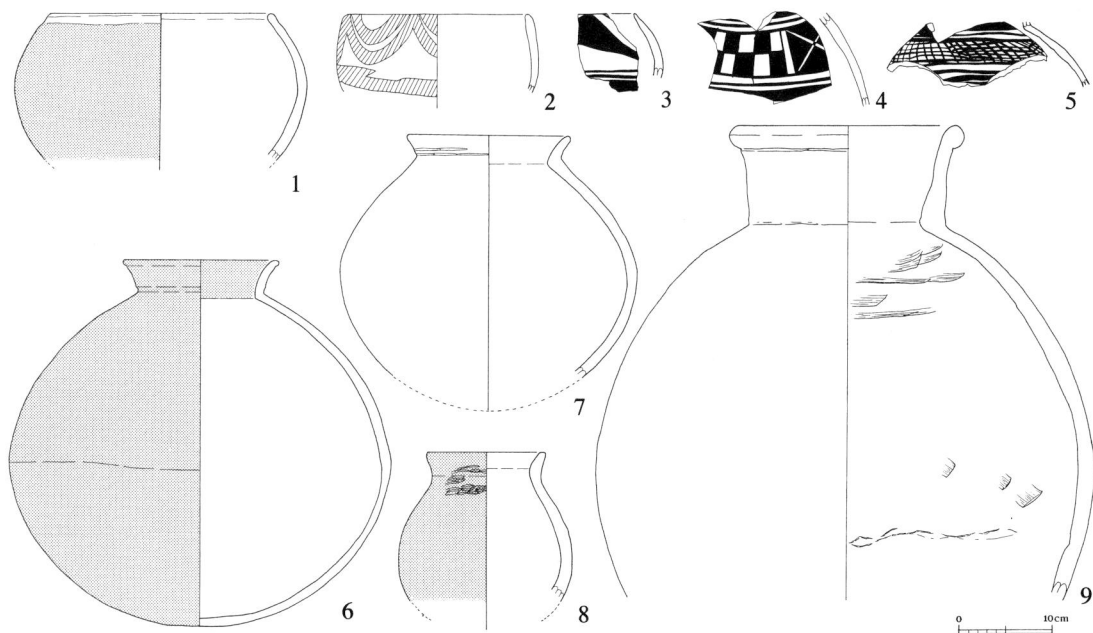

Fig.4.14 Ground level of B504.
1-9: Pottery vessels from the foundation deposits of the Room B504 floor.

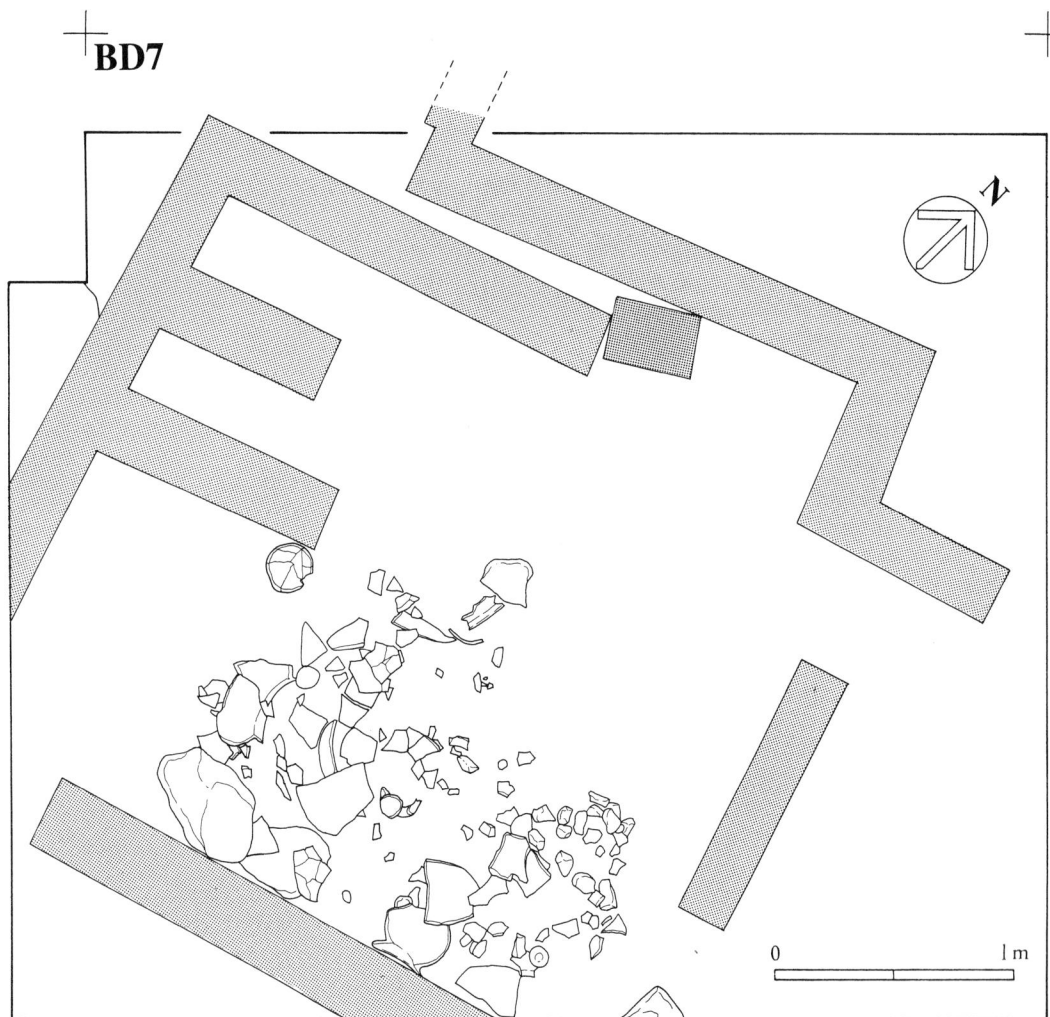

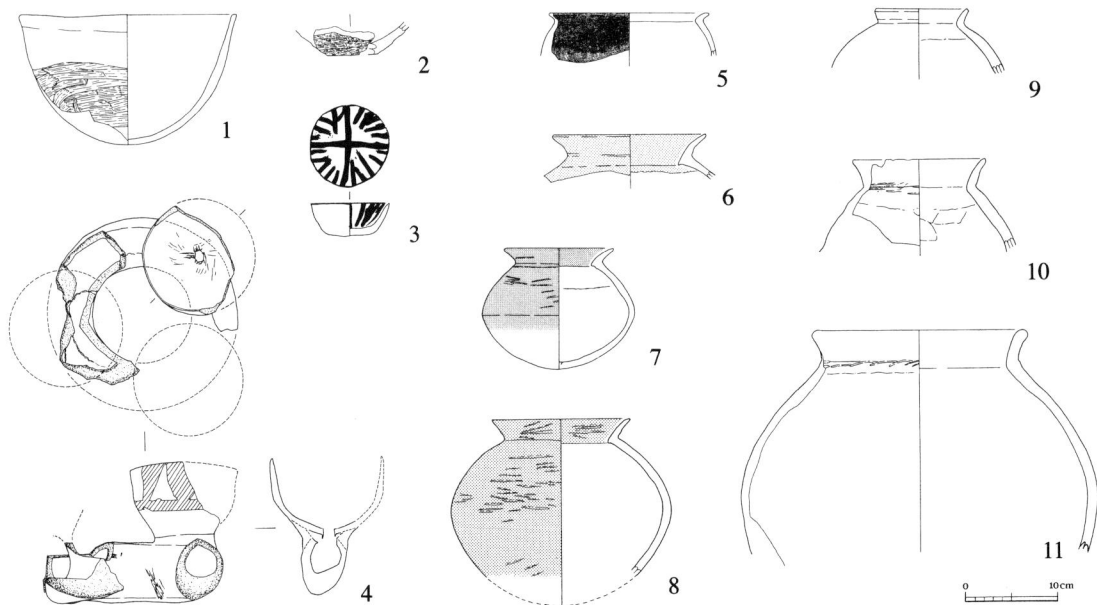

Fig.4.15 Floor of B504.
1-11: Pottery vessels discovered on the Room B504 floor.

1 and 2). The pavement was about 7 m long by 1 m wide and 20 cm deep. It overlaid the B603 stone complex constructed in the previous level.

B503 was separated from B504 and B505 by walls extending over the northern part of Sector B (Pl. 4.9: 2). The floor of B503 was tightly packed and contained charcoal inclusions. A small circular pit (B506) about 70 cm by 40 cm diameter, had been dug 30 cm into the floor. A storage jar, surrounded by a dense grayish olive, fill with many charcoal inclusions, was found in the pit.

The eastern side of B501 was completely open to hold fuel supply, and faced B504, a square room (3 m x 3 m) with a well preserved wall rising to a height of 1.4 m. The wall had three entrances. The foundation of B504 had been modified so that it was the same level as that of B501 (Fig. 4.14). The entire space, including the foundations of B501 and B504, had been filled to a depth of about 10 cm with a tight packing of debris including large sherds (from which we were able to reconstruct vessels; Fig. 4.14: 1-9), some unfired clay blocks, and a cylinder seal (cf. Nishiaki *et al.* 1999: Fig. 17: 11). The southern wall of the room was reinforced by several cobbles (40 to 50 cm in diameter) set against the wall.

A floor above ground level was covered with a compact fill of ashy and charcoal debris, flint flakes or chips, and some nearly complete vessels (Fig. 4.15: 1-11; Pl. 4.12). Ground and floor levels extended towards B505 which was adjacent to B504. The function of all areas related to pottery production. B504 seems to have been a storage space for the preparation of pottery vessels for firing. Bitumen fragments with negative impressions of some type of vegetable such as reeds were found on the floor of B504 (BD7-46) possibly used to make the roof beams rainproof.

A burnt surface, filled with black, loose ash suggesting a hearth, was revealed in the northern part of B505. This feature appears to have had the same function as B610 in Level 6. In the southern area of B505, a series of large stones (2.4 m long, by 70 cm wide and 35 cm high) had been placed beside the eastern wall of the building complex to reinforce the structures (Pl. 4.13: 3). The southern and eastern areas of B505 remained unclear due to the limit of excavation and later erosion.

4.2.5 *Level 4* (Fig. 4.16; Pl. 4.14)

After the workshop complex of Levels 6 and 5 had been abandoned, an 80 cm to 1 m-thick layer brownish gray fill had accumulated. Except for a few fragments of stone foundations, no substantial structures were uncovered in this level. A stone complex (B401), consisting of a concentration of limestone cobbles, covered an area of 1.8 m long and more than 2.2 m wide in the eastern part of Sector B. Most of the cobbles were 10 to 20 cm in diameter, and there were far fewer sherds than in the previous building complex. B402, a small pit (50 cm in diameter and 25 cm deep) was filled with loose, grayish yellow soils. Loose soils and a few artifacts formed the fill of B403, a shallow depression of 1.1 m by 0.9 m in diameter.

4.2.6 *Level 3* (Fig. 4.17; Pl. 4.15)

The foundations of the few architectural remains of this level were set on the previous layers, and concentrated mainly in the northern part of Sector B. The complex was far less well preserved than the Levels 6 and 5 complexes.

B301 was a stone foundation of limestone cobbles (10 to 30 cm in diameter), surrounded by an accumulation of white soil patches (2 to 3 cm in diameter), with charcoal inclusions and sherds. Structures on this foundation were poorly preserved.

B302 comprised stone and mudbrick walls, little of which remained, and with few clear boundaries except on the western side (Pl. 4.15: 1). The stone wall was 3 m long, 30 - 70 cm wide, and 90 cm high. The brick wall, composed of 3 rows of mudbricks stacked to 8 courses, was adjacent to the eastern side of the stone wall. The mudbricks were usually 45 - 50 x 25 - 30 x 7 - 8 cm in size, slightly less thick than those of Levels 6 and 5.

Room B303 was located in the northern area of the building complex. A closely packed, brown to light brown fill with charcoal and abundant gravel debris (less than 5 mm in diameter) had accumulated on the floor of B303. It had a brick-lined oven (B305) with a diameter of 1.8 m and a height of 0.5 m. The oven was sunk into the ground in a shallow pit foundation, faintly visible except for the northeast section of Square BD7 (Fig. 4.5;

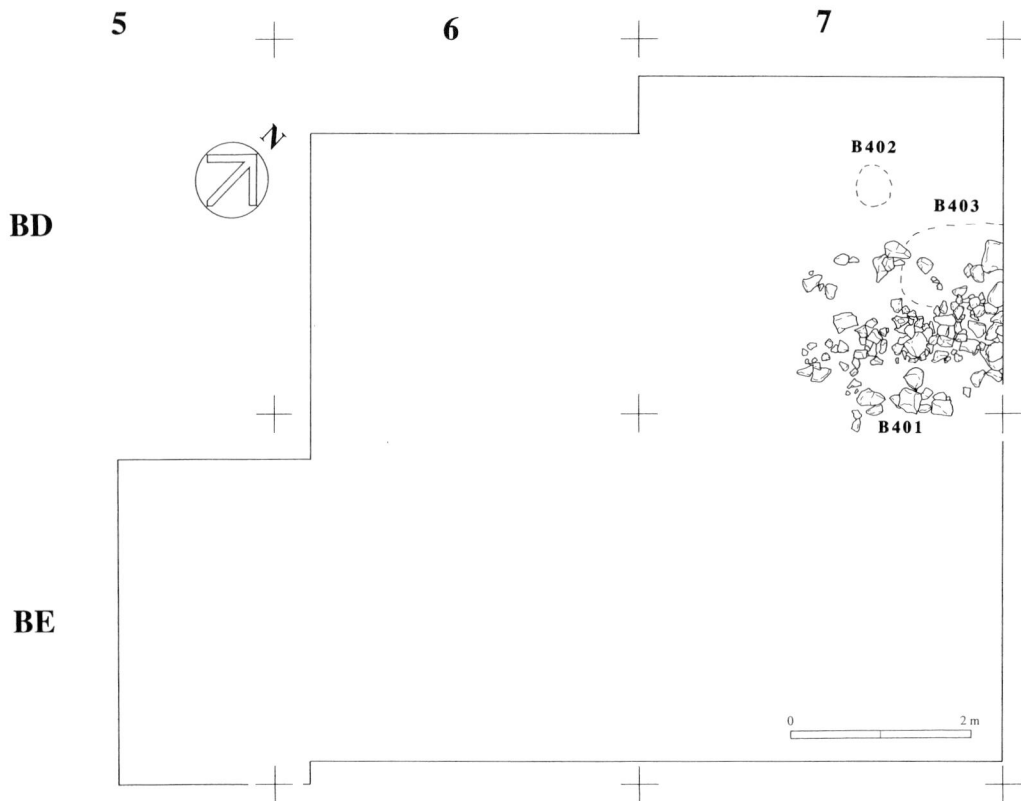

Fig.4.16 Level 4 plans of Sector B.

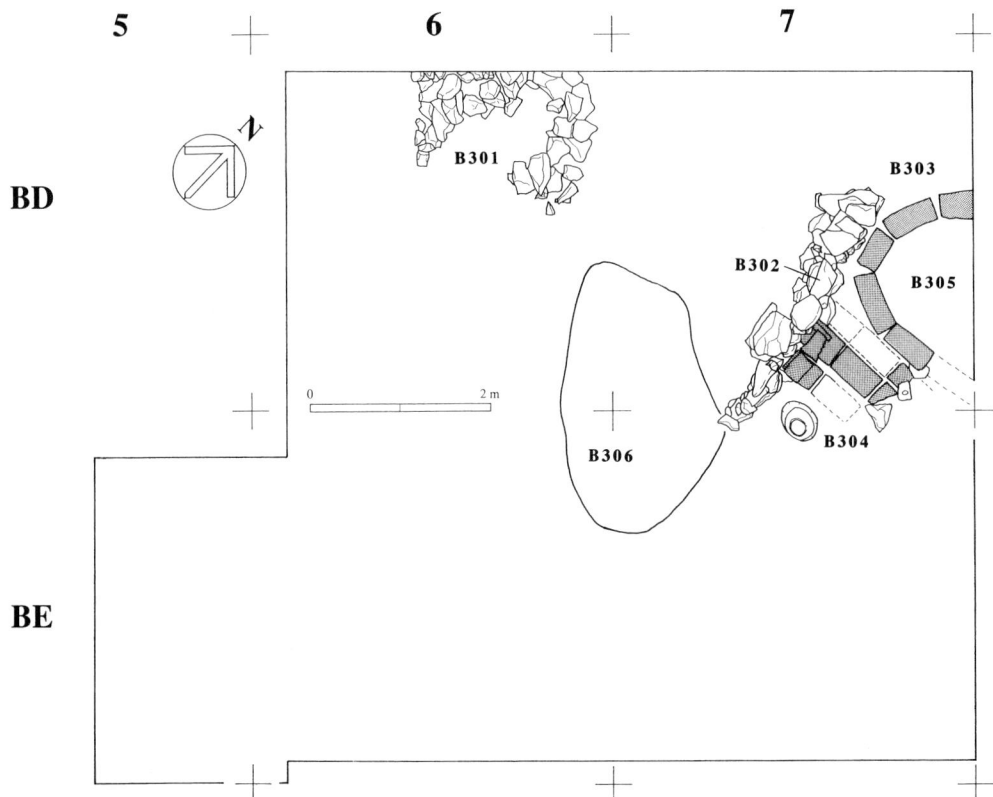

Fig.4.17 Level 3 plans of Sector B.

Pl. 4.15: 3). The oven seems to have had a dome-like structure of *pisé* (Fig. 4.5). B305 had a loose fill consisting of black ash with charcoal inclusions, and abundant burnt brick, probably the broken remains of part of the dome. The oven may have been used for domestic purposes.

Room B304 (measuring more than 1.2 m x 1.2 m), which was contemporaneous with B305 was located in the southern area of the architectural complex. The room had a slightly loose, dull brown fill, unlike that of B303, with small cobble inclusions of 2 to 5 cm in diameter. A complete jar (maximum diameter 33 cm and 27 cm high) was found in a shallow pit dug from the floor of B304 (Pl. 4.15: 2). The pit (50 cm x 40 cm and 10 cm deep) was filled with many sherds.

B306 was a large oval pit of 2.9 m x 1.8 m and 80 cm deep. It was packed with a loose, light gray to brownish gray fill with many sherds, and seems to have been exploited for clay or soil for the construction of buildings in Level 3.

4.2.7 *Level 2* (Fig. 4.18; Pl. 4.16: 1)

The occupation area of this level was preserved only in the northwestern part of Sector B. The remaining excavated squares appeared to have been eroded by later, intrusive cultivation or disturbance. The architectural remains consisted of mudbrick walls and a stone foundation of relatively larger and more irregular cobbles than those found in the Ubaid levels of Sector A.

B201 was a square architectural complex (2.5 m sides and 50 cm high) consisting of mudbrick wall and stone foundation. The wall was 1.7 m long, 40 cm wide, and 21 cm high and brick size was from 40 - 60 cm x 20 - 25 cm x 20 cm. The stone foundation (2.7 m by 2 m) was constructed of large (70 - 90 cm in diameter), medium sized (30 - 40 cm), and small cobbles (less than 25 cm in diameter). The structure of B201 was particularly conspicuous as the bricks and stones were horizontally arranged; the relationship between them is represented by a blank on the fig-

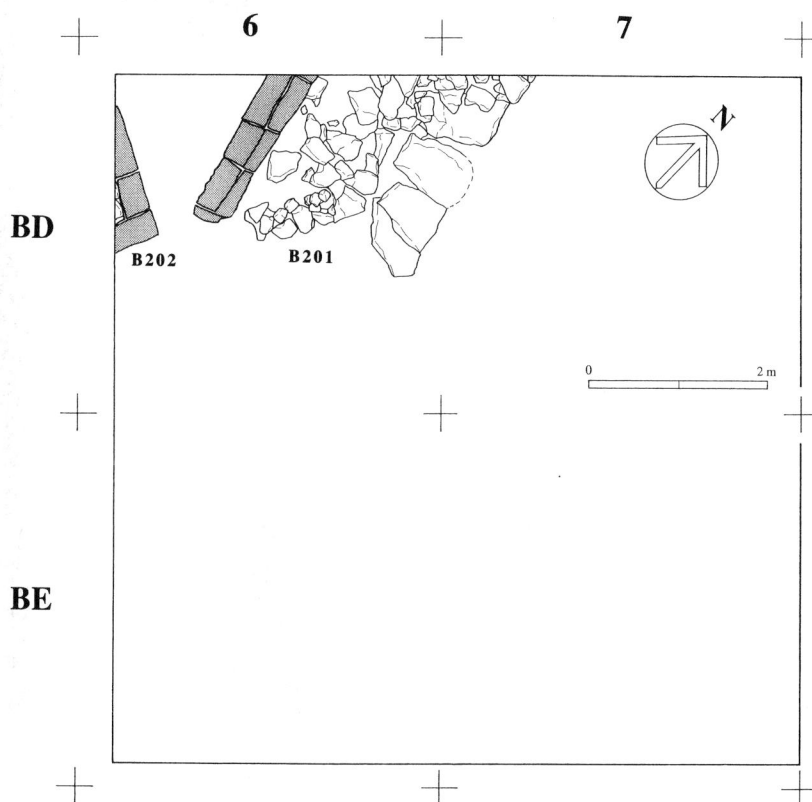

Fig.4.18 Level 2 plans of Sector B.

ure, although more stones could have been laid there originally (Fig. 4.1). No floor of B201 was observed and the superstructure had been disturbed by preparation for the foundation of later buildings. Residues of ash and charcoal were found in the open space between B201 and B202, possibly the result of work-related activities.

B202 was a mudbrick wall that probably formed part of a room next to B201. The wall stood on thin layered foundations with cobbles on the inner corner (Fig. 4.3). Mudbrick size ranged from 40 - 70 x 25 - 30 x 15 - 20 cm.

4.2.8 Level 1 (Fig. 4.19; Pl. 4.16: 2)

The building in this level consisted of mudbrick walls and stone foundations in the northwestern half of Sector B. Most of the rest of the area had been destroyed by erosion or disturbance as in previous Levels 3 and 2.

B101 was a stone and mudbrick building complex. The stone foundation of limestone cobbles (with a diameter of 20 - 50 cm) extended from west to east. The mudbrick structure had three walls, a longer one and two shorter ones. Although the joins between the bricks could be observed faintly in plan, other information from the section allowed us to determine that the building had been constructed primarily of rectangular bricks, similar to those in earlier levels, and in addition, "riemchen"-like bricks (Fig. 4.1). As seen from the section, mudbricks ranged in size from 30 - 40 x 10 x 7 - 10 cm, and were stacked in five courses. No floor level or any indication of plaster was detected, although the dark reddish brown fill was densely packed and contained some charcoal inclusions.

B102 was a room or space adjacent to the northern wall of B101. It appeared to be square or rectangular with sides greater than 50 cm. The remaining walls, joining the B101 wall, had probably formed only a small part of the complex,

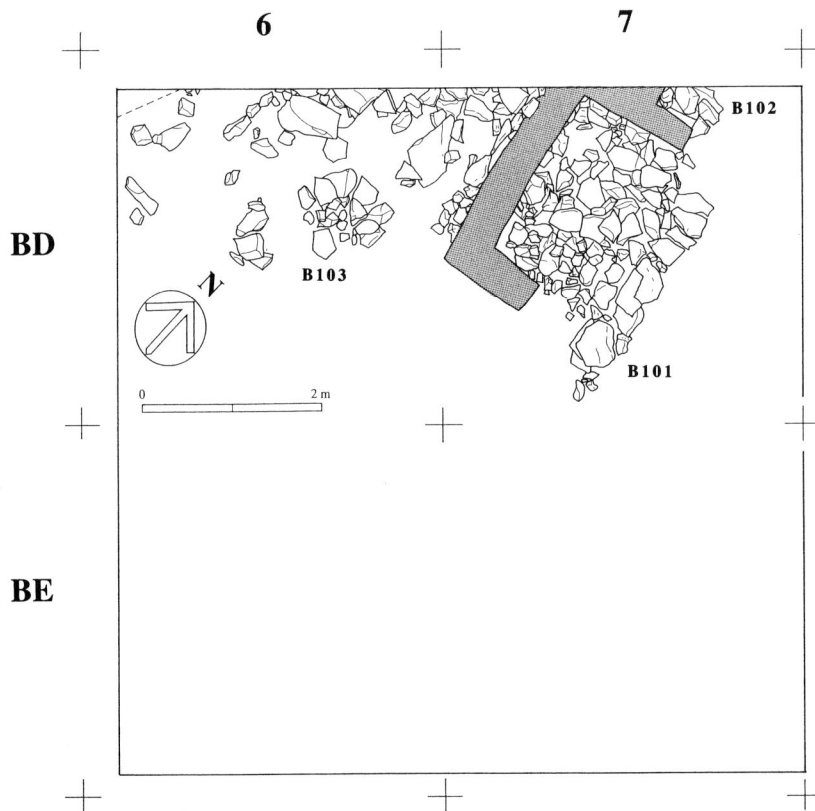

Fig.4.19 Level 1 plans of Sector B.

the rest of which had been eroded by later disturbance. Mudbrick size was similar to that of B101. B102 had a loose, dull reddish brown fill with fewer sherds than those of B101.

B103 was a stone foundation extending westwards in Sector B that joined the B101 foundation. No structure had been preserved on this foundation although slight evidence of a mudbrick wall was revealed in the corner of Sector B (Figs. 4.1 and 4.3). The mudbrick wall could be part of a building complex consisting of B103 and other remains. The B102 and B103 foundation complex, extending 6 m from west to east and 5 m from north to south, was formed mainly of cobbles that were 10 to 50 cm in diameter with a few larger ones of more than 70 cm.

The present surface of Sector B has been eroded by cultivation or strong westerly winds. As the lands are privately owned, no further investigations were possible in the eastern area of Sector B. No architectural remains have been found below the surface of the mound.

4.3 Discussions

4.3.1 Architectural sequence of Sector B

The schematic sequence of architectural complexes in Sector B is represented in Fig. 4.20, with Level 8 the earliest and Level 1 the latest. Level 8 consisted of pits and a hearth, but no buildings. Neolithic pottery sherds were mostly recovered from this level suggesting a Pottery Neolithic formed on virgin soil when the first occupation of Tell Kosak Shamali occurred.

Huge sherds of Early Ubaid to Terminal Ubaid pottery were recovered from the pits or depressions and stone concentrations in Level 7, indicating a Terminal Ubaid period. The area preserved up to this level had been frequently used as a peripheral zone for the discard of sherds throughout the Ubaid periods.

Pottery workshops were the predominant discoveries from Levels 6 and 5. These architectural remains were the earliest building complexes found in Sector B. The main axes of the workshops were aligned virtually north to south. The workshop complex had probably been located in the southeastern periphery of the mound, separated by the ditch or pavement from other areas in the center of the mound. As most sherds recovered in the workshop were clearly neither Ubaid nor Uruk, the pottery assemblages of Levels 6 and 5 were assigned to the Post-Ubaid entity in the Early Uruk-related period, sometimes referred to as the Early Uruk or Late Chalcolithic entity. The Post-Ubaid entity is comparable to the Early Uruk period in southern Mesopotamia, in that the former includes different cultural elements from the southern true Uruk entity. The term Post-Ubaid applied in the present paper really represents the cultural assemblages of the Early Uruk-related period in northern Syria. Although we distinguish this entity from the period, in the strict sense of the meaning, for the sake of convenient usage and simple expression, the term Post-Ubaid is also applied to periodization in this paper (see Chapter 5).

Level 4, in which only stone concentrations and pits were revealed, represents a temporary break in the building complex after the workshop had been abandoned. The main strata of Level 4 consisted of occupational debris and rubbish, unrelated to any building structures. While the accumulated layers of nearly 1 m thick, observed in the trench, might indicate that this level had been used for some period of time, the other areas had also been occupied. As sherds from Level 4 were mostly Post-Ubaid to Middle Uruk in northern Mesopotamia, the level seems to represent the Middle Uruk period.

The mudbrick walls and stone foundations in Level 3 differed from those of the previous level. The Level 3 building complex had been used for domestic purposes, indicated by the complete cooking pot found in situ on the floor of B304. As most sherds, including the cooking pot, were probably Middle Uruk in northern Mesopotamia, Level 3 had formed during the Middle Uruk period.

The unique structure B201 in Level 2 appears to have formed a surrounding wall on the southeastern edge of the mound. The architectural remains were much larger than those of the workshop or domestic areas of Sector B through time; the outer face of B201 was located on the edge of the terrace and its eastern slope; the mudbrick wall was added to the inner side of the stone foundation on nearly horizontal ground, in con-

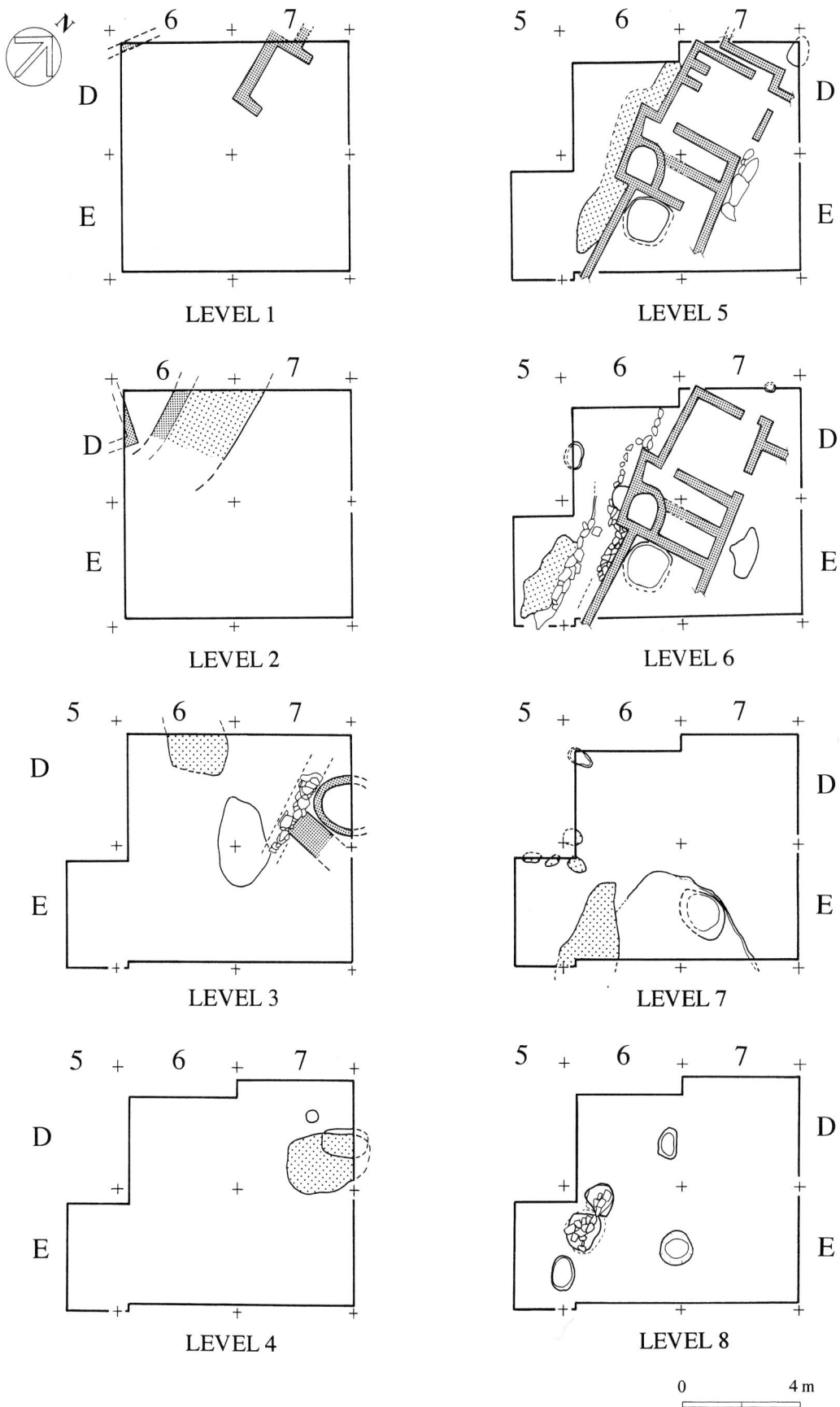

LEVEL 1

LEVEL 2

LEVEL 3

LEVEL 4

LEVEL 5

LEVEL 6

LEVEL 7

LEVEL 8

0   4 m

Fig.4.20 Schematic plans of Sector B.

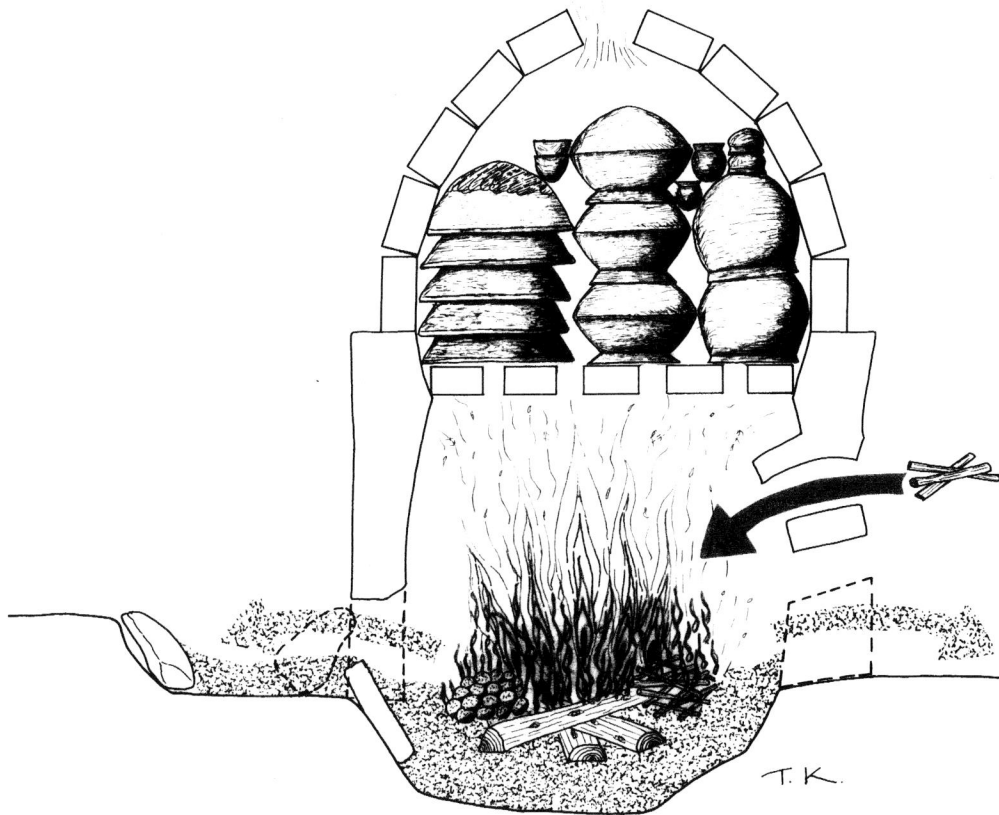

Fig.4.21 Schematic section of B601.

trast to the usual architectural complex style where mudbrick walls were placed on stone foundations, supported by stones (Fig. 4.1).

The fortification-like architectural structure of the Level 2 settlement in Tell Kosak Shamali is reminiscent of the city walls in Levels 6-13 of Tell Sheikh Hassan and Habuba Kabira Süd, Northern Syria (Boese 1995: 123; Strommenger 1980: 35). The B201 wall is slightly narrower (2.5 m wide) than the other fortified walls which are over 3 m thick, and it was not as well preserved. We can presume, however, B201 was distinctive in the architectural sequence in Sector B of Tell Kosak Shamali, and that the qualitative change in the building complex within the settlement was related to social development during the 4th millennium BC.

Level 1 represents the latest phase of the architectural sequence in Sector B, although relatively little of the building complex remains. The complex differs from that of Level 2 in its sturdy construction of upper mudbrick walls and lower stone foundations. It was preserved up to a height of 1 m from the bottom of the stone foundation to the top of the mudbrick wall, making it the sturdiest building structure in Sector B (Fig. 4.1). The sturdy stone foundation, mudbrick buildings and surrounding abundant cobbles may have had a special function other for workshop or domestic use, but this assumption needs to be further researched.

4.3.2 Workshop in Level 6

The pottery workshop of Levels 6 and 5 is one of the most notable discoveries in Sector B. The remarkable, updraught pottery kiln (B601) is comparable with others found in Ubaid to Post-Ubaid or Uruk sites: K-3 of Level I at Tell Songor B, kiln no. 7 of Level I at Tell Abada, R21: 404 of the Protoliterate period at Chogha Mish, and a pottery kiln of Stratum 10 at Tell Habuba Kabira (Matsumoto and Yokoyama 1995: Fig. 32; Jasim 1985: Fig. 36; Alizadeh 1996: Pl. 273; Strommenger 1980: Abb.74 and 75). B601 appears to be an improvement on those of the Ubaid periods found at Tell al-'Abr near Tell Kosak Shamali on the Upper Euphrates. These pottery kilns were horse-shoe-shaped at the base, with few remains of any superstructure (Hammade and Koike 1992: Figs. 10 and 11). B 601 at Tell Kosak Shamali is probably one of the most well-preserved pottery kilns in Ancient West Asia.

The structural remains have allowed us to reconstruct a schematic outline of the firing process of the Level 6 workshop (Fig. 4.21). First, the potters set the perforated clay grate on the inner ledges of the kiln wall. Then they piled a vast number of pottery vessels, which were dry enough to be fired, on the grate. After this, they covered the firing chamber with bricks to make a temporary dome-like vault with some smoke holes. Then they inserted fuel, such as wood, straw or dung which had been temporarily stocked in room B606, through the triangular opening. Finally, after the firing, the potters removed four to five courses of brick blocks that formed the square opening below the fuel supply, and swept the abundant ash from the combustion chamber into ditch B603 on the other side of the mudbrick wall. After some time, when the square opening began to function less effectively, the potters cut an additional semicircular opening on the lower face of the western wall of B601, to enable them to sweep the ash out of the chamber directly into the ditch.

An example comparable to the clay levigation structure B602 has been reported from the Uruk level of Ur; a circular basin in Square D5 built of outwardly extending stepped courses of cement bricks measuring 44 x 16 x 9 - 10 cm (Woolley 1955: 66). We suggest that, although this circular basin at Ur was thought to be for clay pudding, it could have functioned for clay levigation because the circular mudbrick structure is similar to B602 at Tell Kosak Shamali. Few examples of clay levigation structures have been reported, although some evidence for clay storage in a workshop is partially known from several sites of the Halaf to Uruk periods: B-14 in Level IV of Tell Songor B (Halaf), a space near K3 in Level 6 of Tell al-'Abr (Ubaid), and rooms 1012 and 1013 in Level 9 of Tepe Ghabristan (Uruk-related) (Matsumoto and Yokoyama 1995: 34; Hammade and Koike 1992: 115, Fig. 11; Majidzadeh 1989: 161-164).

However, pottery manufacture was less evident in the Level 6 workshop than the clay preparation and firing processes described above. Judging from the location of the rooms and their remarkable finds, however, we can propose probable functions. Room B604, including B602, was the area in which vessels were formed from the fine clay produced in the clay levigation structure. A few pottery making tools were found in B604.

There were very few unfired clay blocks and no pottery making tools on the floor of B609 so that it can be assumed that the room was used for drying pottery vessels before firing. The burnt surface with ash fill from B610 located to the south of B609 supports this hypothesis; potters might have subjected those vessels not dry enough to be fired, to a preliminary firing before loading

them into the kiln B601. At the same time, Room B605 was most likely used for loading vessels into kiln B601. Similar locations of pottery production are known from the pottery workshop like Room 63 and others found at Sarepta, Levant, although the workshop dates to the Phoenician period (Anderson 1987: Fig. 9).

As the preparation of floors B501 and B504 in Level 5 destroyed the upper fill of B607, most pottery vessels preserved at ground level must have been used and abandoned in a final phase of Level 6. These vessels included many different forms with several unique paintings (Fig. 4.14). B607 seems to have been used as a storage room for fired vessels, given that few unfired clay samples and pottery making tools were found in the fill of B607 or the foundation layer of B501 and B504.

Generally, very few pottery production tools were recovered from rooms B604 - B609 in Level 6; it appears that those manufacturing tools had been curated because they were probably precious to the potters who used them for a short time in Level 6.

4.3.3 Workshops in Level 5

In Level 5, too, the pottery production complex continued to be used. B501 is another good example of an updraught pottery kiln with a supporting wall for a grate. It is comparable to one found from Level II (early Uruk-related period) of Tell Qalinj 'Agha in Northern Mesopotamia. The updraught kiln, mentioned as a circular pottery kiln in the report, had a partition wall in the combustion chamber, which was probably a support for a clay grate (Al-Soof 1969: 4, Pl. III). Two pottery kilns have been reported from the Uruk-related level of Tall-i-Bakun in Iran; one with a partition wall is similar to B501 at Tell Kosak Shamali (Langsdorf and McCown 1942: Fig. 6). All these comparable examples were, however, circular in plan and clearly different from B501. The rectangular plan with supporting wall added to the pre-existing wall in Level 5 of Tell Kosak Shamali was distinctive of pottery kiln structures through the 5th to 4th millennium BC in West Asia.

Until the stone pavement of B502 was constructed in Level 5, the semicircular opening for ash removal had been closed while B601 was in use. It seems that B601 was heavily worn by long use for firing in Level 6; the accumulated waste and debris from pottery production in B603 was the same height as the B601 ash fill, suggesting it had not been swept out as well as in former periods (Fig. 4.2). After the heavily worn B601 chamber had been abandoned in Level 5, a huge amount of broken sherds, disturbed clinker, and pottery production tools such as clay ring-scrapers had been discarded. At the same time the northern wall of B606 had been broken down, and B605 was no longer used to load pottery vessels into B601. After B601 had been abandoned, however, the pre-existing structure B602 and Room B604 seems to have been used for pottery manufacturing through Level 5.

Pottery production tools such as clay ring scrapers and clay smoothers were distinctly concentrated in the fill of the heavily worn kiln B601. It is likely, therefore, that a room such as B604, including the clay levigation structure B602 joining B601, was used for vessel formation. Potters probably manufactured vessels in B604 and then discarded the worn-out tools in the adjacent B601. It is also notable that the work area was located slightly away from Kiln B501 and Room B504. A similar spatial pattern of effective workshop rooms has been recognized in the ceramic industry of Sarepta where workshops for the manufacture of vessels were located behind the kilns, or slightly away from the stoking rooms (Anderson 1987: Figs. 6-9). The rarity of manufacturing tools in B504 suggests that it may have functioned as a stoking room under a roof made rainproof with bitumen as mentioned above.

A fragment of a clay ring scraper was also found in the southern part of B505, an area which may have had a similar function to B604. In the northern area of B505, on the other hand, a fired surface was revealed suggesting a preliminary firing of unevenly dried vessels before loading them into B501, as was the case for B610 in Level 6. Therefore, a couple of stages in the pottery production process in Level 5 probably took place in B505.

Furthermore, B503 was distinguished from the

B504 and B505 complex by the two rows of a mudbrick wall extending northwards in Sector B. The floor of B503 was tightly packed and contained a storage jar in a circular pit (B506). Fine, white clay was deposited above the floor, although the exposed level was higher than that of Level 5 so that the clay deposits might have been placed there in preparation for pottery manufacture. The B503 area could, therefore, have been an additional room of another workshop complex located adjacent the B501, B502, B504, and B505 complex.

4.3.4 Pottery production in Levels 6-5

The ditch and pavements of B603 and B502 in Levels 6 to 5 of Sector B clearly separated the workshop complexes from the residential areas that may have been located in the center of the settlement. This workshop location certainly differs from that of the Ubaid periods in Sector A, when pottery production had probably taken place in an open area within the settlement rather than away from the residential zones (Chapter 3). It was not until Levels 6 - 5 of Sector B that the pottery workshop was moved to a peripheral area. Comparable examples are known from such early Uruk-related periods as Level 1c in Tell Musharifa, northern Mesopotamia, Level II of Tell Qalinj 'Agha and Level 9 of Tepe Ghabristan, and from the Late Uruk period in Habuba Kabira Süd (Oguchi 1987: Fig. 12; Al-Soof 1969: Pl. III; Majidzadeh 1989: Fig. 23; Strommenger 1980: Abb. 16). It is emphasized that this resulted from spatial divisions of the settlements related to function in the early Uruk-related, Post-Ubaid, period. The pottery workshop of the Post-Ubaid period seems to have been moved away from settlement center for some reasons.

Pottery production in Levels 6 - 5 of Sector B at Tell Kosak Shamali could have been a full-time activity rather than restricted to the dry season; bitumen fragments, with traces of vegetable-like materials such as reeds, were found on the floor of B504 and B505, suggestive of their use to seal roof beams when rainproofing the structure. Moreover, bitumen traces were evident on the surface of large jar sherds found near the bottom of the northern combustion chamber of B501. Some reinforced roof beams might have been burnt down by workshop fires, resulting in the traces of bitumen on the floor revealed during excavation. Kiln B501, the adjoining rooms B504 and the northern part of B505 seem to have been originally covered by a roof. This remarkable reconstruction indicates that production was not restricted to the dry season, but that the full-time production continued up to the rainy season. Therefore, it is stressed that specialized pottery production appears to have already been undertaken by full time potters in the Post-Ubaid period of Tell Kosak Shamali.

4.4 Conclusions

The above discussions concerning the building complexes in Sector B provide a brief history of the architectural sequence. Initial occupation appears to have taken place on virgin ground in Level 8 in the Pottery Neolithic, leaving no evidence of structures. Level 7 witnesses peripheral use of the settlement until the Terminal Ubaid period. The mudbrick pottery workshop complex in Levels 6 to 5 was active on an almost full-time basis during the 4th millennium BC Post-Ubaid period. After the pottery workshop had been abandoned, the area once again became a peripheral or non valuable zone of the settlement in Level 4, during the early phase of Middle Uruk period. Moreover, domestic use of the tell is seen in Level 3 during the Middle Uruk period. Fortifications are evident in the Level 2 settlement, while solid architecture was introduced in Level 1 through the late Middle Uruk period.

References

Alizadeh, A. (1985) A Protoliterate pottery kiln from Chogha Mish. *Iran* 23: 39-50.

Alizadeh, A. (ed.) (1996) *Chogha Mish Vol. I: The First Five Seasons of Excavations 1961-1971.* Oriental Institute Publications, Vol. 101. Chicago: The Oriental Institute.

Anderson, W. P. (1987) The kilns and workshops of Sarepta (Sarafand, Lebanon): Remnants of a Phoenician ceramic industry. *Berytus* 35: 41-66.

Boese, J. (ed.) (1995) *Ausgrabungen I Tell Sheikh Hassan I, Vorläufige Berichte über die Grabungskampagnen 1984-1990 und 1992-1994.* Schriften zur Vorderasiatischen Archäologie 5. Saarbrücken.

Hammade, H. and Y. Koike (1992) Syrian archaeological expedition in the Tishreen Dam Basin: Excavations at Tell al-'Abr 1990 and 1991. *Damaszener Mitteilungen* 6: 109-175.

Jasim, S. A. (1985) *The Ubaid Period in Iraq: Recent Excavations in the Hamrin Region, 2vols.* BAR i.s. 267. Oxford: British Archaeological Reports.

Koizumi, T. (2000) Specialisation of pottery production in the Ubaid to Uruk periods: Pottery-making techniques and workshop locations (written in Japanese). *Journal of West Asian Archaeology* 1: 11-31.

Langsdorff, A. and D.E. McCown (1942) *Tall-i-Bakun A: Season of 1938.* Oriental Institute Publications 59. Chicago: The Oriental Institute.

van Loon, M. (ed.) (1988) *Hammam et-Turkman I.* Istanbul: Nederlands Historisch-Archeologisch Instituut te Istanbul.

Majidzadeh, Y. (1977) The development of the pottery kiln in Iran from prehistorical periods. *Paléorient* 3: 207-221.

Majidzadeh, Y. (1989) An early Industrial proto-urban center on the central plateau of Iran: Tepe Ghabristan. In: *Essays in Ancient Civilization presented to Helene J. Kantor,* edited by A. Leonard Jr. and B. B. Williams, pp.157-173. Studies in Ancient Oriental Civilization 47. Chicago: The Oriental Institute.

Matsumoto, K. and S. Yokoyama (1995) Excavations at Tell Songor B. *Al-Rāfidān* 16: 1-273.

Molist, M. (1998) Espace collectif et espace domestique dans le Néolithique des IXème et VIIIème millénaires B.P. au Nord de la Syrie: Apports du site de Tell Halula (Vallee de l'Euphrate). In: *Espace Naturel, Espace Habité en Syrie du Nord (10e-2e millénaires av. J.-C.),* edited by M. Fortin and O. Aurenche, pp. 115-130. Lyon: Maison de l'Orient Méditerranéen.

Nishiaki, Y., T. Koizumi, M. Le Mière, and T. Oguchi (1999) Prehistoric occupations at Tell Kosak Shamali, the Upper Euphrates, Syria. *Akkadica* 113: 13-68.

Oguchi, H. (1987) Working report on first season of Japanese archaeological excavation, Saddam Salvage Project, Tell Musharifa. In: *Researches on the Antiquities of Saddam Dam Basin Salvage and Other Researches,* pp.49-55. Baghdad: State Organization of Antiquities and Heritage.

Postgate, J. N. (1990) Excavations at Abu Salabikh, 1988-89. *Iraq* 52: 95-106.

Schwartz, G. M. (1988) *A Ceramic Chronology from Tell Leilan: Operation 1,* edited by H. Weiss. Yale Tell Leilan Research I. New Haven: Yale University Press.

al-Soof, B. A. (1969) Excavations at Tell Qalinj Agha (Erbil), summer 1968. *Sumer* 25: 3-42.

Strommenger, E. (1980) *Habuba Kabira: eine Stadt vor 5000 Jahren.* Mainz am Rhein: Verlag Philipp von Zabern.

Woolley, C. L. (1955) *Ur Excavations, Vol. IV: The Early Periods.* Publication of the Joint Expedition of the British Museum and of the Museum of the University of Pennsylvania to Mesopotamia. Philadelphia: University Museum / London: British Museum.

Pl. 4.1 Sections of Sector B.
1. The SW-NE section of Squares BD6 and BD7 (from the southeast).
2. The SE-NW section of Squares BD6 and BE6 (from the northeast).
3. The NW-SE section of Squares BD7 and BE7 (from the southwest).

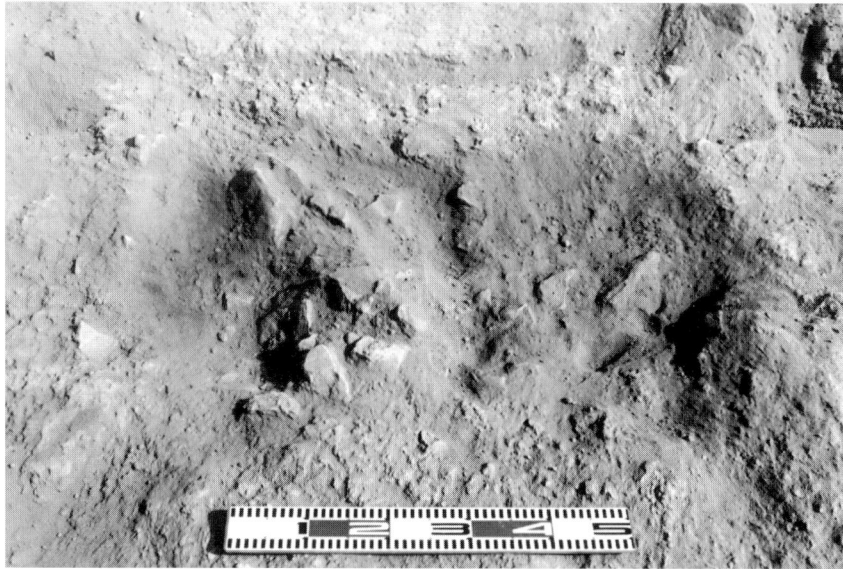

Pl. 4.2 Architectural remains and artifacts of Sector B (Level 8).
1. Hearth B801 (from the southwest).
2. Limestone cobbles in Pits B803 and B804 (from the east).
3. Pits B803 and B804 (from the west).

Pl. 4.3 Architectural remains of Sector B (Level 8).
1. Jar in Pit B804 (from the north).
2. Stone concentration in Pit B802 (from the southeast).
3. Stone concentration B806 (from the southeast).
4. Virgin surface of Sector B (from the southwest).

Pl. 4.4 Architectural remains of Sector B (Level 7).
1. Shallow depression B701 (from the southeast).
2. Stone pavement B704 (from the northeast).
3. Stone concentration B705 (from the northeast).

Pl. 4.5 Architectural remains of Sector B (Levels 6 and 5).
1. Ground level of the workshops of Levels 6 and 5 (from the north).
2. General view of the workshops of Levels 6 and 5 (from the west).

Pl. 4.6 Architectural remains of Sector B (Level 6).
1. Pottery kiln B601(from the northeast).
2. Ash removal of Pottery kiln B601 (from the west).

Pl. 4.7 Architectural remains of Sector B (Level 6).
1. The N-S section of B601 (from the east).
2. Kiln wall of B601 (from the south).
3. Mudbrick wall between Compartments B605 and B606 (from the southeast).

Pl. 4.8 Architectural remains of Sector B (Level 6).
1. Basin for clay levigation B602 (from the southeast).
2. Kiln wall of B601 and Ditch B603 (from the northwest).
3. Ditch B603 (from the south).

Pl. 4.9 Architectural remains of Sector B (Levels 6 and 5).
1. Compartments B605, B606, and B607 (from the west).
2. Compartments B503, B504, and B505 (from the southeast).
3. Burnt surface B610 (from the east).

Pl. 4.10 Architectural remains of Sector B (Level 5).
1. *Workshop of Level 5 (from the west).*
2. *Pottery kiln B501 (from the east).*
3. *Ground level of B501 (from the southeast).*

Pl. 4.11 Architectural remains of Sector B (Level 5).
1. The N-S Section of B501 (from the east).
2. Kiln wall of B501 (from the south).
3. Broken chamber of B501 (from the southeast).

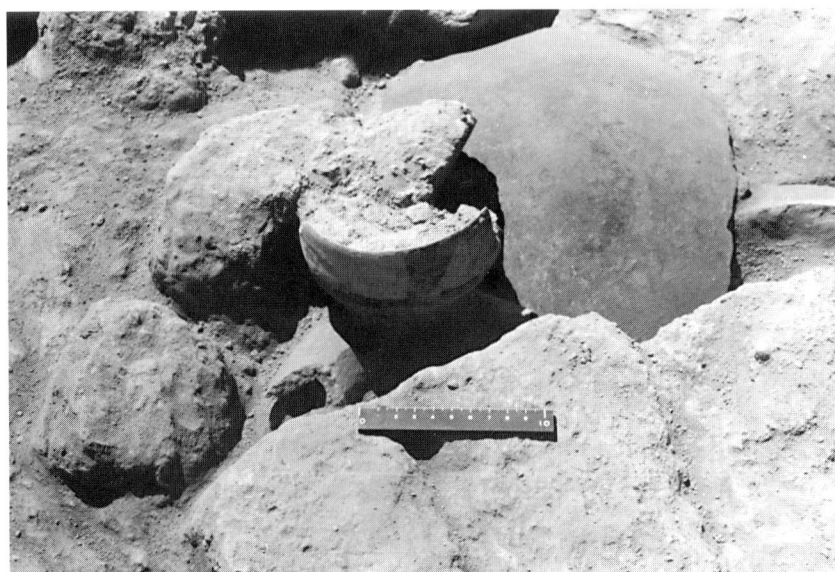

Pl. 4.12 Architectural remains and artifacts of Sector B (Level 5).
1. Ground level of B504 (from the east).
2. Floor of B504 (from the northwest).
3. Kernos in B504 (from the northeast).

1

2

3

Pl. 4.13 Architectural remains of Sector B (Level 5).

1. Southern part of Stone pavement B502 (from the south).
2. Northern part of Stone pavement B502 (from the south).
3. Building complex B505 (from the north).

Pl. 4.14 Architectural remains of Sector B (Level 4).
1. General view of Level 4 (from the north).
2. Stone concentration B401 (from the northwest).

Pl. 4.15 Architectural remains and artifacts of Sector B (Level 3).
1. Building complex B302 (from the north).
2. Cooking pot in B304 (from the southwest).
3. Oven B305 (from the southeast).

Pl. 4.16 Architectural remains of Sector B (Levels 2 and 1).
1. Architectural structure B201 (from the north).
2. Building complex B101 (from the west).

5

Radiocarbon dates and the absolute chronology of Tell Kosak Shamali

Yoshihiro Nishiaki

5.1 Introduction

The archaeological sequence of Tell Kosak Shamali yielded a total of 13 radiocarbon dates. They represent the first series of this kind of data for the Ubaid and Post-Ubaid occupations in the Upper Euphrates valley, which enables us to consider the late prehistoric chronology of this particular area in a larger regional context. This relatively large number of dates became available only through the introduction of the AMS method (TKa series), since the preservation of organic materials was generally poor for most of the levels. Processing by the conventional β counting method was possible for four samples only (TK series; see Appendix).

Table 5.1 shows the provenance and condition of the samples, their conventional BP and calibrated BC dates. Calibration was based on Radiocarbon Calibration Program, CALIB rev. 4.3 (Stuiver and Reimer 1993). The dates obtained are generally concomitant with stratigraphic order, but the inconsistency in a few cases require some comments.

5.2 Early Northern Ubaid and the Late Neolithic

The most secure samples are those from Level 10 of Sector A, all of which consist of carbonized plant remains recovered *in situ* on the floor of the burnt building. Accordingly the dates for them should be considered more reliable than others, and give us a good starting point for discussion. Three actually show the same date, 6050 BP (TK-1000, TKa-11656, 11860), while the rest (TKa-11859) indicates a slightly older date. The latter was taken from a charred large wood beam from Room 10A03, which perhaps once formed part of the ceiling structure. There are a number of local ethnographic observations showing reuse through generations of this sort of ceiling beam for house building, and

would explain the present case. The date of 6050 BP (ca. 5190-4800 BC) can thus be reasonably adopted for Level 10. The date from Level 11 (TK-999), 6080 BP (ca. 5210-4810 BC) is slightly older but very close in age to that of Level 10, matching our expectation from stratigraphic observation (Chapter 3). These dates all accord well with our ceramic periodization, which places Level 10 at the end of the early northern Ubaid (Nishiaki *et al.* 1999), around 5000 BC. They are virtually identical to the dates from equivalent layers of Stratum III at Tell Mashnaqa in the Khabur valley (Thuesen 2000).

Two dates from the underlying levels are clearly inconsistent with the above. The samples were both taken from the fill not associated with any structural remains. In addition, despite their lower stratigraphic position, the sampled layers were not so deep, the sample for TK-998 only about 35 cm and that for TK-997 approximately 55 cm below the present surface. Contamination from modern environments might have effected the dates of these samples.

The date for Pit 1805 of Level 18 (TKa-11668), or 6140 BP (ca. 5280-4860 BC), is obviously unacceptable for the Neolithic period. Level 18 is a poorly defined one, consisting of pit deposits only, whose ceramic assemblages indicate a very short period of occupation, perhaps dated at ca. 7250-7150 BP on a typological basis (Chapter 7). Pit 1805 is one of the pits whose top had been scraped by the Ubaid layers of Level 17, and an animal burrow had cut its northeastern part. These suggest some later deposits could have intruded into this pit, although the associated pottery remains were all Neolithic ones (Chapter 7). The date thus should be better considered as that for an intrusive material from an overlying early Ubaid level.

Identification of dates for the earliest Ubaid levels in Sector A of Tell Kosak Shamali have a crucial

Table 5.1 Radiocarbon dates for Tell Kosak Shamali.

Laboratory No.	Level	Conventional date BP	Calibrated date BC (1 sigma)	Calibrated date BC (2 sigma)	Sample provenance	Material
Sector A						
TKa-11660	1	5900+/-150	4940(4775, 4747,4736) - 4553	5209(4775, 4747,4736) - 4404	95KSL AD4-3	charcoal from the fill of Room 101
TK-1000	10	6050+/-90	5054(4939, 4868,4861) - 4804	5256(4939, 4868,4861) - 4719	94KSL A10-3a	charcoal from the floor of Room 10A09
TKa-11656	10	6050+/-100	5191(4940, 4867,4862) - 4800	5278(4940, 4867,4862) - 4713	96KSL AE6-17	carbonized grain from Feature 10A27
TKa-11860	10	6050+/-100	5192(4940, 4867,4862) - 4800	5279(4940, 4867,4862) - 4713	96KSL AD5-99-10	charcoal from Room 10A02
TKa-11859	10	6130+/-110	5259(5051) - 4855	5320(5051) - 4739	96KSL AE6-19-1	charcoal from Room 10A03
TK-999	11	6080+/-120	5208(4958) - 4805	5303(4958) - 4695	94KSL C10-3	charcoal from the fill of Level 11 (95KSL AF3-8)
TK-998	12	5790+/-100	4774(4685, 4676,4675, 4635,4621) - 4501	4899(4685, 4676,4675, 4635,4621) - 4374	94KSL A11-7 Upper	charcoal from the fill of Level 12 (95KSL AF4-7)
TK-997	13	5330+/-150	4335(4220, 4196,4161, 4121,4110, 4090,4081, 4059,4053) - 3975	4456(4220, 4196,4161, 4121,4110, 4090,4081, 4059,4053) - 3796	94KSL A11-7 Lower	charcoal from the fill accumulated on Feature 1309 (95KSL AF4-9)
TKa-11668	18	6140+/-120	5279(5055) - 4855	5360(5055) - 4733	95KSL AG5-9	charcoal from the fill of Pit 1805
Sector B						
TKa-11674	3	4360+/-100	3256(2921) - 2844	3354(2921) - 2699	95KSL BE7-5	ash from the floor of Room B304
TKa-11655	5	5710+/-120	4709(4539) - 4371	4830(4539) - 4334	96KSL BD7-46	ash from the floor of Room B504
TKa-11678	6	5550+/-120	4496(4360) - 4259	4674(4360) - 4053	94KSL B9-T	ash from the combustion room of Kiln B601
TKa-11664	6	5910+/-160	4948(4779, 4746,4743) - 4553	5255(4779, 4746,4743) - 4402	96KSL BD6-28	ash from the fill of Feature B603

importance in understanding the time and process of the Ubaid expansion into the Upper Euphrates from south Mesopotamia. On the basis of the radiocarbon dates from Tell Mashnaqa, the Khabur basin, Thuesen (2000: 76) argued that the earliest Ubaid occupations could have appeared in the Khabur region, around 5200 BC, and advanced towards the Balikh and the Upper Euphrates in the next few hundred years. However, a contrary view, suggesting an earlier expansion to the Balikh and the west rather than to the Khabur, has also been presented (Hole 1998: 43; cf. Akkermans 1988: 226). The date of the earliest Ubaid level of Tell Kosak Shamali may shed new light upon the argument of the Ubaidian expansion processes.

Considering the best grounded dates for Levels 10 and 11, the thickness of the underlying deposits, the identified number of architectural levels, and the suggested occupational break of an unknown period between Levels 14 and 13 (Chapter 3), the date of TKa-11668 seems to represent a minimum date for Level 17. It is rather likely that Level 17 be assigned to a period close to or even earlier than that of the oldest Ubaid occupation in the Khabur region. Supports for this interpretation come from the ceramic typology as well. The lowest Ubaid levels of Sector A certainly contained Halafian elements, suggesting that the Ubaid penetration was made when the local Halafian settlements still existed in this region. Further they included pottery resembling the vessels known from the Ubaid 2 to early Ubaid 3 levels of southern Iraqi sites such as Ras al 'Amiya and Eridu (Nishiaki *et al.* 1999: 31). The curious structure reminiscent of a Halafian tholos also belongs to this stage (Level 14; Chapter 3). From these, although we tentatively refer to all the lower levels of Sector A (Levels 17 to 10) as "the Early Northern Ubaid", they may in fact contain levels corresponding to a Halaf-Ubaid contact period on the Upper Euphrates. Unfortunately the exact dates for the beginning of this contact or the onset of the "true" Ubaid at Tell Kosak Shamali can not be fixed by the present radiocarbon measurements, but are left for discussion in the artifactual analyses to be presented in the forthcoming volumes of this report.

5.3 Late Northern Ubaid to the Middle Uruk

In the upper sequence of the Ubaid, we have a single date (TKa-11660) only. It comes from the "Terminal Northern Ubaid" of Level 1. In the literature on the Khabur basin excavations, the youngest date for the Ubaid and the oldest date for the Post-Ubaid from Tell Kuran, Tell Ziyada and Tell Mashnaqa, point to around 5750 BP (ca. 4770-4460 BC; Hole 1999). However a difficulty exists in determining the date of the end of the Ubaid from the publications, partly because of inconsistency of terminology. This report refers to the "Terminal Northern Ubaid" to indicate the latest phase of the local Ubaidian cultural entity, while some authors apparently use the term as a synonym as, or as including the "Post-Ubaid" of the present report (Hole 2000: 22-23; Thuesen 2000: 75-76). Our "Terminal Northern Ubaid" may correspond to the earlier part of that period for others. Consequently the current dates published for the "Terminal Ubaid" or the "Post-Ubaid" of other sites should be regarded with caution. Nevertheless it is logically possible to stress that the date for Level 1 (5900 BP: ca. 4940-4550 BC) is within the latest range of the Ubaid, and is somewhat older than its real end. It implies that Level 1 of Tell Kosak Shamali does not represent the terminal stage *sense lato* of the Ubaid. As a matter of fact there are a lot of unexcavated deposits in the north of Sector A, which might well have contained even later Ubaidian occupations levels.

One of the dates for Level 6 of Sector B (TKa-11664; 5910BP: ca. 4950-4550 BC) is very similar to that of Level 1 of Sector A. It is too old for the Post-Ubaid period. One possible explanation is the occurrence of sample contamination from the older deposits, for the sample was the ash filled in a ditch dug into the underlying Ubaid level. Level 7 of Sector B consists of disturbed layers including the late to the terminal Ubaidian artifacts (Chapter 4).

The other date for Level 6 (TKa-11678) and the one for Level 5 (TKa-11635), i.e., 5550 BP (ca. 4550-4260 BC) and 5710 BP (ca. 4710-4370 BC) both fit in the earliest range of the "Post-Ubaid" dates from the Khabur basin sites (Hole 1999). However, they are in the reverse of their stratigraphic position. The samples were obtained *in situ* from a combustion chamber of a kiln, and a room floor respectively. In consideration of the unlikelihood of secondary disturbance in the combustion chamber, which was covered with a massive accumulation of ash enclosed within mudbrick walls about 120 cm high, the former date (TKa-11678) may be more reasonably accepted. It relates the "Post-Ubaid" levels of Tell Kosak Shamali to the Late Chalcolithic 1 of the Santa Fe chronology (ca. 4500-4200 BC; Algaze *et al.* 1998).

The date for Level 3 (TKa-11674) of the Middle Uruk is too late, even if we consider the occupational gap of an unknown period of time after the "Post-Ubaid" settlement was abandoned. The sample was not recognizable plant remains but ash discovered on a floor level, which may partly have contributed to this erroneous measurement.

5.4 Conclusion

Fig. 5.1 presents the dates in relation to the archaeological sequence of Tell Kosak Shamali, together with the estimated dates from the literature. The Ubaidian occupation at Tell Kosak Shamali started perhaps, at least one hundred and a half years or more before 5000 BC and lasted to around 4400/4500 BC, when the "Post-Ubaid" entity appeared as a local evolution. This reconstruction essentially fits in the chronological framework developed by the recent radiocarbon dating and its calibration studies (Evin 1995), in which Ubaid 3 is placed into 5400 to 5000 BC and Ubaid 4 into 5000 to 4500 BC.

As described in Chapters 3 and 4 the levels at Tell Kosak Shamali were defined strictly on an architectural basis. A considerable amount of effort was made in separating levels in as much detail as possible, identifying such minute episodes of building activities as rebuilding of and annexing to the existent construction. Each level, about 30 cm thick in average in Sector A, perhaps represents a period of not much more than 30 - 50 years. This estimate finds support from the radiocarbon dates, as well as the ethnographic evidence on the durability of traditional mudbrick work.

References

Akkermans, P.M.M.G. (1988) Period IV pottery. In: *Hammam et-Turkman I, Report on the University of Amsterdam's 1981-1984 Excavations in Syria, Vol. I,* edited by M. N. van Loon, pp. 181-285. Istanbul: Nederlands Historisch-Archaeologisch Instituut.

Algaze, G., T. D'Altroy, M. Frangipane, H. Nissen, H. Pittman, S. Pollock, M. Rothman, G. Schwartz, G. Stein, and H. Wright (1998) *http://www.science.widener.edu/ssci/mesopotamia/.*

Evin, J. (1995) Possibilité et nécessité de la calibration des datations C-14 de l'archéologie du Proche-Orient. *Paléorient* 21(1): 5-16.

Hole, F. (1997) Paleoenvironment and human society in the Jezireh of Northern Mesopotamia 20,000 - 6,000 BP. *Paléorient* 23(2): 39-49.

Hole, F. (ed.) (1999) *Miscellaneous Papers of the Yale University Khabur Basin Project, Northeast Syria, 1986-1997.* Unpublished manuscript. New Haven: Yale University.

Hole, F. (2000) The prehistory of the Khabur. *Subartu* 7: 17-27.

Nishiaki, Y., T. Koizumi, M. Le Mière and T. Oguchi (1999) Prehistoric occupations at Tell Kosak Shamali, the Upper Euphrates, Syria. *Akkadica* 113: 13-68.

Stuiver, M. and P.J. Reimer (1993) High-precision bidecadal calibration of the radiocarbon time scale, AD 1950-500 BC and 2500-6000 BC. *Radiocarbon* 35(1): 215-230.

Thuesen, I. (2000) Ubaid expansion in the Khabur: new evidence from Tell Mashnaqa. *Subartu* 7: 71-79.

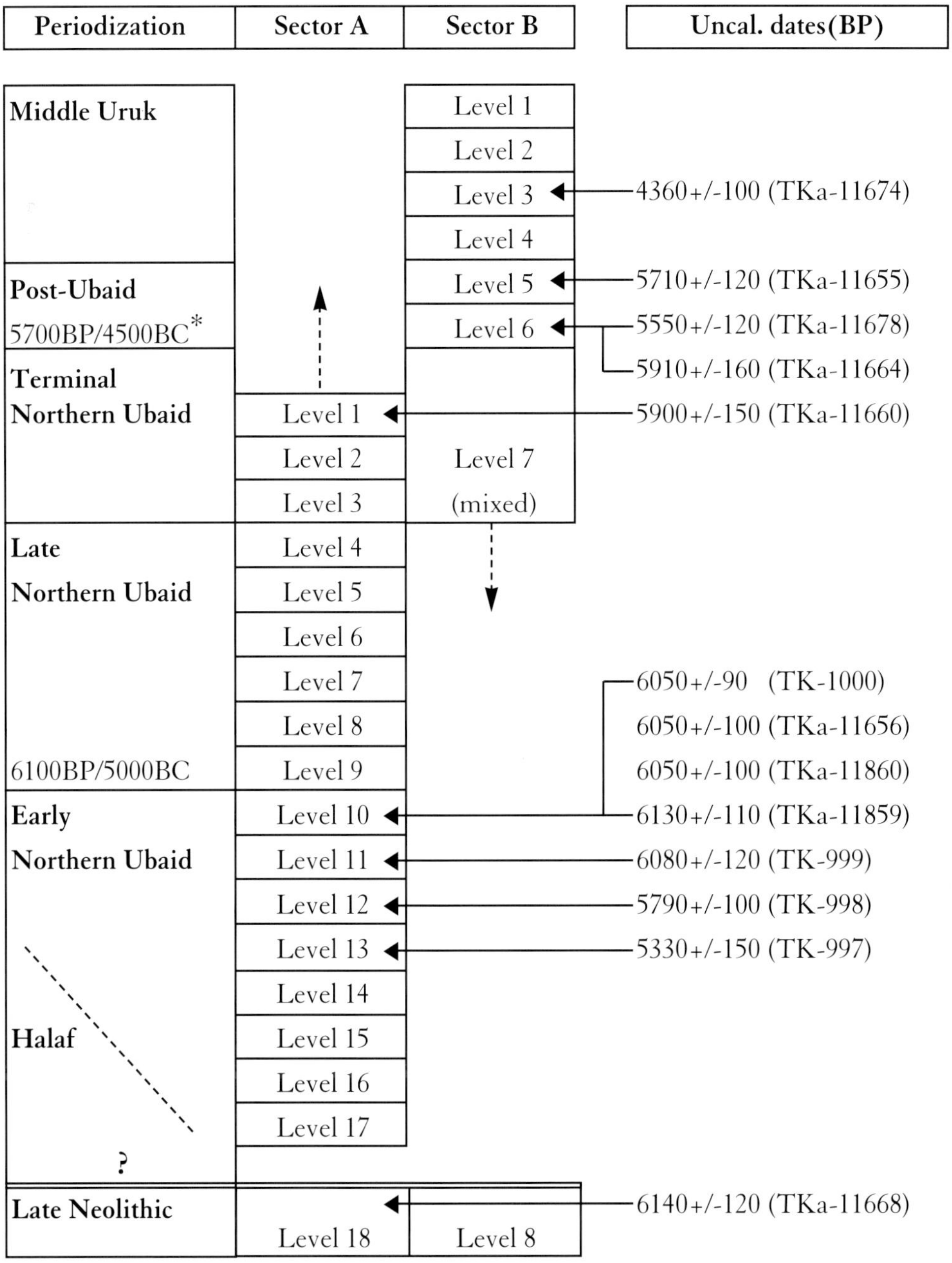

Periodization	Sector A	Sector B	Uncal. dates(BP)
Middle Uruk		Level 1	
		Level 2	
		Level 3 ◄	—4360+/-100 (TKa-11674)
		Level 4	
Post-Ubaid 5700BP/4500BC*		Level 5 ◄	—5710+/-120 (TKa-11655)
		Level 6 ◄	—5550+/-120 (TKa-11678)
			—5910+/-160 (TKa-11664)
Terminal Northern Ubaid	Level 1 ◄		—5900+/-150 (TKa-11660)
	Level 2	Level 7	
	Level 3	(mixed)	
Late Northern Ubaid	Level 4		
	Level 5		
	Level 6		
	Level 7		—6050+/-90 (TK-1000)
	Level 8		6050+/-100 (TKa-11656)
6100BP/5000BC	Level 9		6050+/-100 (TKa-11860)
Early Northern Ubaid	Level 10 ◄		6130+/-110 (TKa-11859)
	Level 11 ◄		6080+/-120 (TK-999)
	Level 12 ◄		5790+/-100 (TK-998)
	Level 13 ◄		5330+/-150 (TK-997)
	Level 14		
Halaf	Level 15		
	Level 16		
	Level 17		
?			
Late Neolithic	Level 18 ◄	Level 8	—6140+/-120 (TKa-11668)

Fig.5.1 The archaeological sequence and the radiocarbon dates.
* The estimated dates are based on Evin (1995).

*Kunio Yoshida and
Yumiko Miyazaki*

APPENDIX | # Methods of radiocarbon dating at Tell Kosak Shamali

Samples

Four samples were received on November 11, 1994, 3 samples were received on February 6, 1996 and 10 samples were received on February 4, 1999. Most of the 1996 samples were charcoal only, but the 1994 and 1999 samples were mixtures of charcoal, ash, sand and soil. The amount and the sample condition are shown in Table 5.2.

The first four samples were dated by β-counting method, in which case the Laboratory No. is described as "TK-No." and the others were dated by AMS method as "TKa-No."

General manner for pretreatment

Archaeological samples for dating may be contaminated by ^{14}C at several stages. There will have been *in situ* absorption of CO_2 gas, carbonate and organic materials, and similar contamination occurs during sample preparation for dating.

Prior to the following sample preparation, samples were checked carefully to remove contaminating foreign materials such as rootlets or grains of soil etc. by handpicking. Grains of soil on surface were removed using a surgical knife under a microscopic observation. It was cut off around the sample.

β-counting method

Sample preparation

Charcoals were boiled in 1% NaOH solution for a few hours to remove dissolved humic acid and lignin, followed by boiling in dil. HC1 solution to remove carbonates. CO_2 was produced by combustion in the oxygen stream.

Samples were converted into acetylene by a conventional method, as $CO_2 \rightarrow CaCO_3 \rightarrow SrCO_3 \rightarrow SrC_2 \rightarrow C_2H_2$ reaction. The overall yield in the conversion of CO_2 to C_2H_2 was 62~67%. In this case, charcoals in the samples were insufficient, and samples were diluted with dead carbon in carbonate form at the $CaCO_3$ stage. The dilution is expressed in a dilution factor, "f", which is the ratio of the final weight to the original weight (TK-997; f=8.14, TK-998; f=3.29, TK-999; f=5.61, TK-1000; f=3.11). The chemical yield of purified $CaCO_3 \rightarrow SrCO_3$ reaction is almost 100% in our system.

Counting

Our laboratory uses a proportional counter with an actual volume of 1.2 liter. A ring guard counter of 1 liter of surrounding the central counter is arranged in anti-coincidence.

The counter is shielded with iron 25cm thick and paraffin 5cm thick. Purified acetylene gas was introduced into the counter for counting at a pressure at 1 atm at room temperature (23°C).

Background is reduced to 0.7 cpm and the counting rate of the NBS old oxalic acid (SRM4990) is 15.4 cpm at the normal counting pressure. The activity of each sample was counted for 20 cycles of 100 min. at three times at long intervals. The "modern" value for all dates is 95% of the activity of the NBS oxalic acid. All dates are based on the Libby value, 5568 yr, for the half-life. The ages are expressed in years before 1950, denoted by BP.

The ages are the average values of dates which agree with each other within 2 σ. The errors given include the standard deviation of the counting rate of the NBS standard, of unknown samples, and of the background.

AMS method

Sample preparation (see Fig. 5.2)
AAA treatment 【*Acid-Alkali-Acid treatment*】
Samples were treated to remove contamination during being buried. The supernatant solution was separated using a centrifuge and taken off using a pasteur pipet. Samples were treated in glass tubes (10ml) during the sequence.

(1) Acid pretreatment (mainly for removing carbonate made or contaminated during being buried)
The solution of 1M HCl was poured into the glass tube, and heated at 80°C for 8 hours. Afterwards the sample was cleansed using Milli-Q water.
(2) Alkali pretreatment (for removing the acidic matter, especially humic acid etc.)
The solution of 0.001~0.05M NaOH was poured into a glass tube according to the state of each sample, and suitable heat treatment (room temperature~80°C) was applied. Afterwards the sample was cleansed using Milli-Q water.
(3) Acid pretreatment (for removing carbonate made during alkali pretreatment)
The solution of 1M HCl was poured into a glass tube, and heated at 80°C for 8 hours. Afterwards, the sample was cleansed using Milli-Q water.
(4) Drying
The sample was dried in the glass tube by heating at 80°C.

Oxidation
The sample was put in a small quartz glass cup (6mm $\phi \times$50mm) with 1g copper (II) oxide. At this time, it is better to be mixed the sample and copper oxide well. The small cup was inserted into a Vycor tube (9 $\phi \times$400mm) and silver foil was put on the small cup. The Vycor tube was connected to a vacuum line and evacuated to be attained high vacuum level (10^{-6}mmHg). The tube was cut to be sealed at an appropriate position for each sample with a propane torch and oxygen gas. The Vycor tube was then heated at 500°C for 30 minutes and 850°C for 2 hours continuously, and oxidized carbon in the sample changed to CO_2 completely.

Purification of carbon dioxide
Once again the Vycor tube of sample was connected to the vacuum line, and water and other impurities were removed and CO_2 was purified by difference temperatures between cooled ethyl alcohol (solid? liquid) (-114°C) and liquid nitrogen (-195.8°C).

Reduction
One **g** of Fe powder (99.9+%: <325 mesh (40 μ m), Aldorich reagent) was

put in a small quartz glass cup (6 ϕ × 15mm), and inserted into a Vycor tube (9 ϕ ×300mm). Reducing Fe powder in advance this tube was connected to a vacuum line, and evacuated until a high vacuum was attained. 0.5 atm of pure H_2 (99.99999%) was introduced into the tube, which was then heated at 450°C for 1 hour. As a result, Fe powder was reduced from its oxidized surface to pure metal, after which it was evacuated again. Purified CO_2, was introduced into the tube to get 1mg carbon after reduction and 2.1 times as much pure H_2 gas as sample CO_2 was added to the amount of substance (mol). The tube was sealed with a torch. The bottom of the sealed tube was heated at 650°C for 10 hours. Thus, CO_2 gas was changed to graphite. Taking care of mixing broken piece of glass with the mixture of graphite and Fe powder, Vycor tube was broken. The mixture of graphite and Fe powder was removed and pressed (50kg f) into a 1mm-diameter hole in an aluminum target holder. This completed the sample for measurement.

The recovery and the yield in chemical treatment are shown in Table 5.3.

Measurement by AMS

The measurements by AMS were done at MALT (Micro Analysis Laboratory, Tandem accelerator, Research Center for Nuclear Science and Technology, the University of Tokyo). A5MV tandem accelerator (Pelletron 5UD, National Electrostatics Corp. USA) is equipped with AMS facility. The ion source, MC-SNICS (Multi-Cathode Source of Negative Ions by Cesium Sputtering) can be loaded with 40 samples on a rotating cathode wheel. The three negative ions, $^{13}C^-$, $^{12}C^-$, $^{14}C^-$, are injected and accelerated sequentially and repeated in the time sequence of 0.001, 0.0003, and 0.1sec. The sequence is repeated 6000 times. It is equal to 600sec for counting time of ^{14}C. The terminal voltage was set at 5.000MV. The ratio of $^{14}C/^{12}C$ and that of $^{14}C/^{12}C$ are obtained using C^{4+} after charge exchanging. The current of $^{12}C^{4+}$ and

that of $^{13}C^{4+}$ are measured by the Faraday cup and the number of $^{14}C^{4+}$ is counted by the detector system (thin metal foil + SSD).

HOx II (SRM4990C, NIST) is used for the standard sample and ANU sucrose (IAEAC6) is supplementary one.

All samples are measured for 3 times including standard samples. The larger error is adopted, comparing the standard deviation of three rations with the statistical error based on counts of ^{14}C.

The value of $\delta\ ^{13}C$ was measured by MAT252 (Finnigan MAT) installed at the Department of Earth & Planetary Science, the University of Tokyo. The standard gas is the commercial CO_2 gas (Oztech Trading Corp.; $\delta\ ^{13}C$=-10.09‰ PDB).

The ratios of $^{14}C/^{12}C$ and $^{14}C/^{12}C$ are normalize to $\delta\ ^{13}C$=-25.0‰ except TK-series.

Calibration

The conventional radiocarbon ages are calibrated by the INTCAL98 calibration curve.

Calibrated ages are calculated by using the computer program CALIB 4.3. In the calculation, the Method A (Intercepts with curve) is mainly employed, and the results are checked by the Method B (Probability distribution).

The examples of calibration are shown in Fig.5.3 and calibrated ages at Sector A and B are shown in Fig.5.4. Results of 1 sigma ranges are expressed by a full line, and those of 2 sigma ranges are by dashed lines. A cross mark in the graph represents the intercept of the conventional age to the calibration curve.

References

"INTCAL98: CALIBRATION ISSUE", *Radiocarbon* 40 (1998).
Stuiver, M., P.J. Reimer, E. Bard, J.W. Beck, G.S. Burr, K.A. Hughen, B. Kromer, G. McCormac, J.v.d. Plicht and M. Spark (1998) *Radiocarbon* 40: 1041-1083.
Stuiver, M. and P.J. Reimer (1998) *CALIB 4.3*. Seatle: University of Washington.

Table 5.2 The amounts and the state of samples.

Sample No	Amt. received (g)	Amt. picked (mg)	Amt. the rest of charcoals	The state of samples
94KSL A11-7 Lower	47.97	6.45g	almost nothing	Almost all charcoals were picked among the mixture of themselves and soil.
94KSL A11-7 Upper	78.15	11.96g	almost nothing	Almost all charcoals were picked among the mixture of themselves and soil.
94KSL C10-3	59.49	10.58g	almost nothing	Almost all charcoals were picked among the mixture of themselves and soil.
94KSL A10-3a	47.33	18.28g	almost nothing	Almost all charcoals were picked among the mixture of themselves and soil.
96KSL AE6-17	46.26	410.72	most of the rest of this sample	Several grains of carbonized wheat were picked. Although they are soft, they are very pure (They are not mixed with soil etc.).
96KSL AE6-19-1	31.14	324.34	most of the rest of this sample	Charcoals are very pure, although they are soft. They are not mixed with soil etc. Some of them were picked.
96KSL AD5-99-10	25.45	303.07	most of the rest of this sample	Charcoals are very pure, although they are soft. They are not mixed with soil etc. A part of them were picked.
94KSL B9-Floor	11.173	Unable to be picked up		Picking was stopped, because most of the sample seemed to be ash.
94KSL B9-T	13.087	186.20	160mg approx.	Samples, except charcoals, are almost ash, soil and resin.
96KSL BD6-28	0.695	414.81	a few (not weighed)	Only solid charcoals were selected. There are a few charcoals in the rest of sample.
95KSL BD7-25	2.764	Unable to be picked up		This sample almost consists of lumps of resin. There are very few charcoals. So charcoals were passed up to pick.
95KSL BD7-26	7.735	Unable to be picked up		Picking was stopped, because most of the sample seemed to be ash.
95KSL BE7-5	4.184	87.20	almost nothing	There are few charcoals in the rest of this sample. There was about 3g resin in it.
96KSL BD7-46	1.728	305.46	the rest of sample	Charcoals are rather solid. A part of the sample was picked up.
96KSL BD7-48	79.009	Unable to be picked up		Picking was stopped, because most of the sample seemed to be ash.
95KSL AD4-3	5.558	501.73	the rest of sample	Charcoals are rather solid. A part of the sample was picked up.
95KSL AG5-9	40.195	265.85	much (not weighed)	Charcoals are rather solid. A part of the sample was picked up.

Table 5.3 The recovery and the yield in a chemical treatment.

Sample No	Amt. picked (mg)	Amt. after AAA (mg)	Recovery after AAA (%)	Amt. oxidation (mg)	Amt. CO₂ (oxidized) (mg C)	Yield oxidized (%)
94KSL A11-7 Lower	6.45g	1.27g	19.69	1.27g	0.53g	41.73
94KSL A11-7 Upper	11.96g	2.80g	23.41	2.80g	1.30g	46.43
94KSL C10-3	10.58g	1.74g	16.45	1.74g	0.75g	43.10
94KSL A10-3a	18.28g	2.61g	14.28	2.61g	1.36	52.11
96KSL AE6-17	410.72	242.36	59.01	8.48	4.17	49.17
96KSL AE6-19-1	324.34	103.75	31.99	7.40	4.60	62.16
96KSL AD5-99-10	303.07	94.15	31.07	12.7	7.93	62.44
94KSL B9-T	186.20	72.29	38.82	8.93	5.40	60.47
96KSL BD6-28	414.81	222.33	53.60	8.30	5.45	65.66
95KSL BE7-5	87.20	47.45	54.42	6.14	3.68	59.93
96KSL BD7-46	305.46	203.78	66.71	9.31	5.79	62.19
95KSL AD4-3	501.73	370.28	73.80	9.31	6.20	66.60
95KSL AG5-9	265.85	143.08	53.82	8.43	5.36	63.58

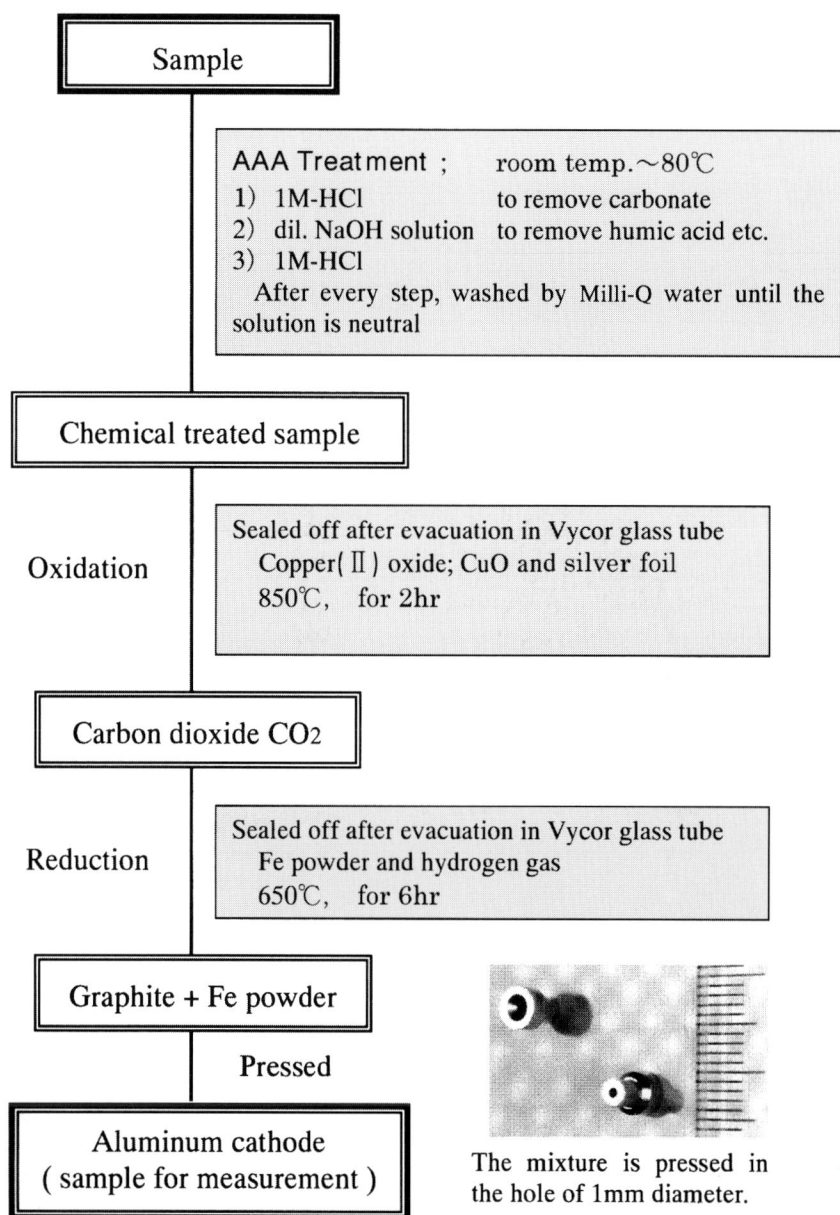

```
┌─────────────────────┐
│       Sample        │
└─────────────────────┘
          │
          │   ┌──────────────────────────────────────────────────┐
          │   │ AAA Treatment ;      room temp.~80℃              │
          │   │ 1) 1M-HCl            to remove carbonate          │
          │   │ 2) dil. NaOH solution  to remove humic acid etc.  │
          │   │ 3) 1M-HCl                                         │
          │   │    After every step, washed by Milli-Q water until the │
          │   │ solution is neutral                               │
          │   └──────────────────────────────────────────────────┘
┌─────────────────────┐
│ Chemical treated sample │
└─────────────────────┘
          │
          │        ┌──────────────────────────────────────────────┐
   Oxidation        │ Sealed off after evacuation in Vycor glass tube │
          │        │    Copper( II ) oxide; CuO and silver foil    │
          │        │    850℃,   for 2hr                            │
          │        └──────────────────────────────────────────────┘
┌─────────────────────┐
│ Carbon dioxide CO2  │
└─────────────────────┘
          │
          │        ┌──────────────────────────────────────────────┐
   Reduction        │ Sealed off after evacuation in Vycor glass tube │
          │        │    Fe powder and hydrogen gas                 │
          │        │    650℃,   for 6hr                            │
          │        └──────────────────────────────────────────────┘
┌─────────────────────┐
│ Graphite + Fe powder │
└─────────────────────┘
          │
       Pressed
          │
┌─────────────────────┐
│  Aluminum cathode    │
│ ( sample for measurement ) │
└─────────────────────┘
```

AAA Treatment ;   room temp.~80℃
1) 1M-HCl   to remove carbonate
2) dil. NaOH solution   to remove humic acid etc.
3) 1M-HCl
   After every step, washed by Milli-Q water until the solution is neutral

Oxidation

Sealed off after evacuation in Vycor glass tube
Copper(II) oxide; CuO and silver foil
850℃,   for 2hr

Reduction

Sealed off after evacuation in Vycor glass tube
Fe powder and hydrogen gas
650℃,   for 6hr

Pressed

The mixture is pressed in the hole of 1mm diameter.

Fig. 5.2 Schematic diagram for sample preparation.

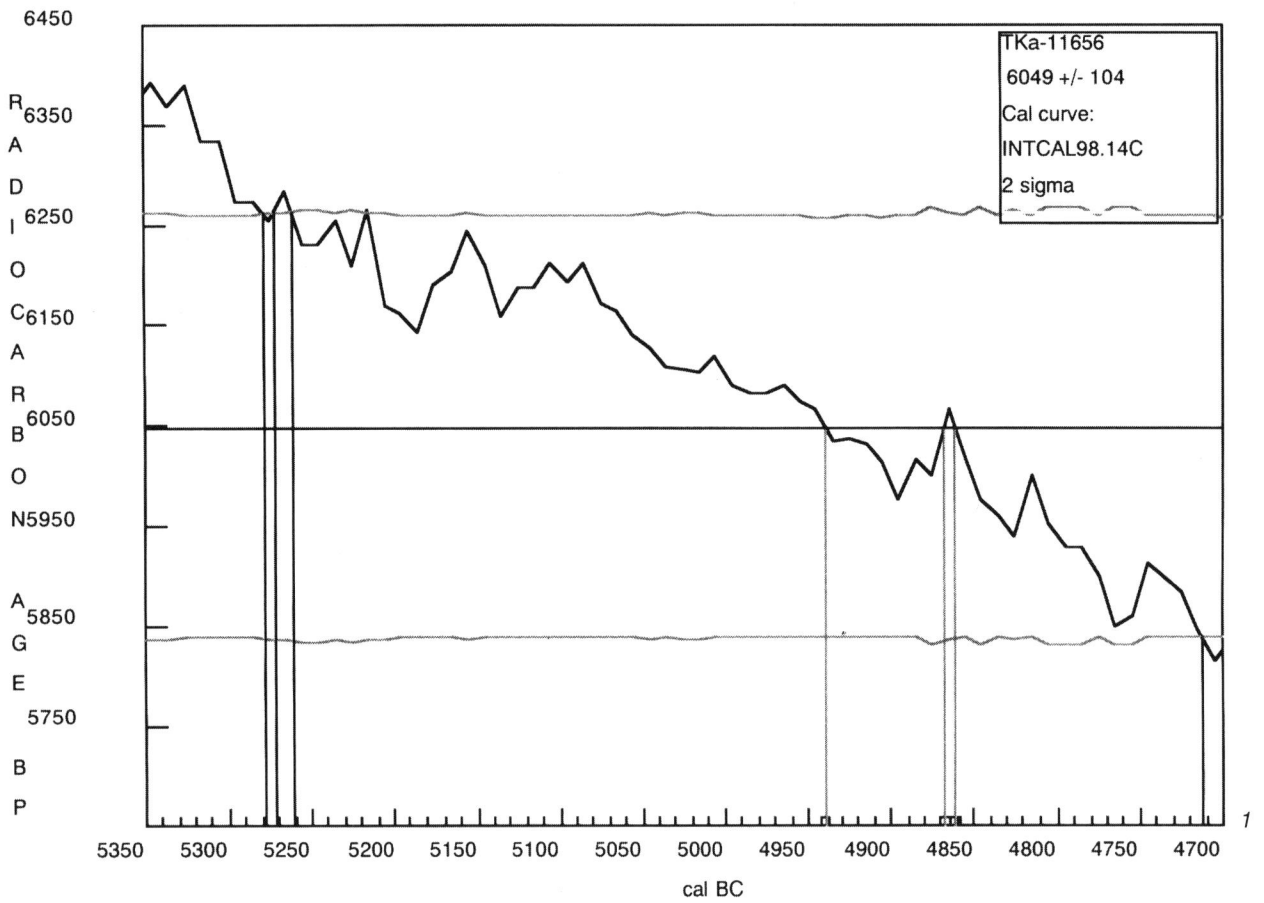

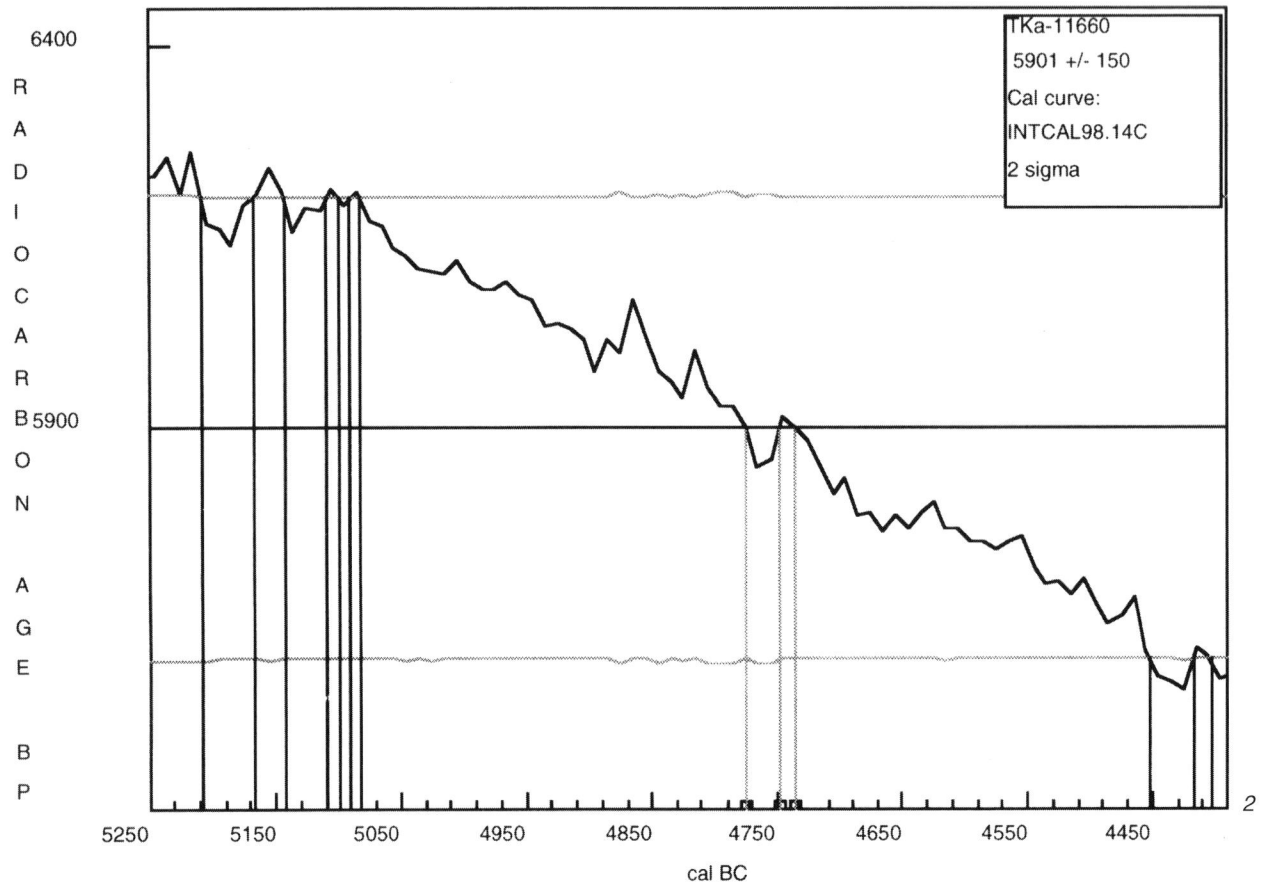

Fig. 5.3 Examples calibration of radiocarbon dates from Tell Kosak Shamali.
1. TKa-11656, 2. TKa-11660

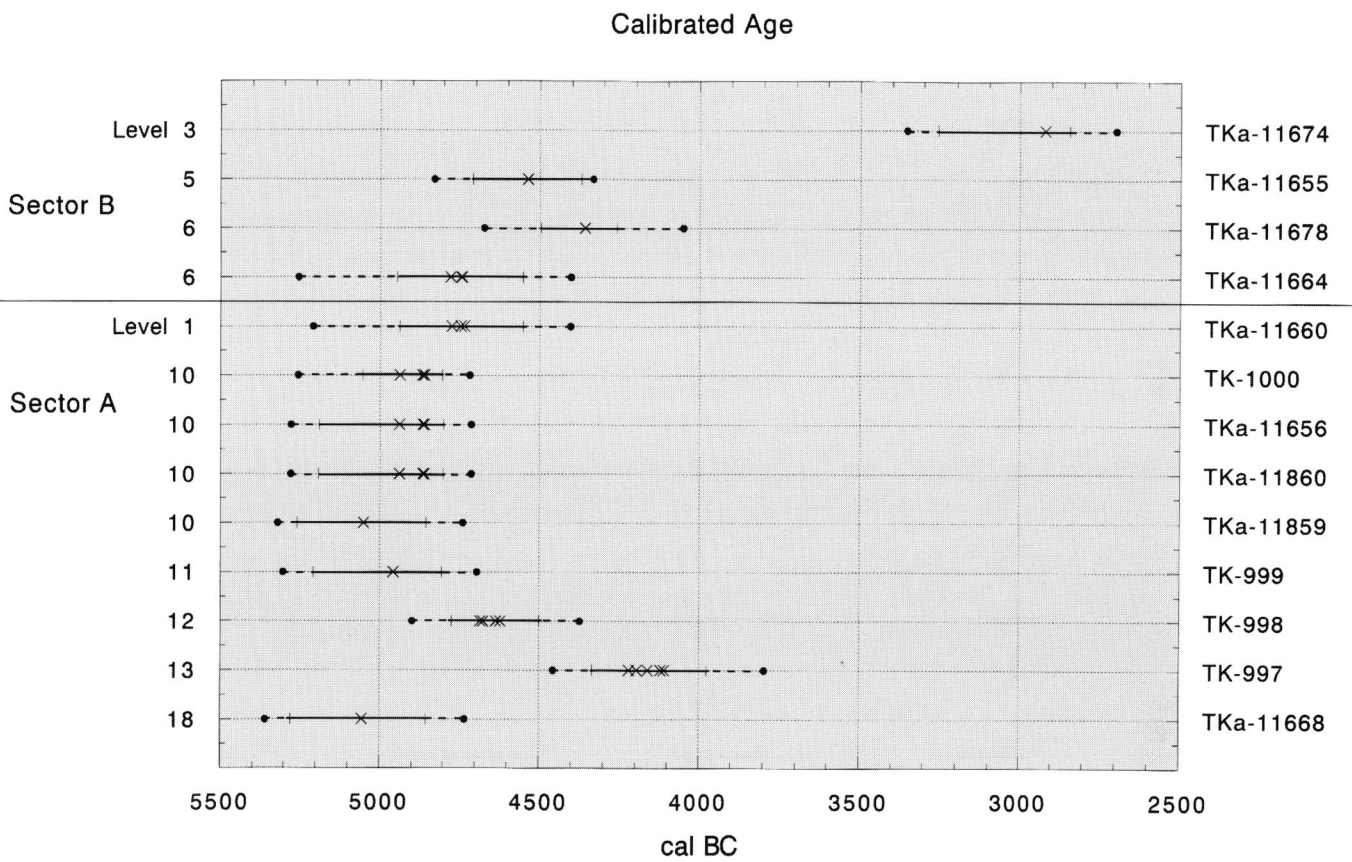

Fig. 5.4 *Calibrated ages of radiocarbon dates from Tell Kosak Shamali.*

6 The Palaeolithic artifacts from Tell Kosak Shamali

Yoshihiro Nishiaki

6.1 Introduction

Substantial human occupation at Tell Kosak Shamali began during the late Pottery Neolithic and is evident in both excavation areas. However, excavations revealed traces of Palaeolithic occupation as well; some Lower, Middle and Epi-Palaeolithic flint artifacts were found as intrusive materials in most Neolithic to Chalcolithic levels (Table 6.1). The Palaeolithic flints were distinguishable from later ones by their significantly deeper patination and more weathered surface condition, as well as particular techno-typological characteristics. The selection of Lower and Middle Palaeolithic pieces was thus relatively easy to recognize, albeit discovered out of their original contexts, but a difficulty was often met when separating Epi-Palaeolithic lithics from those of the Neolithic and Chalcolithic because of the comparatively smaller differences in surface condition and techno-typology. To avoid a too subjective sampling, only deeply patinated and/or weathered specimens with the definite Epi-Palaeolithic techno-typological characteristics were identified as Epi-Palaeolithic in the present study; featureless pieces such as simple blades and flakes were left with later materials, even if their surface conditions are suggestive of an Epi-Palaeolithic origin. Accordingly, the accounts shown under the Epi-Palaeolithic column in Table 6.1 should be understood as representing the minimum number of such pieces discovered at Tell Kosak Shamali.

Several possible explanations can be proposed for the presence of Palaeolithic artifacts in the Neolithic to Chalcolithic levels. Firstly, they could well have been dug up from "virgin soil" by later inhabitants, particularly when in search of building materials. Geomorphological research indicates that the terrace on which Tell Kosak Shamali stood consisted of late Upper Pleistocene deposits containing colluvial sediments derived from the steep hillslopes behind the mound (Chapter 1). Therefore, it is not surprising that the "virgin soil" would have originally contained Palaeolithic artifacts. In fact, it cannot be entirely ruled out that it once had some intact Palaeolithic occupation levels. A second explanation is that Neolithic and Chalcolithic inhabitants intentionally brought in earlier flint artifacts from neighboring areas to use as raw materials for tools, as might be the case with a handaxe recovered from Level 14 (Fig. 6.1; Pl. 6.1: 1). This heavily rolled, typologically late Acheulean handaxe showed some later secondary flaking at the tip, probably by an Ubaidian knapper testing its flaking quality for future use.

Typological analysis shows that most Palaeolithic artifacts from Tell Kosak Shamali are either Middle or the Epi-Palaeolithic. The Lower Palaeolithic is represented by a single piece - the above-mentioned handaxe.

6.2 Middle Palaeolithic

Sectors A and B yielded 119 and 77 identifiable Middle Palaeolithic flint artifacts respectively (Table 6.2), of which 108 specimens were examined in detail (Table 6.3). As these pieces, which exclude those that are too water-rolled or damaged, are all secondary materials isolated from primary contexts, they will be described collectively below.

The raw material is a buff-brown to whitish brown patinated flint, which must have originally been grayish brown, as seen on the occasional fresh breaks. Today similar flint pebbles are easily available on the nearby terraces and banks of the Euphrates. The surface generally exhibits a weathered and slightly glossed appearance, an obvious indicator of secondary derivation contexts, further suggested by the presence of heav-

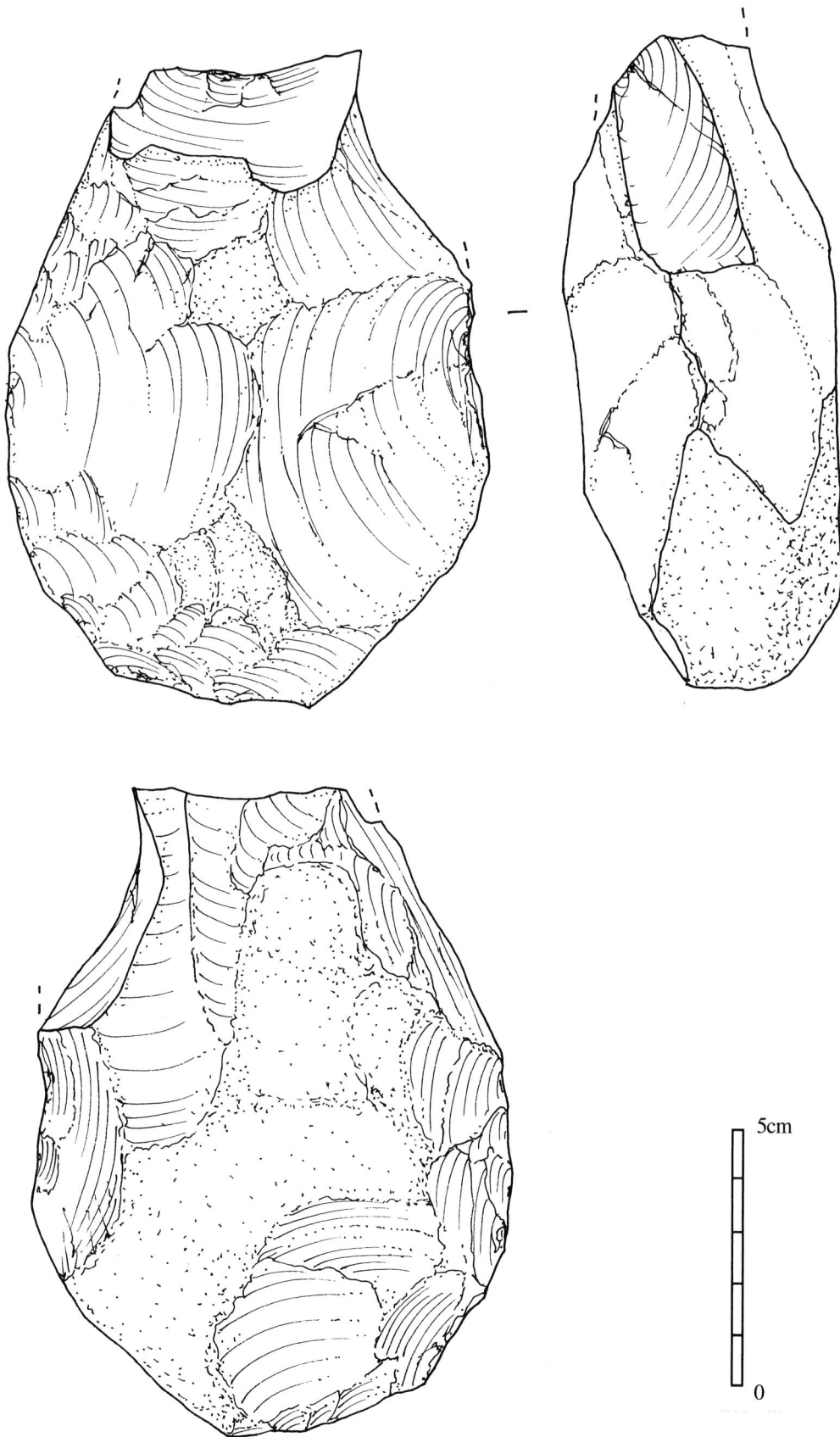

Fig. 6.1 Lower Palaeolithic flint artifact.
Acheulean handaxe, reused as a core in the Ubaid period (97KSL-AE5-5-3; Fill; Level 14 of Sector A).

ily rolled pieces.

There are nine cores in the present collection (Table 6.3). Five are Levallois, two flake cores (Fig. 6.2: 1 and 2) and three point cores (Fig. 6.2: 3-5; Pl. 6.1: 2 and 3). Uni-directional convergent preparation scars are more often observable than radial ones. The remaining cores are Non-Levallois, consisting of a single-platform prismatic core, a globular, change-of-orientation core, and two, unifacial, multi-platform/discoidal cores (Fig. 6.2: 6). These are all flake cores and the absence of cores with definite traces of blade production characterizes the core assemblage of the present collection.

The debitage is composed of core-edge pieces (flakes retaining the core-edge), cortical flakes, partially cortical flakes, flakes, partially cortical blades and fragments (Table 6.2). The greater part of the debitage consists of flakes with or without cortex. There are no non-cortical blades. This feature well reflects the technological traits observed on the cores.

Levallois debitage is included in the tool catego-ry (Table 6.2). Levallois pieces comprise about one-third of the tool assemblage (10/30). Levallois flakes (Fig. 6.3: 3; Pl. 6.1: 5) are more common than Levallois points (Fig. 6.3: 1 and 2; Pl. 6.1: 4 and 6), and no unretouched Levallois blades are present. As seen from dorsal scar patterning, the short, triangular Levallois points were produced by the uni-directional convergent method. The only blade in the present collection is a tip fragment of an elongated retouched Levallois point (Fig. 6.3: 5; Pl. 6.1: 7).

Truncated-faceted flakes (Fig. 6.3: 7 and 8) constitute the most common type of retouched tool, although their tool status has been a matter of controversy. They could also have functioned as cores (cf. Nishiaki 1985; Goren-Inbar 1988). Most are manufactured on Levallois type flakes. The second most commonly retouched pieces are side-scrapers. The collection includes two single straight (Fig. 6.3: 6), one single-convex, and one double straight-convex scrapers (Fig. 6.3: 4). Again, they are mostly Levallois products. Retouched flakes also constitute a relatively common tool category. These are flake-shaped pieces with secondary modification along their edges

Table 6.1 Palaeolithic artifacts from Tell Kosak Shamali*.

Sector A	Level																				
	1	2	3	4	5	6	7	8	9	10	11	12	13	14	15	16	17	18	Later pits	Mixed	Total
Neolithic to Chalcolithic	283	312	322	1826	1228	1609	1838	2151	1296	2560	2496	1833	2353	668	345	71	184	167	72	183	21799
Flint	(283)	(311)	(321)	(1819)	(1225)	(1608)	(1827)	(2142)	(1291)	(2548)	(2481)	(1818)	(2328)	(651)	(341)	(67)	(183)	(167)	(72)	(183)	(21664)
Obsidian	(0)	(1)	(1)	(7)	(3)	(1)	(11)	(9)	(5)	(12)	(17)	(15)	(25)	(17)	(4)	(4)	(1)	(0)	(0)	(0)	(133)
Palaeolithic	1	2	1	3	2	4	5	3	3	7	7	8	19	14	15	3	25	11	0	2	135
Epi-Palaeolithic	(0)	(0)	(0)	(0)	(0)	(0)	(0)	(0)	(0)	(0)	(1)	(0)	(2)	(4)	(3)	(0)	(3)	(3)	(0)	(0)	(16)
Middle Palaeolithic	(1)	(2)	(1)	(3)	(2)	(4)	(5)	(3)	(3)	(7)	(6)	(8)	(17)	(10)	(12)	(3)	(22)	(8)	(0)	(2)	(119)
Total	284	314	323	1829	1230	1613	1843	2154	1299	2567	2505	1841	2372	682	360	74	209	178	72	185	21934

Sector B	Level										
	1	2	3	4	5	6	7	8	Later pits	Mixed	Total
Neolithic to Chalcolithic	465	330	797	2311	2041	3908	1148	271	51	287	11609
Flint	(464)	(329)	(796)	(2302)	(2028)	(3905)	(1143)	(269)	(51)	(287)	(11574)
Obsidian	(1)	(1)	(1)	(9)	(13)	(3)	(5)	(2)	(0)	(0)	(35)
Palaeolithic	1	1	1	13	9	11	23	8	0	10	77
Epi-Palaeolithic	(0)	(0)	(0)	(0)	(0)	(0)	(0)	(0)	(0)	(0)	(0)
Middle Palaeolithic	(1)	(1)	(1)	(13)	(9)	(11)	(23)	(8)	(0)	(10)	(77)
Total	466	331	798	2324	2050	3919	1171	279	51	297	11686

*Palaeolithic artifacts reused by the later inhabitants are not listed in this table.

Table 6.2 Middle Palaeolithic artifacts from Tell Kosak Shamali.

Sector A	Level																		Later pits	Mixed	Total
	1	2	3	4	5	6	7	8	9	10	11	12	13	14	15	16	17	18			
Cores																					
Levallois, flake	0	0	0	0	0	0	0	0	0	0	0	0	0	0	1	0	0	0	0	0	1
Levallois, point	0	0	0	0	0	0	0	0	0	0	0	0	1	1	0	0	0	0	0	0	2
Single-platform, Prism	0	0	0	0	0	0	0	0	0	0	0	0	0	0	1	0	0	0	0	0	1
Change-of-orientation, Globular	0	0	0	0	0	0	0	0	0	0	0	0	0	0	1	0	0	0	0	0	1
Multi-platform, Uniface	0	0	0	0	0	0	0	0	0	0	0	0	0	0	1	0	0	0	0	0	1
Debitage																					
Core-edge pieces	0	0	0	0	0	0	0	0	0	0	0	0	1	0	0	0	0	0	0	0	1
Cortical flakes	0	0	0	0	0	0	1	0	1	1	4	1	2	0	0	0	2	0	0	0	12
Partially cortical flakes	0	0	0	0	0	3	0	1	0	0	2	2	0	0	2	0	0	2	0	0	12
Flakes	0	0	0	1	0	0	1	0	0	0	0	1	0	1	3	0	0	2	0	0	9
Partially cortical blades	0	0	0	0	0	0	0	0	0	1	0	0	0	0	0	0	0	0	0	0	1
Blades	0	0	0	0	0	0	0	0	0	0	0	0	0	0	0	0	0	0	0	0	0
Fragments	0	0	0	0	0	0	0	0	0	0	0	0	2	1	0	0	0	0	0	0	3
Tools																					
Levallois Flakes	0	0	0	0	0	0	0	0	0	1	0	0	0	1	0	0	0	0	0	0	2
Levallois Points	0	0	0	0	0	0	0	0	0	0	0	0	1	0	0	0	0	1	0	0	2
Retouched Levallois point	0	0	0	0	0	0	0	0	0	0	0	0	0	0	0	0	1	0	0	0	1
Side-scraper	0	0	0	0	0	1	0	0	0	0	0	0	0	0	0	0	0	0	0	0	1
Truncated-Faceted flakes	0	0	0	0	0	0	0	0	0	0	0	0	3	0	2	0	1	0	0	1	7
Retouched flakes	0	0	0	0	0	0	0	0	0	0	0	0	0	1	0	0	0	1	0	0	2
Tool fragments	0	0	0	0	0	0	0	0	0	0	0	0	0	0	0	0	1	0	0	0	1
Total	0	0	0	1	0	4	2	1	1	3	6	4	10	5	11	0	5	6	0	1	60

Table 6.2 Continued.

Sector B	Level								Later pits	Mixed	Total
	1	2	3	4	5	6	7	8			
Cores											
Levallois, flake	0	0	0	0	0	0	0	0	0	1	1
Single-platform, Prismatic	0	0	0	1	0	0	0	0	0	0	1
Change-of-orientation, Globular	0	0	0	0	0	0	0	0	0	0	0
Multi-platform, Uniface	0	0	0	0	0	0	0	1	0	0	1
Debitage											
Core-edge pieces	0	0	0	0	0	0	1	0	0	1	2
Cortical flakes	0	0	0	0	0	0	2	1	0	1	4
Partially cortical flakes	1	0	1	1	0	2	3	2	0	1	11
Flakes	0	0	0	1	2	2	2	2	0	1	10
Partially cortical blades	0	0	0	0	0	1	1	3	0	0	5
Blades	0	0	0	0	0	0	0	0	0	0	0
Fragments	0	0	0	0	0	0	0	0	0	0	0
Tools											
Levallois flakes	0	0	0	0	1	0	3	0	0	2	6
Levallois points	0	0	0	0	0	0	0	0	0	0	0
Retouched Levallois point	0	0	0	0	0	0	0	0	0	0	0
Side-scraper	0	0	0	0	0	0	0	1	0	2	3
Truncated-Faceted flakes	0	0	0	0	0	0	0	0	0	0	0
Retouched flakes	0	1	0	0	0	0	1	2	0	0	4
Tool fragments	0	0	0	0	0	0	0	0	0	0	0
Total	1	1	1	3	3	5	13	12	0	9	48

Table 6.3 Comparison of the Middle Palaeolithic artifacts from Sectors A and B.

	Sector A	%	B	%	Total	%
Cores						
Levallois, flake	1	16.7	1	33.3	2	22.2
Levallois, point	2	33.3	0	0.00	2	22.2
Single-platform, Prismatic	1	16.7	1	33.3	2	22.2
Change-of-orientation, Globular	1	16.7	0	0.0	1	11.1
Multi-platform, Uniface	1	16.7	1	33.3	2	22.2
(Total)	(6)	(100.0)	(3)	(100.0)	(9)	(100.0)
Debitage						
Core-edge pieces	1	2.6	2	6.3	3	4.3
Cortical flakes	12	31.6	4	12.5	16	22.9
Partially cortical flakes	12	31.6	11	34.4	23	32.9
Flakes	9	23.7	10	31.3	19	27.1
Partially cortical blades	1	2.6	5	15.6	6	8.6
Blades	0	0.0	0	0.0	0	0.0
Fragments	3	7.9	0	0.0	3	4.3
(Total)	(38)	(100.0)	(32)	(100.0)	(70)	(100.0)
Tools						
Levallois flakes	2	12.5	6	46.2	8	27.6
Levallois points	2	12.5	0	0.0	2	6.9
Retouched Levallois point	1	6.3	0	0.0	1	3.4
Side-scraper	1	6.3	3	23.1	4	13.8
Truncated-Faceted flakes	7	43.8	0	0.0	7	24.1
Retouched flakes	2	12.5	4	30.8	6	20.7
Tool fragments	1	6.3	0	0.0	1	3.4
(Total)	(16)	(100.0)	(13)	(100.0)	(29)	(100.0)
Total	60		48		108	

Table 6.4 Epi-Palaeolithic artifacts from Tell Kosak Shamali.

Level	Sector A 11	12	13	14	15	16	17	18	Total
Core									
Single-platform, Blade, Prismatic	0	0	0	0	1	0	0	0	1
Tools									
Lunates	0	0	0	1	0	0	2	2	5
Lunates	(0)	(0)	(0)	(1)	(0)	(0)	(2)	(1)	(4)
Lunates, Helwan	(0)	(0)	(0)	(0)	(0)	(0)	(0)	(1)	(1)
Microburin	0	0	0	1	0	0	0	0	1
Backed bladelets	0	0	0	0	2	0	0	0	2
Rectangle	(0)	(0)	(0)	(0)	(1)	(0)	(0)	(0)	(1)
Triangle	(0)	(0)	(0)	(0)	(1)	(0)	(0)	(0)	(1)
Burins	0	0	1	2	0	0	1	1	5
Dihedral	(0)	(0)	(0)	(1)	(0)	(0)	(0)	(0)	(1)
Transversal	(0)	(0)	(1)	(0)	(0)	(0)	(0)	(0)	(1)
Angle, on break	(0)	(0)	(0)	(0)	(0)	(0)	(1)	(0)	(1)
Truncation	(0)	(0)	(0)	(1)	(0)	(0)	(0)	(1)	(2)
Endscrapers	1	0	1	0	0	0	0	0	2
Total	1	0	2	4	3	0	3	3	16

but without a standardized techno-morphological feature that places them into any formal tool type. Many are edge-damaged pieces with nibbling retouch or a few isolated retouch scars. Finally, there is one fragment of a retouched piece too heavily broken to show its original form.

In sum, the common use of Levallois core reduction methods typifies the Middle Palaeolithic artifacts from Tell Kosak Shamali. The conventional Bordesian Levallois index is 25.0 (25/100). The Levallois methods known from cores and products in this small collection share the following traits: the predominance of uni-directional/convergent flaking for blank removal; the relatively frequent manufacture of Levallois points, and rare traces of elongated blanks production. These traits would place the Tell Kosak Shamali material, when dealt with as if representing a homogeneous industry (which is probably not wise), in the broad context of the Levantine Mousterian cultural phenomenon.

The Upper Euphrates valley in which Tell Kosak Shamali is located has been subjected to a number of archaeological surveys since the 1970s with an emphasis on recording the Palaeolithic human occupation (e.g. Copeland 1981, 1985; Yalçinkaya 1995). They have amply documented the ubiquitous distribution of Middle Palaeolithic flint artifacts on the Pleistocene valley terraces. The most comprehensive report is that made by L. Copeland (1981) on the basis of her survey conducted in 1975, which lists over ten find spots. She comments on "the extraordinary abundance of Palaeolithic artifacts in this region" (Copeland 1981: 248), stretching from the Sajour valley to the Middle Euphrates.

In the Tishreen dam flood zone two sites were mentioned. Tellik is a small hillslope located about 35km north of Tell Kosak Shamali, where typical Levallois specimens, including radially prepared cores, were collected. Ja'ade, about 10km north of Tell Kosak Shamali, where a relatively large amount of Middle Palaeolithic artifacts were collected, was described in greater detail. Of the 303 pieces examined, 55 were cores including 23 Levallois type specimens. The Levallois cores consisted of both radial and single-axis preparation types, although the latter predominated. The debitage, consisting of 186 pieces, also included

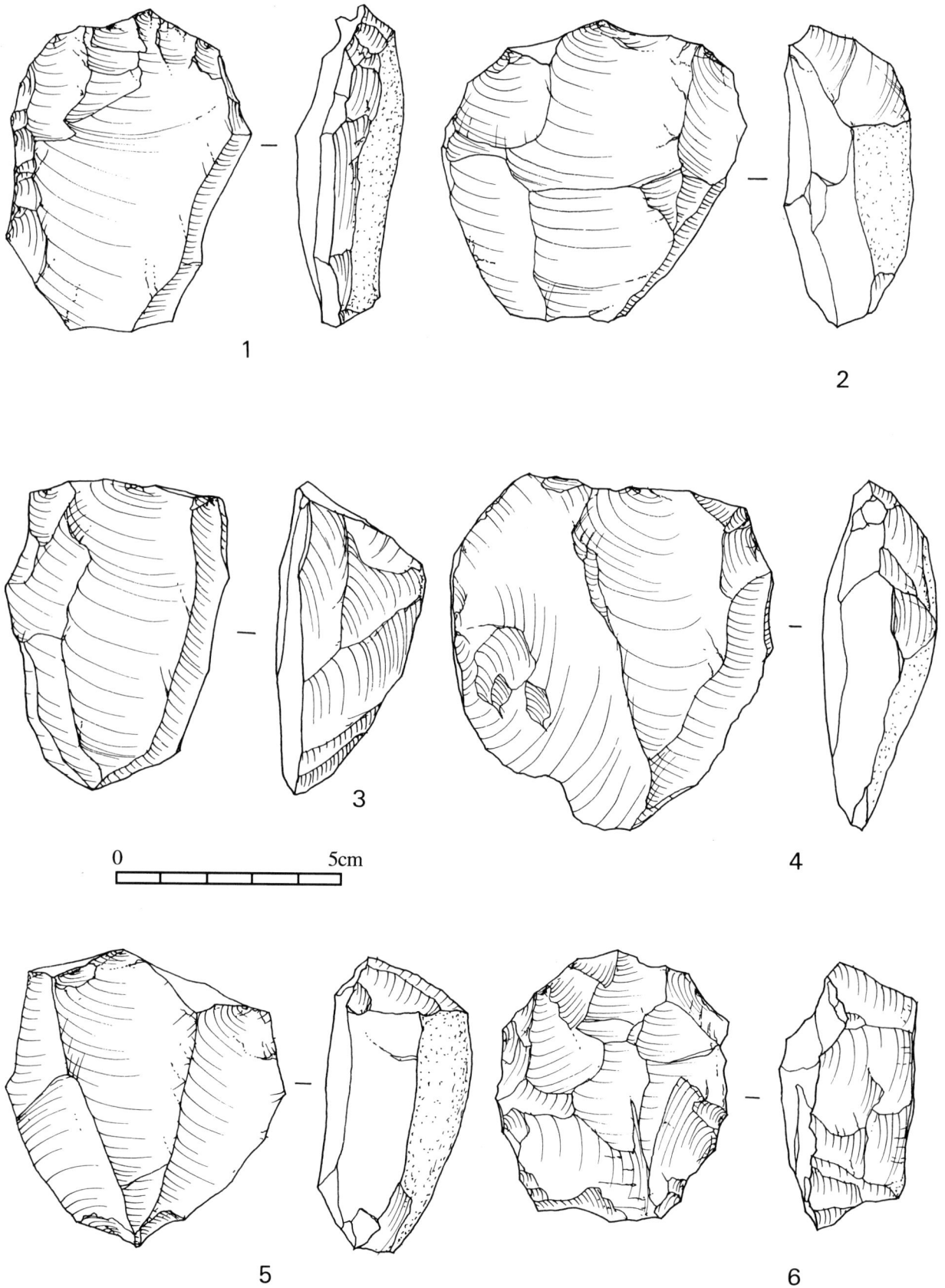

Fig. 6.2 Middle Palaeolithic flint cores.
1. Levallois flake core with multi-directional preparation scars (95KSL-AG4-8; Level 15 of Sector A).
2. Levallois flake core with uni-directional preparation scars (97KSL-BE5-topsoil; Surface of Sector B).
3. Levallois point core with uni-directional preparation scars (94KSL-A12-5; 1310; Level 13 of Sector A).
4. Levallois point core with uni-directional preparation scars, on a flake (95KSL-AG5-8; 1408; Level 14 of Sector A).
5. Levallois point core with bi-directional preparation scars (97KSL-BE7-35; Fill; Level 8 of Sector B).
6. Multi-platform discoidal flake core with unifacial flaking scars (97KSL-BD6-30; Fill; Level 8 of Sector B).

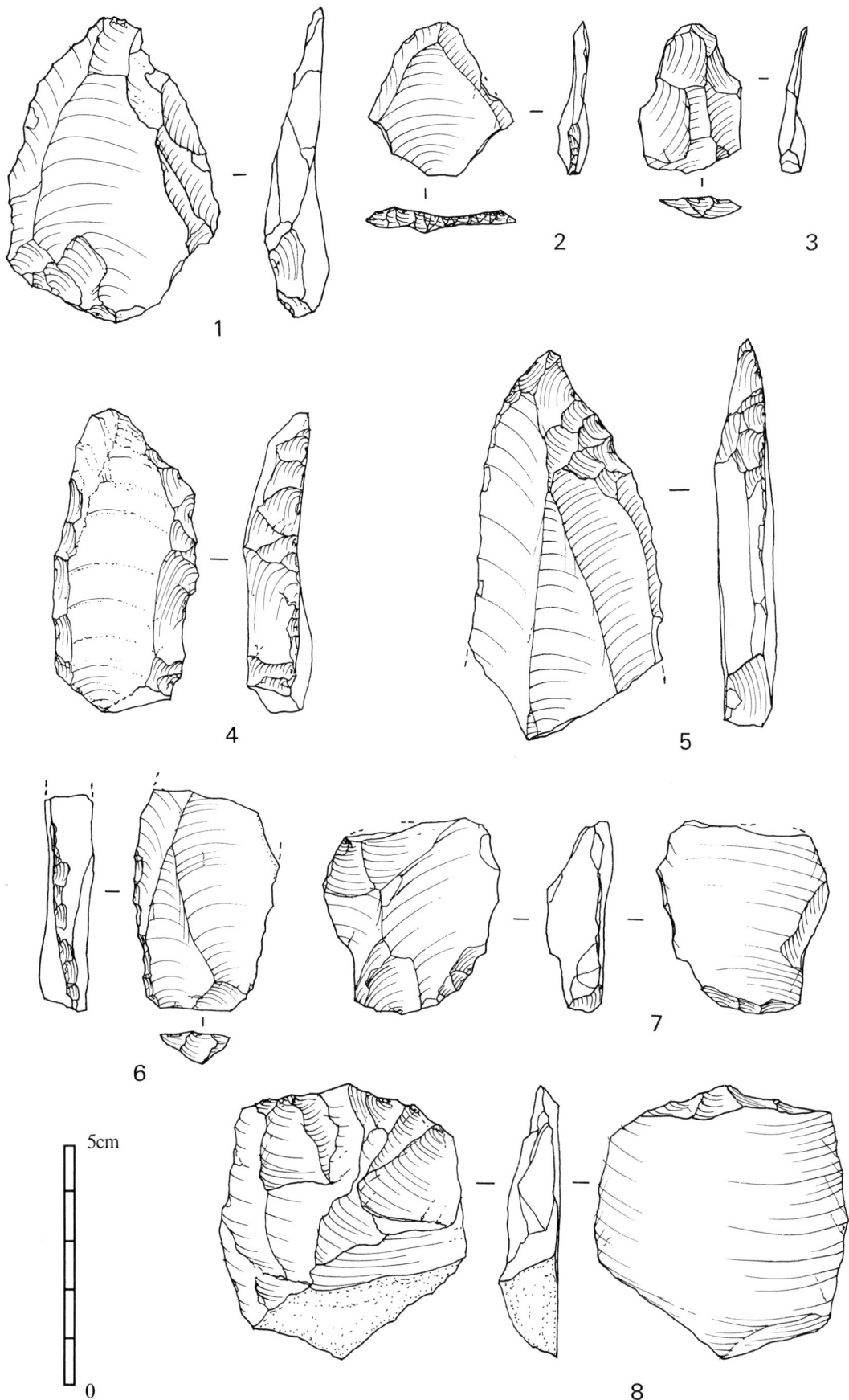

Fig. 6.3 Middle Palaeolithic flint artifacts.

1. Levallois point with uni-directional convergent preparation scars (94KSL-A12-6; 1805; Level 18 of Sector A).
2. Levallois point with uni-directional convergent preparation scars (95KSL-AF5-9; 1309; Level 13 of Sector A).
3. Levallois flake with multi-directional preparation scars (95KSL-AG5-8; 1408; Level 14 of Sector A).
4. A double convex side-scraper, on a Levallois flake with double patina (97KSL-AE4-27; 10A19; Level 10 of Sector A).
5. An elongated Levallois retouched point (94KSL-A14-1; Fill; Level 17 of Sector A).
6. A single straight edge side-scraper on a Levallois flake (97KSL-BD6-34; Fill; Level 8 of Sector B).
7. Truncated-faceted flake on a non-Levallois flake (94KSL-A10-7; Fill; Level 13 of Sector A).
8. Truncated-faceted flake on a non-Levallois flake (97KSL-BD7-60; Fill; Level 8 of Sector B).

Levallois pieces but in comparatively low proportions (11/186). Many had been detached from non-prepared plain butts. Retouched tools were rarely present. On this basis, Copeland suggested the workshop nature of the Ja'ade site, and considered it slightly earlier than the proper Levantine Mousterian within the Middle Palaeolithic.

In the northern Syrian Euphrates, similar flake-oriented assemblages are known in the Sehremuz Sirti region of southern Turkey. Yalçinkaya (1995) reports over 20 sites with Middle Palaeolithic artifacts in a survey area of 5km x 2.5km. About 400 pieces were analyzed resulting in a Levallois index of 22.75. The core assemblage of 81 pieces included 37 Levallois cores, showing traces of both unilinear and recurrent reduction methods. According to Yalçinkaya's graph in the report, Levallois flakes dominate the Levallois products. The ratio of flake-blade-point was approximately 5-1-2.

In the southern part of the valley, smaller collections of typical Levantine Mousterian artifacts, probably in secondary contexts, were collected at several localities (Copeland 1981). Many cores, abundant cortical flakes, but few retouched tools were found at Rhayat, near the confluence of the Balikh and Euphrates rivers. These were considered as an indication of the workshop character of this spot. The Levallois index was 16.6. Similar finds were also made at nearby Chnine West 3. An important trait of these collections was the relatively common occurrence of blade elements on both cores and products (Copeland 1981). The surface material reported by M. Perves (1964) from the vicinity of Deir ez-Zor, in the Middle Euphrates, may also be comparable in its abundance of elongated pieces.

These surface materials, except for the probably earlier Ja'ade assemblage, suggest the presence of at least two facies of Levantine Mousterian in this region: one characterized by the abundant production of blade elements, and the other by the more common emphasis on flake production. The collection from Tell Kosak Shamali, as well as that from Sehremuz Sirti, clearly belong to the flake-dominated group. At present, the relationship between these two facies or groups is unclear because of the nature of the survey mate-

rials in general, and the lack of excavated materials in this region. However, if we refer to the stratified evidence from the El-Kowm basin sites (Boëda and Muhesen 1993), from Douara Cave, Palmyra (Akazawa 1979; Nishiaki 1987), and the Tabun D-C-B tripartite system for technological division, established at Tabun Cave, Israel (Copeland 1975), the flake facies such as that from Tell Kosak Shamali would be ascribable to the later phase.

The presence of "substantial" blade elements on the Middle Euphrates near Raqqa raises an interesting problem in the regional perspective. Recent surveys further north and east beyond the Euphrates, such as the Khabur basin, emphasize the rarity of blade elements at Middle Palaeolithic sites (Nishiaki 2000). The same holds true for survey results from the Anatolian plateau (Algaze et al. 1991) and the Turkish Euphrates regimes (Yalçinkaya 1995). Blade-rich industries of the Levantine Mousterian, which are often referred to as Tabun D type Mousterian, are known to have a denser distribution in the southern Levant and the inland desert apparently stretching towards northern Syria. The Euphrates valley currently appears to represent the northernmost area of their distribution, and deserves further investigation to increase our understanding of the regional variablity of Levantine Mousterian assemblages.

6.4 Epi-Palaeolithic

The next stage of Palaeolithic occupations at Kosak Shamali relates to the Epi-Palaeolithic. The lithic collection from the Neolithic and the lowest Ubaidian levels in Sector A produced lunates and other tools characteristic of the Natufian. They were only found in Sector A, especially from Squares AF and AG located at the southwestern edge of the mound. This rather limited distribution is in marked contrast to that of the rather ubiquitous occurrences of Middle Palaeolithic pieces, which may indeed suggest the presence of a small Natufian settlement somewhere in the mound beneath the later deposits.

Table 6.4 shows the stratigraphic distribution of these 16 intrusive Epi-Palaeolithic artifacts. Added to them is one bifacial tool re-used as a core in the Ubaid period (Level 6; see below). Most of these specimens are in chocolate brown fine-grained flint with a dull glossy, patinated surface. Similar flint was occasionally used in the Neolithic, but rarely in the Ubaid and later. The collection includes a single-platform prismatic core (Fig. 6.4: 1), whose main flaking surface is on one side of a biface, on which microlithic blade scars originate from a roughly prepared platform. The axis of the main flaking surface is set at a slightly slanted angle to the axis of the core blank. In overall appearance the core is reminiscent of carinated scrapers of Abu Hureyra (Olszweski 2000), and in fact, could have functioned as such.

The tool category can be divided into two major groups: microlithic and non-microlithic tools. Microlithic tools consist of five lunates (Fig. 6.4: 2-6; Pl. 6.2: 3-7) and two backed bladelets (Fig. 6.4: 7 and 8; Pl. 6.2: 1 and 2), none of which exhibit visible gloss along their cutting edges. As suggested by one piece that has a burinated fracture at the tip (Fig. 6.4: 2), they seem more likely to have been utilized as projectile elements. The largest lunate is 30.0 x 7.2 x 3.1 mm, while the smallest is 18.0 x 4.5 x 2.5 mm, and all have one side steeply retouched to form a curved back. One specimen was shaped with bifacial or Helwan retouch (Fig. 6.4: 6; Pl. 6.2: 4). Both backed bladelets have a series of rather straight and abrupt retouch along one edge, and one has a pointed tip (Fig. 6.4: 8; Pl. 6.2: 2), perhaps a fragment of a geometric triangle. Of particular interest is a microburin (Fig. 6.4: 9; Pl. 6.2: 12), a rather wide fragment of a blade butt, with microburin scars at the distal end.

Non-microlithic tools include end-scrapers, burins and a heavy-duty tool. The end-scrapers are on blades with a rounded scraping distal edge (Fig. 6.4: 10 and 11). Burins are varied: a dihedral burin (Fig. 6.5: 1; Pl. 6.2: 8), a transversal burin on a truncation (Fig. 6.5: 2), an angle burin on a break (Fig. 6.5: 3; Pl. 6.2: 11), and two truncation burins on narrow blades (Fig. 6.5: 4 and 5; Pl. 6.2: 9 and 10). The dihedral burin is on a thick flake with relatively wide fluting scars, and may also have served as a microblade core.

Finally, mention should be made of a heavy-duty tool with double-patina (Fig. 6.5: 6; Pl. 6.2: 13) that closely resembles the "gouges" at Abu Hureyra

(Olszewski 2000). The dorsal surface of one end is radially retouched to form a high back, while the other surface has one large removal that created a rather flat surface. These scars are all water-rolled. The opposite end is covered with either radial or parallel flake scars along the longer axis, and is fresh. As this piece was found in a Late Northern Ubaid level (Level 6), the fresh flake scars perhaps indicate its re-use as a core or a type of biface by an Ubaidian knapper.

The above-mentioned core tools and their manufacturing techniques all show evident affinities with those reported from the Epi-Palaeolithic assemblages of Tell Abu Hureyra, a well-known site situated about 40 km south from Tell Kosak Shamali (Moore et al. 2000). The Epi-Palaeolithic of Abu Hureyra, or Abu Hureyra 1, has been dated to the Late Epi-Palaeolithic, spanning approximately 11,500 -10,000 BP (uncalibrated radiocarbon dates). The flaked stone assemblages of Abu Hureyra 1 are reported to consist of geometrics and non-geometrics in a variety of forms including lunates, scrapers, borers, burins, notches/denticulates, gouges and others. The present collection has a much more limited range of tool types, but this must be a mere artifact of our sampling procedure; flake tools such as scrapers, notches and denticulates generally do not display characteristics that are distinctive enough to allow separation from the Neolithic and Chalcolithic. As flake tools were more common in Abu Hureyra 1 (Olszweski 1991), it is quite plausible that more Epi-Palaeolithic flint tools are mixed with later pieces at Tell Kosak Shamali.

Sites with similar materials, whether or not called Natufian, are also known slightly to the north of Abu Hureyra, e.g. Nahr Homr (Boerma and Roodenberg 1977) and Dibsi Faraj East (Wilkinson and Moore 1978). These sites indicate that the steppic-riverine environment along the Upper Euphrates valley was quite commonly exploited by late Epi-Palaeolithic people. The materials from Tell Kosak Shamali, although incomplete and from secondary contexts, add a further example of such settlements to our database.

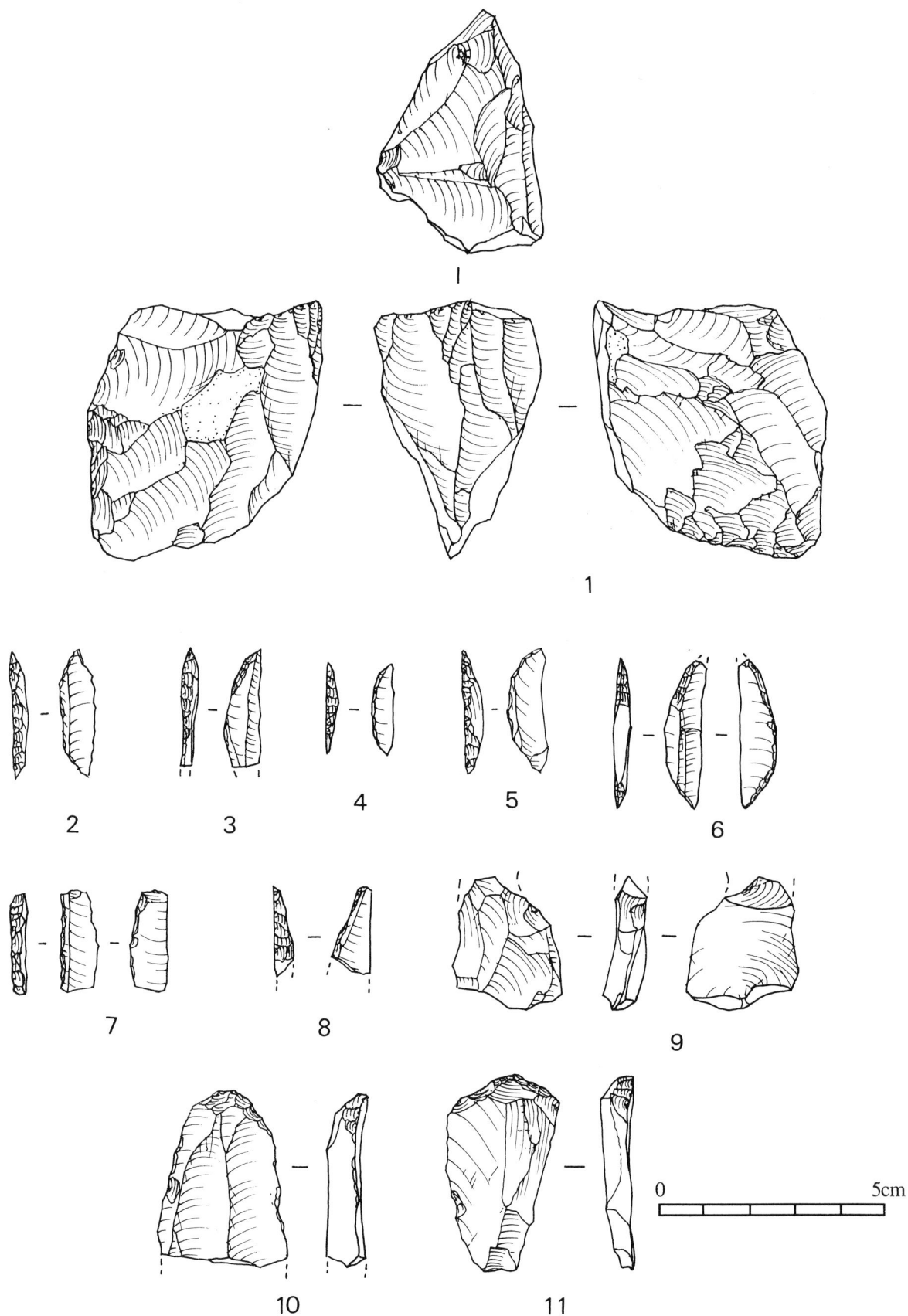

Fig. 6.4 Epi-Palaeolithic flint artifacts.

1. Blade core with blade removals at an edge of bifacially prepared blank
   (95KSL-AF5-32; Fill; Level 15 of Sector A).
2. Lunate with a burinated fracture at point (95KSL-AF3-22; Fill; Level 17 of Sector A).
3. Lunate with one end broken (95KSL-AF3-22; Fill; Level 17 of Sector A).
4. Lunate (95KSL-AG5-6; Fill; Level 14 of Sector A).
5. Lunate (94KSL-A12-6; 1805; Level 18 of Sector A).
6. Lunate with Helwan retouch (94KSL-A12-6; 1805; Level 18 of Sector A).
7. Backed bladelet with both ends broken (95KSL-AF5-30; 1501; Level 15 of Sector A).
8. Backed bladelet with one end broken (95KSL-AF5-30; 1501; Level 15 of Sector A).
9. Microburin (95KSL-AG5-8; 1404; Level 14 of Sector A).
10. End-scraper, on blade (95KSL-AF3-8; Fill; Level 11 of Sector A).
11. End-scraper, on blade (95KSL-AF3-12; Fill; Level 13 of Sector A).

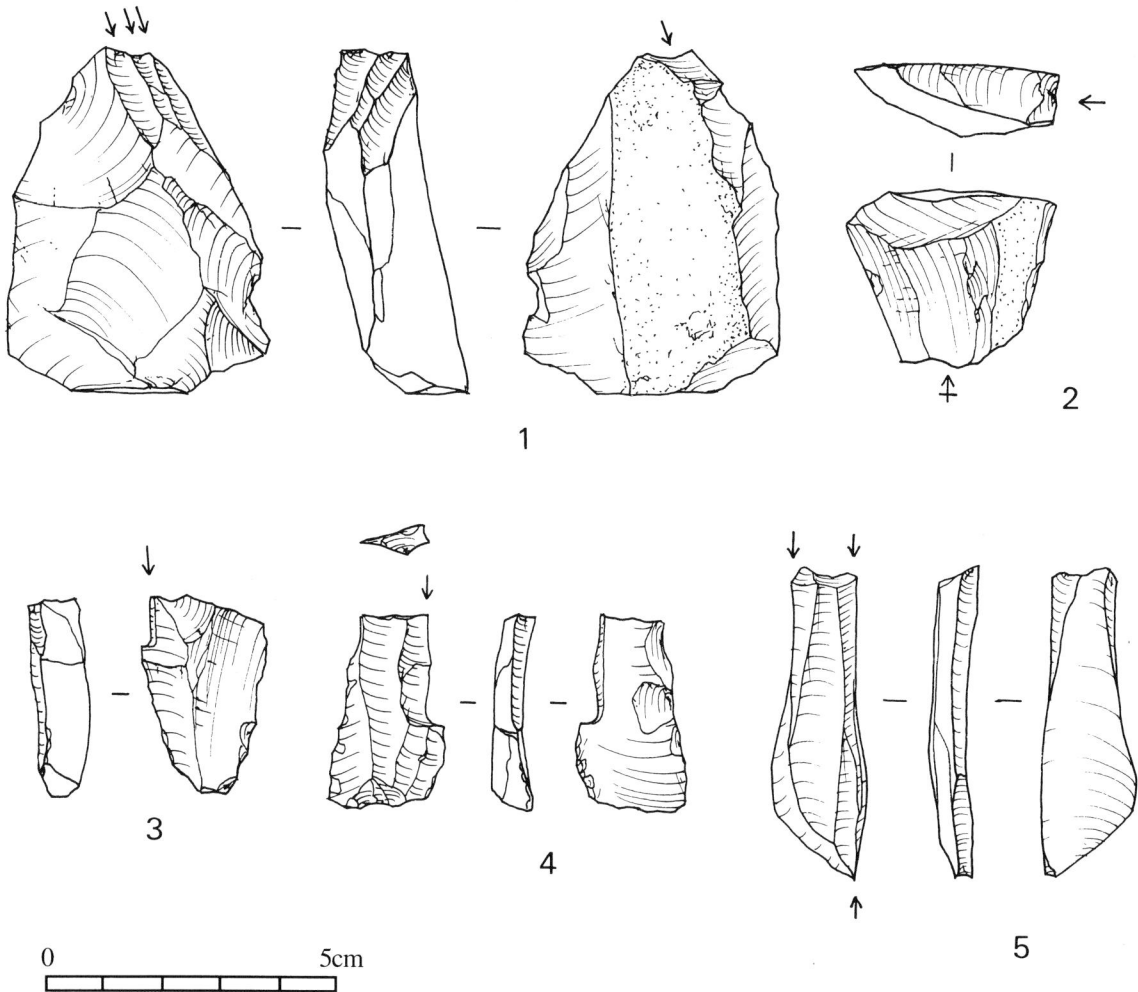

Fig. 6.5 Epi-Palaeolithic flint artifacts.
1. Dihedral burin (95KSL-AG5-6; Fill; Level 14 of Sector A).
2. Transversal burin (95KSL-AE5-48; 1313; Level 13 of Sector A).
3. Burin on a break (95KSL-AF3-21; Fill; Level 17 of Sector A).
4. Truncation burin (95KSL-AF5-34; 1803; Level 18 of Sector A).
5. Truncation burin (95KSL-AG5-6; Fill; Level 14 of Sector A).
6. Gouge with double patina, partly reused probably as a core
   in the Late Northern Ubaid period (95KSL-AD4-10; Fill; Level 6 of Sector A).

6.4 Conclusion

The Palaeolithic collection described in this chapter demonstrates that exploitation of the area of Tell Kosak Shamali started much earlier than the formation of the mound. Traces of Middle and the Epi-Palaeolithic occupation are particularly well represented. Such traces and the lack of Upper Palaeolithic evidence, have often been encountered in previous surveys and excavations in inland north Syria. For instance, in the same valley, Middle and Epi-Palaeolithic, and even some Neolithic traces have been reported on a small terrace at Dibsi Faraj (Wilkinson and Moore 1978). The evidence from Tell Kosak Shamali confirms that this pattern of settlement distribution was prevalent in inland Levant.

Tell Kosak Shamali is located at the edge of a Pleistocene terrace of the Euphrates, at the edge of the large flood plain and the northern bank of the Sarine River. Immediately to the east are higher terraces supporting scrub and trees today. It is assumed that this advantageous site-location, in an area of a variety of easily accessible resources, was enjoyed by prehistoric hunter-gatherers, and was a reason for the location of a settlement or camp in this place.

References

Akazawa, T. (1979) Prehistoric occurrences and chronology in Palmyra basin. In: *Paleolithic Site of the Douara Cave and Paleogeography of Palmyra Basin in Syria, Part II,* edited by K. Hanihara and T. Akazawa, pp. 201-220. Tokyo: University of Tokyo Press.

Algaze, G., R. Breuninger, C. Lightfoot and M. Rosenberg (1991) The Tigris-Euphrates archaeological reconnaissance project: a preliminary report of the 1989-1990 seasons. *Anatolica* 17: 175.340.

Boëda, E. and S. Muhesen (1993) Umm el-Tlel (El Kowm, Syrie): Étude prelinminaire des industries lithiques du Paléolithique Moyen et Superiueur 1991-1992. *Cahiers de l'Euphrates* 7: 47-92.

Boerma, J.A.K. and J.J. Roodenberg (1977) Une deuxieme industrie Épipaléolithique sur le Nahr el-Homr. *Palaeohistoria* 19: 8-17.

Copeland, L. (1975) The Middle and Upper Palaeolithic of Lebanon and Syria in the light of recent research. In: *Problems in Prehistory: North Africa and the Levant,* edited by F. Wendorf and A.E. Marks, pp. 317-350. Dallas: Southern Methodist University Press.

Copeland, L. (1981) Chronology and distribution of the Middle Palaeolithic, as known in 1980, in Lebanon and Syria. In: *Préhistoire du Levant,* edited by J. Cauvin and P. Sanlaville, pp. 239-264. Paris: C.N.R.S.

Goren-Inbar, N. (1985) Too small to be true? Reevaluation of cores on flakes in Levantine Mousterian assemblages. *Lithic Technology* 17(1): 37-44.

Moore, A.M.T., G. C. Hillman and A. J. Legge (2000) *Village on the Euphrates: From Foraging to Farming at Tell Abu Hureyra.* Oxford: Oxford University Press.

Nishiaki, Y. (1985) Truncated-faceted flakes from Levantine Mousterian assemblages. *Bulletin of Department of Archaeology, the University of Tokyo* 4: 215-326.

Nishiaki, Y. (1987) Middle Palaeolithic assemblages from the Douara Cave: 1984 excavations. In: *Paleolithic Site of the Douara Cave and Paleogeography of Palmyra Basin in Syria, Part IV: 1984 excavations,* edited by T. Akazawa and Y. Sakaguchi, pp. 61-96. Tokyo: University of Tokyo Press.

Nishiaki, Y. (2000) The Palaeolithic and Neolithic industries from the prehistoric survey in the Khabur basin. In: *Prospection Archéologique du Haut-Khabur Occidental (Syrie du N.E.), Volume I,* edited by B. Lyonnet, pp.77-124. Beyrouth: Bibliothèque Archéologique et Historique.

Olszewski, D. (1991) The lithic evidence from Abu Hureyra 1 in Syria. In: *The Natufian Culture in the Levant,* edited by O. Bar-Yosef and F.R. Valla, pp. 433-444. Ann Arbor: International Monographs in Prehistory.

Olszewski, D. (2000) The chipped stone. In: *Village on the Euphrates: From Foraging to Farming at Tell Abu Hureyra,* edited by A.M.T. Moore, G. C. Hillman and A. J. Legge, pp. 133-154. Oxford: Oxford University Press.

Perves, M. (1964) La préhistoire de la région du Moyen Euphrate. *Bulletin de la Société Préhistorique* 61: 422-435.

Wilkinson, T.J. and A.M.T. Moore (1978) A prehistoric site near Dibsi Faraj in Syria. *Levant* 10: 26-36.

Yalçinkaya, I. (1995) Thoughts on Levallois technique in Anatolia. In: *The Definition and Interpretation of Levallois Technology,* edited by H.L. Dibble and O. Bar-Yosef, pp. 399-412. Madison: Prehistory Press.

Plate 6.1 Lower and Middle Palaeolithic artifacts from Tell Kosak Shamali.

1. Acheulean handaxe (cf. Fig. 6.1).
2. Levallois point core (cf. Fig. 6.2: 3).
3. Levallois point core (cf. Fig. 6.2: 4).
4. Levallois point (cf. Fig. 6.3: 2).
5. Levallois flake (cf. Fig. 6.3: 3).
6. Levallois point (cf. Fig. 6.3: 1).
7. Levallois retouched point (cf. Fig. 6.3: 5).

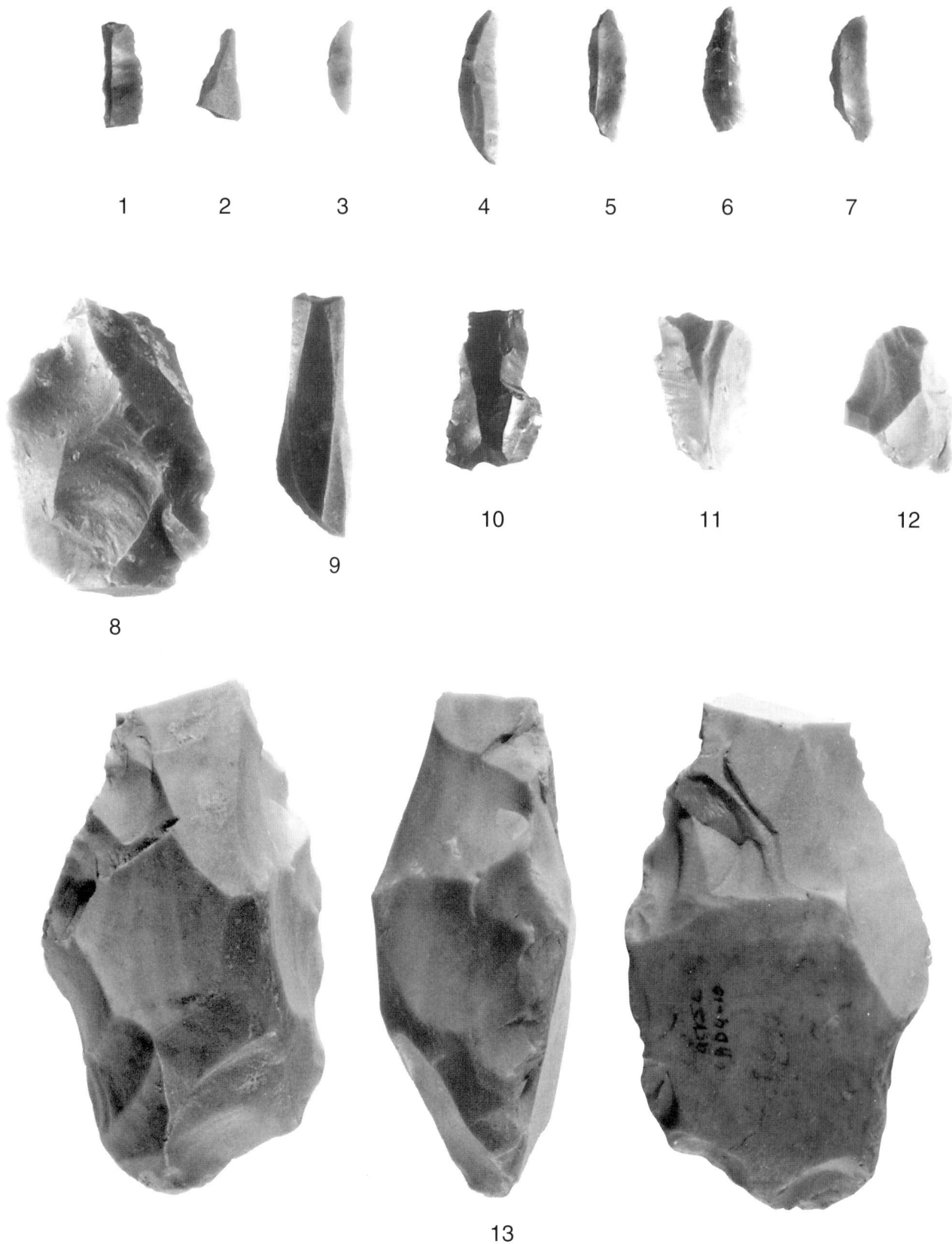

Plate 6.2 Epi-Palaeolithic artifacts from Tell Kosak Shamali.
1. Backed bladelet (cf. Fig. 6.4: 7).
2. Backed bladelet (cf. Fig. 6.4: 8).
3. Lunate (cf. Fig. 6.4: 3).
4. Lunate (cf. Fig. 6.4: 6).
5. Lunate (cf. Fig. 6.4: 2).
6. Lunate (cf. Fig. 6.4: 3).
7. Lunate (cf. Fig. 6.4: 5).
8. Burin (cf. Fig. 6.5: 1).
9. Burin (cf. Fig. 6.5: 5).
10. Burin (cf. Fig. 6.5: 4).
11. Burin (cf. Fig. 6.5: 3).
12. Microburin (cf. Fig. 6.4: 9).
13. Gouge (cf. Fig. 6.5: 6).

7 The Neolithic pottery from Tell Kosak Shamali

Marie Le Mière

7.1 Introduction

The Neolithic pottery comes from both sectors of the excavation, A and B (Table 7.1). The Neolithic settlement in Kosak Shamali consists mainly of pits dug into the virgin soil in both sectors of excavation, except fragments of the stone foundation of a building of unknown shape in Sector B (see Chapter 4). As explained in Chapters 3 and 4, very few Neolithic areas are undisturbed by later occupants of the site. About a third of the material comes from Neolithic layers, Level 18 in Sector A and Level 8 in Sector B (Table 7.1). As seen in Table 7.1, the proportion of material from Neolithic levels is much higher in Sector B than Sector A. In both sectors, only very few Neolithic contexts were without later material. The amount of pottery from these undisturbed contexts (147 sherds) is too small to be studied apart from the rest of the material and, furthermore, the number of sherds from Neolithic levels is also rather restricted (504). For this reason, and also because the preliminary investigations show this material to be rather homogeneous, we will describe all contexts as a whole. Nevertheless, we have systematically established comparisons: firstly, between the pottery from Neolithic levels and that from later ones; secondly, the material, between Sector A and Sector B in the Neolithic levels; thirdly, between the pottery of Neolithic levels as a whole and that from the undisturbed contexts. The differences which became apparent in these comparisons will be presented in the conclusion, except for those comparisons concerning condition of pottery which is directly related to its stratigraphic position.

The Neolithic collection from Kosak Shamali amounts to 1609 pieces, of which only 2 complete pots and another complete profile could be reconstructed. Furthermore, it should be emphasized that Neolithic pottery is rather simple, often uneven and still mostly unstandardized, making it difficult to describe on the basis of types. Therefore, a description of individual characteristics has been undertaken and the characteristics further combined to allow available data to be used to maximum effect. With such material, only quantitative data will provide any results which, in most cases, will show only relative trends and rarely clear differences (all differences further mentioned take into consideration intervals of confidence). The different fields of this description are: condition of pottery, technological characteristics, shape, decoration and measurements. To the system of description previously used for Bouqras and Sabi Abyad material and yet published (Le Mière and Nieuwenhuyse 1996: 123-125) some more characteristics have been added in the present study for the description of decoration.

Three rather clear wares, already identified at other sites, can be described separately from the bulk because they are quite unusual in many respects: Dark-Faced Burnished Ware, Gray Black Ware and Mineral Coarse Ware. The remaining material is extremely variable, and no characteristic or combination of characteristics can be used to define *a priori* wares or categories. For this reason, we will study as one group all the pottery not belonging to one of the three wares, in order to characterize it as clearly as possible and to determine categories, should they do exist. This material represents over 90% of the pottery collection and is provisionally named "the bulk" (Table 7.2).

Table 7.1 Distribution of the Neolithic sherds by sector and context.

Sector	A	B	Total
Undisturbed Neolithic contexts	113	34	147
Disturbed Neolithic contexts	37	320	357
Later levels	796	309	1105
Total	946	663	1609

7.2 Condition of the pottery

About 50% of the entire collection is damaged (concretions, rolling...). This is a rather high percentage, which rises to about 60% if simple blunting is also considered. Such a high percentage could be due to the provenance of most of the material whether from disturbed Neolithic contexts or as loose sherds in the fill of the upper layers. This hypothesis is supported by the fact that less than 25% of the material from undisturbed Neolithic contexts is damaged. These contexts are mainly pits which could explain such a low percentage, as well as the rather large size of many sherds: pits are usually favorable to good preservation of the material. If we consider only the pottery found whether in Neolithic disturbed contexts or in later deposits, the material from Sector B is much more often damaged than that from Sector A (respectively 74% and 58%). And we must mention that there are much more sherds coming from later deposits, in which one could expect Neolithic sherds to be more damaged, in Sector A than in Sector B. The difference noticed between both sectors could be due to the fact that Neolithic level was exposed shorter to erosion in Sector A since this part of the site was reoccupied yet during the early Ubaid period when Sector B Neolithic level kept exposed to erosion till the terminal Ubaid period.

7.3 Dark-Faced Burnished Ware

This ware was first identified and named by R. J. Braidwood for the Amuq Plain material (Braidwood and Braidwood 1960: 49). As has already been discussed (Le Mière and Nieuwenhuyse 1996: 126-127), the Amuq material to which this term corresponds is probably not completely homogeneous and could be composed of two, or perhaps more, different wares. It seems to be necessary to return to this question. When the term "Dark-Faced Burnished Ware" refers to surface color and treatment, the main characteristic of the ware is fabric: plant inclusions are absent, mineral inclusions are abundant, very large (>1mm and often >2mm) and mainly black, although not exclusively so; fabric color ranges from black to red, rarely dark buff, and mainly dark gray or chocolate brown; surface color range is the same as that seen in the fabric. The words "Dark-Faced" suggests that the dark-color of the surface was a deliberate act, but in the category described here, surface color is rarely darker than fabric color which seems to rule out a systematic use of such a technique. We have already seen it in other ware found on many other sites (see Gray Black Ware below), as well as a small group of the Dark-Faced Burnished Ware (see end of this paragraph). The dark color of the fabric and surface, in the case of Dark-Faced Burnished Ware, is due to the chemical composition of this ware: very low in calcium and very high in iron (Bader *et al.* 1994: Table 2; see also below). Such fabric, even when completely oxidized, never turns a light color such as beige or light buff. On the basis of the chemical composition, we maintain the term "Dark-Faced Burnished Ware", which in addition to the Amuq material has been recognized at many other sites in North-Western Syria and in Cilicia (Ras Shamra, Tell el-Kerkh, Mersin, Sakçe Gözü, ...). Furthermore, the chemical composition of this ware corresponds to a specific geological environment, ophiolithic areas, found in exactly the same region of North-Western Syria and Cilicia (Le Mière and Picon 1987: 136). Consequently, it is highly probable that this pottery was imported from this area, justifying the continued use of the term "Dark-Faced Burnished Ware" (hereafter termed DFBW), although it does not fit very well with the strict meaning of the words.

Table 7.2 Amount of sherds of the "bulk" and the wares.

	"Bulk"	Dark-Faced Burnished Ware	Gray Black Ware	Mineral Coarse Ware	Mineral Coarse Ware-like	Total
Frequency	1495	31	46	11	26	1609
Percentage	92.9	1.9	2.9	0.7	1.6	100.0

DFBW was found in Kosak Shamali in restricted quantities (31 sherds), not too surprising as it was imported on to the site (see below p. 189). General fabric characteristics are as indicated above for most (25) of the DFBW sherds but the 6 other ones show peculiar characteristics. They are not included in the group described now. The outside surface is always burnished and in two cases slipped and burnished. Mean thickness is 6.3mm. While such a small collection of sherds is not very informative about shape, one carination and three neck sherds were present. Many of these DFBW sherds are decorated; one is incised (pattern unidentified); 9 have red painted decoration, although the pattern is unclear because the sherds are too small, and also because DFBW is commonly decorated with a pattern of large (3 cm or more) bands of which we mostly find fragments (Fig. 7.11: 16 and 17).

As yet mentioned six of the sherds from the Kosak Shamali material do not strictly belong to DFBW as defined above: they correspond exactly to the term "Dark-Faced Burnished Ware" as the surface has been deliberately darkened and also burnished. This group is very homogenous (possibly because there are so few pieces), and shares the range in fabric color seen in DFBW, also due to a chemical composition extremely low in calcium. But this composition is very different from that of DFBW (see below). The color of the mineral inclusions is the same as in DFBW, but they are only medium or large in size (<1mm) which occurs only occasionally in DFBW. Thickness is smaller (m=5mm) too. Shape cannot be determined from these sherds. Four have comb impressed decoration. Although very restricted in number, this group seems to have definite characteristics and should be considered separately.

7.4 Gray Black Ware

Gray Black Ware is defined first by its dark surface: black, gray or brown. The chemical composition of this ware includes a rather high percentage of calcium which cannot be responsible for the color. In this case, color is due to a reducing atmosphere at the final stage of the pottery firing process, and evident on many sherds with a fabric lighter in color than the surface. The second characteristic, which combined with color contributes to define Gray Black Ware, is a very fine fabric containing,

in general, a few, small sized plant inclusions. Mineral inclusions are fine (invisible) and very rarely medium in size (<0.5mm). We should stress that the bulk of the Kosak Shamali pottery is of a rather fine fabric so that some sherds could have been mistaken for Gray Black Ware when they are not, as Gray Black Ware sherds do not all show deliberate darkening of the surface because of reoxydization problems. The number of sherds (46) for this ware could be somewhat too high.

The Gray Black Ware from Kosak Shamali is mostly burnished and in 2 cases slipped and burnished. Walls are thin with an average thickness of 6.7mm. The shape of a rather high proportion of rims can be determined, possibly because of the rather small size of Gray Black Ware vessels. There are only 2 neck fragments; carination appears to be characteristic of the ware. One sherd has brown painted decoration (pattern unknown) and another is impressed and incised (3 lines of grain shape impressions on the shoulder and an incised dotted triangle below; Fig. 7.10: 6).

7.5 Mineral Coarse Ware

This ware has already been defined (Le Mière and Nieuwenhuyse 1996: 128) and is clearly recognizable. The main characteristics are the large quantity, size (>1mm) and type (calcite, either crushed or not) of mineral inclusions. Other characteristics include surface burnishing, wall thickness and vessel shape (usually closed, frequently with lugs). The use of this ware for cooking is suggested not only by the fabric with very large calcite inclusions, which is one of the solutions to the problem of resistance to thermal shock (Le Mière and Picon 1998: 17), but also by shape and black traces (probably soot) frequently found on the ware. In fact, cooking ware is present in Neolithic as well as later assemblages. If a few sherds can clearly be identified as Mineral Coarse Ware, the fabric of others is comparable with that of Mineral Coarse Ware but without the other characteristics. As has already been mentioned, most Neolithic material was mixed with later material. Although this group of Mineral Coarse Ware-like sherds has not been recognized as belonging to one of the later assemblages, it raises some suspicion, because the number (26) would bring the Mineral Coarse Ware count up to 37 sherds, a higher than usual proportion for this ware. Furthermore, if we compare this group of sherds with the 11 Mineral Coarse Ware sherds, differences in several characteristics are apparent: half the group is not burnished while, except for one sherd, the Mineral Coarse Ware is always burnished; wall thickness is smaller (m=10.6) than in Mineral Coarse Ware (m=11.8); no sherd had mineral inclusions of crushed calcite; two closed rims and a lug (Fig. 7.4 : 20) were found among the 11 Mineral Coarse Ware sherds but neither of these elements appear in the other group. Therefore, it seems justified to analyse this group of sherds separately, and not to include them as Mineral Coarse Ware even if we still keep them provisionally as Neolithic.

7.6 "The bulk"

7.6.1 Technology

(1) General description
The bulk comprises 1495 sherds, most of which (95%) are plant tempered[1]. About 55% contain large plant inclusions, 40% small ones, and hardly any very large ones (Table 7.3). Sherds with rare and large plant temper represent 0.2% of the bulk, while those with rare and small plant temper represent 8%. Rounded traces of plants, identified as husks (S. Forni and G. Willcox, pers. com.), have been found in 8% of the bulk; husks can be predominant but they are usually found together with other plant parts. They are included in the count of the large plant inclusions group since they appear to have no specific link with characteristics other than those associated with the large plant inclusions. Mineral inclusions are mostly very small and visible in less than 10% of the sherds (Table 7.4). Surface color is mainly pink/reddish (53%) and beige/buff (33%) (Table 7.5). Over 70% of the sherds have a gray core corresponding to the high percentage of plant tempering: gray cores are twice as frequent in plant tempered sherds than others. As a matter of fact core color depends on the intensity of reoxydation during the final stage of the firing process, and it is the presence of plant inclusions, whatever their size or quantity, which really makes the difference. Wall thickness ranges from 3 to 25mm (m=9.2). Burnishing is the most common form of surface treatment (55%; Table 7.6), often producing a very even and glossy surface, either because of very heavy and careful burnishing, or

*Table 7.3 Presence and size of plant inclusions of the "bulk" *.*

	No plant inclusions	Rare and small plant inclusions	Abundant and small plant inclusions	Large plant inclusions	Very large plant inclusions	Total
Frequency	71	118	483	816	3	1491
Percentage	4.8	7.9	32.4	54.7	0.2	100.0

*The quantity of plant inclusions, which was roughly estimated, turned out to be significant only in the case of the small and rare ones, so we will introduce this character only in this case.

Table 7.4 Size of mineral inclusions of the "bulk".

	Small (invisible)	Middle and Large (<1 mm)	Very large (>1 mm)	Total
Frequency	1383	42	60	1485
Percentage	93.1	2.8	4.0	100.0

[1] Comment on the terms inclusions and temper: we use both terms temper and inclusions for plant inclusions because these were clearly added and most likely to serve as temper; for mineral inclusions it is more difficult to determine whether they were added to the clay or whether they were originally in it, so we use only the term inclusions.

possibly because of clay quality. Other surface treatment included smoothing (33%), and red or brown-slipping plus burnishing (12%) (slipping was always burnished except on 1 sherd).

(2) Significant technological characteristics

The presence/absence of plant inclusions is usually the main element used to define fine and coarse pottery. However, with such a high percentage of plant tempered sherds it is clearly necessary to use other criteria to determine whether they are all coarse or whether some could be considered as fine pottery. Therefore, size and quantity of plant inclusions is included, and fineness of sherds without plant inclusions will also be considered. Whereas size and quantity of mineral inclusions, surface treatment and wall thickness were seen to be significant characteristics, surface and fabric color were much less meaningful, although important elements for the identification of DFBW and Gray Black Ware (see above).

The very low percentage of visible mineral inclusions is clearly related to the high percentage of plant tempered pottery; less than 5% of plant tempered sherds have visible mineral inclusions in contrast to the about 70% seen in non-plant tempered sherds: it is important to stress the proportion (40%) of very large inclusions (>1mm) in non-plant tempered pottery even though the group as a whole is rather small (71 sherds), because it does not correlate with fineness usually associated with the absence of plant inclusions. Furthermore, if we consider wall thickness and its relationship to mineral inclusion size (divided into 3 groups: invisible, <1mm, and >1mm) (Table 7.7), it is evident that in non-plant tempered sherds, wall thickness in the latter two groups, respectively m=8.9mm and m=11mm, is comparable for the first one and even bigger for the last one than that of the plant tempered group. Wall thickness of non-plant tempered sherds with invisible mineral inclusions (m=7.6mm) is much smaller. These are the only non-plant tempered sherds that can be considered as fine. Quantity of mineral inclusions does not appear to be significant in relation to size and quantity of plant temper, nor with wall thickness.

Wall thickness does not appear affected by the presence/absence of plant inclusions: mean thickness of 9.2mm for the plant tempered group and 9.4mm for the non-plant tempered group, which is probably due to the high proportion of sherds without plant inclusions with very large mineral inclusions. But among the plant tempered group inclusion size is clearly related to wall thickness: mean of 9.9mm for the large plant inclusions group and 8.1mm for the small inclusions. And, as already noticed in the non-plant tempered pottery, mineral inclusion size could also be related to thickness but

Table 7.5 Surface colors of the "bulk".

	Black	Gray	Brown	Beige/Buff	Pink/Reddish	Total
Frequency	2	46	158	488	796	1490
Percentage	0.1	3.1	10.6	32.8	53.4	100.0

Table 7.6 Surface treatment of the "bulk".

	None*	Smoothing	Burnishing	Slipping	Total
Frequency	12	444	749	157	1362
Percentage	0.9	32.6	55.0	11.5	100.0

*On some sherds we could not recognize any surface treatment and the condition of the sherds does not seem to be responsible for that, nevertheless such a small group is not really representative and we just mention it but do not get any conclusion out of it.

the number of sherds containing visible inclusions is very small and a larger sample would be necessary to confirm this tendency (Table 7.7).

Surface treatment is not related to the presence/absence of plant inclusions nor to the size and quantity of plant inclusions as much as might be expected (Table 7.8). While smoothing and burnishing are rather in comparable percentages for each category, slipping occurs more frequently on non-plant tempered pottery and on pottery with rare and small plant inclusions; it occurs also a little more frequently on pottery with abundant and small plant inclusions and definitely less frequently on large plant-tempered pottery.

Wall thickness of smoothed and burnished pottery is similar (m=9.1 and m=9.3 respectively) but slipped sherds are much thinner (m=7.9), regardless of the size and quantity of plant inclusions.

7.6.2 Shape

As well as those wall sherds which are large enough to indicate body shape (convex, straight or concave), 348 pieces including the two complete vessels and other complete profile pieces, already mentioned, provide some indication of shape. They form a quarter of the total sherds which is a rather high proportion. Nevertheless, the number of sherds representing each characteristic is not large and when considered together, the number of occurrences becomes too small to be significant, preventing a detailed description of shape. Therefore, the few generalizations presented below must be treated with caution.

(1) General description

Two oval shapes have been clearly recognized indicating that such shapes exist, although nothing can be said about their real importance in the Kosak Shamali material because of the proportion of small sherds.

Among the 74 rims of recognizable direction, nearly 50% are open (Fig. 7.5), over 30% are vertical and 20% are closed (Fig. 7.4). These latter types do not include collared shapes (see below), so that when taken as a whole, closed shapes are by far the most numerous, although hole-mouth closed shapes are not too abundant. Rim diameter of non-collared shapes (mesured in 57 cases),

Table 7.7 Mean thickness of plant inclusions groups linked with mineral inclusions ones.

	No plant inclusions	Small plant inclusions	Large plant inclusions
Invisible	m=7.6	m=8.2	m=9.8
<1 mm	m=8.9	m=9.1	m=10.1
>1 mm	m=11.0	m=9.2	m=10.7

Table 7.8 Surface treatment linked with plant inclusions.

	No plant inclusions	Small and rare plant inclusions	Small plant inclusions	Large plant inclusions	Total
Smoothing	18	31	135	258	442
Frequency	4.1	7.0	30.5	58.4	100.0
Burnishing	33	53	242	419	747
Frequency	4.4	7.1	32.4	56.1	100.0
Slipping	17	21	66	53	157
Frequency	10.8	13.4	42.0	33.8	100.0

ranges from 9 to 38cm (m=20.0).

186 sherds, that is more than half the sherds showing some element of shape, indicate the presence of a neck (Figs. 7.6 and 7.7: 1). Only 29 show a complete neck profile with direction and shape; 103 sherds are body fragments from the junction between neck and shoulder. Neck direction is either open (17 cases) or vertical (12 cases), with one example of a closed neck. Shape (determined in 82 necks) is concave, except for 4 straight necks and a convex one. Almost all combinations of diverse directions and shapes exist. Neck height is variable ranging from 2 to 10cm, and neck diameter (measurable on 30 sherds), ranges from 7 to 20cm (m=13.5), with one much larger example (35cm).

Body shape, described for 1230 sherds, is nearly always convex (97%), very rarely straight (2.5%) and in very few cases concave. The small proportion of straight shapes is probably related to the large number of collared shapes, which are generally convex. Carinated sherds are rare (19 pieces) (Fig. 7.4: 9-11). Rims are mostly extremely simple, indistinct (95%) and rounded (over 90%).

The number of base sherds (44) (Fig. 7.7: 2-13) is rather low compared to those pieces showing some element of shape (12.6%), probably due to the 9 clearly recognizable, convex bases possibly suggesting the presence of further bases of this type, although not identifiable because of small sherd size. Apart from these convex bases, all other bases are flat; only 4 are distinct. It was possible to measure just one diameter. A fragment of the base of a finger-impressed Husking Tray was present; it is flat but so damaged that it does not provide further information on shape or measurement. No handle of any sort was found in the whole bulk.

(2) Link between shape and technological features
Fabric characteristics do not seem to correlate greatly with shape except that the proportion of oriented rims is higher in the group with small plant inclusions than in the large inclusion group. One might hypothesize this to be due to the slightly higher proportion of closed shapes (providing fewer rim sherds than open ones) and/or deeper shapes in the latter group. The proportion of neck sherds is the same in every plant tempered group and is slightly lower in the non-plant tempered group.

While there is very little evidence of smoothing on the rims of uncollard shapes, when present it is more frequently seen on closed shapes. This element, together with a possibly high proportion of large plant inclusion, a mean thickness greater than the large plant tempered group, suggests a certain "coarseness" of hole-mouth closed shapes. All carinated sherds, (admittedly few in number) are burnished or slipped. Necks are also more frequently burnished or slipped than smoothed. It is difficult to estimate the significance of such a link because of the few sherds (11) which have both neck and body characteristics, thus preventing assessment of whether the neck surface was treated more carefully than the rest of the vessel, or whether there are more collared shapes in the burnished and slipped group than in the smoothed one. We will discuss this question further in relation to decoration (see below).

7.6.3 Decoration

(1) General description
A very large proportion of the bulk is decorated (33%) with a limited array of techniques: impression, painting and incision (Table 7.9). Some sherds are both impressed and painted; they are included in the impressed group for the description, except

Table 7.9 Techniques of decoration.

	Impressions	Impressions and painting	Painting	Incisions	Total
Frequency	452	14	67	1	534
Percentage	84.6	2.6	12.5	0.2	100.0

when other specified. Examples of incision are limited to two rather shallow lines on one sherd. Impression is by far the most important mode of decoration, present on over 30% of the pottery in contrast to the 4.2% with painted decoration.

Painted decoration (Fig. 7.11) is red or brown, and black in two cases (both sherds very likely belong to the same vessel). Most pieces are burnished. Patterns identifiable on 26 sherds were most often plain or hatched, sometimes alternating, triangles. The organization of patterns visible on larger sherds show one row, or a few superimposed rows of triangles along the rim (Fig. 7.11: 9-15). Other patterns consist of a single or several simple parallel bands, or one band at the base of the neck. The pattern on the two black painted sherds, mentioned above, appears to be sinuous, more or less parallel, vertical lines. The previously mentioned painted decoration along the rim never appears on the neck, except as a band at the base.

Over 90% of impressions were made with a comb (Figs. 7.8, 7.9 and 7.10: 1-5). Smooth or sharp points, nails, smooth tools in a variety of shapes (round, oval . . .), angular tools and hollow stems were also used (Fig. 7.10: 7-21), but less often (evident on 3 to 11 sherds at most). These diverse impressions often appear to be organized in parallel lines, but the sherds are usually too small to provide good data on patterning.

Combs consisted of between 3 and 22 teeth, although very long ones are rare. Impressions are straight or, less frequently, curved. On those sherds where organization of impressions identifiable, 335 out of 375 show parallel impressions, 18 parallel rocker ones, 7 zigzags (horizontal or vertical) and 10 have no clear organization. About half the sherds with bands of impressions show some organization of these bands. Most are horizontal, oriented in the same (60%) or opposite (40%) direction, the latter sometimes forming chevrons when very close to each other; a dozen are vertical, and in one case horizontal and vertical bands appear together. In 3 cases, comb has been trailed rather than impressed (Fig. 7.10: 5).

Impressions never appear along the rim nor the neck, and even when they cover a very large part of the body, they do not appear on the lowest part of the vessel. Impressions frequently do not start directly at the base of the neck on collared vessels but lower on the shoulder, the upper part being either burnished or painted and burnished. Painting on painted and impressed sherds (14 pieces) appears as a band on the shoulder and/or at the base of neck. On the sole example of a complete neck, painting covers the neck as well as the uppermost part of shoulder, suggesting that a painted neck would have been rather common among the painted and impressed group. No clear painted pattern appeared on the few (4) painted and impressed sherds which are not part of a neck, due to the small size of these pieces.

(2) Links between decoration and technological features

Painting and impressions are found in every category of pottery, whether with or without plant inclusions, although there seems to be some relationship between decoration and fabric. The proportion of non-plant tempered, impressed pottery is rather low (7% compared with 30% for the bulk as a whole), while the percentage in every group, with either large, small, or rare and small plant inclusions, does not differ from the general pattern. Furthermore, painting occurs less frequently in the group with large plant inclusions than in that with small ones, indicating another link between decoration and size of plant inclusions.

In every group of plant inclusions (different sizes) impressed sherds are slightly thinner than the bulk as a whole. The same applies to painted sherds, with the exception of the small inclusions group, although this observation is made with caution because of the small number of sherds in each group.

Surface treatment on both groups of decorated pottery is quite different to general surface treatment. Two thirds of the impressed sherds are smoothed, twice that of the bulk of pottery. This may be explained by the fact that burnishing is applied to a leather dry surface while impressions would have probably already been made by this stage of drying. It may also have been the potter's choice not to burnish impressed pottery or, at least that part of the vessel which was impressed; there are 2 cases with burnishing on the lower part of the vessel, below the impressed area. In two thirds of the cases, shoulder and/or neck sherds are burnished. Painted pottery is rarely smoothed (about 5%) but, despite the small size of the painted group, it appears that burnishing was the usual surface treatment accorded it.

(3) Links between decoration and shapes

We mentioned earlier that impressed decoration never appears along the rim; in fact none of the impressed group has rims except for two collared pieces, and none is carinated. Therefore, there is no proof of impressed pottery having rims other than collared. The proportion of neck sherds is comparable with that seen in general, but since necks themselves are never impressed, many neck sherds could be from the impressed group, but impossible to identify as such. If correct, our suspicion that a rather large proportion of burnished or painted necks are part of the impressed group would explain the large proportion of burnished and slipped necks in the bulk as a whole (see above, p. 185). Impressed bases, are quite rare (3). As already noted on two pieces, the lowest part of the vessel was not decorated which might explain this small number. It suffices to mention that two of the three bases are convex.

There are numerous rims in the painted group (18), 15 of which could be oriented. None are closed. Two carinations and 10 neck sherds were found in this group. One very small neck sherd had a painted band at the base of the neck and may have been part of an impressed and painted vessel, given that we do not know whether the body was impressed or not. Only one base (convex) is associated with the painted group. As we have already noted that painting was applied mainly along the rim, and as several sherds (7) were large enough to show that the lower part of the vessel was not decorated, the large number of rim sherds and single base of the painted group are not surprising.

7.7 Chemical analyses

51 samples have been analysed [2] (Table 7.10): 44 samples of pottery, 1 sample of mudbrick and 6 samples of clay. Pottery is represented by samples of DFBW, both usual and peculiar types (see above p. 180), Gray-Black Ware, "Mineral Coarse Ware-like" (see above p. 181) and by samples of the bulk. As explained above (p. 183) the mere presence/absence of plant inclusions is not sufficient to distinguish coarse ware from fine ware, so bulk samples are classified on the base of the presence and also the size of plant and mineral

Table 7.10 List of analyzed samples by type.

Type	Sample nos.
" Bulk " with large plant inclusions	KSL 1, 2, 4, 5, 7, 8, 11, 12, 14, 16, 17, 20, 26, 27, 48
" Bulk " with small plant inclusions	KSL 3, 6, 9, 10, 13, 18, 19, 21, 22, 28
" Bulk " without plant inclusions (small mineral inclusions)	KSL 15, 23, 24, 25, 38
" Mineral Coarse Ware-like "	KSL 29, 30, 31
"Gray-Black Ware "	KSL 32, 33, 34, 51
Usual Dark-Faced Burnished Ware	KSL 37, 39, 47
Peculiar Dark-Faced Burnished Ware	KSL 35, 36, 49, 50
Mudbrick	KSL 41
Clay	KSL 40, 42, 43, 44, 45, 46

---

[2] Analyses have been carried out in the Laboratoire de Céramologie de Lyon - CNRS, and the interpretation of the results of analyses was made by M. Picon whom I should like to thank.

inclusions: either without plant inclusions (with invisible mineral inclusions) or with small plant inclusion or with large plant inclusions. Let us precise that one of these sherds is not Neolithic but Ubaid (n°15) and two others (n°23-24) are somewhat doubtful from this point of view as well as the Mineral Coarse Ware-like ones (see below p. 191). The mud-brick sample (n°41) comes from an Ubaid level. The clay samples are coming from the Euphrates bank (n°44-46) or from the Nahar Sarine bank (n°42-43); n°40 is a sample of clay coming from a floading level in the archaeological deposit, therefore it is very likely Nahar Sarine clay since this river flow by the tell.

Analyses have been carried out by X-ray fluorescence. Ten main elements have been analysed (Na₂O, K₂O, MgO, CaO, MnO, Al₂O₃, Fe₂O₃, SiO₂, TiO₂, P₂O₅), as well as ten trace elements (Rb, Sr, Ba, Ni, Zn, Cr, Zr, La, Ce, V). Chemical analyses data have been processed by cluster analysis for which only 17 elements have been used, the other ones (Na, P, La) being discarded because of some incertainty of the analyses.

The dendrogram (Fig. 7.1) shows a large group, group B, which would represent the main local production together with the sherds of group C, the composition of which is rather comparable. Within these two groups we find all the plant tempered sherds: sherd n°22 is isolated because of problems of alteration (fixation of barium) but it actually belongs to the groups B/C as probably does sherd n°27 which is also classified apart for the same reason; sherd n°5 could be an exception and not belong to the groups B/C, though it is plant tempered, because its composition is marginal, but this one is not extremely different of the composition of groups B/C and it is not impossible that it also belongs to these groups. Only one sample of these groups is not plant tempered and it happens to be also Ubaid; unfortunately too few later sherds have been analysed to make possible any further interpretation. The size of groups B/C and the proportion of plant tempered sherds which is the main group of pottery on the site are two arguments to hypothesize groups B/C as representing the local production.

Even if clays n°44 and 45 (Euphrates bank) show a composition somewhat different of that of groups B/C, it is probable that the pottery of these groups have been made of Euphrates clays, when they are clearly not made of Nahar Sarine clay (n° 40, 42, 43): the ratio Cr/Ni is much higher in the Nahar Sarine clay samples than in the Euphrates ones (Tables 7.11 and 7.12). Since the Nahar Sarine flows by the tell of Kosak Shamali which is situated further from the Euphrates (650 m) we expected the pottery from the site to be made of the clay of the Nahar Sarine, so it is worth noticing that it is not the case. Though, we must mention the fact that the Nahar Sarine clay samples we analysed have a very high percentage of calcite (up to 35% of CaO) which is not so suitable to make pottery. The only sample of mudbrick which has been analysed (n°41) has very probably been made with Nahar Sarine clay, which was even more expectable since architecture requires a very large quantity of clay usually taken as near as possible from the place where it will be worked out; and, as a matter of fact, calcareous clay is rather suitable to make mudbricks (Guest-Papamanoli 1978).

Nevertheless a small group of pottery, group D, could have, with some probability, been made of Nahar Sarine clay also: it is composed of samples of pottery without plant inclusions and of samples of "Mineral Coarse Ware-like". Amongst them sample n°25 has the highest proportion of chromium (Cr) and could have been made with Nahar Sarine clay but not in Kosak Shamali, possibly upper stream, nearer to the volcanic region from where Nahar Sarine flows and which explains the ratio chromium/nickel (Cr/Ni) and the high proportion of chromium of its clays. The composition of samples n°23 and 38 are marginal of group D, nevertheless they can be better compared with that of Nahar Sarine clays than with that of Euphrates clays. These two samples could be included in group D. The possibility, mentioned above, that n°25 could have been not locally made should be considered as well for all the group D and sherds n°23 and 38: this hypothesis was suggested by the model encountered on several sites previously studied (amongst them Bouqras and the Sinjar sites; Bader *et al.* 1994: 67) in which, beside a large group of local production and some samples clearly imported, possibly from far away, appears a group of fine ware (without plant inclusions) which is not local but could have been imported from not far distance. If this model is the rule on Near Eastern Neolithic sites then the group D could correspond to this regional production imported in Kosak Shamali. But it should be verified.

Beside this group possibly not locally made, two small groups have been clearly imported in Kosak Shamali: group A and group F. They are composed respectively of peculiar DFBW samples and of usual DFBW ones. The two groups have quite distinct chemical composition and this is one of the reasons mentionned above (p. 180) when considering these two groups separately. If both groups have rather low percentages of calcium their composition are quite different. Unfortunately the composition of the peculiar DFBW group (group A) does not give any indication about the geological type of area where it could come from. This is not the case of the usual DFBW group which is yet known from many different sites (Le Mière and Picon 1987: 144; Bader *et al.* 1994: 67; Le Mière 2000: 132) and, as explained above, presents certain characters of composition which indicate an origin in an ophiolithic area: this type of geological zone can be found in the Southern part of the Taurus, not further east than the area of Malatya, and also in a not so large zone along the Mediterranean sea, a few kilometers back inland, far south to Latakia. This is precisely in this region of North-Western Syria - Cilicia that this ware is the most abundant (up to 80% or more in the material from Amuq, Ras Shamra and Tell el-Kerkh) when it never reaches 5% in the other regions. Unfortunately we can't precise better the area from where the usual DFBW was exported. We must simply indicate that the usual DFBW samples from Kosak Shamali contains a very low proportion of titanium, characteristic rather rare in clays, and yet encountered in the composition of DFBW samples from many different sites (Bader *et al.* 1994: 67; Le Mière 2000: 132). So this material should come from a rather small region which has exported its production in many directions and rather far away.

The Gray-Black Ware samples belong to the group B and don't show any special composition: it is worth noticing it because we mentioned the

Table 7.11 Mean concentrations and standard deviations of groups B/C (Fig. 7.1).

a. Major and minor elements expressed as oxydes (percent)

n=27	Na2O	K2O	MgO	CaO	MnO	Al2O3	Fe2O3	SiO2	TiO2	P2O5
m	1.57	3.2	5.9	14.7	0.147	14.1	8.4	50.6	0.85	0.27
σ	0.2	0.3	0.9	2.2	0.016	0.4	0.5	1.2	0.06	0.15

b. Trace elements (ppm)

n=27	Rb	Sr	Ba	Ni	Zn	Cr	Zr	La	Ce	V
m	74	461	326	301	126	297	157	19	60	156
σ	9	48	85	76	11	34	16	7	7	9

Table 7.12 Mean concentrations and standard deviations of groups D/E1/E2 and samples nos. 23 and 38 (Fig. 7.1).

a. Major and minor elements expressed as oxydes (percent)

n=11	Na2O	K2O	MgO	CaO	MnO	Al2O3	Fe2O3	SiO2	TiO2	P2O5
m	1.32	2.9	4.7	24.9	0.093	11.8	6.7	46.2	0.93	0.3
σ	0.48	0.9	0.5	5.5	0.026	1.2	0.7	3.7	0.13	0.19

b. Trace elements (ppm)

n=11	Rb	Sr	Ba	Ni	Zn	Cr	Zr	La	Ce	V
m	69	569	297	157	110	372	186	12	70	161
σ	6	156	84	17	16	92	13	8	7	26

fact that it is not always so easy to clearly identify Gray-Black Ware in Kosak Shamali material (see above p. 181) when on sites previously studied Gray-Black Ware can clearly be identified and shows also peculiar (or at least marginal) chemical compositions which let suspect, if not a foreign origin, possibly a specialized production (Bader *et al.* 1994: 67). In Kosak Shamali Gray-Black Ware could simply be a part of the usual production.

So the chemical analyses show that most part of the Neolithic pottery used in Kosak Shamali would have been locally produced, very probably all the plant tempered one and possibly also some of the non-plant tempered one. The surely foreign production would be only composed of two different groups. This picture is somewhat simpler than the picture previously encountered when studying other Near Eastern Neolithic materials, but it could be simply due to the yet mentioned general homogeneity of Kosak Shamali pottery.

7.8 Discussion

The primary result of this study confirms that no technological characteristic (type, size and quantity of inclusions; surface treatment; thickness) of shape or decoration can in itself categorize Kosak Shamali pottery, and that none of the modalities of each characteristic is exclusive, although certain combinations of characteristics appear to be significant. Therefore, this material is highly variable and no ware other than the three previously identified (Dark-Faced Burnished Ware, Gray Black Ware and Mineral Coarse Ware) could be defined.

During the above description, we mentioned the question of fineness and coarseness of the pottery. In fact, while the pottery is usually categorized as fine or coarse, such characterizations are also significant when trying to set Kosak Shamali pottery in the evolutionary context of Neolithic pottery. The general evolution of Neolithic pottery shows firstly a trend to diversification and variability, followed by a decrease in variability and emergence of clearly defined categories announcing standardization. While this evolution is very progressive, the long sequence of Sabi Abyad provides elements of comparison.

In contrast to current opinion, the absence of plant inclusions did not appear to be a criteria of fineness as such, but only in relation to the size of mineral inclusions. If the small size of mineral inclusions is characteristic of fineness, the small size of plant inclusions is also clearly relevant since it is linked to a small mean thickness. Slipping, the most elaborate surface treatment, is related to the absence or small quantity of plant inclusions together with small thickness, and seems to be a rather good criteria of fineness, even if not exclusively applied to this particular type of pottery.

Only one shape characteristic is linked with coarseness and fineness: hole-mouth closed shapes often seem to combine characteristics of coarseness which could correspond to the use of such shapes as better adapted to storage (or preparing food), than the other shapes.

Decoration is often indicative of some degree of fineness and, in fact, the slightly smaller thickness of impressed sherds may be relevant, but beyond this, impressions are not linked with any other characteristic of fineness. Painted sherds appear to present more of such characteristics: smaller thickness, a large proportion of small plant inclusions and burnished surfaces except for rare cases of smoothing.

On the basis of these diverse elements it is possible to designate part of the bulk as "finer", that is those sherds without plant inclusions but with small mineral inclusions, and slipped or painted sherds with small (and rare) plant inclusions. Together they represent 10% of the bulk.

Although we have stressed the variability of the bulk, we must nevertheless point out the specific characteristics of a large part of this material; the impressed pottery. Technologically it is quite variable and cannot be seen as the result of specialized production, but it seems limited to collared shapes. This group of pottery is to a certain extent rather homogeneous. Because of its numbers (over 30% of the bulk), specific shape and certain characteristics due to decorative technique such as surface treatment (mainly smoothing), we must take it into consideration in our comparisons with other sites where it is not so well represented.

Before comparing the Kosak Shamali pottery with that of other sites, we must indicate a few differences between the various stratigraphic units. Differences between Neolithic and later levels, such as the smaller proportion of non-plant tempered sherds (together with a smaller proportion of sherds containing very large mineral inclusions), could be due to misidentification of some sherds as Neolithic as they are not very typical of any period. We have already mentioned this possibility with reference to the group of "Mineral Coarse Ware-like" sherds (see above p. 181), which are comparable to the sherds discussed here. That this difference is also noticeable between Neolithic levels from both Sector B and Sector A might be explained by the fact that later levels from each sector differ (Ubaid in Sector A and mainly Post-Ubaid in Sector B), the questionable sherds possibly belonging to the Ubaid assemblage and not to Post-Ubaid one. We must emphasize that only two Mineral Coarse Ware - like sherds were found in Neolithic levels (1 in each sector) and that all the others (24) come from later levels in Sector A.

The higher proportion of sherds with small plant inclusions in Neolithic levels than in later ones enhances the general fineness of the Neolithic pottery discussed previously.

With reference to shape, the proportion of oriented rims in Neolithic levels is twice that in later levels. Furthermore, 8 out of the 9 convex bases come from the Neolithic levels. This is probably due to better preservation of material from Neolithic levels, where sherds are bigger, than later levels where the material is mainly in the form of loose sherds in the filling.

Finally, the proportion of impressed pottery is the same in the Neolithic levels of both sectors, and is the same in Neolithic and later levels, but is slightly higher in the undisturbed Neolithic levels. The presence of an important proportion of impressed pottery is thus confirmed as a definite characteristic of Kosak Shamali pottery.

In summary, there are no great differences suggesting different Neolithic assemblages in the various stratigraphic units. Disturbance of Neolithic levels and subsequent mixing of material has been noticed, but is not to such an extent as to prevent us from considering the Neolithic

collection as homogeneous. We will use it for comparative purposes with other sites, while at the same time taking into account the few doubtful elements.

As might be expected from its geographical position, Kosak Shamali belongs to the North Syria - Cilicia ceramic area; characteristics of shape and decoration at the site conform with the general characteristics of this area (Nishiaki *et al.* 1999: 25) (Fig. 7.2). But the area is rather extensive (Fig. 7.3) and at least two zones, an eastern (from the Balikh to the Euphrates) and a western (west of the Euphrates), have already been recognized. Further divisions are possible once better documentation is available for the period. Differences between the two zones are based on color and temper: light-colored and plant tempered in the east, dark-colored without plant temper in the west (Le Mière and Picon 1998: 15). Differences are also based on the dominant decorative technique, when it appears: painting in the east and impressions in the west, apparently associated with all fabric categories. To date, the boundary between these zones seems to be the Euphrates valley. Kosak Shamali (where most of the pottery is light-colored and plant-tempered) seems to belong to the eastern zone, but the very high proportion of impressed decoration suggests the Euphrates valley to be intermediate between both zones (Faura and Le Mière 1999: 290). The Pottery Neolithic period is not yet very well documented in the Upper-Euphrates valley, where Kosak Shamali is located, as excavation is still in progress at two nearby sites, Tell Halula and Ja'ade. The sequence at Halula, which appears to be quite long, has not yet been fully documented, while at Ja'ade, poor preservation of the sole pottery level, at the top of the archaeological deposit, provides only limited possibilities for comparison (Faura and Le Mière 1999; Faura in press). Investigations have just begun at two promising sites upstream to the north: Akarçay (N. Balkan, Y. Miyake and M. Molist, pers. com.) and Teleilat (M. Özdoğan, pers. com.), which currently provide no more than a few elements of comparison. The Sajour valley was surveyed and a few sites provided some Neolithic pottery but not abundant and characteristic enough for precise comparisons (Contenson 1985; Moore 1985). The Balikh valley, to the east, is much better known, in particular the site of Sabi Abyad (Le Mière and Nieuwenhuyse 1996). Almost no Pottery Neolithic sites have been found downstream to the south, except for Abu Hureyra (Moore 1975) which is not very informative. Finally, the nearest area to the west providing elements of comparison is the Qoueiq valley, which unfortunately has only been surveyed (Mellaart 1981). The coastal area, with Ras Shamra (Contenson 1992), Tell el-Kerkh (Tsuneki and Miyake 1996; Tsuneki et al. 1998), the Amuq plain sites (Braidwood and Braidwood 1960) and Mersin (Garstang 1953), are more distant from Kosak Shamali, but nevertheless we will also make comparisons with the pottery of these sites, if not directly then through comparison with other sites.

As verified again with the Kosak Shamali material, characterization of Neolithic pottery (and its evolution) is based on variation in proportions and not on the presence or absence of certain characteristics, so that a quantitative study is necessary to establish close comparisons. Although we cannot compare quantity exactly, trends visible in a sequence are significant. Therefore, we will begin with comparisons with the Sabi Abyad material for which we have some quantitative data and a long sequence.

The characteristics of pottery from the lowest level (Level 11) of Sabi Abyad indicate primarily the second stage of pottery development (Le Mière and Picon 1998:14-16), although some characteristics indicate a late phase of this stage (Le Mière and Nieuwenhuyse 1996: 141). The diversity of fabrics at Kosak Shamali, the abundance of more elaborate shapes such as collared pieces, and the evolved decoration do not correspond to this stage but to the subsequent one, represented at Sabi Abyad by the pottery of levels 10 to 4. In this part of the sequence, pottery evolves from very simple to increasingly diversified, followed by a decrease in diversity, to the rather standardized Halaf production. The appearance of new wares, proven not to have developed from traditional Sabi Abyad production, marks the beginning of the Transition from the Pre-Halaf to Halaf periods (levels 6-4). None of these wares are represented at Kosak Shamali so that we must look for comparable material in the pre-transition levels of Sabi Abyad (levels 10-7). As the first impressed sherds were found only in Level 8, a comparison between the pottery of both sites should be possible whether with Level 8 or with Level 7. The three defined wares (Dark-Faced Burnished Ware, Gray Black Ware, Mineral Coarse Ware) are all present in both Levels 8 and 7 at Sabi Abyad: the percentage of Dark-Faced Burnished Ware at Kosak Shamali is closer to that of Level 8 than to that of level 7 where it is twice as high. The percentage of Gray Black Ware, similar in both levels, is higher in Kosak Shamali but may be overestimated (see above p. 181). Mineral Coarse Ware is present in comparable percentages at Kosak Shamali and Sabi Abyad Levels 8 and 7. When the "bulk" is considered, the percentage of sherds with small plant inclusions is the same (around 40%) in Level 8 as at Kosak Shamali; it decreases rapidly from Level 7 where it is two times less frequent than in Level 8 and continues to decrease in Level 6. The general trends in surface treatment at Sabi Abyad show an increase of smoothing and decrease of burnishing and slipping, so that Kosak Shamali compares more favorably with Level 8 in which the proportion of smoothing is lower and that of burnishing and slipping higher. However, the value of this comparison is limited by the fact that Level 8 is not too different from Level 7 and that the main change occurs between Levels 7 and 6. Furthermore, the Kosak Shamali pottery differs in surface treatment from that at Sabi Abyad Level 8: burnishing and slipping are more than twice as frequent and smoothing occurs nearly twice less frequently at Kosak Shamali, when we might have expected a much higher proportion of smoothing because of the high percentage of impressed sherds at Kosak Shamali (see above p. 186). Shape is of no help as a comparative tool between Sabi Abyad and Kosak Shamali as these characteristics show no clear changes or even evolutionary trends from Levels 8 to 6: we can simply state that the different shapes present on one site are present on the other, and that the more typical characteristics of Level 6 (S-shape profile and neck with a marked shoulder) are either absent (the former) or very rare (1 case of the later) at Kosak Shamali. As already mentioned, impressed pottery is much more abundant at Kosak Shamali than Sabi Abyad, regardless of level considered: the highest percentage, in Level 7, is about 2% but more than 30% at Kosak Shamali. While painting also occurs more frequently at Kosak Shamali (4.5%) than Sabi Abyad (about 1% in Level 8 and about 2% in Level 7), nevertheless, it is more comparable. Decoration seems to increase throughout the pre-Transition sequence, and from this perspective Kosak Shamali, although different, resembles Level 7 more than Level 8. With regard to decoration, impressed and painted patterns are very similar at both sites. When considering the combination of impressions and painting, it is evident that comb impressed horizontal bands alternating with painted horizontal bands on the vessel body do not occur at Kosak Shamali. The cross-hatched painted pattern, which appears in Level 6 at Sabi Abyad, is not present at Kosak Shamali.

The detailed comparison between Kosak Shamali and Sabi Abyad (somewhat limited by the preliminary nature of the Sabi Abyad report) shows that most of the general pottery characteristics from both sites are the same. The absence of wares appearing at the Transition clearly distinguishes Kosak Shamali from Sabi Abyad Level 6, and this is confirmed by several other elements. The pottery from Sabi Abyad Level 8 provides the best parallel with Kosak Shamali pottery but, while some arguments are compelling, others are less so and the difference between Levels 8 and 7 is not always very clear. We must stress that the specificity of Kosak Shamali pottery, in particular the proportion of impressed pottery and the proportions of each surface treatment, may have hampered the comparison.

In the Qoueiq valley to the west (Mellaart 1981), 26 sites were surveyed which provided Neolithic pottery corresponding to our third stage of pottery development. The second stage has not been clearly identified, although a few elements suggest its presence and some sites might reveal earlier levels not indicated from surface material. Two types of assemblages, Qoueiq A and Qoueiq B, have been recognized, based mainly on comparisons with the Amuq sequence, and correspond to Amuq A and Amuq B assemblages. But they are not similar. The main group of Qoueiq pottery, Monochrome Burnished Ware, is equivalent to Dark-Faced Burnished Ware, sometimes impressed and differing only by the generally somewhat lighter color of DFBW fabric; impressed decoration is much more frequent on plant tempered pottery, while impressed plant tempered pottery does not exist in the Amuq assemblage. Mellaart mentions the small quantity of coarse, undecorated, plant tempered ware in the Qoueiq assemblages but it actually forms a very small part (around 10%) of the Amuq pottery. He also notices the absence of plastic bands, ledge handles and knobs associated with this

ware, but it should be noticed that these features also occur on Dark-Faced Burnished Ware in the Amuq assemblage but are completely absent in the Qoueiq material, whatever the ware. The general composition of the Qoueiq assemblage differs greatly to that at Kosak Shamali because of the predominance of the DFBW-like group (Monochrome Burnished Ware) and the rather restricted amount of plant tempered pottery. Nevertheless the significant group of impressed plant tempered pottery is an element linking the Qoueiq material with Kosak Shamali. The shapes of impressed DFBW-like pottery are rather variable, open, closed, collared (seemingly with short necks) as in the Amuq material, but the impressed plant-tempered group contains predominantly, and possibly exclusively, collared shapes with no non-collared rims present, a point of similarity with Kosak Shamali. The scarcity of flat bases and the hint of a possible important proportion of convex bases is another common feature. As with the Qoueiq material, there is no plastic band or ledge-handle in Kosak Shamali except for one Mineral Coarse Ware lug, a characteristic feature of this ware. Mellaart distinguished a "very fine thin overfired variant" among the DFBW-like group, but unfortunately he did not give a detailed description of the ware. However, it could correspond to our small group of unusual DFBW described above (see p. 180). This needs to be checked but if correct would form a further parallel between the Qoueiq sites and Kosak Shamali, because, as Mellaart mentioned, this ware is not recorded from Amuq and, to date, nor from any other site. It would also be interesting to determine if these sherds are imported into the Qoueiq area as they are at Kosak Shamali. The painted decoration of Kosak Shamali has no equivalent in the Qoueiq material. However, should the seemingly sinuous vertical and parallel lines (only two fragmentary examples) be such a pattern, it would constitute another link between Kosak Shamali pottery and that of Qoueiq where it is a common pattern of the Early painted pottery, which is similar to the Brittle painted ware from the Amuq. In our comparison with Sabi Abyad material, we did not discuss pattern burnish decoration. There is no evidence of it at Kosak Shamali despite the presence of one doubtful sherd. At Sabi Abyad it exists but in very small quantities (one sample in each level 8 and 7), so that the absence of this decorative technique at Kosak Shamali might simply be due to the limited amount of pottery found on the site. Nevertheless, we must address the question of chronology raised by the Qoueiq assemblages. Pattern burnish appears only in Amuq B levels; it was not found at those Qoueiq sites in which later elements such as Early painted ware or Coarse incised ware were missing, and which together with pattern burnish appear for the first time in Amuq B. At Kosak Shamali pattern burnish and coarse incised pottery are also missing, so that the absence of pattern burnish could be due to the restricted amount of material from this site, but it might also have chronological significance. It should be noted that the "very fine thin overfired variant" of DFBW, suspected in Kosak Shamali, was not found associated with any later element either in the Qoueiq assemblages.

The comparison between Kosak Shamali pottery and that from the Qoueiq sites is limited in that the Qoueiq sites have only been surveyed and assemblages tentatively established; no quantitative data are available and, as explained above, many elements of comparison are rather hypothetical. Nevertheless, it is useful to provisionally consider these potential links, at least as a working hypothesis. The elements concerned are mainly those which differentiate the Qoueiq material from the coastal area (with large quantities of impressed plant tempered pottery, the absence of plastic bands or ledge-handles, the possible presence of "the very thin overfired variant" of DFBW, and the possible abundance of convex bases). The fact that some elements are not found either in the Balikh or in the coastal area, suggests an intermediate zone including the Euphrates and the area west of it, but this has to be further corroborated.

Akarçay and Teleilat, two new sites currently being investigated upstream, will, in the future, certainly provide important data concerning this point. At present, the information available from Akarçay provides no element for close comparison with Kosak Shamali. This is not the case for Teleilat where some clear links are already apparent from the precise illustrations and information kindly provided by M. Ozdoğan (pers. com.). The main element for comparison is: a very high percentage of impressed, plant tempered pottery; impressions are very similar to those found in Kosak Shamali, although they are more variable, possibly due to the abundance of material; painting (or "slip") is associated with impressed decoration, whether on the neck or around a possible rim but not on the lower body; illustrations indicate a predominance of collared shapes among impressed plant-tempered pottery, as occurs at Kosak Shamali. Painted pottery is also present in Teleilat, mainly in the form of geometric patterns, many of which appear at Kosak Shamali but some, such as cross-hatching, are more elaborate which may correspond to later levels, given the long sequence at Teleilat. We should mention some examples of sinuous vertical lines, a pattern also possibly present at Kosak Shamali. Preliminary results of the evolution of the decorative techniques are important: impression is the earliest at Teleilat, later associated with painting (or "slip") later still impressions disappear and are replaced by "red coating occasionally with painted designs"; after this, painted decoration develops extensively. At Kosak Shamali impressed and painted pottery were found together, but as the material was found as secondary deposits and not in any clear architectural context within the sequence, we can only hypothesize that, had the material been in sequence it may have been divided into two different units. A better knowledge of Teleilat assemblages with quantitative data is needed which can be used to determine if there are other evolutionary elements, for example shape, which can be used to establish closer comparisons with Kosak Shamali.

Tell Halula (Faura 1996; Faura and Le Mière 1999; Faura in press), located on the right bank of the Euphrates, a few kilometers downstream from Kosak Shamali, has a long sequence from Pre-Pottery Neolithic to the Halaf period. This sequence has not yet been fully documented and none of the assemblages found to date strictly resemble the Kosak Shamali material. However, it is likely that Kosak Shamali pottery has parallels with the phase III pottery from Halula: if phases II and III correspond to the third stage of pottery development as at Kosak Shamali, the presence of impressed plant-temperd sherds (in very small quantity) as well as undecorated necks in phase III, make it more comparable with Kosak Shamali than phase II. Forthcoming detailed studies of the Halula material (Faura in press) will certainly provide further elements for a more precise comparison.

Ja'ade (Faura and Le Mière 1999), a few kilometers upstream on the left bank of the Euphrates, is primarily a Pre-Pottery Neolithic site. Pottery was found in the upper level only. Results of a very preliminary study indicate that it shares many common characteristics with the Kosak Shamali material: a very large proportion of plant-tempered pottery (90%), the presence of Dark-Faced Burnished Ware, Gray Black Ware and Mineral Coarse Ware, a certain abundance of necks, and impressed as well as painted decoration. Nevertheless, the presence of carinations among a rather small collection of shape diagnostic sherds, and also the presence of painted cross-hatched patterning, suggest Ja'ade to be a somewhat later assemblage though still pre-Transition (following Sabi Abyad reference), the confirmation of which can only be made when the material has been studied more closely.

Two main results are coming out of these comparisons: the first one concerns the chronological position of Kosak Shamali assemblage which could be not so late in the third stage of development of the pottery, since it can be provisionnally compared more probably with Level 8 than with any other level of Sabi Abyad sequence, possibly better with Amuq A/Qoueiq A than with Amuq B/Qoueiq B and which is very probably earlier than Ja'ade assemblage; the second result concerns the possible existence, in the large ceramic region of North-Syria-Cilicia, of an intermediary zone between the eastern zone, mainly the Balikh valley, and the western one, the coastal area: this intermediate zone would be the Euphrates and Qoueiq valleys. Current works in the Euphrates sites should provide new arguments to verify this hypothesis.

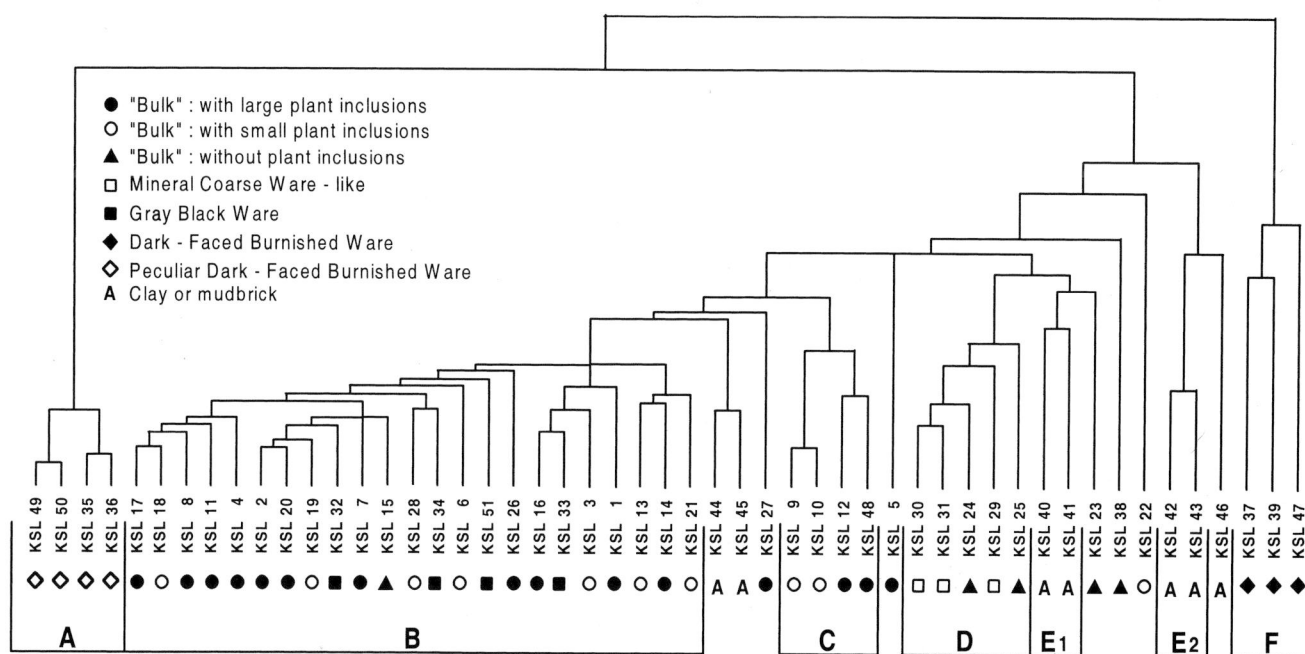

Fig. 7.1 Cluster analysis dendrogram of pottery and clay samples from Tell Kosak Shamali.

References

Bader, N.O., V.A. Bashilov, M. Le Mière and M. Picon (1994) Productions locales et importations de céramique dans le Djebel Sinjar au VIe millénaire. *Paléorient* 20 (1): 61-68.

Braidwood, R.J. and L. Braidwood (1960) *Excavations in the Plain of Antioch I.* Oriental Institute Publications 56. Chicago: The University of Chicago Press.

Contenson, H. de (1985) Le matériel archéologique des tells. In: *Holocene Settlement in North Syria,* edited by P. Sanlaville, pp. 99-161. BAR i.s. 238. Oxford: British Archaeological Reports.

Contenson, H. de (1992) *Préhistoire de Ras Shamra.* Ras Shamra-Ougarit VIII. Paris: Editions Recherche sur les Civilisations.

Faura, J.M. (1996) La cerámica Pre-Halaf. In: *Tell Halula (Siria): Un Yacimiento Neolítico del Valle Medio del Éufrates Campañas de 1991 y 1992,* edited by M. Molist, pp. 91-97. Madrid: Ministerio de Educación y Cultura.

Faura, J.M. (in press) La primeras cerámica neoliticas de Tell Halula: estudio tipològico y morfológico. In: *El Asentiamento Neolítico de Tell Halula (Valle del Éufrates, Siria): memoria de la campañas 1993-1994,* edited by M. Molist. Madrid: Ministerio de Educación y Cultura.

Faura, J.M. and M. Le Mière (1999) La céramique néolithique du Haut Euphrate syrien. In: *The Archaeology of the Upper Syrian Euphrates, The Tishrin Dam Area,* edited by G. del Olmo Lete and J.-L. Montero Fenollós, pp. 281-298. Barcelona: Editorial Ausa.

Garstang, J. (1953) *Prehistoric Mersin.* London: Clarendon Press.

Guest-Papamanoli, A. (1978) L'emploi de la brique dans le domaine égéen à l'époque néolithique et à l'Age du Bronze. *Bulletin de Correspondance Hellénique* 102: 3-24.

Le Mière, M. (2000) L'occupation proto-Hassuna du Haut-Khabur occidental d'après la céramique. In: *Prospection Archéologique du Haut-Khabur Occidental (Syrie du N.E.), Vol. I,* edited by B. Lyonnet, pp. 127-149.

Le Mière, M. and O. Nieuwenhuyse (1996) The prehistoric pottery. In: *Tell Sabi Abyad, the Late Neolithic Settlement. Report on the Excavations of the University of Amsterdam (1988) and the National Museum of Antiquities Leiden (1991-1993) in Syria,* edited by P.M.M.G. Akkermans, pp. 119-284. Istanbul: Nederlands Historisch-Archaeologisch Instituut te Istanbul

Le Mière, M. and M. Picon (1987) Production locale et circulation des céramiques au VIe millénaire au Proche-Orient. *Paléorient* 13 (2): 133-147.

Le Mière, M. and M. Picon (1998) Les débuts de la céramique néolithique au Proche-Orient. *Paléorient* 24 (2): 5-26.

Mellaart, J. (1981) The Prehistoric pottery from the Neolithic to the beginning of E.B.IV (c. 7000-2500 B.C.). In: *The River Qoueiq, Northern Syria and its Catchment,* edited by J. Matthers, pp. 131-319. BAR i.s. 98(I). Oxford: British Archaeological Reports.

Moore, A.M.T. (1975) The excavation of Tell Abu Hureyra in Syria: preliminary report. *Proceedings of the Prehistoric Society* 41: 50-77.

Moore, A.M.T. (1985) The archaeological survey of 1977. In: *Holocene Settlement in North Syria,* edited by P. Sanlaville, pp. 45-66. BAR i.s. 238. Oxford: British Archaeological Reports.

Nishiaki, Y., T. Koizumi, M. Le Mière and T. Oguchi (1999) Prehistoric occupations at Tell Kosak Shamali, the upper Euphrates, Syria. *Akkadica* 113: 13-68.

Tsuneki, A., J. Hydar, Y. Miyake *et al.* (1998) Second preliminary report of the excavations at Tell el-Kerkh (1998), Nothwestern Syria. *Bulletin of the Ancient Orient Museum* XIX: 1-40.

Tsuneki, A. and Y. Miyake (1996) The earliest pottery sequence of the Levant: new data from Tell el-Kerkh 2, Northern Syria. *Paléorient* 22 (1): 109-123.

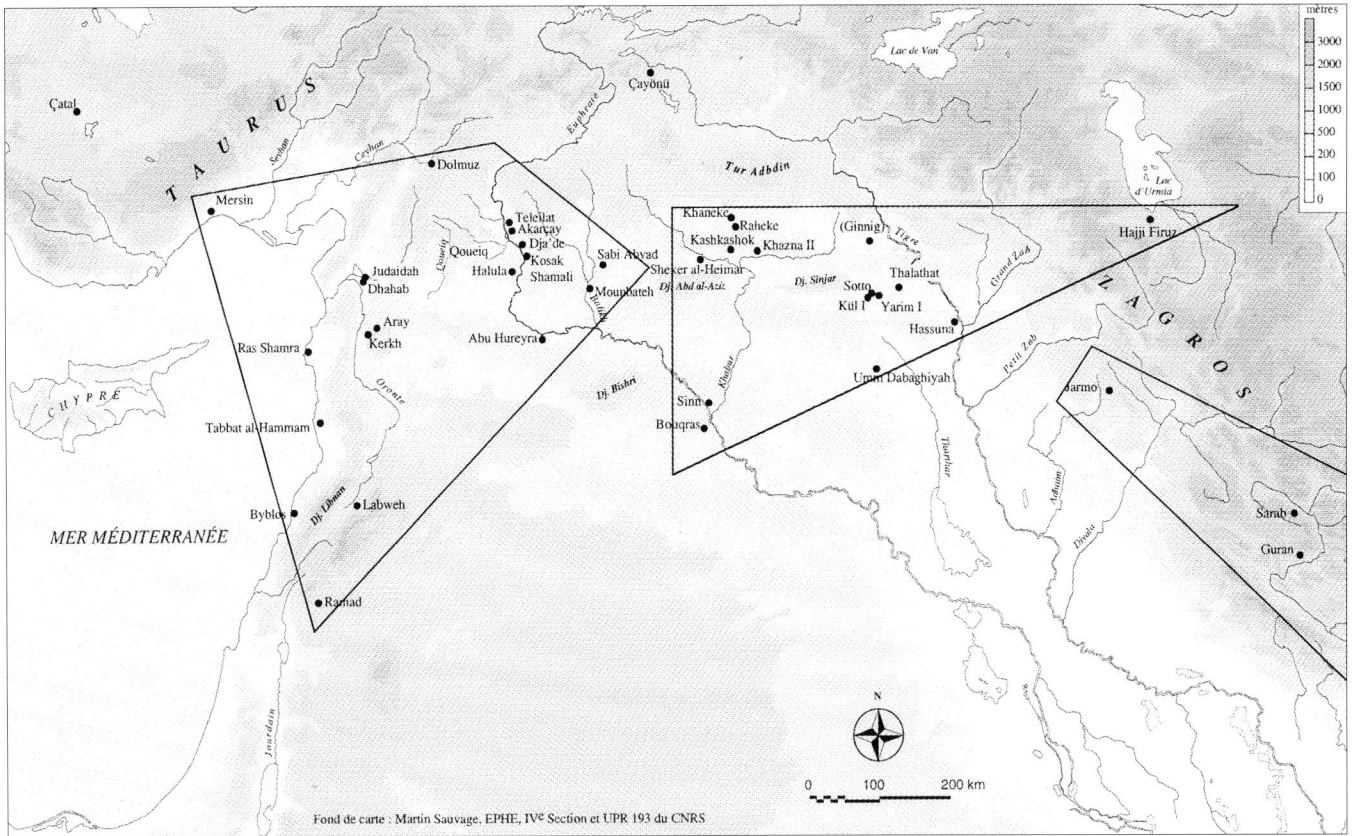

Fig. 7.2 Map of the Near Eastern Neolithic pottery sites at the third stage of development of the technique. *Only the main sites are indicated.*

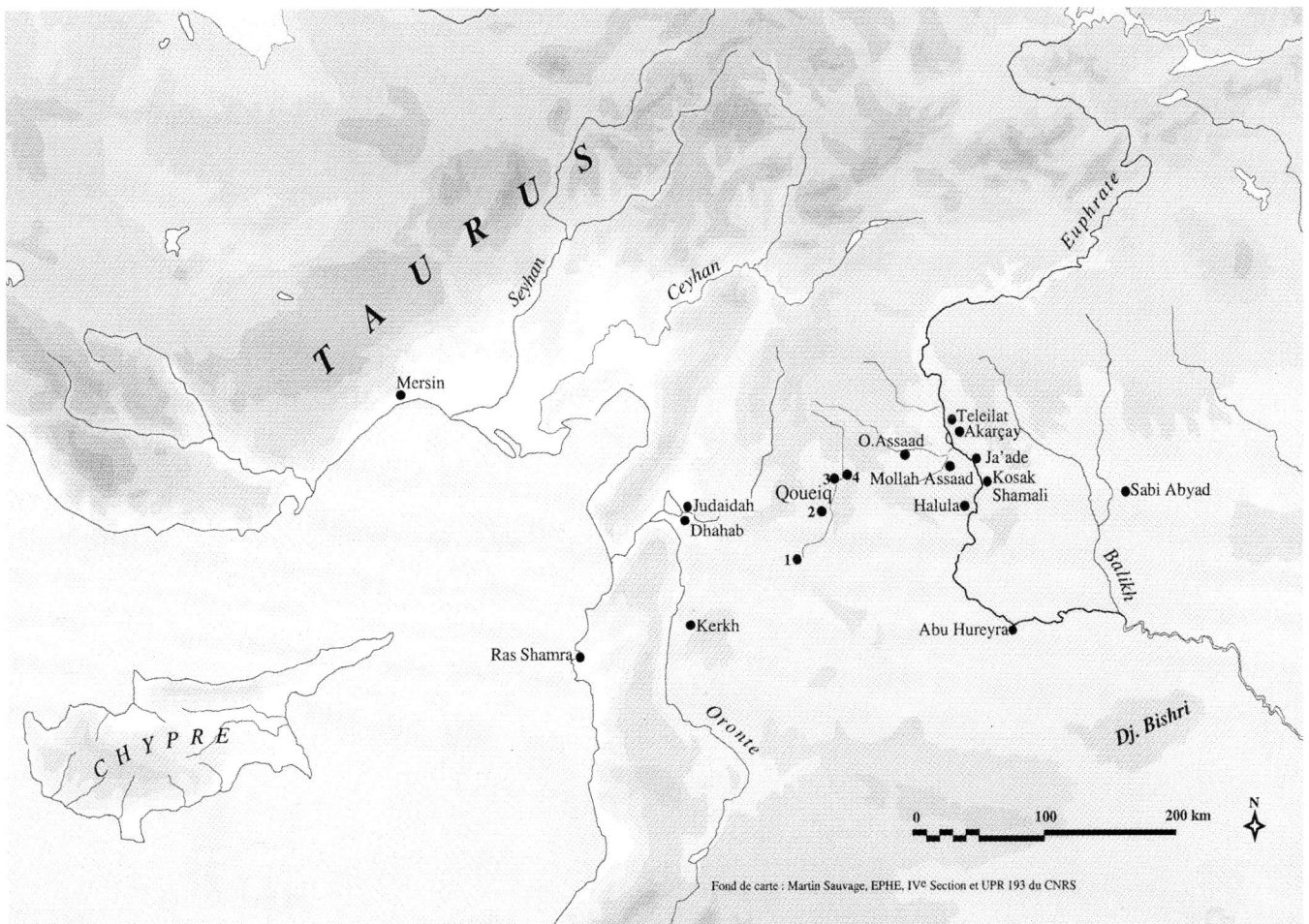

Fig. 7.3 Map showing the sites mentioned in the text. *Qoueiq valley sites (1-4); Ouadi Assaad and Mollah Assaad; Sajour valley sites.*

Fig. 7.4 Neolithic pottery - closed, carinated and vertical shapes.
1. Pot, plant tempered, beige core, pink/red surface, burnishing (94KSL-A12-6; Level 18 of Sector A).
2. Pot, plant tempered, beige core, pink/red surface, burnishing (97KSL-BE6-42; Level 8 of Sector B).
3. Pot, no plant temper, brown core, brown surface, burnishing, Mineral Coarse Ware
   (95KSL-AF5-9; Level 13 of Sector A).
4. Pot, plant tempered, gray core, pink/red surface, burnishing (95KSL-AF5-19; Level 14 of Sector A).
5. Pot, plant tempered, gray core, pink/red surface, red burnished slip (96KSL-BD6-26; Level 8 of Sector B).
6. Pot, plant tempered, beige core, pink/red surface, burnishing (97KSL-BE5-17; Level 8 of Sector B).
7. Pot, plant tempered, gray core, pink/red surface, smoothing (96KSL-BD7-48; Level 5 of Sector B).
8. Pot, plant tempered, gray core, gray surface, burnishing, Gray Black Ware (94KSL-A12-6; Level 18 of Sector A).
9. Pot, plant tempered, gray core, gray surface, red burnished slip (95KSL-AF4-11; Level 13 of Sector A).
10. Body, plant tempered, gray core, beige surface, burnishing (95KSL-AF6-10; Level 16 of Sector A).
11. Body, plant tempered, gray core, brown surface, burnishing (97KSL-BE7-34; Level 6 of Sector B).
12. Bowl, plant tempered, gray core, beige surface, red burnished slip (97KSL-BE6-41; Level 8 of Sector B).
13. Bowl, plant tempered, gray core, pink/red surface, burnishing (94KSL-A12-6; Level 18 of Sector A).
14. Bowl, plant tempered, gray core, beige surface, burnishing (95KSL-AF5-15; Level 13 of Sector A).
15. Bowl, plant tempered, gray core, brown surface, burnishing, Gray Black Ware (?)
    (95KSL-AF5-19; Level 14 of Sector A).
16. Bowl, plant tempered, beige core, pink/red surface, burnishing (97KSL-BE6-41; Level 8 of Sector B).
17. Bowl, plant tempered, gray core, pink/red surface, burnishing (95KSL-AF5-19; Level 14 of Sector A).
18. Bowl, plant tempered, gray core, beige surface, burnishing (95KSL-AF4-11; Level 13 of Sector A).
19. Bowl, plant tempered, gray core, pink/red surface, burnishing (97KSL-BE5-18; Level 8 of Sector B).
20. Ledge-handle, no plant temper, pink/red core, brown surface, burnishing, Mineral Coarse Ware
    (97KSL-BE5-18; Level 8 of Sector B).

Fig. 7.5 Neolithic pottery - open shapes.
1. Bowl, plant tempered, gray core, gray surface, burnishing, Gray Black Ware (97KSL-BE6-42; Level 8 of Sector B).
2. Bowl, plant tempered, gray core, pink/red surface, burnishing (95KSL-AF5-26; Level 18 of Sector A).
3. Bowl, plant tempered, gray core, brown surface, burnishing (97KSL-BE6-42; Level 8 of Sector B).
4. Bowl, plant tempered, gray core, beige surface, red burnished slip (97KSL-BE6-42; Level 8 of Sector B).
5. Bowl, plant tempered, gray core, pink/red surface, burnishing (97KSL-BE6-42; Level 8 of Sector B).
6. Bowl, plant tempered, gray core, beige surface, burnishing (95KSL-AF5-9; Level 13 of Sector A).
7. Bowl, plant tempered, gray core, beige surface, burnishing (97KSL-BE5-14; Level 8 of Sector B).
8. Bowl, plant tempered, gray core, pink/red surface (95KSL-AF5-15; Level 13 of Sector A).
9. Bowl, plant tempered, gray core, pink/red surface, burnishing (94KSL-A10-8; Level 14/15/17 of Sector A).
10. Bowl, plant tempered, gray core, pink/red surface, red burnished slip (95KSL-AF5-9; Level 13 of Sector A).
11. Bowl, plant tempered, gray core, pink/red surface, burnishing (94KSL-A10-8; Level 14/15/17 of Sector A).
12. Bowl, plant tempered, gray core, pink/red surface, burnishing (97KSL-BD6-26; Level 8 of Sector B).
13. Bowl, plant tempered, gray core, beige surface, red burnished slip (97KSL-AE5-48; Level 13 of Sector A).
14. Bowl, plant tempered, beige core, beige surface, red burnished slip (97KSL-BD6-33; Level 8 of Sector B).
15. Bowl, plant tempered, gray core, brown surface, burnishing (94KSL-A12-6; Level 18 of Sector A).
16. Bowl, plant tempered, beige core, beige surface, red burnished slip (94KSL-A12-6; Level 18 of Sector A).
17. Bowl, plant tempered, gray core, pink/red surface, burnishing (95KSL-AF5-9; Level 13 of Sector A).
18. Bowl, plant tempered, beige core, pink/red surface, burnishing (94KSL-A12-6; Level 18 of Sector A).
19. Bowl, plant tempered, gray core, pink/red surface, burnishing (94KSL-A10-8; Level 14/15/17 of Sector A).
20. Bowl, plant tempered, gray core, gray surface, burnishing, Gray Black Ware (94KSL-D10-4; Level 15 of Sector A).
21. Bowl, plant tempered, gray core, brown surface, burnishing (95KSL-AF5-19; Level 14 of Sector A).
22. Bowl, plant tempered, pink/red core, pink/red surface, red burnished slip (95KSL-AF5-26; Level 18 of Sector A).

Fig. 7.6 Neolithic pottery - collared shapes.
1. Jar, plant tempered, beige core, pink/red surface, burnishing (95KSL-AF5-9; Level 13 of Sector A).
2. Jar, plant tempered, beige core, beige surface, burnishing (97KSL-BE6-27; Level 7 of Sector B).
3. Jar, plant tempered, pink/red core, pink/red surface, red burnished slip (95KSL-AF6-10; Level 16 of Sector A).
4. Jar, plant tempered, gray core, beige surface, burnishing (97KSL-BE6-20; Level 6 of Sector B).
5. Jar, plant tempered, gray core, pink/red surface, red burnished slip (95KSL-AG5-2; Level 13 of Sector A).
6. Jar, plant tempered, gray core, pink/red surface, burnishing (95KSL-AG5-8; Level 14 of Sector A).
7. Jar, plant tempered, gray core, beige surface, burnishing (95KSL-AF5-19; Level 14 of Sector A).
8. Jar, plant tempered, gray core, beige surface, burnishing (95KSL-AF5-26; Level 18 of Sector A).
9. Jar, plant tempered, gray core, pink/red surface, burnishing (94KSL-A10-8; Level 14/15/17 of Sector A).
10. Jar, plant tempered, pink/red core, beige surface, burnishing (97KSL-BE5-18; Level 8 of Sector B).
11. Jar, plant tempered, gray core, beige surface, smoothing (95KSL-AF5-29; Level 13 of Sector A).
12. Jar, plant tempered, gray core, beige surface, red burnished slip (94KSL-A10-8; Level 14/15/17 of Sector A).
13. Jar, plant tempered, gray core, beige surface, burnishing (96KSL-BD6-26; Level 8 of Sector B).
14. Jar, plant tempered, gray core, beige surface, burnishing (97KSL-BE6-42; Level 8 of Sector B).
15. Jar, plant tempered, gray core, pink/red surface, burnishing (97KSL-BE6-42; Level 8 of Sector B).
16. Jar, plant tempered, gray core, beige surface, burnishing (96KSL-BD6-26; Level 8 of Sector B).
17. Jar, plant tempered, gray core, beige surface, burnishing (97KSL-BE5-18; Level 8 of Sector B).
18. Jar, plant tempered, beige surface, smoothing (95KSL-AF4-11; Level 13 of Sector A).
19. Jar, plant tempered, gray core, beige surface, burnishing (95KSL-AF3-22; Level 17 of Sector A).

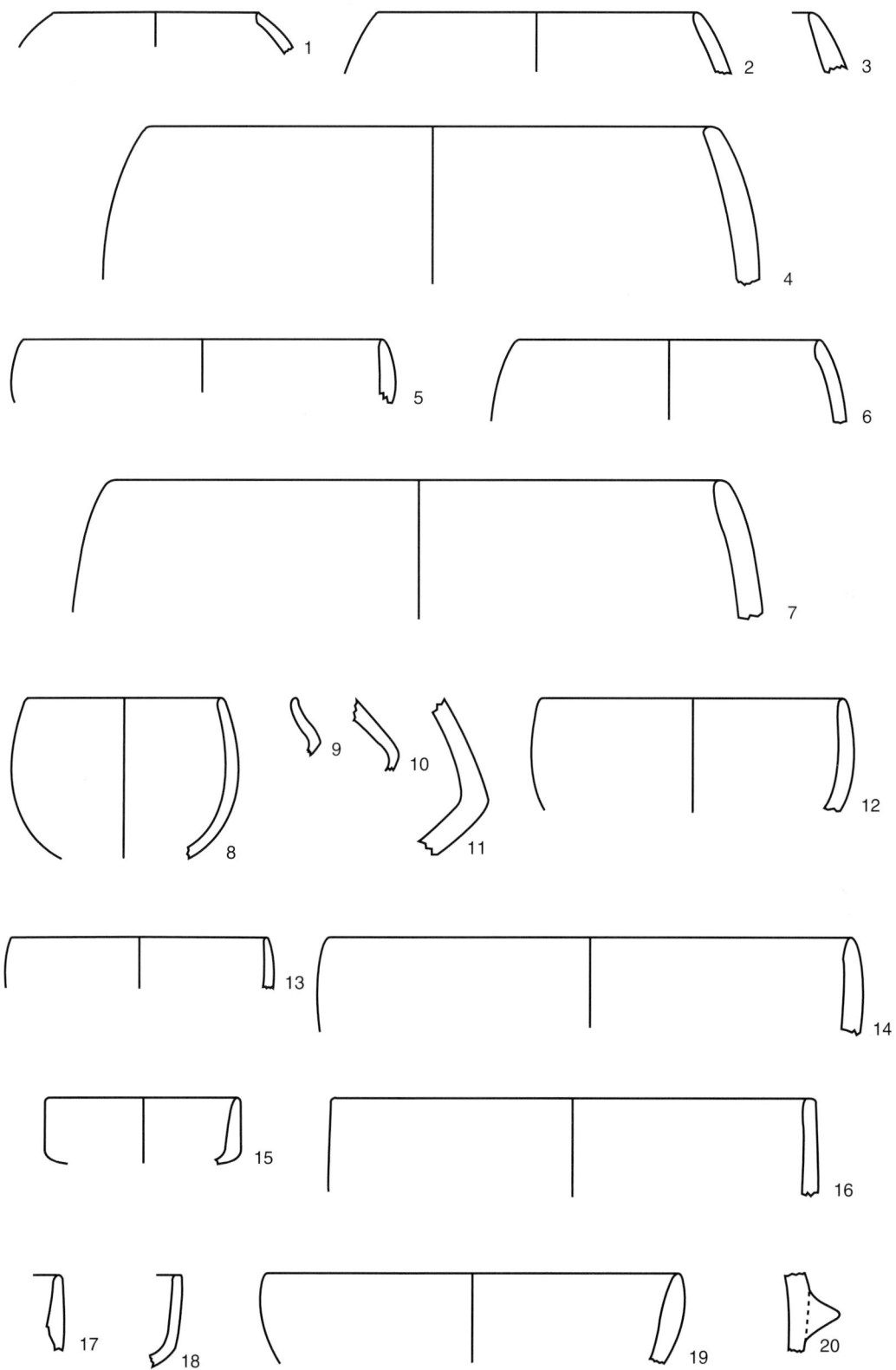

Fig. 7.4 Neolithic pottery - closed, carinated and vertical shapes.

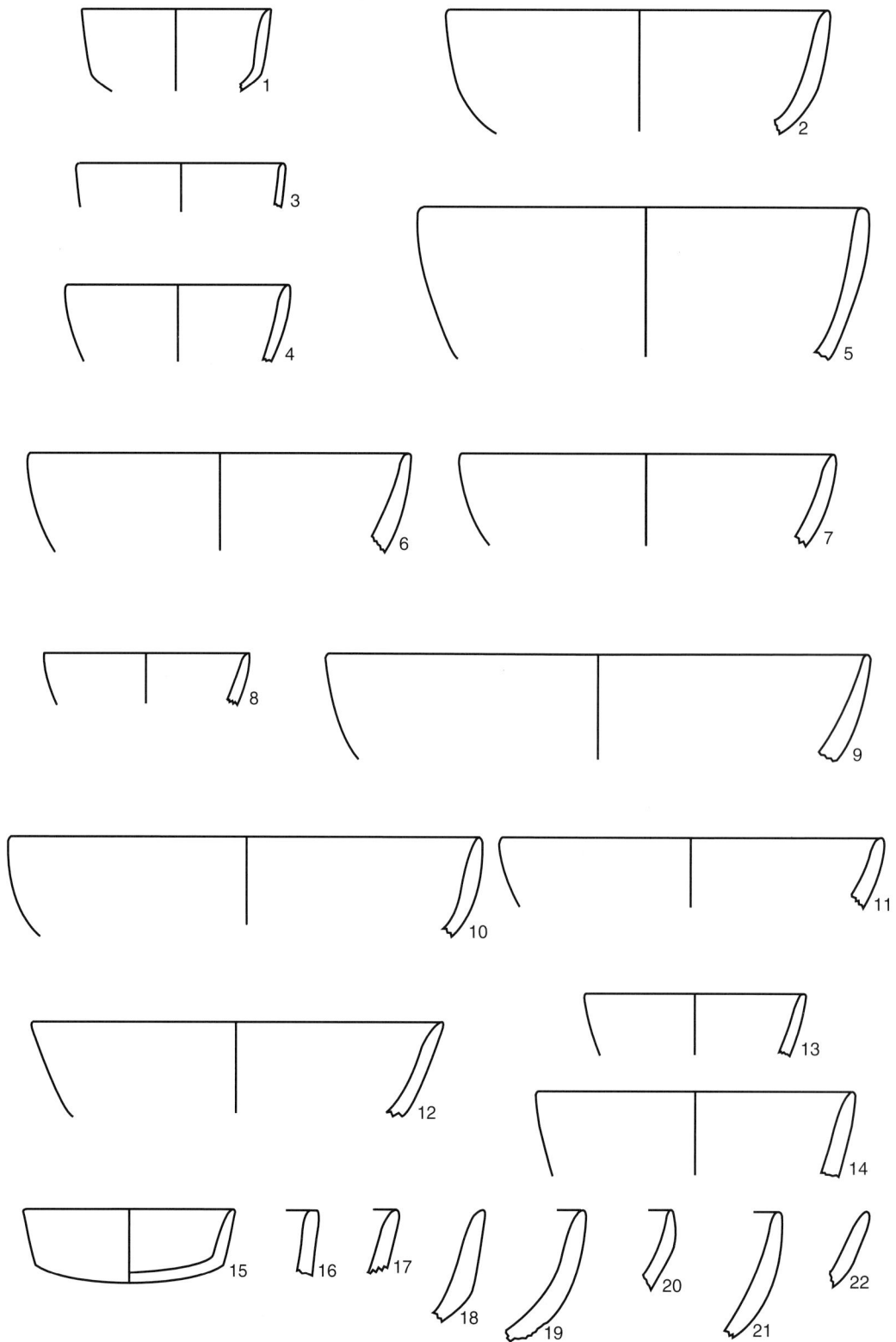

Fig. 7.5 Neolithic pottery - open shapes.

0   10cm

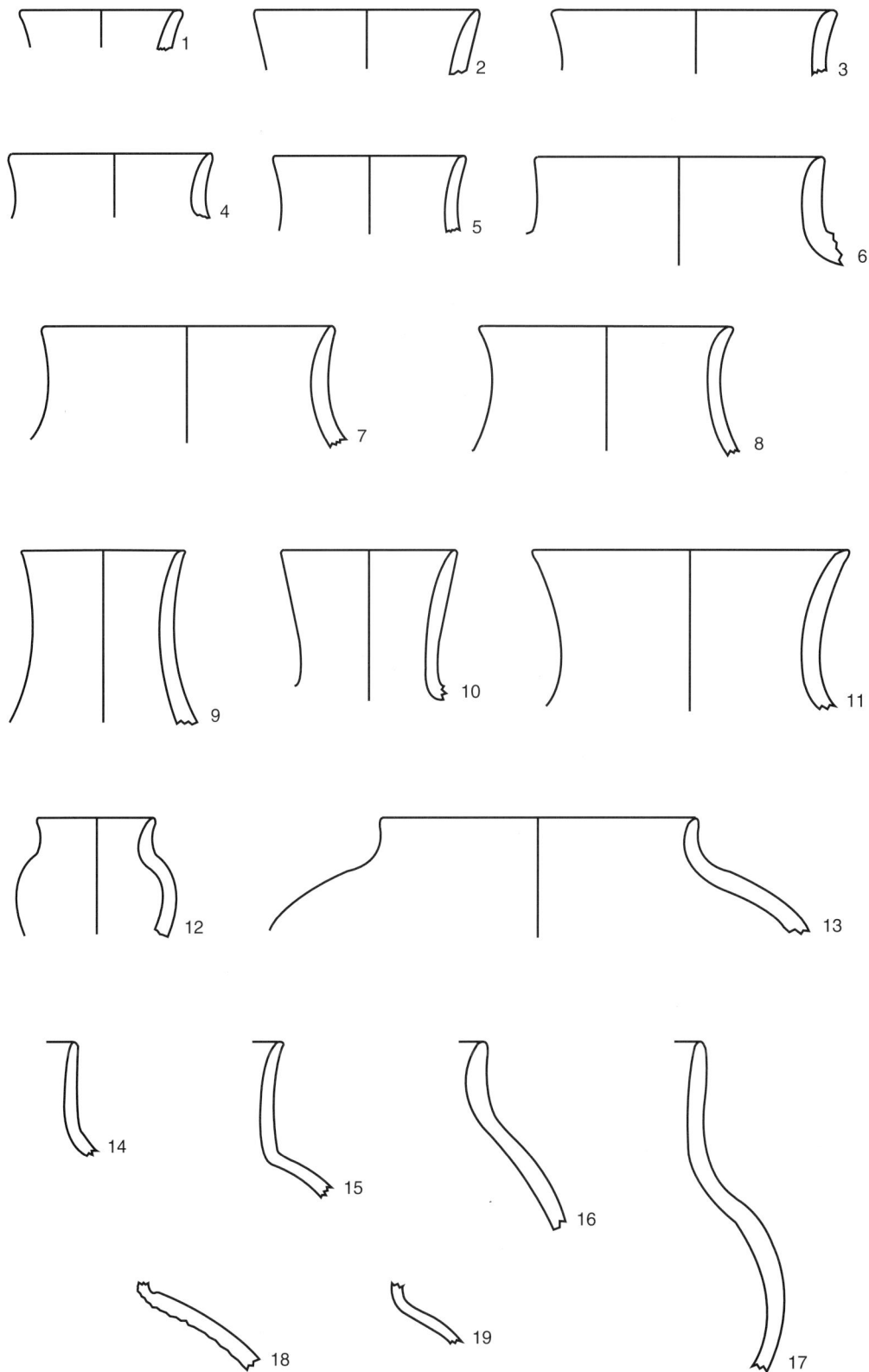

Fig. 7.6 Neolithic pottery - collared shapes.

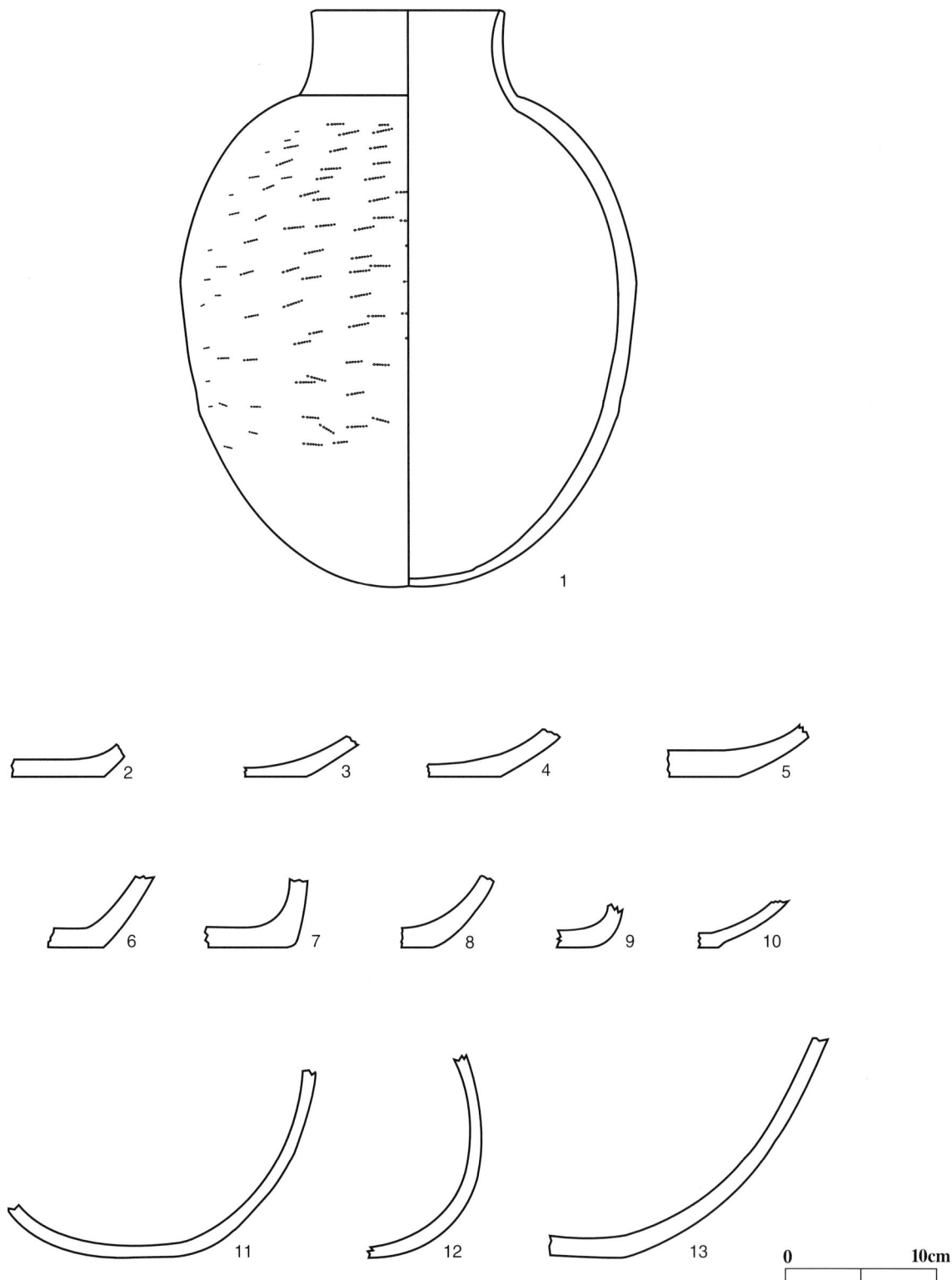

Fig. 7.7 Neolithic pottery - complete jar and bases.
1. Jar, plant tempered, gray core, pink/red surface, burnishing (97KSL-BE5-17; Level 8 of Sector B).
2. Flat base, plant tempered, gray core, pink/red surface, smoothing (94KSL-A12-5; Level 13 of Sector A).
3. Flat base, plant tempered, gray core, pink/red surface, burnishing (94KSL-A10-8; Level 14/15/17 of Sector A).
4. Flat base, no plant temper, beige core, pink/red surface, red burnished slip (94KSL-A12-6; Level 18 of Sector A).
5. Flat base, plant tempered, gray core, pink/red surface, burnishing (94KSL-A12-6; Level 18 of Sector A).
6. Flat base, plant tempered, gray core, brown surface, burnishing (94KSL-D11-6; Level 15 of Sector A).
7. Flat base, plant tempered, light beige core, light beige surface, overfired, smoothing (97KSL-BE6-27; Level 7 of Sector B).
8. Flat base, no plant temper, gray core, pink/red surface, burnishing (95KSL-AF5-20; Level 15 of Sector A).
9. Flat base, plant tempered, gray core, beige surface, burnishing (97KSL-BE6-41; Level 8 of Sector B).
10. Flat base, plant tempered, gray core, pink/red surface, burnishing (97KSL-BE5-17; Level 8 of Sector B).
11. Convex base, plant tempered, gray core, brown surface, smoothing (97KSL-BE6-41; Level 8 of Sector B).
12. Convex (?) base, plant tempered, gray core, pink/red surface, burnishing (97KSL-BE6-42; Level 8 of Sector B).
13. Flat base, plant tempered, gray core, brown surface, burnishing (96KSL-BD6-26; Level 8 of Sector B).

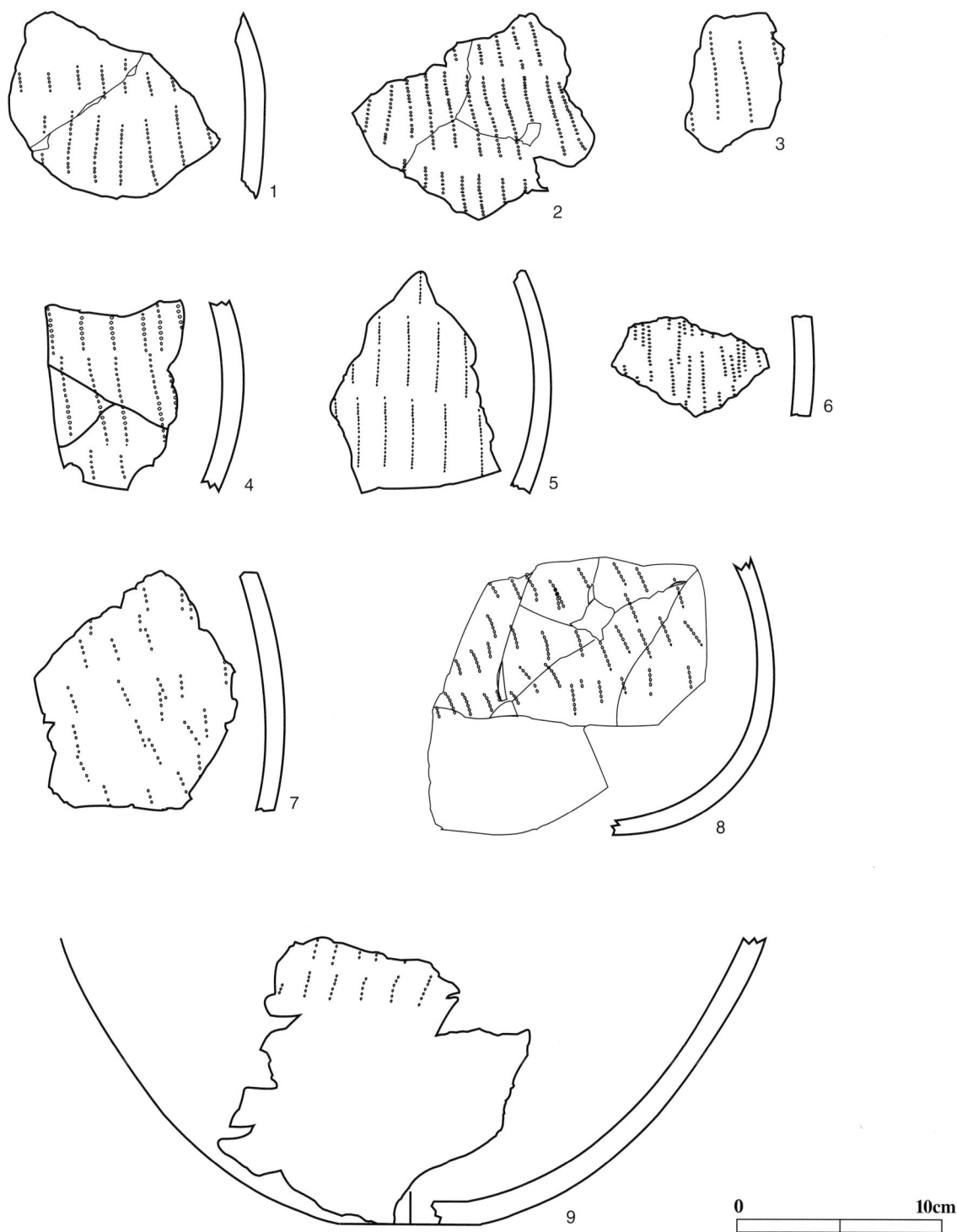

Fig. 7.8 Neolithic pottery - impressed decorations.
1. Body, plant tempered, gray core, beige surface, burnishing (97KSL-BE6-42; Level 8 of Sector B).
2. Body, plant tempered, beige core, beige surface, smoothing (94KSL-A12-6; Level 18 of Sector A).
3. Body, plant tempered, gray core, beige surface, burnishing (95KSL-AF5-9; Level 13 of Sector A).
4. Body, plant tempered, pink/red core, beige surface, smoothing (97KSL-BE6-35; Level 8 of Sector B).
5. Body, plant tempered, gray core, brown surface, smoothing (97KSL-BE7-34; Level 6 of Sector B).
6. Body, plant tempered, gray core, pink/red surface, burnishing (95KSL-AF5-20; Level 15 of Sector A).
7. Body, plant tempered, gray core, beige surface, smoothing (95KSL-AF5-20; Level 15 of Sector A).
8. Body, plant tempered, gray core, pink/red surface, burnishing (97KSL-BE6-42; Level 8 of Sector B).
9. Flat base, plant tempered, gray core, brown surface, burnishing (95KSL-AF5-9; Level 13 of Sector A).

Fig. 7.9 Neolithic pottery - impressed decorations.
1. Body, plant tempered, gray core, pink/red surface, smoothing (96KSL-BD6-29; Level 5 of Sector B).
2. Body, plant tempered, gray core, beige surface, smoothing (95KSL-AF5-24; Level 18 of Sector A).
3. Body, plant tempered, gray core, pink/red surface (95KSL-AF6-10; Level 16 of Sector A).
4. Body, plant tempered, gray core, pink/red surface, burnishing (95KSL-AF5-19; Level 14 of Sector A).
5. Body, plant tempered, gray core, beige surface, smoothing (95KSL-AF5-19; Level 14 of Sector A).
6. Body, plant tempered, gray core, pink/red surface, smoothing (95KSL-AF5-19; Level 14 of Sector A).
7. Body, plant tempered, gray core, pink/red surface, smoothing (95KSL-AF5-22; Level 15 of Sector A).
8. Body, plant tempered, gray core, pink/red surface, smoothing (95KSL-AF5-9; Level 13 of Sector A).
9. Jar, plant tempered, gray core, pink/red surface, burnishing (97KSL-BE6-35; Level 8 of Sector B).
10. Jar, plant tempered, gray core, beige surface, burnishing (94KSL-B8-5: Level 4 of Sector B).
11. Jar, plant tempered, beige core, beige surface, burnishing (94KSL-A10-8; Level 14/15/17 of Sector A).
12. Body, plant tempered, gray core, pink/red surface, smoothing (97KSL-BE5-18; Level 8 of Sector B).
13. Body, plant tempered, gray core, beige surface, burnishing (94KSL-A12-6; Level 18 of Sector A).
14. Body, plant tempered, gray core, pink/red surface, burnishing (94KSL-A10-8; Level 14/15/17 of Sector A).
15. Body, plant tempered, gray core, pink/red surface, burnishing (97KSL-BE5-18; Level 8 of Sector B).
16. Body, plant tempered, gray core, pink/red surface, smoothing (95KSL-AF5-20; Level 15 of Sector A).
17. Body, plant tempered, gray core, pink/red surface, burnishing (95KSL-AF5-22; Level 15 of Sector A).
18. Body, plant tempered, gray core, pink/red surface, smoothing (95KSL-AF6-4; Level 13 of Sector A).
19. Body, plant tempered, gray core, pink/red surface, smoothing (95KSL-AG5-9; Level 18 of Sector A).
20. Body, plant tempered, gray core, beige surface, smoothing (95KSL-AF5-19; Level 14 of Sector A).
21. Body, plant tempered, gray core, beige surface, burnishing (95KSL-AF5-9; Level 13 of Sector A).
22. Jar, plant tempered, gray core, pink/red surface, burnishing (94KSL-A10-8; Level 14/15/17 of Sector A).
23. Jar, plant tempered, gray core, pink/red surface, burnishing (94KSL-A10-8; Level 14/15/17 of Sector A).
24. Body, plant tempered, gray core, pink/red surface, burnishing (94KSL-A10-8; Level 14/15/17 of Sector A).

Fig. 7.10 Neolithic pottery - impressed decorations.
1. Body, plant tempered, beige core, beige surface, burnishing (95KSL-AG5-9; Level 18 of Sector A).
2. Body, plant tempered, gray core, beige surface, burnishing (94KSL-A10-8; Level 14/15/17 of Sector A).
3. Body, plant tempered, gray core, pink/red surface, smoothing (97KSL-BE6-31; Level 8 of Sector B).
4. Body, plant tempered, gray core, pink/red surface, burnishing (94KSL-A12-5; Level 13 of Sector A).
5. Body, plant tempered, gray core, beige surface, smoothing (94KSL-A10-8; Level 14/15/17 of Sector A).
6. Body, plant tempered, gray core, gray surface, burnishing and traces of a possible red slip, Gray Black Ware
(96KSL-BD6-29; Level 5 of Sector B).
7. Body, plant tempered, gray core, beige surface, smoothing (97KSL-BE6-41; Level 8 of Sector B).
8. Body, plant tempered, gray core, beige surface, smoothing (95KSL-AG5-9; Level 18 of Sector A).
9. Body, plant tempered, gray core, beige surface, burnishing (94KSL-A12-6; Level 18 of Sector A).
10. Body, plant tempered, gray core, beige surface, smoothing (95KSL-AG4-9; Level 13 of Sector A).
11. Body, plant tempered, gray core, beige surface, smoothing (95KSL-AG4-9; Level 13 of Sector A).
12. Body, plant tempered, pink/red core, pink/red surface, burnishing (95KSL-AF5-9; Level 13 of Sector A).
13. Body, plant tempered, gray core, pink/red surface, smoothing (96KSL-BD6-29; Level 5 of Sector B).
14. Body, plant tempered, gray core, brown surface, smoothing (94KSL-A10-8; Level 14/15/17 of Sector A).
15. Body, plant tempered, beige core, pink/red surface, burnishing (95KSL-AG3-8; Level 13 of Sector A).
16. Body, plant tempered, beige core, pink/red surface, smoothing (95KSL-AF5-15; Level 13 of Sector A).
17. Body, plant tempered, gray core, brown surface, smoothing (97KSL-BE6-43; Level 8 of Sector B).
18. Body, plant tempered, gray core, beige surface, smoothing (95KSL-AF5-22; Level 15 of Sector A).
19. Body, plant tempered, gray core, pink/red surface, smoothing (95KSL-AF3-16; Level 13 of Sector A).
20. Body, plant tempered, gray core, brown surface (96KSL-BD7-48; Level 5 of Sector B).
21. Jar, plant tempered, beige core, pink/red surface, smoothing (97KSL-BD6-30; Level 8 of Sector B).

Fig. 7.11 Neolithic pottery - painted decorations.
1. Jar, plant tempered, gray core, beige surface, burnishing (95KSL-AF5-8; Level 13 of Sector A).
2. Body, plant tempered, gray core, beige surface, burnishing (94KSL-A10-8; Level 14/15/17 of Sector A).
3. Body, plant tempered, pink/red core, pink/red surface, burnishing (94KSL-A12-6; Level 18 of Sector A).
4. Jar, plant tempered, gray core, pink/red surface, burnishing (94KSL-A10-8; Level 14/15/17 of Sector A).
5. Body, plant tempered, gray core, beige surface, burnishing (95KSL-AF5-9; Level 13 of Sector A).
6. Body, plant tempered, gray core, pink/red surface, burnishing (95KSL-AG5-2; Level 13 of Sector A).
7. Body, plant tempered, beige core, beige surface, burnishing (95KSL-AF5-9; Level 13 of Sector A).
8. Bowl, plant tempered, gray core, pink/red surface, burnishing (95KSL-AF5-9; Level 13 of Sector A).
9. Jar, plant tempered, gray core, beige surface, burnishing (95KSL-AG5-9; Level 18 of Sector A).
10. Bowl, plant tempered, beige core, beige surface, burnishing (94KSL-D11-6; Level 15 of Sector A).
11. Bowl, plant tempered, gray core, pink/red surface, burnishing (97KSL-BE5-17; Level 8 of Sector B).
12. Bowl, plant tempered, gray core, beige surface, burnishing (97KSL-BE6-21; Level 7 of Sector B).
13. Bowl, plant tempered, gray core, pink/red surface, burnishing (97KSL-BE6-41; Level 8 of Sector B).
14. Jar, plant tempered, gray core, pink/red surface, burnishing (97KSL-BE6-31; Level 8 of Sector B).
15. Jar, plant tempered, gray core, beige surface, burnishing (95KSL-AF3-22; Level 17 of Sector A).
16-17. Body, no plant temper, brown core, brown surface, burnishing, Dark-Faced Burnished Ware
(95KSL-AF3-2; Level 10A of Sector A).
18. Body, plant tempered, gray core, brown surface, burnishing (97KSL-BE6-35; Level 8 of Sector B).

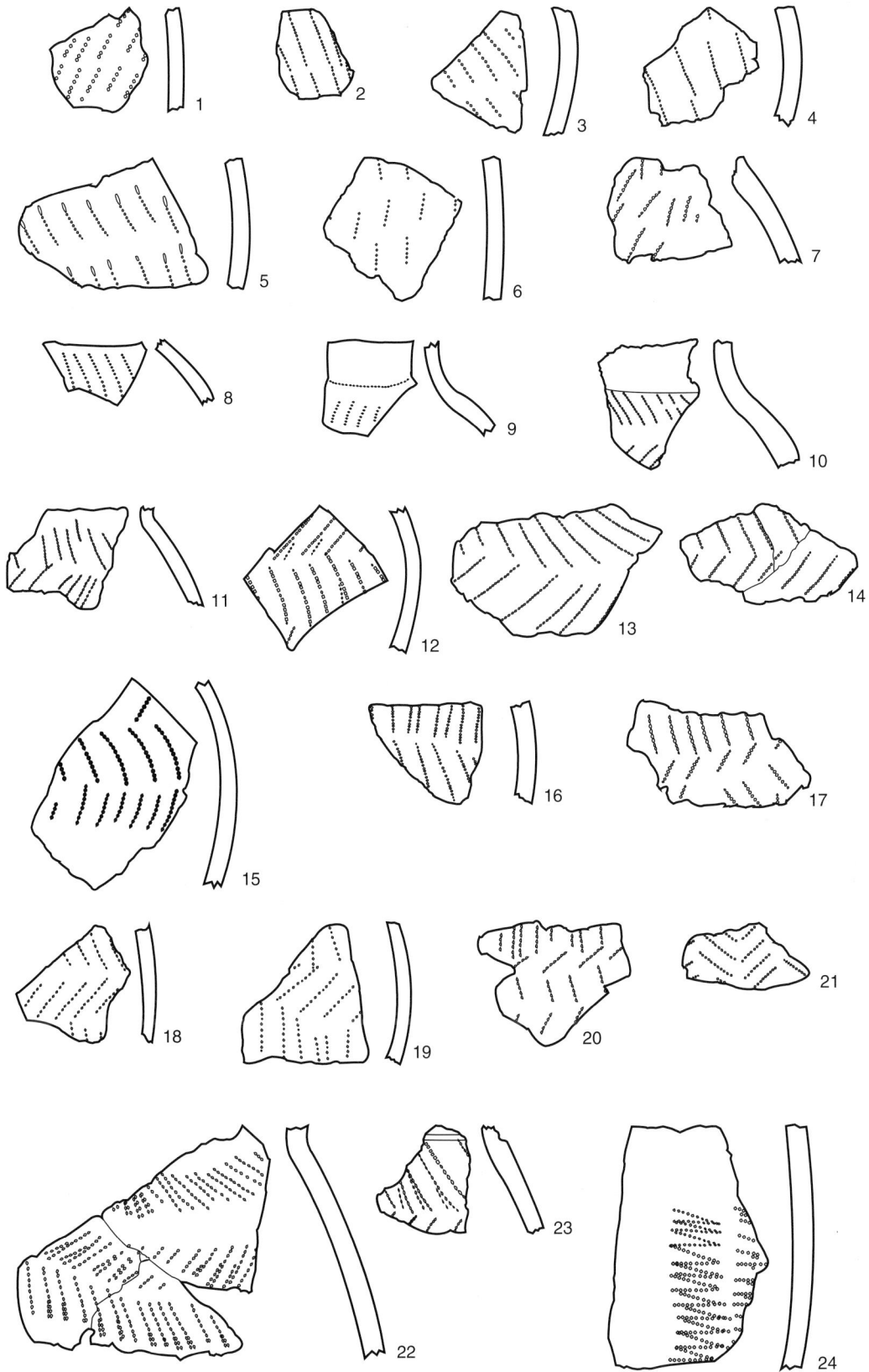

Fig. 7.9 Neolithic pottery - impressed decorations.

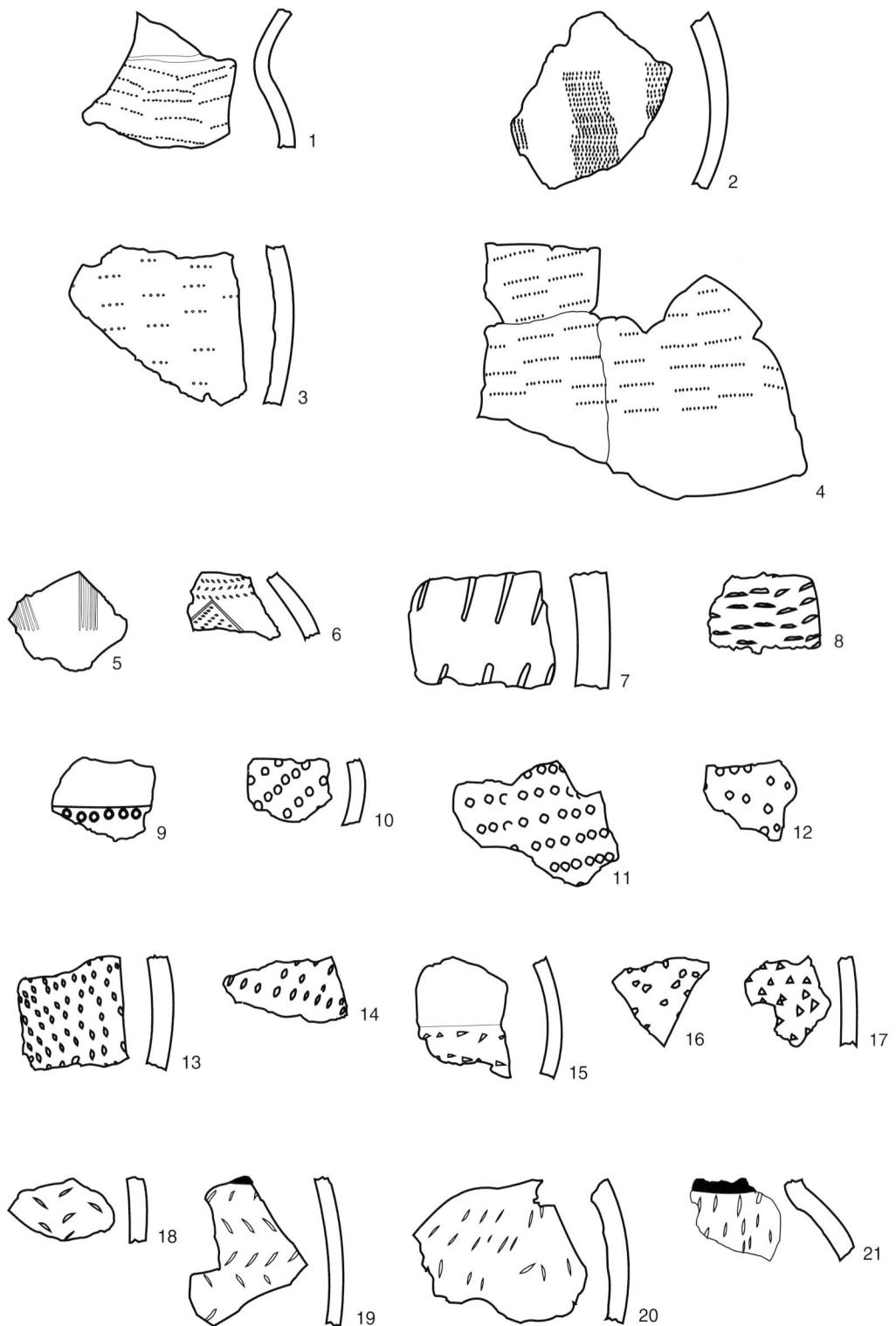

Fig. 7.10 Neolithic pottery - impressed decorations.

0   10cm

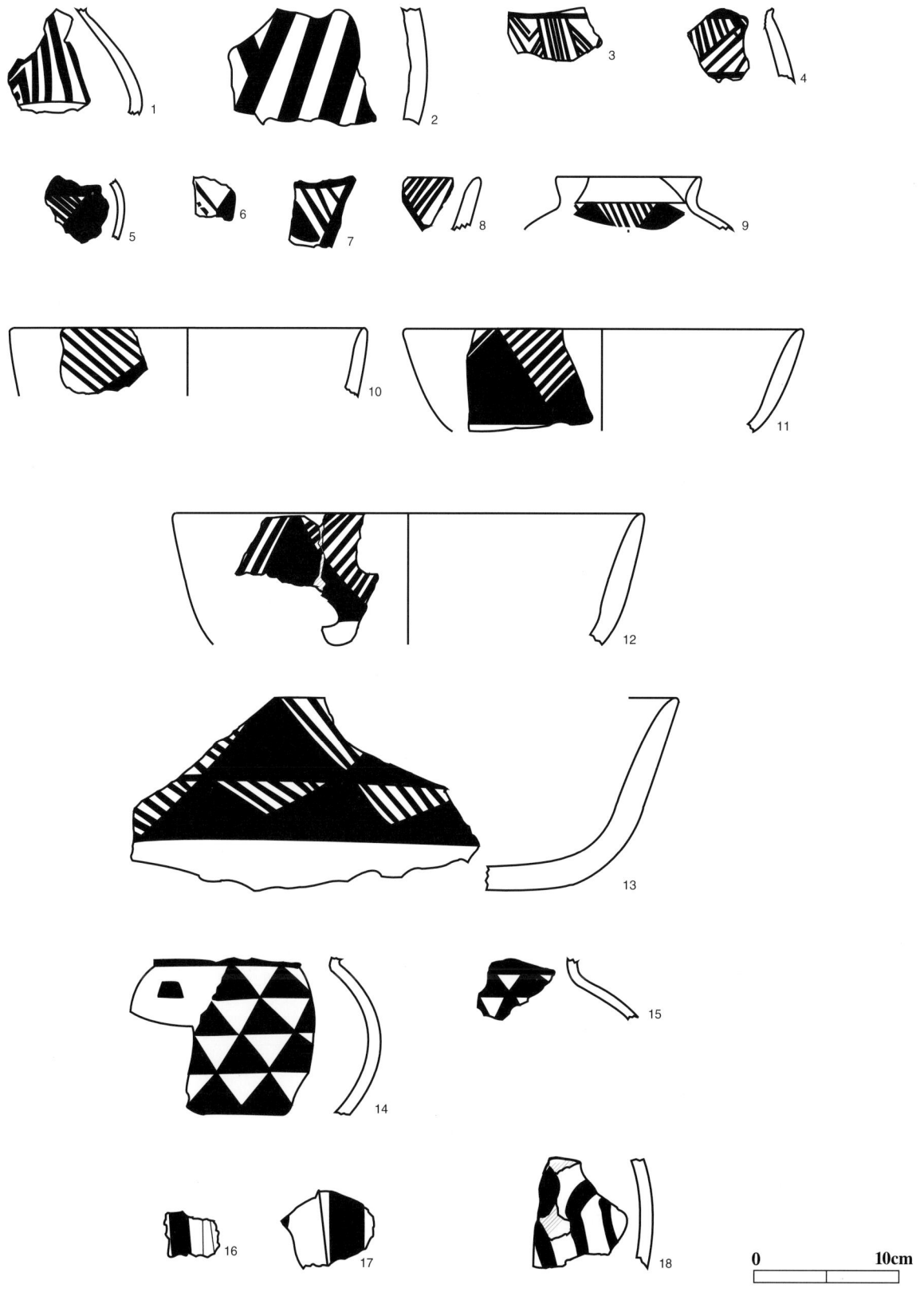

Fig. 7.11 Neolithic pottery - painted decorations.

Plate 7.1 Neolithic pottery from Tell Kosak Shamali.
1. Jar (cf. Fig. 7.7: 1).
2. Bowl (cf. Fig. 7.5: 15).

Plate 7.2 Neolithic pottery from Tell Kosak Shamali.

1. Jar (cf. Fig. 7.6: 10).
2. Jar (cf. Fig. 7.6: 13).
3. Jar, plant tempered, gray core, pink/red surface, burnishing (97KSL-BE6-42; Level 8 of Sector B).
4. Jar, plant tempered, gray core, pink/red surface, burnishing (96KSL-BD6-26; Level 8 of Sector B).
5. Bowl, plant tempered, gray core, beige surface, red burnished slip (97KSL-BE6-43; Level 8 of Sector B).
6. Pot (cf. Fig. 7.4: 9).
7. Bowl, plant tempered, gray core, beige surface, burnishing (97KSL-BD6-30; Level 8 of Sector B).
8. Jar, plant tempered, gray core, pink/red surface, red burnished slip (96KSL-BD6-26; Level 8 of Sector B).
9. Pot (cf. Fig. 7.4: 5).
10. Ledge-handle, no plant temper, pink/red core, brown surface, burnishing, Mineral Coarse Ware
    (97KSL-BE5-18; Level 8 of Sector B).

Plate 7.3 Neolithic pottery from Tell Kosak Shamali.

1. Body (cf. Fig. 7.11: 3).
2. Body (cf. Fig. 7.11: 2).
3. Body (cf. Fig. 7.10: 9).
4. Body, plant tempered, beige core, beige surface, smoothing
   (94KSL-A12-6; Level 18 of Sector A).
5. Body (cf. Fig. 7.10: 6).
6. Jar (cf. Fig. 7.10: 21).
7. Body (cf. Fig. 7.10: 17).
8. Body (cf. Fig. 7.10: 13).
9. Body, plant tempered, gray core, pink/red surface, smoothing
   (97KSL-BE7-35; Level 7/8 of Sector B).

Plate 7.4 Neolithic pottery from Tell Kosak Shamali.
1. Body (cf. Fig. 7.9: 24).
2. Body (cf. Fig. 7.10: 2).
3. Body, plant tempered, gray core, brown surface, smoothing (97KSL-BE6-41; Level 8 of Sector B).
4. Body (cf. Fig. 7.9: 13).
5. Body, plant tempered, pink/red core, pink/red surface, smoothing (94KSL-B10-3; Level 6 of Sector B).
6. Jar (cf. Fig. 7.9: 22).
7. Body (cf. Fig. 7.8: 8; upside down).
8. Body (cf. Fig. 7.8: 8).
9. Body (cf. Fig. 7.8: 8).
10. Body, plant tempered, gray core, pink/red surface, smoothing (96KSL-BD6-29; Level 5 of Sector B).
11. Body, plant tempered, gray core, beige surface, smoothing (97KSL-BD6-26; Level 8 of Sector B).

8 The Neolithic flaked stone artifacts from Tell Kosak Shamali

Yoshihiro Nishiaki

8.1 Introduction

Traces of the Neolithic occupation at Tell Kosak Shamali were discovered in Level 18 of Sector A and Level 8 of Sector B. As discussed in Chapters 3 and 4, few architectural remains survived in these levels apart from several pits and depressions dug into virgin soil in Level 18 of Sector A and Level 8 of Sector B, although remnants of collapsed stone walls were uncovered from the latter. This poor preservation of architecture was undoubtedly a result of later erosional processes, including intensive building activities of the Chalcolithic people. The artifact assemblages also reflect such disturbances. As the pottery analysis shows (Chapter 7), many of the "Neolithic" excavation contexts in these levels contained later materials. As a matter of fact the undisturbed contexts were essentially limited in both sectors to several of the basal pits only. The undisturbed materials, to be described below, thus comprise about a third of the total (209 pieces; Table 8.1).

Under these circumstances any spatial or particular activity-related analysis would be impractical. Accordingly the description below deals with them by level rather than by specific feature or stratum within a level, and focuses on their general technological and typological aspects viewed from a chronological perspective.

The overlying Ubaid to Post-Ubaid levels in both sectors also occasionally contained a small number of Neolithic lithics, most notable among them being flint arrowheads and obsidian side-blow blade-flakes. These intrusive materials will also be described below.

8.2 Method of description

As the system employed for artifact classification basically follows that developed and published by the present author for the Late Neolithic industries of North Syria (Nishiaki 1992, 2000), there is no

Table 8.1 Neolithic flaked stone artifacts from Tell Kosak Shamali.

Contexts	Undisturbed						Disturbed						Total		
	Sector A		Sector B		Total		Sector A		Sector B		Total				
	18	%	8	%		%	18	%	8	%		%		%	%
Flint	140	100.0	69	100.0	209	100.0	28	100.0	344	100.0	372	100.0	581	100.0	99.7
Cores	(6)	4.2	(10)	14.5	(16)	7.5	(3)	11.5	(42)	12.2	(45)	21.2	(61)	10.5	
Debitage	(130)	90.9	(57)	82.6	(187)	88.2	(22)	84.6	(269)	78.2	(291)	137.3	(478)	82.3	
Tools	(4)	2.8	(2)	2.9	(6)	2.8	(3)	11.5	(33)	9.6	(36)	17.0	(42)	7.2	
Obsidian	0	-	0	-	0	-	0	-	2	100.0	2	100.0	2	100.0	0.3
Cores	(0)	-	(0)	-	(0)	-	(0)	-	(0)	0.0	(0)	0.0	(0)	0.0	
Debitage	(0)	-	(0)	-	(0)	-	(0)	-	(1)	50.0	(1)	50.0	(1)	50.0	
Tools	(0)	-	(0)	-	(0)	-	(0)	-	(1)	50.0	(1)	50.0	(1)	50.0	
Total	140		69		209		28		346		374		583		

need to repeat full details here. A brief outline is summarized below.

The lithics were divided into three major categories: cores, debitage and tools. Each category was then subdivied according to its own techno-morphological traits. For convenience sake, cores were classified into three general groups according to the estimated stage of abandonment in the reduction sequence: early, middle and late. Strictly speaking, all cores are considered to have been abandoned at their last stage of operation. "Early" stage cores are those that are non-flaked and semi-flaked. Non-flaked cores, i.e. flint nodules or blocks are referred to as chunks, and cores with a few flake scars as semi-flaked cores. Cores in the "middle" stage group show variable traces of blank production. They can be classified by the shape of major flake scars on the main flaking surface (blade or flake), the number and location of platforms (single-, opposed-, change-of-orientation, or multi-platform), and the overall shape resulting from blank production (flat, prismatic, etc.). Cores of the "final" stage, which no longer retain their original technological traits due to repeated flaking, are described as exhausted cores.

The term debitage is used to refer to pieces detached from cores and left unmodified. They consist of core trimming pieces, flakes, blades, chips and fragments. Flakes and blades can also be classified by the overall shape and the amount of surface cortex. The latter attribute is expected to reflect a general stage in the reduction sequence. The division between cortical and partially cortical pieces depends on whether or not more than half the dorsal surface is cortical.

In principle, tools denote flaked pieces with intentional retouch. However, unmodified pieces with possible traces of use, such as those with gloss and nibbling on an edge, are also included in this category. Retouch or use-wear patterns result in a number of particular types but retouched tools from the undisturbed contexts were so few at Tell Kosak Shamali that detailed classification was impractical.

8.3 Flaked stone artifacts from Tell Kosak Shamali

8.3.1 Level 18 of Sector A

The excavation of this level yielded a total of 168 flint artifacts from disturbed and undisturbed contexts (Table 8.1). The undisturbed materials (140 pieces) were mostly from Pit 1805. Over 90% are debitage (130/140), with only a small number of cores and tools. The raw material is mostly medium-grained flint, with a variety of surface colors ranging from gray, dark gray, grayish brown, purple brown to reddish brown. The much finer grain-textured chocolate brown flint which was often used in PPNB assemblages of this region, is virtually absent. No obsidian pieces were discovered.

Cores

There are six cores. All but one semi-flaked core had been abandoned in the middle reduction stage. They include two single-platform blade cores with regular blade removals; one has its main flaking surface on one face only (flat type), while the flaking surface of the other extends to one side (prismatic type). The piece in Fig. 8.1: 1 is an example of the former type showing well-developed core preparation. The left face has a series of flake scars preceeding blade removals, indicating that core reduction had begun with the making of a crested ridge. Small scars originating from the distal end probably represent attempts to avoid overshot errors.

The remaining cores are flake cores showing relatively simple preparation and blank production. They consist of one single-platform core, one opposed-platform core, and one change-of-orientation core. The single-platform core belongs to the prismatic type (Fig. 8.1: 2). The opposed-platform core, definitely not a Naviform type, is an irregular core with the main flaking surface on one face only. The change-of-orientation core has two main flaking surfaces, one of which uses the other as its striking platform (Fig. 8.1: 3). As the number of blank production surfaces indicates, the core results from a simple rotated reduction of a single-platform core.

Debitage

The debitage assemblage consists of core-trimming pieces, flakes, blades, chips and fragments. The core-trimming pieces are all simple flakes retaining an edge of their parent core at one side. They do not include crested blades, although cores suggest their use (see above). The flakes and blades group is dominated by flakes, nearly half of which are wholly or partially cortical (Table 8.3). Blades comprise a small percentage at 3.8 % (4/105).

Tools

The collection from Level 18 of Sector A includes four retouched tools: one arrowhead, two sickle elements, and one retouched blade (Table 8.4).

The arrowhead is a tang fragment from a Byblos point (Fig. 8.1: 4; Pl. 8.1: 7), on which both sides of the tang are modified by abrupt retouch.

The sickle elements from Tell Kosak Shamali both have abrupt backing and/or truncating retouch. No simple snapped blades or flakes were present. They show gloss (Fig. 8.1: 5 and 6) running almost parallel along the longer axis, suggesting that these elements were hafted parallel to their handle.

The retouched blade shown in Fig. 8.1: 7 is a regular blade with a nibbling retouch along the left edge. While no visible gloss exists, this specimen could also have been used as a sickle element.

8.3.2 Level 8 of Sector B

(1) Flint

A slightly larger flint collection of 415 pieces was retrieved from Level 8 of Sector B (Table 8.1) However, pieces from the undisturbed contexts account for a much smaller portion (69 specimens only) of the whole assemblage than in Level 18 of Sector A. The pattern is the same as that noted for the pottery assemblages (Chapter 7). The heavier disturbance to the Neolithic level in Sector B perhaps reflects the longer exposure for erosion: the Neolithic settlement had been left uncovered there until the construction of a workshop in the Post Ubaid period (Level 6).

As in the collection from Level 18 of Sector A, debitage prodominates the small undisturbed assemblage (82.6 %), followed by cores (14.5 %) and tools (2.9 %). Raw material differs little from that of Sector A, mostly grayish brown to dark brown, medium-grained flint.

Cores

The assemblage consists of 10 cores of similar types to those of the Sector A assemblage (Table 8.2), but with a more simple type composition. No blade cores are present, and all the flake cores except one belong to the single-platform type. Core reduction using single-platform cores thus

Table 8.2 Cores from Neolithic levels of Tell Kosak Shamali.

Level	Sector A		Sector B			
	18	%	8	%	Total	%
(Early stage)						
Semi-flaked	1	16.7	1	10.0	2	12.5
(Blade cores)						
Single-platform	2	33.3	0	0.0	2	12.5
Flat	(1)		(0)		(1)	
Prismatic	(1)		(0)		(1)	
(Flake cores)						
Single-platform	1	16.7	8	80.0	9	56.3
Flat	(1)		(4)		(5)	
Prismatic	(0)		(4)		(4)	
Opposed-platform	1	16.7	0	0.0	1	6.3
Uniface	(1)		(0)		(1)	
Biface	(0)		(0)		(0)	
Change-of-orientation	1	16.7	1	10.0	2	12.5
Simple	(1)		(0)		(1)	
Globular	(0)		(1)		(1)	
Total	6	100.0	10	100.0	16	100.0

Table 8.3 Debitage from Neolithic levels of Tell Kosak Shamali.

Level	Sector A		Sector B			
	18	%	8	%	Total	%
Core trimming pieces						
Core-edge pieces	8	6.2	1	1.8	9	4.8
Flakes and Blades						
Cortical flakes	16	12.3	4	7.0	20	10.7
Partially cortical flakes	39	30.0	19	33.3	58	31.0
Flakes	46	35.4	16	28.1	62	33.2
Partially cortical blades	0	0.0	3	5.3	3	1.6
Blades	4	3.1	2	3.5	6	3.2
Chips and fragments	17	13.1	12	21.1	29	15.5
Total	130	100.0	57	100.0	187	100.0

Table 8.4 Retouched tools from Neolithic levels of Tell Kosak Shamali.

Level	Sector A		Sector B			
	18	%	8	%	Total	%
Arrowhead	1	25.0	0	0.0	1	12.5
Retouched blade	1	25.0	0	0.0	1	12.5
Sickle elements	2	50.0	2	100.0	4	50.0
Glossed	(2)		(1)		(3)	
Non-glossed	(0)		(1)		(1)	
Total	4	100.0	2	100.0	6	100.0

characterizes the Sector B assemblage. Flat and prismatic types (Fig. 8.2: 1) are equally represented in the single-platform cores. The remaining is a change-of-orientation core (Fig. 8.2: 2). It retains blank production scars originating from three platforms, demonstrating repeated changes of knapping direction. No other cores but a semi-flaked one are discovered.

Debitage

The debitage assemblage of Level 8 of Sector B shows basically the same features as that of Sector A (Table 8.3). Flakes predominate (nearly 90 %). Blades are slightly more common (11.4 % or 5/44), but the small sample size precludes any conclusive statement. Proportions of cortical, partially cortical, and non-cortical pieces are virtually the same between these two levels, indicating that similar core reduction processes tool place in Sectors A and B.

Tools

There are only two retouched pieces in the undisturbed collection. One is a sickle element with a silica gloss on one edge (Fig. 8.2: 3). The opposite edge is partially backed with steep retouch. The other specimen is a flake with a steeply retouched back (Fig. 8.2: 4). It shows no gloss on the working edge, but the overall shape suggests its use as a sickle element.

(2) Obsidian

The material from Level 8 of Sector B contains two pieces of obsidian, comprising 0.3% of the total (Table 8.1), but they are both from disturbed contexts. One is a side-blow blade-flake (Fig. 8. 2: 5), and the other is a thin fragment of flake shatter or chip (Fig. 8. 2: 8). The side-blow blade-flake was detached from the proximal end of parent blade. It shows no subsequent retouch. While the side-blow blade-flake definitely belongs to the Neolithic industry, the derivation of the flake shatter is uncertain.

8.3.3 Derived materials

As with the Palaeolithic pieces described in Chapter 6, Neolithic lithic artifacts had also intruded into the Chalcolithic levels (Fig. 8.3). However it was not always easy to identify them as, in most cases, the physical conditions of the Neolithic and Chalcolithic flints were indistinguishable from each other. Therefore, only typologically distinct pieces are mentioned here, and should be considered as a few examples out of many.

Six arrowhead fragments were present: five were excavated from Ubaid levels of Sector A, and the sixth was from a Post-Ubaid level of Sector B. Except for one piece, which seems to be an Amuq point (Fig. 8.3: 3; Pl. 8.1: 1), most are probably from Byblos points (Fig. 8. 3: 1, 2, 4, 5 and 6; Pl. 8.1: 2-6). They share the following general technological traits: the proximal end of the blank is modified by bifacial retouch to make a tang, the mid part is fashioned by direct retouch, and the tip is pointed by inverse retouch. The use of pressure flaking is not evident. It should be noted that two arrowheads are made on blades with bidirectional dorsal scars (Fig. 8.3: 1 and 5), a blank form that would not have been produced from the cores mentioned in the above.

The blade segment illustrated in Fig. 8.3: 7 is on an exceptionally fine-grained brown flint, reminiscent of the raw material popular in the PPNB industries of this region. One corner of the distal end on the ventral surface has multi burin-like facets at an oblique angle. In overall morphology this piece is comparable to the "Damishliyya piece" originally designated at the final PPNB assemblages of Tell Damishliyya, the Balikh valley (Nishiaki 1992).

Finally, but of great interest, is a Naviform core (Fig. 8.3: 8; Pl. 8.1: 8), in a fine-grained chocolate brown flint, although thermal action had changed the surface color to brownish gray. Although the main flaking surface shows only unidirectional flake scars, it is obvious that this core is an opposed-platform type with the Naviform shape. Platforms have been set up at both ends, and the back has been modified to form a short zigzag ridge. The Naviform core and the burin mentioned above, were both found in the lowest Ubaidian level (Level 17) of Sector A.

Among the obsidian artifacts are two side-blow blade-flakes: one from Ubaid (Fig. 8.2: 6), and the other from Post-Ubaid (Fig. 8.2: 7) levels of Sector B. They have received no subsequent modification retouch after detachment from their parent blade.

8.4 Discussion

Because of their overall techno-typological similarities and the small sample size, the assemblages from the lowest levels of Sectors A and B can be discussed collectively. General features indicate that they represent a single industry of the Pottery Neolithic (cf. Chapter 7), based on the production of flake blanks from single-platform cores on small flint pebbles. In the course of reduction, cores were often rotated a couple of times resulting in change-of-orientation cores when abandoned. Blade production was minimal and produced from single-platform cores. Naviform cores were not found in the relevant contexts. The only notable standardized tools were arrowheads and sickle elements. The primary assemblages included a single Byblos point fragment. Sickle elements were on flakes or blades with truncation and/or backing retouch. Among the rare obsidian pieces were a few side-blow blade-flakes. These are diagnostic of the Pottery Neolithic of northern Mesopotamia, and indicate links with the east. Tell Kosak Shamali is one of the westernmost sites within the distribution region of side-blow blade-flakes (cf. Nishiaki 1996).

These flaked stone assemblages show that after the mound of Tell Kosak Shamali had been abandoned in the late Epi-Palaeolithic (see Chapter 6), it was occupied again in the Pottery Neolithic. While Pottery Neolithic settlements are not uncommon on the Upper Euphrates (cf. Copeland and Moore 1985; de Contenson 1985), only a handful have been excavated. In the Tishreen Dam flood zone, excavations have been in progress at Tell Halula, a large multi-stratified mound located on the opposite bank of the Euphrates, where a long sequence spanning the middle PPNB to the Halafian periods has been exposed (Molist and Ferrer 1996; Ferrer *et al.* 1996). Excavations at Ja'ade Mughara, about 10km north of Tell Kosak Shamali, have also yielded traces of Pottery Neolithic above the PPNB levels (Coqueugniot 1999). In the south, excavations in the 1970s at Tell Abu Hureyra yielded Pottery Neolithic materials in Abu Hureyra 2 (Moore *et al.* 2000).

Unfortunately the lithic materials from these sites have not been fully published yet. The best information available so far, although still in a preliminary form, is that from Tell Halula.

According to Molist and Ferrer (1996) and Ferrer *et al.* (1996), the Pottery Neolithic lithic assemblages from Tell Halula have the following features: medium-grained local flint was exploited at the expense of the finer-grained exotic flint common in the PPNB period; the core reduction technology of the Pottery Neolithic was directed towards flake production from amorphous single-platform cores; Naviform blade technology of the PPNB was no longer used; a variety of flake tools such as scrapers and denticulates dominated the retouched tools of the Pottery Neolithic; arrowheads were still manufactured but in much smaller quantities; sickle elements, made primarily on flakes by abrupt retouch, were important.

The description of the Tell Halula assemblages is applicable to the Neolithic lithics of Tell Kosak Shamali. Furthermore, they match the characteristics of Pottery Neolithic assemblages from northern Syria in general (Nishiaki 1992). The lithics from Tell Halula and those of Tell Kosak Shamali demonstrate that the Pottery Neolithic lithic manufacturing tradition of the Upper Euphrates region can be understood within the same broader contexts of cultural processes of the North Syrian Neolithic.

The flaked stone industries of North Syria underwent great changes in the late 9th millennium BP. New industries with different sets of techno-typological features and the different approaches to raw material use became popular in a rather short period of time. This rapid industrial shift is considered to reflect the dynamic processes of cultural change that occurred between the Late PPNB and early Pottery Neolithic, the nature of which has been discussed from a variety of view-points (cf. Nishiaki 2000). Their relationship to later industries, i.e. the transition from Pottery Neolithic to Halafian has not been sufficiently documented, largely because of the unavailability of lithic assemblages bridging these periods. However, recent research in the Balikh valley is beginning to shed new light on this problem. Studies of the material from Tell Damishliyya and the lowest level of Tell Sabi Abyad I (Level 11) provide detailed data on the early Pottery Neolithic industry (Nishiaki 2000; Copeland 1996), and those of the upper levels of Tell Sabi Abyad I allow an examination of the development from the late Pottery Neolithic

(Levels 10-7), the Transitional (Levels 6-4) to the early Halafian periods (Levels 3-1; Copeland 1989, 1996). Together these provide a general view of the complete industrial sequence. Although a strong continuity is evident for this time period, Copeland (1996) has pointed out some changes as well. Technologically, the late Pottery Neolithic industries were characterized by an even stronger emphasis on flake production. Blades of Levels 10-7 account for less than 10 % of the debitage category. The change was also reflected in typological aspects; blade tools such as arrowheads and burins significantly diminished in numbers and were replaced by rather amorphous flake tools such as denticulates and notches. Furthermore, new types appeared in the Transitional and the Early Halafian levels, distinguishing them from the earlier periods. Arrowheads on blades were virtually replaced by smaller and often transversal arrowheads. The Tile knife, a new type of scraper, joined the menu of flake scrapers. In addition, the obsidian side-blow blade-flakes and corner-thinned blades popular in the Late Pottery Neolithic, almost completely disappeared in subsequent periods.

In light of this general sequence documented in the Balikh valley, the flaked stone assemblages from Tell Kosak Shamali can be seen as comparable to the late Pottery Neolithic. Needless to say the general similarities of blank production technology, the absence of tools characterizing the Transitional and later periods, such as Tile knives and transversal arrowheads, also supports this comparison.

In addition, a typological comparison of sickle elements points out another similarity between the late Pottery Neolithic of Sabi Abyad and Tell Kosak Shamali. The common use of backed and/or truncated elements, often shaped into a crescentic form, is typical of both assemblages. In the Balikh valley, a change of the sickle element technology over a period of the late PPNB to early Pottery Neolithic has been documented, using the data from Tell Damishliyya (Nishiaki 1997, 2000). Rectangular or crescent-shaped sickle elements on blades were popular forms in the late PPNB, but they were increasingly replaced by crescent-shaped pieces on flake blanks in the latest PPNB and early Pottery Neolithic. The later samples of Tell Sabi Abyad (Copeland 1996) clearly show that this changing pattern continued into the late Pottery Neolithic and the Transitional periods. The Tell Kosak Shamali specimens, consisted of predominantly crescent-shaped or backed flake types, suggest that the similar change was also in progress on the Upper Euphrates. The observed changes of the sickle technology in the Balikh valley included that of a hafting technique as well. It has been suggested that many of the sickle elements were hafted to a handle obliquely in the Pottery Neolithic (Nishiaki 1997). However the distribution pattern of silica gloss indicates that the parallel hafting was popular at Tell Kosak Shamali. But it will be certainly unwise to generalize or emphasize this point with such a small sample. In fact, at Tell Sabi Abyad too, the published drawings show that sickle elements probably hafted in a parallel way were not uncommon in the late Pottery Neolithic and the Transitional samples (cf. Figs. 4.4: 4 and 4.8 in Copeland 1996).

8.5 Conclusion

Typologically and technologically, the two Neolithic flaked stone assemblages of Tell Kosak Shamali resemble each other closely. It is likely that together they represent a single industry of the Late Pottery Neolithic, probably dating from the late-8th millennium uncalibrated BP. The flaked stone tools of this stage of the Pottery Neolithic have received relatively little attention in the literature. In this respect, the Tell Kosak Shamali collection, which is small but a rare sample from this region, hopefully helps to understand the continuous processes of industrial change in the Pottery Neolithic period of North Syria.

A final comment is needed on the derived materials in the Tell Kosak Shamali Neolithic collection. It is important to note that they include pieces suggesting different traditions. The Naviform core and arrowheads made on blades produced from opposed-platform cores suggest that PPNB occupations could also have existed somewhere at this small mound.

References

Coqueugniot, E. (1999) Tall Gadat al-Mugara. In: *Archaeology of the Upper Syrian Euphrates, the Tishreen Dam Area,* edited by G. del Omo Lete and J.-L. Montero Fenollós, pp. 41-55. Barcelona: Universitat de Barcelona.

Copeland, L. (1989) The flint and obsidian artifacts of Tell Sabi Abyad. In: *Excavations at Tell Sabi Abyad: Prehistoric Investigations in the Balikh Valley, Northern Syria,* edited by P.M.M.G. Akkermans, pp. 237-284. BAR i.s. 468. Oxford: British Archaeological Reports.

Copeland, L. (1996) The flint and obsidian industries. In: *Tell Sabi Abyad: The Late Neolithic Settlement,* edited by P.M.M.G. Akkermans, pp. 285-338. Istanbul: Nederlands Historisch-Archaeologisch Instituut te Istanbul.

Copeland, L. and A.M.T. Moore (1985) Inventory and description of sites. In: *Holocene Settlement in North Syria,* edited by P. Sanlaville, pp. 41-98. BAR i.s. 238. Oxford: British Archaeological Reports.

Copeland, L. and M. Verhoeven (1996) Bitumen-coated sickle-blade elements at Tell Sabi Abyad II, Northern Syria. In: *Neolithic Chipped Lithic Industries of the Fertile Crescent and Their Adjacent Regions,* edited by S.K. Kozlowski and H.G. Gebel, pp.327-330. Berlin: ex oriente.

de Contenson, H. (1985) Le materiel archéologique des tells. In: *Holocene Settlement in North Syria,* edited by P. Sanlaville, pp. 99-161. BAR i.s. 238. Oxford: British Archaeological Reports.

Ferrer, A., J. Mateu, M. Molist and A. Palomo (1996) Industria litica tallada. In: *Tell Halula (Siria): Un Yacimiento Neolitico del Valle Medio del Eufrates Campanas de 1991 y 1992,* edited by M. Molist, pp. 73-90. Barcerona: Ministerio de Educacion y Cultura.

Molist, M. and A. Ferrer (1996) Industries lithique pendant la periode 8000-7500 B.P. a Tell Halula dans d'Euphrate moyen Syrien. In: *Neolithic Chipped Lithic Industries of the Fertile Crescent and Their Adjacent Regions,* edited by S.K. Kozlowski and H.G. Gebel, pp.431-442. Berlin: ex oriente.

Moore, A.M.T., T. Legge and G. Hilman (2000) *Village on the Euphrates: From Foraging to Farming at Abu Hureyra.* Oxford: Oxford University Press.

Nishiaki, Y. (1992) *Lithic Technology of Neolithic Syria: A Series of Analyses of Flaked Stone Assemblages from Douara Cave II, Tell Damishliyya, Tell Nebi Mende and Tell Kashkashok II.* Ph.D. Dissertation, University College London, London University.

Nishiaki, Y. (1993) Lithic analysis and cultural change in the late Pre-pottery Neolithic of North Syria. *Anthropological Science* 101(1): 91-109.

Nishiaki, Y. (1996) Side-blow blade-flakes from Tell Kashkashok II, Syria: a technological study. In: *Neolithic Chipped Lithic Industries of the Fertile Crescent and Their Adjacent Regions,* edited by S.K. Kozlowski and H.G. Gebel, pp.311-325. Berlin: ex oriente.

Nishiaki, Y. (1997) Neolithic sickle elements from the Balikh valley, North Syria. *Al-Rafidan* 18: 59-67.

Nishiaki, Y. (2000) *Lithic Technology of Neolithic Syria.* BAR.i.s. 840. Oxford: Archaeopress.

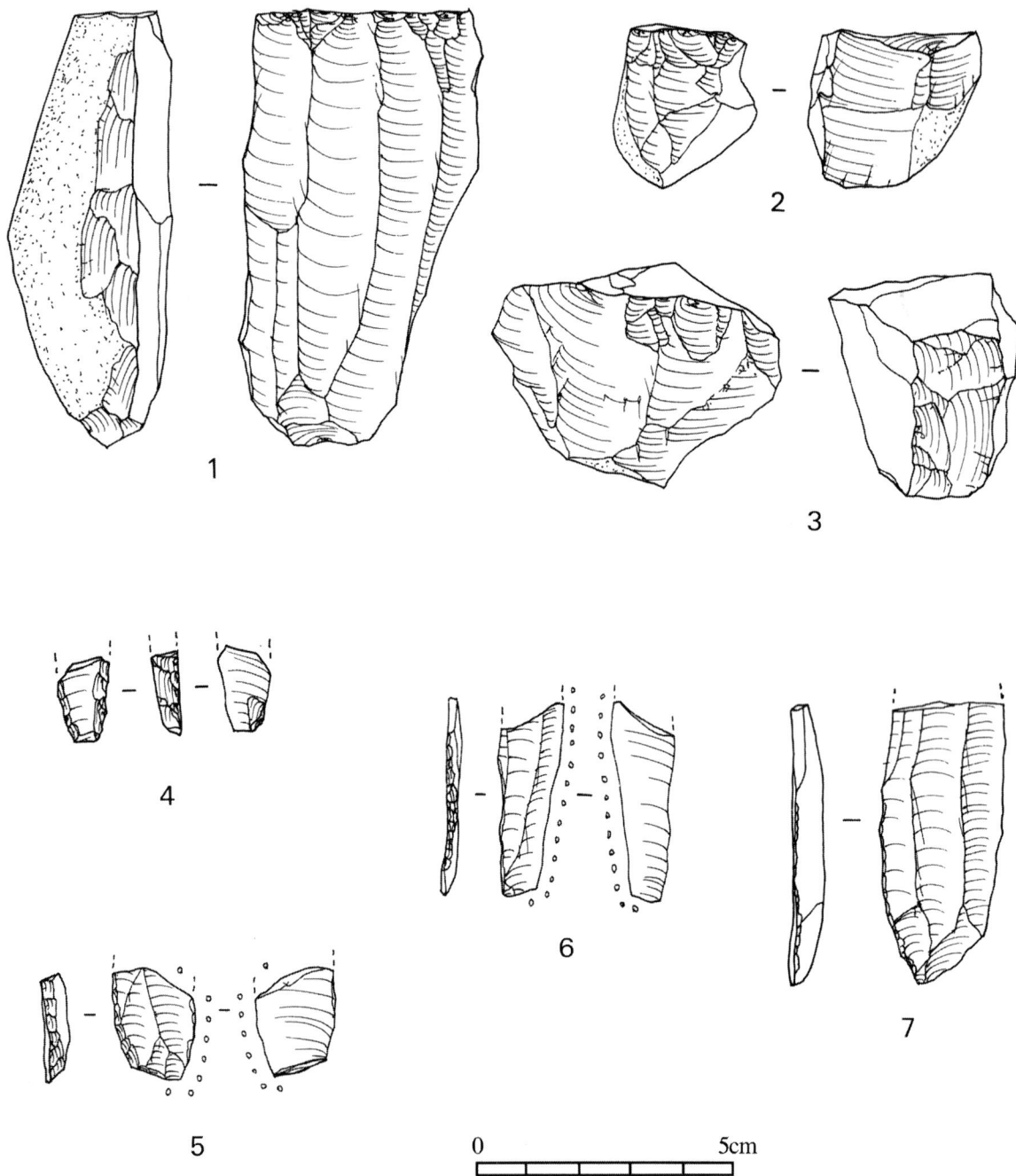

Fig. 8.1 Neolithic flint artifacts from Level 18 and later levels of Sector A.

1. Single-platform blade core, flat type (94KSL-A11-8-pit; 1805; Level 18 of Sector A).
2. Single-platform flake core, prismatic type (95KSL-AG5-9; 1805; Level 18 of Sector A).
3. Change-of-orientation flake core, simple type (95KSL-AF5-24; 1803; Level 18 of Sector A).
4. Arrowhead, tang fragment, Byblos point (94KSL-A11-8-pit; 1805; Level 18 of Sector A).
5. Sickle element, fragment (94KSL-A12-6; 1805; Level 18 of Sector A).
6. Sickle element, backed, on blade (94KSL-A12-6; 1805; Level 18 of Sector A).
7. Retouched blade, nibbled along the left edge (94KSL-A11-8-pit; 1805; Level 18 of Sector A).

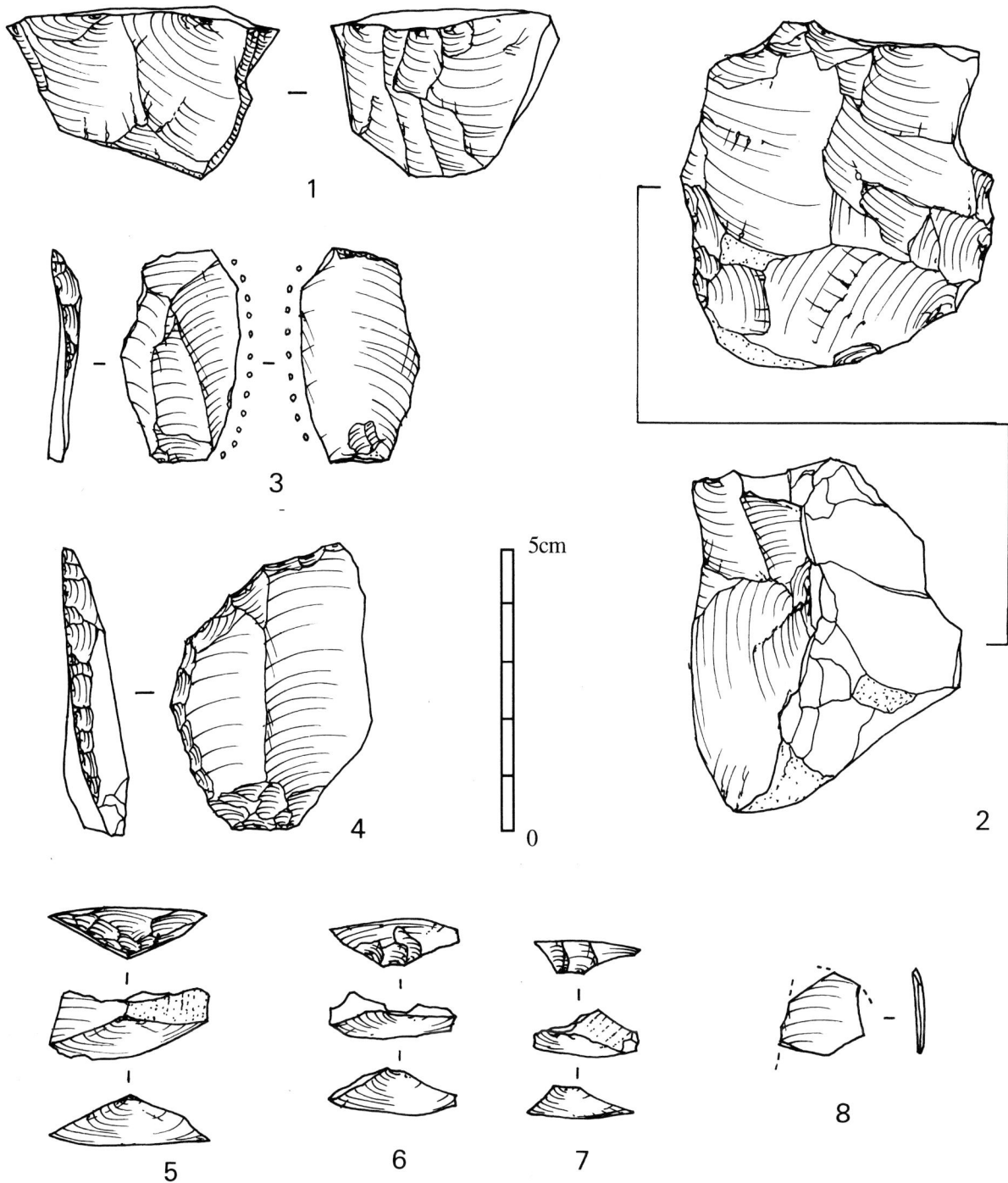

Fig. 8.2 Neolithic flint and obsidian artifacts from Level 8 and later levels of Sector B.
1. Single-platform flake core, prismatic type (97KSL-BE6-41; B803; Level 8 of Sector B).
2. Change-of-orientation flake core, globular type (97KSL-BE6-35; B802; Level 8 of Sector B).
3. Sickle element, partially backed, on flake (97KSL-BE6-42; B804; Level 8 of Sector B).
4. Sickle element (?), gloss invisible (97KSL-BE6-42; B804; Level 8 of Sector B).
5. Side-blow blade-flake, flaked from the proximal end of parent blade (97KSL-BE6-41; B803; Level 8 of Sector B).
6. Side-blow blade-flake, flaked from the proximal end of parent blade (96KSL-BD6-25; B703; Level 7 of Sector B).
7. Side-blow blade-flake, flaked from the proximal end of parent blade (96KSL-BE7-21; Fill; Level 5 of Sector B).
8. Flake, shatter (97KSL-BD6-30; Fill; Level 8 of Sector B).

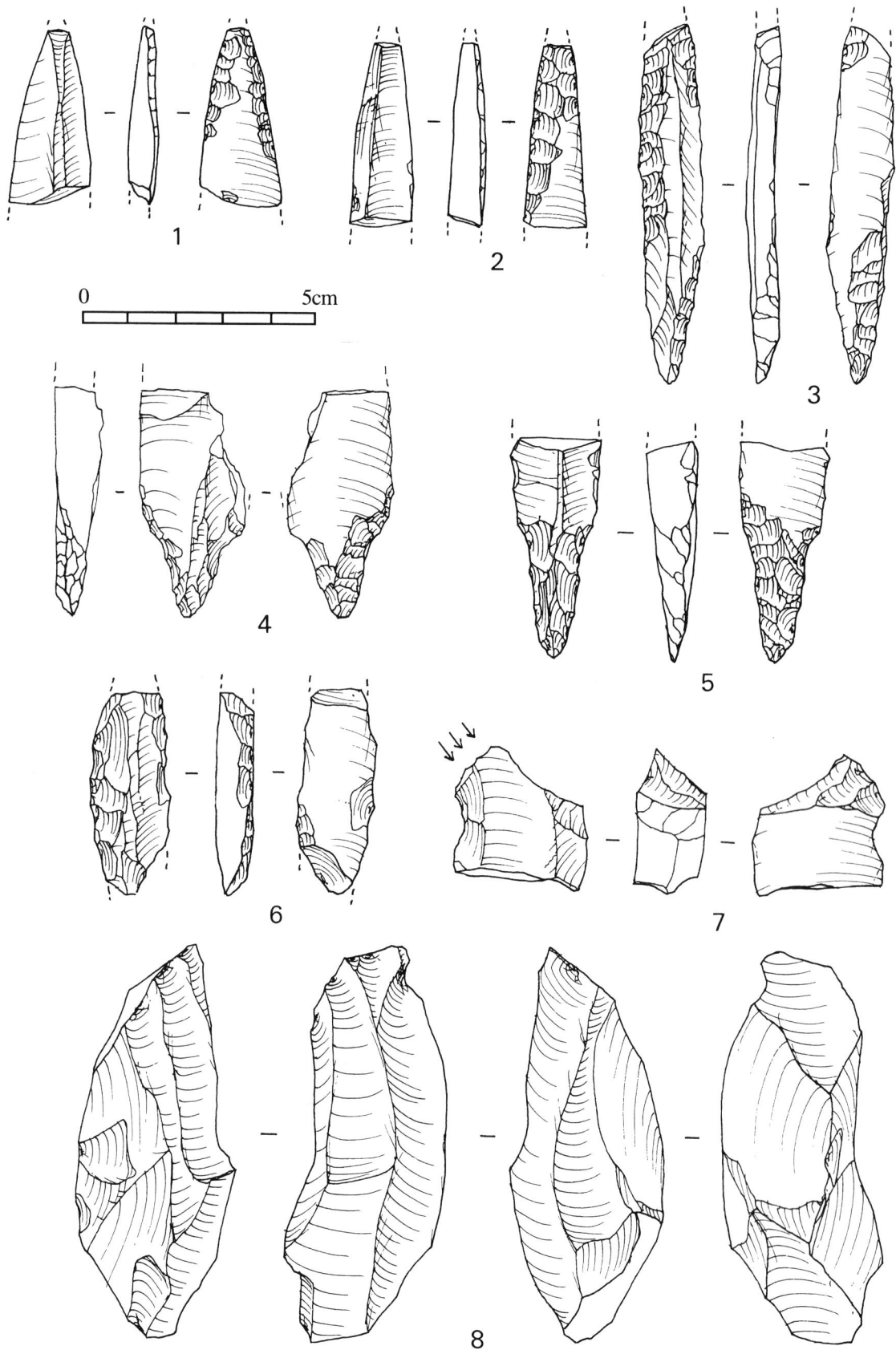

Fig. 8.3 Neolithic flint artifacts from later levels of Sectors A and B.
1. Arrowhead, tip fragment, with impact fracture, Byblos point (97KSL-AD4-50; 1303; Level 13 of Sector A).
2. Arrowhead, tip fragment, Byblos point (97KSL-AD5-114; 1302; Level 13 of Sector A).
3. Arrowhead, tang fragment, Amuq point (94KSL-surface; surface collection from Sector A).
4. Arrowhead, tang fragment, thermally fractured, Byblos point (95KSL-AG5-4; 1309; Level 13 of Sector A).
5. Arrowhead, tang fragment, Byblos point (94KSL-C10-2; Fill; Level 11 of Sector A).
6. Arrowhead, middle fragment, Byblos point (97KSL-BE5-4; B603; Level 6 of Sector B).
7. Burin, proximal end broken (95KSL-AF5-23; Fill; Level 17 of Sector A).
8. Naviform core, chocolate brown flint (95KSL-AF5-23; Fill; Level 17 of Sector A).

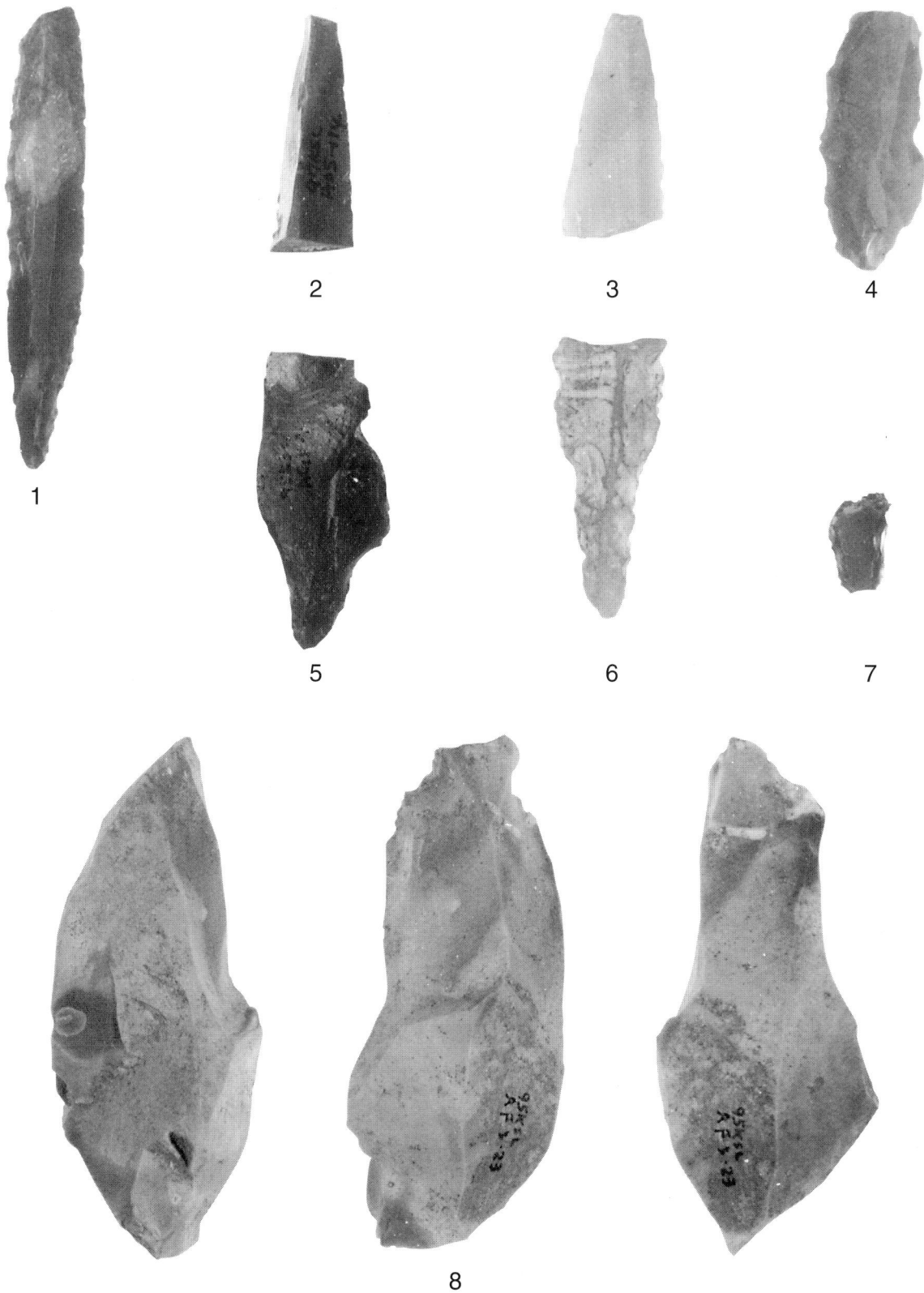

Plate 8.1 Neolithic flint artifacts from Tell Kosak Shamali.

1. Arrowhead (cf. Fig. 8.3: 3).
2. Arrowhead (cf. Fig. 8.3: 2).
3. Arrowhead (cf. Fig. 8.3: 1).
4. Arrowhead (cf. Fig. 8.3: 6).
5. Arrowhead (cf. Fig. 8.3: 4).
6. Arrowhead (cf. Fig. 8.3: 5).
7. Arrowhead (cf. Fig. 8.1: 4).
8. Naviform core (cf. Fig. 8.3: 8).

CHAPTER **9** The other Neolithic finds
from Tell Kosak Shamali

Yoshihiro Nishiaki, Hiroshi Sudo and Seiji Kadowaki

9.1 Introduction

This chapter addresses a variety of artifact classes other than pottery and flaked stone from the Neolithic levels of Tell Kosak Shamali. They are described under the headings of ground stone tools, stone objects, bone tools and a clay object. The sample is very small reflecting the limited area of excavation and the relatively thin deposits of the Neolithic period, but it is hoped that the description will enrich our understanding of the Neolithic material culture represented at the site.

As the pottery and flaked stone assemblages (Chapters 7 and 8), the assemblage of other objects also suffered from the contamination problem. Any attempt to separate Ubaid and Neolithic objects of this kind on a typological basis alone would be too subjective. Therefore we shall report the artifacts from the supposedly undisturbed contexts only, i.e. several of the bedrock pits. The exception is a clay object from Level 8 of Sector B. It was discovered in a disturbed Neolithic context, but could be typologically a Neolithic piece (see below).

9.2 Ground stone tools

The Neolithic levels of Tell Kosak Shamali yielded 24 ground stone tools: 1 from Level 18 of Sector A, and 23 from Level 8 of Sector B (Table 9.1). Useful typologies for these artifact classes, generally based on a combination of morpho-technological and functional features, have become available in the recent literature (e.g. Gopher and Orrelle 1995; Wright 1992; Mazlowski 1997). The present report follows principally the typology developed by Wright (1992), with some simplification to accommodate the smaller morphological diversity of the present collection. Upper stones, or stones used in active motion are grouped into handstones, pounders and pestles. Lower stones, or passive tools, showing very limited morphological variability, are classified into grinding slabs. The absence of mortars may correlate with the relative scarcity of pounders and pestles in the upper stone assemblages.

These ground stone tools are often related to grain processing activities, but the possibility of their use for other purposes like flint working can not be ruled out.

Handstones

These are tools believed to have been used as an upper stone to grind or polish other materials. They are in a variety of raw materials, all easily available in the vicinity of Tell Kosak Shamali today. Basalt and limestone were most commonly used, but flint and sandstone were also used. Use-traces from grinding or polishing were generally observed on limited areas of the surface or edges, but occasionally cover the whole surface. They could also have been used for pounding. Three morphological types were discernible: elongated, disc and globular. Elongated pieces were characterized by their length being one and a half times longer than their width. Disc and globular pieces were distinguished from each other by their relative thickness. Disc-shaped handstones comprised specimens with a

Table 9.1 Neolithic ground stones from Tell Kosak Shamali.

Level	Sector A		Sector B			
	18	%	8	%	Total	%
Handstones						
Elongated	0	0.0	6	26.1	6	25.0
Disc-shaped	1	100.0	1	4.3	2	8.3
Globular	0	0.0	2	8.7	2	8.3
Pounders	0	0.0	2	8.7	2	8.3
Pestles	0	0.0	2	8.7	2	8.3
Grinding slab	0	0.0	1	4.3	1	4.2
Fragments	0	0.0	9	39.1	9	37.5
Total	1	100.0	23	100.0	24	100.0

width/thickness ratio larger than 1.5, while globular ones had a ratio equal to or smaller than 1.5.

Pounders
Pounders refer to stone tools used for pounding or crushing. They are a globular shape, with a length/width ratio smaller than 1.5. Signs of battering are visible at least at part of the surface. Two specimens were found from Level 8 of Sector B; one was flint (Fig. 9.1: 1), and the other basalt (Fig. 9.1: 2). The flint piece with signs of more extensive battering might have functioned as a hammerstone for the manufacturing flint tools.

Pestles
Pounding tools that have a length/width ratio equal to or larger than 1.5 are referred to as pestles. Only two pieces were identified as such in the present collection. One, of limestone, was pre-shaped by flaking at the sides and showed signs of battering at one end (Fig. 9.1: 3). The other (Fig. 9.1: 4), of basalt, was similar morphologically but the possible working edge was missing, perhaps through breakage.

Grinding slab
These are stone tools probably used as lower stones for handstones. Only one small fragment, basalt, was found in the present collection (Fig. 9.1: 5). The upper surface, with a shallow depression, clearly shows traces of grinding.

Fragments
The collection from the undisturbed Neolithic contexts of Sector B included nine basalt fragments of unknown shape. Our preliminary survey shows that basalt rocks are available nowadays in the riverbed and the bank of the Nahar Sarine (see Chapter 1). They are rare near the mound, but are common about a few kilometers or more upstream. The basalt usually occurs as large blocks. The fragments discovered at Tell Kosak Shamali could consist of not only broken ground tools but also debris from initial shaping of basalt blocks.

9.3 Stone objects

Celt
An elongated polished greenstone celt was discovered from a Neolithic pit in Sector A (Fig. 9.2: 2; Pl. 9.1: 2). It is rectangular, tapering slightly towards the butt. It is also roughly rectangular in transverse section. The area close to the working edge is polished perpendicular to the longer axis, while the mid-part of the body is polished primarily in a parallel direction. Scratches indicate perpendicular polishing again on the upper part, but the polishing is incomplete as signs of the initial flaking to shape the piece are still identifiable; it probably represents the area to be hafted. A series of use-damage scars is visible on the working edge. The overall features are similar to those reported as *herminettes* at Tell Bouqras (Roodenberg 1986).

"Truncated conical stone"
A large stone object, tentatively described as a "truncated conical stone", was found in a supposedly Neolithic pit (B802) in Sector B (Fig. 9.2: 1; Pl. 9.1: 1; see Chapter 4, Pl. 4.3: 2). When discovered it was upright, slightly inclined, with the lower part inserted into the pit. It is conical with the top truncated by polishing. The upper part had been polished after it had been scraped in a vertical direction. Battering has shaped the lower part into an irregular column, while the bottom is flat and polished. Nothing can be found in the available literature that refers to a comparable object, and its use or function is presently unknown. It is too heavy to use as an active tool. Perhaps it was laid on the ground as a passive tool or simply as a marker. This interpretation could be supported by the rather rough workmanship of the lower part of the body.

Stone vessel
A fragment of a marble object was retrieved from Pit B802, Sector B (Fig. 9.2: 5; Pl. 9.1: 4). It seems to represent the base of a vessel although the overall shape is unknown. The surface is roughly polished in irregular directions. Comparable round base and wall vessels are known from the Late Neolithic and transitional levels of Tell Sabi Abyad (Spoor and Collet 1996: 422-423). The Tell Kosak Shamali fragment has a relatively thick wall that falls within the thickest group of Tell Sabi Abyad vessels.

9.4 Bone tools

There are only two worked bone implements recovered in proper Neolithic contexts; a spatula from Level 18 of Sector A and an awl from Level 8 of Sector B.

Spatula

This thin spatula (Fig. 9.2: 4; Pl. 9.1: 3) was retrieved from a pit (1805) dug into virgin soil in Sector A. The blank had been made by splitting a long bone, neatly removing the medullary cavity, and then rubbing almost the entire surface of the bone until the desired thinness was achieved. The tip had been worked particularly intensively to create a symmetrical profile.

This type of spatula has been reported only occasionally from related Neolithic sites. The spatulas commonly found are made from ribs, and when made from long bones often retain the medullary cavity in its original condition (cf. Tell Sabi Abyad: Spoor and Collet 1996: 453; Tell Halula: Molist *et al*. 1996: 118). The spatula from Layer XVa of Telul eth-Thalathat, Iraq (PL. 44 in Fukai and Matsutani 1981) is perhaps most similar to the Tell Kosak Shamali piece.

Awl

An awl was found in Sector B in a pit in virgin soil (804). A long bone had been split longitudinally and one end had been tapered (Fig. 9.2: 3). The proximal end was missing due to breakage.

9.5 Clay object

A small baked clay object was found in the fill of Level 8 of Sector B. A cylindrical piece with flat ends (Fig. 9.2: 6; Pl. 9.1: 5), it had a slightly burnished surface. Parallels can be found at Tell Halula, where small conical or cylindrical "teracottas" have been discovered in PPNB levels (Fig. 2: 2, 4 in Molist *et al.* 1996). It may also be compared to the so-called tokens known from transitional levels of Tell Sabi Abyad. However, the latter are unbaked, and more irregularly finished (Fig. 8.5: 2 and 3 in Spoor and Collet 1996).

References

Fukai, S. and T. Matsutani (eds.) (1981) *Telul eth-Thalathat, Vol. III*. Tokyo: The Institute of Oriental Culture, the University of Tokyo.

Gopher, A. and E. Orrelle (1995) *The Ground Stone Assemblages of Munhata, A Neolithic Site in the Jordan Valley, Israel: A Report*. Paris: Association Paléorient.

Mazlowski, R. (1997) *Ground and Pecked Stone Industry in the Pre-Pottery Neolithic of Northern Iraq. Nemrik 9: Vol. 3, Pre-Pottery Neolithic Site in Iraq*, edited by S. K. Kozlowski. Warsaw: Warsaw University.

Molist, M., C. Barrachina and M. Gangonells (1996) Mobiliario diverso. In: *Tell Halula (Siria): Un Yacimiento Neolítico del Valle Medio del Éufrates Campanãs de 1991 y 1992*, edited by M. Molist, pp. 125-133. Barcerona: Ministerio de Educacion y Cultura.

Moore, A.M.T., T. Legge and G. Hilman (1975) The excavations of Tell Abu Hureyra in Syria: a preliminary report. *Proceedings of the Prehistoric Society* 41: 50-77.

Nishiaki, Y, T. Koizumi, M. Le Mière and T. Oguchi (1999) Prehistoric occupations at Tell Kosak Shamali, the Upper Euphrates, Syria. *Akkadica* 113: 13-68.

Roodenberg, J.J. (1986) *Le Mobilier en Pierre de Bouqras*. Istanbul: Nederlands Historisch-Archaeologisch te Instituut.

Spoor, R. H. and P. Collet (1996) The Other small finds. In: *Tell Sabi Abyad: The Late Neolithic Settlement*, edited by P.M.M.G. Akkermans, pp. 452-473. Istanbul: Nederlands Historich-Archaeologisch Instituut te Istanbul.

Wright, K. (1992) A classification system for ground stone tools from the prehistoric Levant. *Paléorient* 18(2): 53-82.

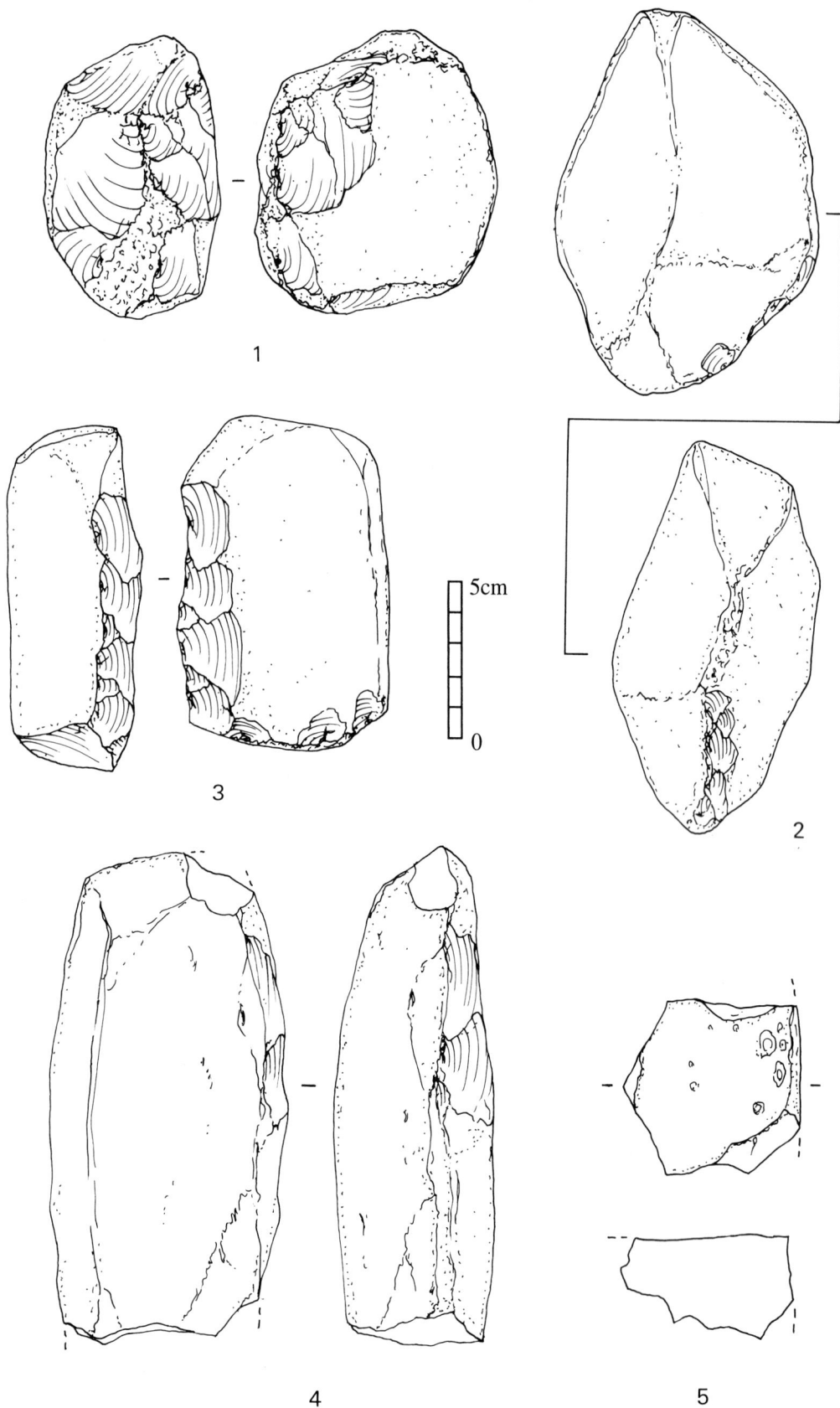

Fig. 9.1 Neolithic ground stone artifacts from Level 8 of Sector B.

1. Pounder, globular, flint, hammerstone for flint working? L: 7.9cm, W: 7.7cm,
   T: 5.6 cm (97KSL-BE6-35; B802; Level 8 of Sector B).

2. Pounder, globular, basalt, L: 11.9cm, W: 8.7cm, T: 6.3cm
   (97KSL-BE6-35; B802; Level 8 of Sector B).

3. Pestle, cylindrical, sandstone, L: 10.2cm, W: 6.5cm,
   T: 3.9cm (97KSL-BE6-41; B803; Level 8 of Sector B).

4. Pestle?, cylindrical, basalt, L: 14.5cm, W: 6.9cm, T: 4.7cm (97KSL-BE5-17;
   B804; Level 8 of Sector B).

5. Grinding slab, basalt, fragment (97KSL-BE6-41; B803; Level 8 of Sector B).

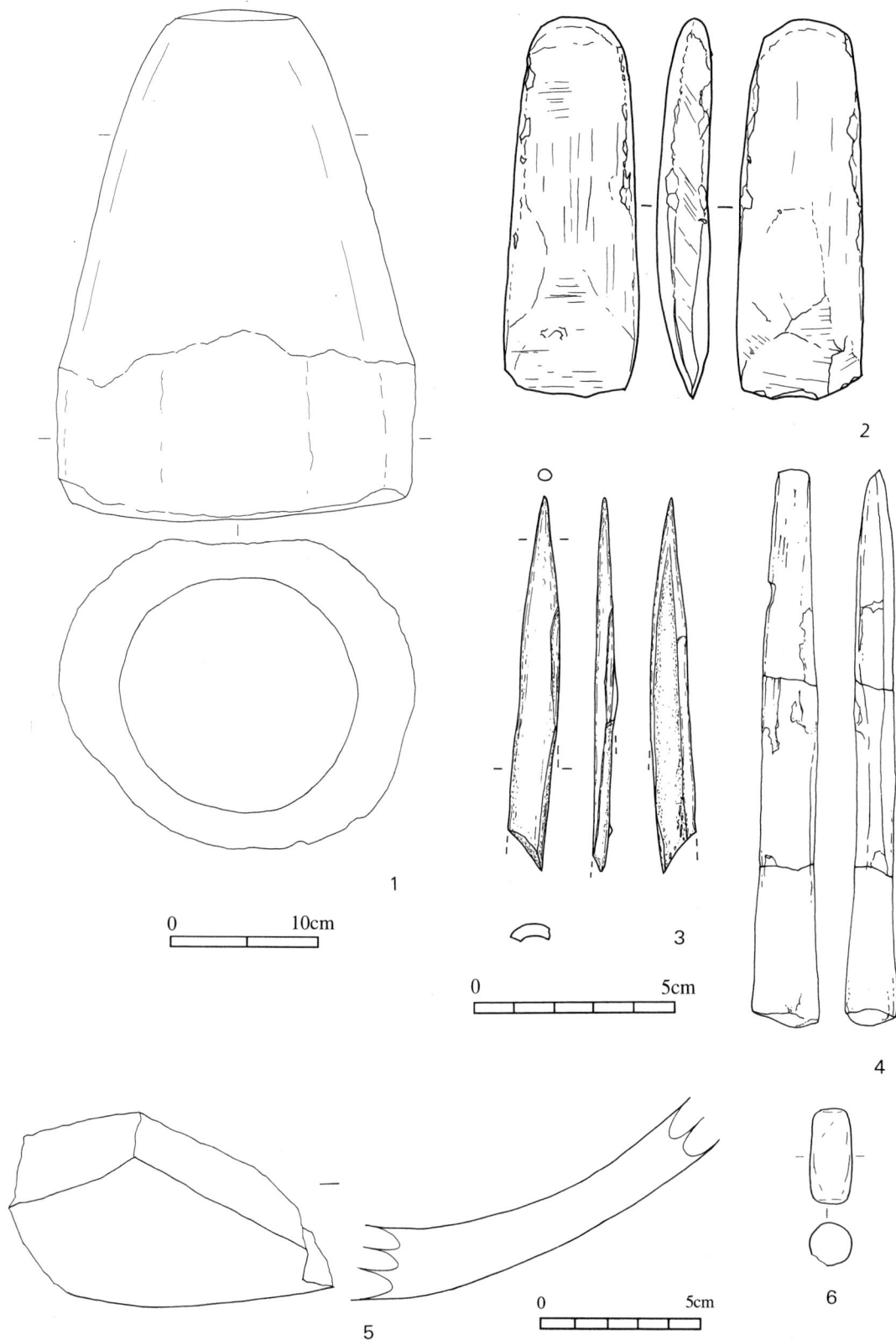

Fig. 9.2 Neolithic bone implements and other small finds from Sectors A and B.
1. Truncated conical stone, limestone, H: 31.7cm, Upper diameter: 14.7cm,
   Lower diameter: 23 cm (97KSL-BE6-35; B802; Level 8 of Sector B).
2. Celt, polished, greenstone, L: 10.1cm, W: 3.8cm, T: 1.4cm
   (94KSL-A12-6; 1805; Level 18 of Sector A).
3. Awl, pointed tip formed by abrasion, made of a split long bone.
   Its proximal end is missing by breakage. L: 8.9cm, W: 1.0cm, T: 0.5cm
   (97KSL-BE6-42; B804; Level 8 of Sector B).
4. Spatula, polished by use, made of a long bone, L: 12.6cm, W: 1.5cm, T: 1.1cm
   (94KSL-A12-6; 1805; Level 18 of Sector A).
5. Stone vessel fragment, whitish orange marble, Maximum thickness: 2.4 cm
   (97KSL-BE6-35; B802; Level 8 of Sector B).
6. Clay object, baked, complete, dull brown paste, L: 2.9cm, Diameter: 1.3cm
   (97KSL-BE6-31; Fill; Level 8 of Sector B).

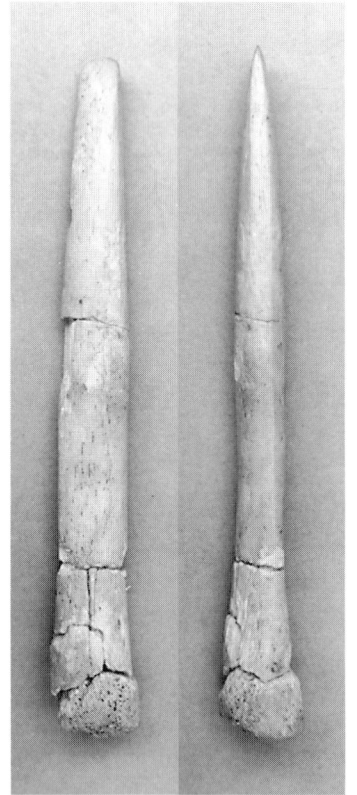
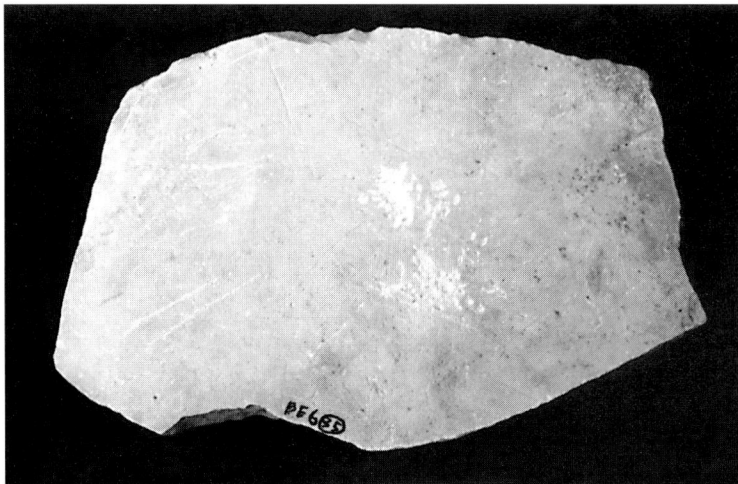

Plate 9.1 Other Neolithic implements from Tell Kosak Shamali.
1. Truncated conical stone (cf. Fig. 9.2: 1).
2. Celt (cf. Fig. 9.2: 2).
3. Bone spatula (cf. Fig. 9.2: 4).
4. Stone vessel fragment (cf. Fig. 9.2: 5).
5. Clay object (cf. Fig. 9.2: 6).

10 Conclusions
Yoshihiro Nishiaki

The University of Tokyo team conducted excavations at Tell Kosak Shamali between 1994 and 1997, and organized two study seasons in 1998 and 1999. The present volume has provided accounts of the excavations, analysis of the Palaeolithic and Neolithic finds, and the geo-archaeological and socio-anthropological research conducted in the surrounding area. Major results are summarized with comments below.

The geo-archaeological research, consisting of field survey, laboratory analysis of the digitized topography maps, provided a detailed account of the geographic setting of the settlement (Chapter 1 and its Appendix). It showed the settlement to have been in a geographically strategic location at the junction of a hilly terrace east of the Euphrates, the northern bank of the Nahar Sarine, and the flood plain of the Euphrates. These different geo-ecological zones offered readily available, diversified resources. In addition, the deep valley of the Nahar Sarine running from the northeast is a further major geo-cultural feature, providing one of the rare crossing points of the Euphrates. The research also attempted to clarify the formation processes of the human related deposits on the mound. It concluded that the site of Tell Kosak Shamali formed at the edge of a Last Glacial terrace (Q4) covered with colluvial deposits, accumulated most probably during Oxygen Isotope Stage 2. A lower, narrow terrace (Q5) located close to the mound and the large Euphrates flood plain (Q6) were considered to have been created by down-cutting of the river in subsequent periods. This implies that, at least at some time in the past, the Euphrates flowed closer to the settlement and that the Euphrates and Nahar Sarine beds were higher than today. This may partly explain the meager preservation of traces of early Holocene occupation (Chapters 3 and 4), when the settlement might well have suffered more serious erosion from flooding by these two rivers. On the other hand, if the flow of the Euphrates was closer to the settlement in the prehistoric period, it would have provided more favorable conditions facilitating exploitation of particular resources such as sedimentary and metamorphic rocks and clay.

Research into the sociological settings at the village of Kosak Shamali (Chapter 2) was designed to provide models that might be useful in understanding prehistoric social interaction as well as to document village life on the Upper Euphrates that has now disappeared due to completion of the Tishreen dam. One of the major discoveries, which could potentially contribute to our understanding of the prehistoric record, concerns the mating network within the modern agrarian society. The network operates primarily east of the Euphrates, and does not extend to the west to the same extent. The Euphrates River, about 80 m wide at its narrowest point today, appears to function as a natural barrier. Although the modern situation should not be directly projected on to the past, it might help interpretation of localized stylistic variability of artifact manufacture expressed in the prehistoric artifactual assemblages.

The first human occupation at the Tell Kosak Shamali region dates to the Palaeolithic period (Chapter 6). It was particularly intensive during the Middle Palaeolithic, as evidenced in the numerous Levantine Mousterian flints in the colluvial deposits washed out from the slopes behind the mound. The industry showed a heavy emphasis on Levallois blank production, sharing such elements as uni-directional core preparation with other Levantine Mousterian assemblages of northern Syria. After a gap in the Upper Palaeolithic, Late Epi-Palaeolithic people arrived at the site. Again, remains of their activity were discovered out of primary context, either in colluvial deposits or in soils of the Chalcolithic period. The lithic artifacts express distinct stylistic features, including the relatively large size of microliths and unusual morphology of gouges, which are almost identical to those of the nearby settlements of Abu Hureyra and Dibsi Faraj, but differ from the characteristics of the Natufian homeland to the south. The material enhances the presence of a particular Late Epi-Palaeolithic community on the Upper Euphrates.

The settlement was abandoned again in the earlier Neolithic or PPNA period. Traces suggesting sporadic occupation during the PPNB period have been noted, but no substantial architectural remains were found (Chapter 8). A reasonably recognizable settlement appeared only in the late phase of the Pottery Neolithic period in which architecture survived in fragmentary conditions. All standing structures, except a few stone walls, had been destroyed by erosional processes, leaving only pits dug into "virgin soil" (colluvial deposits) and a few fire places. The pits were mostly circular in plan, about 1 to 1.5 m in diameter, some 60 to 80 cm deep and often with steep vertical walls (Chapters 3 and 4). Comparable pits have commonly been reported from the basal levels of Neolithic settlements in North Syria. Their proposed functions or uses include ovens/kilns, storage structures, and quarrying pits for building materials. The Tell Kosak Shamali pits are unlikely to have been ovens or kilns, as none retained traces of fire on the inside. Their rather regular form rules out quarrying pits. Their use as storage structures is also questionable, because no traces of plastering were identified on the inner surface. The use for garbage disposal seems more plausible. Given the absence of rooms or floors and function-specific remains, however, conclusive interpretation of pit function is presently open for further discussion.

The artifact assemblages of pottery (Chapter 7), stone tools (Chapter 8) and other small finds (Chapter 9), are generally poor. However pottery, more than the other artifacts, allows a more precise comparison with related assemblages. The most defining characteristics of Tell Kosak Shamali ware lie in the predominant use of impressed decoration on the plant-tempered pottery and the common manufacture of necked jars. Very similar materials are found to the east and to the north of the site, at Tell Sabi Abyad on the

Balikh and at Akarçay and Teleilat on the upper valley of the Euphrates. Most comparable are those from Levels 7 and 8 of Tell Sabi Abyad, which have been dated to about 6100-6000 BC (ca. 7250-7150 BP). The pottery analysis suggests that the upper Euphrates and the Balikh valleys were a largely common cultural sphere situated midway between the East (northern Mesopotamia including the Khabur region) and the West (the Levant). This sphere may have extended to the west bank of the Euphrates, and even to the Qoueiq valley in the northwest. However, the shared elements significantly decrease, suggesting the Euphrates valley as a possible western border. In fact, the closest parallels to the Tell Kosak Shamali materials do not seem to have been at the nearby site, Tell Halula. At Tell Halula, about 15 km southwest of Tell Kosak Shamali but on the opposite bank, similar pottery occurred in the same period but only in small quantities.

The homogeneous nature of the cultural assemblages, as well as the fragmentary evidence of architecture indicates that the Pottery Neolithic occupation at Tell Kosak Shamali was short. It was perhaps a small hamlet covering less than a half hectare. The subsistence basis of the inhabitants were probably on farming and herding, although no organic remains demonstrating it have survived in the archaeological records. The small settlement of Tell Kosak Shamali can be understood in the context of the social restructuring process that took place on the Upper Euphrates from the late PPNB onwards. Archaeologically this process is characterized by at least two aspects: reduction of settlement size and emergence of more region-specific cultural entities. The available literature shows that the large PPNB settlements of Tell Abu Hureyra and Tell Halula were significantly reduced in size in the Pottery Neolithic period. Furthermore, to date, no comparably large Pottery Neolithic settlements are known in this region. Other sites such as Ja'ade and Tell Hammam Kebir were all apparently small hamlets similar in size to Tell Kosak Shamali. In addition, the nature of the large cultural horizon characterizing the PPNB period of the Levant also changed: north Syria split into more diversified cultural areas in the early Pottery Neolithic. Although the evidence from our excavations is limited, it may help further define this diversification, notably in pottery manufacturing tradition. Tell Kosak Shamali seems to typify Pottery Neolithic settlement in the region, demonstrating that this process of change was still in operation in its latest phase.

The Late Pottery Neolithic of the Balikh valley evolved into the new, Halafian society in the following centuries. However, the settlement at Tell Kosak Shamali was soon abandoned. Occupation might have occurred during the Halafian but, aside from the uncertain architectural remains of Level 14 of Sector A (Chapter 3), this occupation is suggested by only a small number of late Halafian sherds mixed with the earlier Ubaid materials. The mixture may indicate a contact of the early Ubaid inhabitants with the local Halafian society, or a transition from the local Halaf to the early Ubaid. Its implication, as yet unclear, certainly requires a further study.

Clearly Tell Kosak Shamali developed intense settlements during the Ubaid and the Post-Ubaid periods (Chapters 3 and 4). Seventeen levels spanning a thickness of over 5 m accumulated in the southwestern area during the Ubaid period (Sector A). The occupation continued into the Post-Ubaid with a shift of settlement to the southeast (Sector B). This long sequence, spanning nearly a thousand years, provides a valuable opportunity to explore in detail the Chalcolithic of the Upper Euphrates. Thanks to the AMS methods, a relatively large number of radiocarbon dates were obtained for this important sequence. They demonstrate that the first Ubaidian people settled in the site probably slightly after or almost at around 5200 BC, when the Halafian society still flourished, and continued to evolve into the local Post-Ubaidian society at about 4500/4400 BC (Chapter 5 and its Appendix). This local cultural development was interrupted only after the Post-Ubaid period, when at least part of the mound was deserted before the Middle Uruk settlement was constructed.

The Ubaid to Uruk levels produced a number of important architectural remains. One remarkable example was the burnt building of the Ubaid period from Level 10, Sector A (Chapter 3). It allowed us not only to examine details of the architectural techniques but also to analyze the room functions from plenty of *in situ* floor remains. A metric analysis revealed that it was built with the same cubit system as that used at Ubaid settlements of Iraq, demonstrating the penetration of the southern and eastern architectural traditon into this region of Syria fairly in a pure form. The floor remains, on the other hand, indicated that at least parts of the building were worksnops for pottery production and storage. Two storage rooms (10A01 and 10A03), containing a tatal of nearly 200 complete pots, were of particular interest as they provided an usual opportunity to reconstruct the production and consumption patterns of pottery within a socio-economic context of the Early Ubaid period. The fact that facilities for grain storage were equipped with the workshop complex shoud also be stressed, since it attests the use of the burnt building for other activities as well. Indeed association of craft activities with the domestic ones in the same building complexes was a common phenomenon noted in other levels of the Ubaid period too.

Pottery workshops from the Post-Ubaid levels, the most outstanding discoveries from Sector B of Tell Kosak Shamali, displayed a striking contrast to the above situation. The workshops were constructed obviously for the specialized purpose, without any facility for domestic use. They consisted of large updraught kilns, a clay levigation basin, vessel manufacturing areas and so on, all well organized in a way never seen in the preceding Ubaid workshops. A preliminary study suggests that pottery production could have been performed even by full-time potters on a year-round basis (Chapter 4). The Post Ubaid workshops are thus considered representing a significant change of the pottery production system at the end of the Ubaid period, undoubtedly involved with structural changes of the society.

These elements of archaeological evidence, as well as the series of radiocarbon dates, are the first one to be made available at a Chalcolithic site in the Tishreen Dam region. The nature of the settlement at Tell Kosak Shamali in this time period, including the Ubaid expansion processes to the Upper Euphrates and its subsequent social changes, should be better discussed in the forthcoming volumes of this report, in which information about all the finds gets into available.

تل كوساك شمالي يبدو أنه مثل مستوطنة العصر الحجري الحديث للأواني الفخارية في هذه المنطقة، ويوضح بأن هذه العملية للتغيير كانت ما تزال في التشغيل في طورها الأخير.

أن العصر الحجري الحديث للأواني الفخارية الأخير في وادي بليخان تطور نشوئياً في المجتمع الجديد لهالافين في القرون التالية. مع ذلك، تم تجنب مستوطنة تل كوساك شمالي حالاً. وقد تم تقديم أحتلال هالافين، لكن هذا "الأحتلال" كان تلميحات فقط عن طريق رقم صغير من مزيج كسرات فخارية من هالافين الأخير مع مواد من عصر أوبايد المبكر. وبوضوح كانت في عصر أوبايد والفترات ما بعد أوبايد التي تطورت الى مستوطنات مزدحمة في عهد تل كوساك شمالي (فصل ٣و٤). وتم تجميع سبعة عشر مستوى أتساع بأكثر من ٥ متر سمك في الجزء الجنوب الغربي خلال فترة عصر أوبايد (قطاع أ). ويستمر الأحتلال في فترة عصر ما بعد أوبايد مع تحويل المستوطنة الى الجنوب الشرقي (قطاع ب). هذا لا يعيق الأتساع التعاقبي القريب من ألف سنة الذي يعطي فرصة ثمينة لعمل مناقشة تفصيلية عن تطور الحضارة للعصر الحجري النحاسي في أعلى نهر الفرات. بفضل طريقة AMS، الرقم الكبير نسبياً من تواريخ الراديو كاربون تم الحصول عليها لهذه النتائج المهمة. ويبرهنوا بأن شعب أوبايدان الأول القاطن في مكان على الأرجح قليلاً أو غالباً عند حوالي ٥٢٠٠ قبل الميلاد، عندما مجتمع هالافين ما يزال يزدهر، وستمر بالتطور نشوئياً في المجتمع المحلي بعد عصر الأوبايدين في حوالي ٥٤٠٠-٤٤٠٠ قبل الميلاد (الفصل وملحقاته). هذا التطور الحضاري المحلي تم أعاقته بعد فترة ما بعد أوبايد عندما تم تشييد مستوطنة أورك الوسطى.

هذه العناصر من الأيضاحات الأثرية، مثلها سلسلة التواريخ من الراديوكاربون، تكون الأولى من نوعها تصبح متوفرة من موقع العصر الحجري النحاسي في منطقة سد تشرين. إن طبيعة المستوطنة في تل كوساك شمالي في هذه الفترة من الزمن، من ضمنها عمليات توسع أوبايد الى أعلى نهر الفرات وتغيراته الأجتماعية، يجب من الأفضل نقاشها في الفصول الآتية من هذا التقرير، التي معلوماته حول كل ما وجد أصبحت متوفرة.

أن مشروع تل كوساك الشمالي أصبح ممكن من خلال الدعم الكثير والمشكور من عدد من الأفراد والمؤسسات. ومن سرورنا العظيم أن نعبر عن أمتناننا العميق لكل هؤلاء، وخصوصاً الزملاء السوريين التالية أسمائهم. قبل كل شيئ، نود أن نشكر البروفسور الدكتور سلطان محسن، المدير السابق، والدكتور عبد الرزاق مواز، المدير الحالي لمجلس أدارة المتاحف والآثار، بكرمهم بالسماح لنا بتنفيذ مشروعنا ـ ونحن أيضاً مدينون بالكثير للدكتور عدنان بوني، المدير السابق لقسم الحفريات وأخيراً للدكتور ناسب ساليبي والدكتور باسم جاموس، والمدراء المساعدين السابقين لقسم الحفريات، الذين أعطونا المساعدة عند الحاجة. والدكتور محمد قدور مدير المتاحف، أيضاً الذي عبر عن الرغبة بالأستمرار في مشروعنا. والدعم الفعلي من الدكتور وحيد خياط، مدير قسم أليبو للآثار والمتاحف وموظفيه، الدكتور أنطون سليمان، والسيد محمد مسلم، والسيد محمد شباني كانوا من أكثر المساعدين لنا في المجال الحقلي وفي متحف أليبو. وأن عمل ممثلينا السوريين، السيد محمود شقرا (١٩٩٤)، والسيد محمد علي (١٩٩٥-١٩٩٦، ١٩٩٨)، والسيد مأمون شواف (١٩٩٧)، والسيد ناصر شريف (١٩٩٩)، الذين أشرفوا بعناية على عملنا ممتنين لهم بكل تقدير.

كما أن السيد عديد شاهين، مساح قاعدة أليبو، هيأ لنا خريطة تخطيطية ممتازة للموقع. ومهارات التنسيق الواسعة من قبل السيد مصطفى شادي ليس فقط كسائق سيارة فحسب، وأنما أيضاً في متابعة قضايا محلية مختلفة ساعدنا بها كثيراً. ونحن ندين بالعرفان والشكر لهؤلاء الناس جميعهم.

236

لم تترك أي أثار معمارية هامة. ظهرت المستوطنة المميزة تقريباً فقط في المرحلة المتأخرة من عصر الأواني الفخارية للعهد الحجري الحديث. وأن الطراز المعماري لعصر الأواني الفخارية للعهد الحجري الحديث تم أنقاذه بحالات جزئية. كل الهياكل القائمة، عدا القليل من السياجات الصخرية، تم أزالتها بعمليات التآكل، وحفر الحفريات في "تربة بكر" (ترسبات كولفيال) وبعض الأماكن النارية وجد بقايا أجزاء منها. وأغلب الحفريات كانت دائرية في الخطة، مع قطر حوالي ١ الى ١٫٥ متر وبعضها بعمق ٦٠ الى ٨٠ سم (فصل ٣و٤). وكانت السياجات العمودية غالباً على شكل تدرجات. والحفريات من الأنواع المقارنة قد أبلغت عادة عن المستويات الأساسية عن مستوطنات العصر الحجري الحديث في شمال سوريا. ووظائفهم أو أستعمالاتهم المقترحة من ضمنها هذه المتعلقة بالأفران/التنور، وتركيبة المخازن، وحفريات أستخراج الأحجار لمواد البناء. أن الحفريات لتل كوساك شمالي هي مستبعدة أن تكون أفران أو تنور، لأنه لاتوجد آثار حرق أو نار بالداخل. وبالأحرى شكلهم المنتظم يمنع من وضعهم أو تحديدهم الى حفريات أستخراج الأحجار. ومن بين الأحتمالات الأخرى أن تركيبة التخزين تبدو أكثر محتملة لصحة الحالة، بالرغم من أن لاآثار لطبقة البلاستر كانت قد عرفت في السطح الداخلي. على أي حال، يعطي غياب المجالات أو الأرضية وأبقاء وظيفة محددة، تفسير الأدلة المقنعة لوظيفة الحفريات بأن يكون مفتوح بالوقت الحاضر لمناقشات أضافية.

إن مجموعة الأدوات الصناعية، تتألف من الفخاريات (فصل ٧)، الأدوات الحجرية (فصل ٨) وأدوات صغيرة أخرى (فصل ٩)، تظهر تجانس طبيعي جداً في كل الفصائل. وأكثر مقارنة دقيقة مع المجموعة ذات العلاقة هي ممكنة في الفخاريات منها في أضافة الأدوات الصناعية الأخرى. وأغلب الخصائص المعرفة لتل كوساك شمالي يتم أدراكها في الأستعمال السائد لطابع الزخرفة على الأواني الفخارية المعالجة بالنباتات والصناعة المشتركة لأعناق الجرة. ووجدت مواد مشابهة جداً في الشرق والشمال من الموقع، كما في تل سابي أبياد، في بليخان وفي أكار والتليلة في أعلى سهل نهر الفرات. وأكثر قابلة للمقارنة هي هذه من مستويات ٧ و٨ من

تل سابي أبياد، والتي يرجع تأريخها الى حوالي ٦١٠٠-٦٠٠٠ قبل الميلاد (ca.7250-7150BP). وتحليل الأواني الفخارية يقود الى أن أعلى نهر الفرات وسهول بليخان تشكل دائرة حضارية كبيرة مشتركة واقعة في المنتصف بين الشرق (الجزء الشمالي من ميسوبوتاميا من ضمنها منطقة الخابور) والغرب (اليفانت). هذه الدائرة قد تمتد الى الضفة الغربية من نهر الفرات، وحتى الى وادي كوبيك في الجزء الشمال الغربي. لكن العناصر المشتركة تقل بشكل واضح. ويقود الى أن وادي نهر الفرات ممكن أن يكون الحدود الغربية. وأنه بالحقيقة، يبدو أن مواد تل كوساك شمالي ليس لها متوازيات متقاربة في المواقع القريبة، مثل تل هالول. وفي أحدثها، حوالي ٥ كم جنوب غرب تل كوساك شمالي لكن على الجهة من الضفة، قد حصل تشابه في الأواني الفخارية في نفس الفترة لكن فقط في كمية صغيرة.

أن التجانس الطبيعي للمجموعات الحضارية، ومثلها أيضاً أيضاحات الفخارية في تل كوساك شمالي أنتهت فقط في فترة قصيرة جداً. ربما كانت قرية صغيرة تغطي مساحة أقل من نصف هكتار. وأن المستوطنة الصغيرة لتل كوساك شمالي قد تفهم في عملية أعادة التركيبة الأجتماعية التي تطورت في أعلى نهر الفرات من PPNB الأخير وفي ما بعد. حسب علم الآثار هذه العملية قد تتميز بشكلين بالأقل: تقليل حجم المستوطنة ونشوء كينونات أكثر حضارية لمنطقة معينة. وتبين الأدبيات المتوفرة بأن مستوطنات PPNB الكبيرة لتل أبو هوريري وتل هالولي قلل بشكل ملحوظ حجمهم في فترة العصر الحجري الحديث للأواني الفخارية، وأكثر من هذا، لا توجد مستوطنات كبيرة مقارنة للعصر الحجري الحديث للأواني الفخارية معروفة التاريخ في هذه المنطقة. والموقع الأخرى مثل جعادي وتل حامام خبير كانت على ما يبدو قرى صغيرة بحجم مشابهة لتل كوساك شمالي. بالأضافة الى أن ميزة خط الأفق الثقافي الكبير لفترة PPNB ليفانت أيضاً قد غير طبيعته: فأن شمال سوريا أصبح منقسم الى أكثر من منطقة ثقافية مختلفة في العهد المبكر للعصر الحجري الحديث للأواني الفخارية. ولو أن الأيضاحات من حفرياتنا كانت محددة، ولكن تساعد على تعريف هذه الأختلاف بشكل أكثر تفصيل، ويلاحظ هذا في صناعة الأواني الفخارية التقليدية. أن

نفذ فريق جامعة طوكيو عملية الحفريات لتل كوساك من عام ١٩٩٤ الى ١٩٩٧، وقام بتنظيم موسمي دراسة في عام ١٩٩٨ و١٩٩٩. وأعد عديد من التقارير في الوقت الحاضر عن الحفريات نفسها، وتحليل موجودات العصر الحجري القديم والحديث، والجيو–أرتشايولوجيكال (علم الآثار) وتم أجراء بحث سوسيو–أنثروبولوجي في المنطقة المحيطة. كما تم تلخيص النتائج الرئيسية تحت مع بعض التعليقات.

إن بحث الجيو–أرتشايولوجيكال، لا يتألف فقط من دراسة حقلية لكن أيضاً من تحليل مختبري للخرائط الطوبوغرافيا وعينات التربة، وتعريف الأوضاع الجغرافية للمستوطنة تفصيلاً (فصل ١ وملحقاته). كما تظهر بأن المستوطنة تكون واقعة في مكان جغرافي أستراتيجي، وفي نقطة أتصال صف من التلال الكثيرة في شرق نهر الفرات، وفي الضفة الشمالية من نهر سارين، والسهل المعرض للفيضان من نهر الفرات. وكانت الموارد المتنوعة متاحة بسهولة هناك من مناطق الجيو-يكولوجيكا المختلفة هذه بالأضافة لذلك الوادي العميق لنهر سارين. الممتد من الشمال الشرقي، من الممكن ذكره كميزة جيو–حضاريه رئيسية أخرى، ويعطي واحد من نقاط التقاطع النادرة لنهر الفرات. وأن البحث هو محاولة أيضاً لتوضيح عمليات التشكيل للمحيطات الأجتماعية المتعلقة بهذه الهضبة. ويستنتج من أن موقع تل كوساك الشمالي تشكل عند حافة آخر المساكن الجليدية (Q4) المغطاة بتجمعات رسوبية كولفيال الأحتمال الأغلب في المرحلة الثانية من نظائر الأوكسجين. والمساكن السفلية الضيقة (Q5) تقع قريب من الهضبة وسهل الفيضان الكبير لنهر الفرات (Q6) الذي يعتبر من المخلفات التي وجدت من تقطيع النهر في الفترات المتعاقبة. ويلمح بأن نهر الفرات كان يجري قريب جداً الى المستوطنة على الأقل في بعض الأوقات في الماضي، وأن أسس نهر الفرات ونهر سارين كانت أعلى من ما هي اليوم. هذا قد يوضح جزئياً الصيانة الضئيلة لأثر المحتلين في العهد المبكر من عصر هولوسين (فصل ٣ و٤)، عندما عانت المستوطنة من تآكل خطير نتيجة الفيضانات المستمرة لهذين النهرين. من جهة أخرى، الجريان القريب لنهر الفرات قد أعطى حالة مشجعة أكثر لتسهيل الموارد المحددة مثل الصخور الرسوبية والأنسلاخية والطينية في الفترة البدائية.

بحث المحطيات الأجتماعية في القرية في تل كوساك شمالي (فصل ٢) تم تصميمه لكي يحصل على التضمينات حول التفاعلات في المجتمع البدائي، وأيضاً لتوثيق عن حياة القرية في أعالي نهر الفرات التي أختفت بسب أكمال بناء سد تشرين. ومن الأمور الرائدة التي وجدت، والتي ستساهم بفعالية في أدراكنا لسجل المجتمع البدائي، كان ما يتعلق بشبكة التزاوج أثناء العمل بين المجتمع الزاعي الحديث. وتم تشغيل هذه الشبكة غالباً ضمن حدود منطقة شرق نهر الفرات، لكنها لاتمتد الى الغرب منه على نفس الأمتداد. إن نهر الفرات، هو حوالي بعرض ٨٠ متر عند أضيق نقطة في الوقت الحاضر، ويبدو بأنه يؤدي كدور حاجز طبيعي. بالرغم من أن الموقف الحديث لا يعبر عن الماضي مباشرةً، ولكن يساعد على التفسير عبر التغيير الأسلوبي المتمركز للصناعة المعبر عنها بالسجلات البدائية.

إن الحرفة البشرية الأولى في منطقة تل كوساك شمالي يرجع تأريخها الى العصر الحجري (الفصل ٦). كانت مركزة بشكل خاص في وسط العصر الحجري، كما عندما حدثت لعديد من صوانات موستيرايان في الكولفيال وزالت مقدمة المنحدرات خلف التل. وكانت الصناعة قد تسارعت بقوة الى الأنتاج الفاتر لليفالوسي، وتتقاسم العناصر الأساسية كتحضيرات لمركز أحادي الأتجاه مع مجموعات موسيرايان الشرقية الأخرى في شمال سوريا. بعد الفجوة في أعلى العصر الحجري، وصلت شعوب قريبة من العصر الحجري (بالأيولينيك) الأخير الى الموقع. ومرة ثانية تبقى نشاطاتهم المكتشفة خارج عن الموقع الأولية، سواء المتضمن في ترسبات الكولفيال أو في التربة المحفورة من شعوب شالكولينك. وتعرف بالتعبير عنها بصنع الأدوات الحجرية عن السمات الأسلوبية المميزة، من ضمنها الحجم الكبير نسبياً للميكرولينس المورفولوجيا الخاصة بالمظفار، التي تكون تقريباً متماثل لهذه المستوطنات المجاورة لأبو هوريري ودبسي فرج لكن يختلف عن الخصائص لوطن ناتفيان في الجنوب. وأن تحسينها للمادة يكرس حضورها في أعلى نهر الفرات.

تم تجنب المستوطنة مرة ثانية في العهد المبكر للعصر الحجري الحديث أو PPNA. وهناك تتواجد آثار نقود الى بعض الأحتلالات المتفرقة في عهد PPNA (فصل ٨)، لكن

تل كوساك شمالي :
بحوث آثارية عن أعلى نهر الفرات، سوريا

المجلد ١   العمارات في العصر النحاسي
و الآثار في أوائل عصر ما قبل التاريخ

أصدرت من قبل
يوشيهيرو نيشياكي
و
توشيو ماتسوتاني

جامعة طوكيو
٢٠٠١